ADVANCING THE BROADCAST
STORY JOURNALISM
IN A MULTIMEDIA WORLD

1

ADVANCING THE BROADCAST
STORY
JOURNALISM

IN A MULTIMEDIA WORLD

DEBORA HALPERN WENGER and **DEBORAH POTTER**

Virginia Commonwealth University   NewsLab

CQ PRESS

A Division of Congressional Quarterly Inc
Washington, D.C.

CQ Press
1255 22nd Street, NW, Suite 400
Washington, DC 20037

Phone: 202-729-1900; toll-free, 1-866-4CQ-PRESS (1-866-427-7737)

Web: www.cqpress.com

Photo credits:
AP Images: 16
Krystyna Wentz-Graff/The Poynter Institute: 169
Wright's Reprints LLC/Photo-illustration for TIME by Arthur Hochstein, with photographs by
    Spencer Jones—Glasshouse: 303

Cover and interior design: Matthew Simmons
Composition: Naylor Design, Inc

⊗ The paper used in this publication exceeds the requirements of the American National Standard for Information Sciences—Permanence of Paper for Printed Library Materials, ANSI Z39.48-1992.

Printed and bound in the United States of America

11 10 09 08 07   1 2 3 4 5

Library of Congress Cataloging-in-Publication Data

Advancing the story : broadcast journalism in a multimedia world / Debora Halpern Wenger, Deborah Potter.
     p. cm.
  Includes bibliographical references and index.
  ISBN 978-0-87289-463-1 (alk. paper)
  1. Broadcast journalism. I. Wenger, Debora Halpern. II. Potter, Deborah (Deborah A.) III. Title.

PN4784.B75A38 2008
070.1'9--dc22

                                                         2007035553

ABOUT THE AUTHORS ▬▬▬▬▬▬▬▬▬▬

Debora Halpern Wenger, a 17-year broadcast news veteran, is associate professor for media convergence and new media at Virginia Commonwealth University. Prior to her academic appointment, she served as assistant news director at WFLA-TV in Tampa, Fla. She started her career as a reporter/anchor at KXJB in Fargo, N.D., moved on to producing at WBBH in Ft. Myers, Fla., and WMUR in Manchester, N.H., then became executive producer at WSOC in Charlotte, N.C. Wenger conducts multimedia training in newsrooms across the country and is co-author of the broadcast and online journalism curricula for the Society of Professional Journalists' Newsroom Training Program. She has been invited to work as visiting faculty for the Poynter Institute's "Producing Producers" seminar and has been a part of the Committee of Concerned Journalists Traveling Curriculum through the Project for Excellence in Journalism.

Deborah Potter is a veteran journalist and educator who spent 16 years as a network correspondent for CBS News and CNN. She is executive director of NewsLab (www.newslab.org), a non-profit resource for journalists in Washington, D.C., that she founded in 1998. She is a past executive director of the Radio and Television News Directors Foundation. Before joining CBS, Potter was a local TV news producer in Washington, D.C., and a radio news anchor in Philadelphia. She writes a monthly column about broadcast news for American Journalism Review, and leads workshops for journalists in newsrooms across the United States and around the world on writing, storytelling, ethics and news leadership. Potter previously taught journalism at the Poynter Institute, and is the author of Ready, Set, Lead: The Resource Guide for News Managers, and the Handbook of Independent Journalism. She has a BA from the University of North Carolina at Chapel Hill and an MA from American University.

BRIEF CONTENTS

CONTENTS   vii

TABLES, FIGURES AND BOXES   xviii

PREFACE   xxi

1. THE MULTIMEDIA MIND-SET   1

2. REPORTING THE STORY   23

3. MULTIMEDIA NEWSGATHERING   54

4. REPORTING IN DEPTH   81

5. WRITING THE STORY   111

6. VISUAL STORYTELLING   139

7. WRITING FOR THE WEB   167

8. PRODUCING FOR THE WEB   192

9. PRODUCING FOR TV   219

10. DELIVERING THE NEWS   247

11. MULTIMEDIA ETHICS   271

12. GETTING READY FOR THE REAL WORLD   301

NOTES   331

GLOSSARY OF MULTIMEDIA JOURNALISM   336

INDEX   344

CONTENTS

TABLES, FIGURES AND BOXES   xviii

PREFACE   xxi

1. THE MULTIMEDIA MIND-SET   1

Multimedia Basics   2
   A New Approach   2
   Audience First   2

Media on Demand   5
   The Multimedia Industry   5
   Multimedia Journalists   5

Technology Changes Content   7
   Good Journalism Matters   7
   The Power of Multimedia   11

The Best of Broadcast   11
   Immediacy   12
   Impact of Visuals and Emotion   12
   Audience Connection   13

The Power of Print   14
   Depth   14
   Detail   14
   Permanence and Portability   15

The Originality of Online   16
   On Demand   17

ADVANCING THE STORY

Interactivity 18

Innovation 18

Focus on the Future 20

Taking It Home 21

Talking Points 21

eLearning Opportunities 22

2. REPORTING THE STORY 23

Finding Stories 24

Read, Look and Listen 24

Follow Up and Plan Ahead 24

Develop Stories from Topics 26

Story Building Blocks 26

Character 26

Place 27

Emotion 28

Detail 28

Tension or Surprise 28

Research Strategies 28

Follow the Stakeholders 29

Seek Background and Data 30

Consult Experts 30

Research Tools 30

Clips and Scripts 30

Online Sources 31

Phone Calls 33

Sources 34

Multiple, Diverse Sources 35

Source Credibility 36

Interviews 36

Interview Questions 38

Types of Questions 39

Openers and Closers 39

Tough Questions 41

Silence 42

Types of Interviews 43

In-Person Interviews 43

On-Camera Interviews 43

Interviews for the Web 44

Phone or E-Mail Interviews 45

Interview Ground Rules 47

Background Interviews 47

Deep Background and Off-the-Record Interviews 48

Interview Policies 48

Embargoes 49

Note Taking 50

Getting It Right 51

Taking It Home 52

Talking Points 52

eLearning Opportunities 53

3. MULTIMEDIA NEWSGATHERING 54

Thinking across Platforms 55

Putting It Together 56

Sound 58

Equipment 60

Ambience 60

Online Use 61

Video 62

Framing 63

Steady Shots 64

Sequences, Action and Reaction 65

Opens, Closes and Introductions 66

Online Issues 66

Lighting 69

Technical Issues 69

Placement 70

Nonvisual Stories   **71**
   Graphics   72
   Natural Sound Stories   73

Teamwork   **74**
   Story Planning   74
   In the Field   74

Working Alone   **75**
   VJs and Backpackers   75
   Pros and Cons   76

Tools of the Trade   **77**
   Cameras   77
   Audio Recorders   78
   Microphones   79

Taking It Home   **79**
   Talking Points   80
   eLearning Opportunities   80

4. REPORTING IN DEPTH   **81**

Mapping the Community   **82**
   Research and Explore   82
   Read, Listen and Connect   82

Beat Reporting   **83**
   Getting Started   83
   Tracking the Beat   86
   Working the Beat   87

Topical Beats   **88**
   Crime and Justice   88
   Government and Politics   92
   Education   95
   Business and Economics   97
   Health, Science and the Environment   100

Investigative Reporting   **102**
   Using FOI   104
   Computer-Assisted Reporting   105

Undercover Reporting	108
The Multimedia Advantage	108
Taking It Home	**109**
Talking Points	110
eLearning Opportunities	110

5. WRITING THE STORY   111

Finding the Focus	**112**
Focus Questions	112
Focus for Multiple Media	115
Planning Your Story	**116**
Review	116
Select	116
Organize	118
Consider the Extras	118
Story Structure	**120**
Inverted Pyramid	121
Hourglass	122
Diamond	123
Christmas Tree	124
Beginnings and Endings	**126**
Leads	126
Endings	127
Watch Your Words	**128**
Keep It Simple	128
Stay Active	129
Use Powerful Words	129
Be Conversational	131
Preserve Surprise	131
Accuracy	**132**
Attribution	132
Numbers	133
Revising Your Story	**134**
Read Aloud	135

Nuke Wasted Words   135

Check for Errors and Accuracy   137

Taking It Home   **138**

Talking Points   138

eLearning Opportunities   138

6. VISUAL STORYTELLING   **139**

Planning   **140**

Screening and Logging   141

Timing   141

Choosing Sound   **143**

Sound Bite Content   143

Sound Bite Number and Length   144

Natural Sound   145

Choosing Video   **146**

Moments   146

Say It, Prove It   146

Writing to Sound   **147**

Leading In   148

Leading Out   148

Using "Nat Pops"   149

Writing to Video   **150**

Sequence Your Story   151

Show, Don't Tell   151

Draw Attention   152

Parallel Parking   152

Editing   **153**

Video Edits   154

Audio Edits   155

Graphics   **156**

Why Use Graphics?   158

Simple Is Better   158

Shapes and Movement   160

Writing to Graphics   160

Online Graphics   161

Natural Sound Stories   **162**

Slide Shows   **163**

Taking It Home   **165**
    Talking Points   166
    eLearning Opportunities   166

7. WRITING FOR THE WEB   167

How People Use the Web   **168**

When News on the Web Falls Short   **170**
    Broadcast Shovelware   170
    Print Rehash   171

Writing for the Web   **171**
    Grab Their Attention!   172
    Use Time and Tense   172
    Be Relevant   174
    Be Concise and Conversational   174
    Write for the Scanners   175

Print to Online Story   **176**

Converting Broadcast to Online   **179**

Web Headline Writers Wanted   **183**

Web Extras   **186**
    Provide Additional Content   188
    Produce Original Web Content   188
    Produce Web Interactives   189

Taking It Home   **190**
    Talking Points   190
    eLearning Opportunities   191

8. PRODUCING FOR THE WEB   192

The Skill Set   **193**

Continuous Production Mode   **196**
    Breaking News versus Developing Stories   196
    Strategies for Constant Updates   197

Accuracy Matters   198
Producing Webcasts and Podcasts   198

Blogging   **199**

Interactive Tools   **204**
Searchable Data Sets   204
Clickable Maps and Interactive Timelines   206
Online Calculators   207
Polls, Questionnaires and Quizzes   207
Interactive Storytelling   209

Planning the Multimedia Story   **209**
Review Your Plan   210
Storyboards   210
Putting It All Together   212

The Multimedia Team   **212**
Determine Unique Content   213
Communicate and Share Resources   214
Develop a Presentation Plan   215

Citizen Journalism   **215**

Taking It Home   **217**
Talking Points   217
eLearning Opportunities   218

9. PRODUCING FOR TV   **219**

The Journalist Producer   **220**

Show Choreography   **220**
The Lead   222
Flow   225
Pacing   227
Newscast Blocks   228
Timing   228

Audience and Ratings   **229**
Demographics   229
Diaries and Meters   230
Ratings and Share   230

Strategic Producing and Special Reports   **231**

Teases   **233**
    Know the Story   233
    Viewer Benefit and Station Brand   234
    Weather Teases   235
    Sports Teases   235
    Stand-Up and Live Teases   236
    Teasing Pitfalls   237
    Working with Promotion Producers   238
    Promoting Multimedia   240

Working with Newscast Producers   **241**

Web Work   **242**

Newscasts of the Future   **242**

Taking It Home   **245**
    Talking Points   245
    eLearning Opportunities   246

10. DELIVERING THE NEWS   **247**

Voicing   **247**
    Mental Preparation   249
    Intonation   249
    Pacing   251

Stand-Ups   **251**
    Planning a Stand-Up   252
    Solo Stand-Ups   254
    Memorizing   255
    Action   256
    Shooting Stand-Ups   257
    Stand-Ups with Graphics   257

Live Shots   **258**
    Content   260
    The Live Toss   261
    The Live Tag and Anchor Questions   262
    Live Only   263

Talking Heads   **264**

    Preparation   264

    Lessons Learned   266

Podcasting   **266**

Print Pointers   **267**

    Structure   267

    Style   268

Taking It Home   **269**

    Talking Points   270

    eLearning Opportunities   270

11. MULTIMEDIA ETHICS   **271**

Thinking about Ethics   **271**

Multimedia Issues   **272**

    Corrections on the Web   274

    Transparency and Bias   277

    Advertorials and Infomercials   278

    Interview Agreements   280

    Multimedia News Releases   282

Online Issues   **284**

    Blogging   284

    Plagiarism and Copyright   285

    Digital Manipulation of Images   288

Multimedia Solutions   **291**

    Graphic Images and Sound   291

    Access to Information   293

    Access to Sources and Content   294

Diversity   **295**

    Diverse Resources   298

    Partnering with Ethnic Media and Alternative Media   299

Taking It Home   **299**

    Talking Points   300

    eLearning Opportunities   300

12. GETTING READY FOR THE REAL WORLD 301

The Changing Media Landscape 302
The User's Voice 303
Using the Content 303

New Distribution Methods 305
Newsroom Usage 305
Journalism Skills 306

Media Convergence 306
Formal Partnerships 308
Cross-Owned Convergence 309

Multimedia Job Searches 309
Planning 310
Hunting 313
Networking 314

Job Applications 316
Cover Letters 316
Résumés 317
Résumé Tapes 321
Multimedia Portfolios 323
Interviews 323
Hiring Tests 326

Contracts 326

Journalism Entrepreneurs 328

Taking It Home 329
Talking Points 329
eLearning Opportunities 330

NOTES 331

GLOSSARY OF MULTIMEDIA JOURNALISM 336

INDEX 344

TABLES, FIGURES AND BOXES

TABLES

1.1	The Changing Landscape of News	17
8.1	Skills for Online Journalists	193
9.1	Story Flow	225
12.1	Starting Annual Salaries	327

FIGURES

1.1	The More the Merrier	3
2.1	Story Mapping	27
5.1	Inverted Pyramid	122
5.2	Hourglass	123
5.3	Diamond	124
5.4	Christmas Tree	125
6.1	City Spending (bar graph)	159
6.2	City Spending (line graph)	159
9.1	TV Ratings/Shares	232

BOXES

Chapter 1: The Multimedia Mind-Set

Know and Tell—*A New Type of Journalist*	4
Know and Tell—*On the Multimedia Highway with the Reader behind the Wheel*	8

Chapter 2: Reporting the Story

Trade Tools—*Brainstorming Basics*	25
Trade Tools—*Diverse Sources*	35
Trade Tools—*Evaluating Sources*	37
Trade Tools—*Getting an Interview*	38
Know and Tell—*Interview Questions*	40
Know and Tell—*Report: Live Interviews*	46
Trade Tools—*Ground Rules*	49

Chapter 3: Multimedia Newsgathering

Trade Tools—*Platform Pluses*	57
Trade Tools—*Reporting Checklists*	59

Know and Tell—*Capturing Sound*   62

Trade Tools—*Shooting Documents for TV*   72

Trade Tools—*Gear List*   78

Chapter 4: Reporting In Depth

Know and Tell—*Breaking and Entering*   85

Trade Tools—*Crime Glossary*   89

Know and Tell—*The Cop Beat*   90

Trade Tools—*Reporting on Polls*   92

Know and Tell—*Covering Education*   98

Trade Tools—*Beat Reporter Resources*   100

Know and Tell—*Environmental Reporting*   103

Chapter 5: Writing the Story

Know and Tell—*Writing Wisdom*   113

Know and Tell—*The Rosenbaum Method*   117

Trade Tools—*Story Planning*   119

Know and Tell—*The Story "Quest"*   120

Trade Tools—*Types of Leads*   127

Trade Tools—*Writing Tips from CNN's Candy Crowley*   130

Trade Tools—*Revise and Conquer*   137

Chapter 6: Visual Storytelling

Trade Tools—*Logging Shorthand*   143

Know and Tell—*Make It Memorable*   150

Trade Tools—*Words and Pictures*   153

Know and Tell—*One Editor's Wisdom*   157

Chapter 7: Writing for the Web

Trade Tools—*Web Writing Style*   176

Know and Tell—*Online Writing Tips*   180

Trade Tools—*Web Headlines*   184

Chapter 8: Producing for the Web

Trade Tools—*Online Tutorials*   195

Trade Tools—*11 Tips for Better Blogging*   202

Trade Tools—*Storyboarding Questions*   213

Chapter 9: Producing for TV

Trade Tools—*Pitching Stories*   221

Trade Tools—*Producer Skills*   223

Know and Tell—*A News Director's Expectations for Producers*   224

Know and Tell—*Teases "Я" Us*   239

Chapter 10: Delivering the News

Trade Tools—*Sounding Natural*   248

Trade Tools—*Why Do a Stand-Up?*   252

Know and Tell—*Solo Stand-Ups*   255

Know and Tell—*Live Shots*   259

Trade Tools—*Doing TV*   265

Chapter 11: Multimedia Ethics

Know and Tell—*Correcting Mistakes*   274

Trade Tools—*News and Sales: Clarifying the Relationship*   281

Know and Tell—*Fighting the Pirates of the Press*   286

Trade Tools—*Ethics Resources*   296

Chapter 12: Getting Ready for the Real World

Trade Tools—*Getting the Most from an Internship*   312

Trade Tools—*How NOT to Get a Job, in Five Easy Steps*   318

Trade Tools—*Finding a Small-Market TV Job*   322

Know and Tell—*Employer Pet Peeves*   325

Why would anyone want to be a journalist today? The business seems to be imploding. Newspapers are losing readers. Television viewers are tuning out the news. But the truth is, it's a great time to be a journalist, and this book is aimed at helping you be a better one.

As we wrote this text, we sometimes thought about the way journalism was practiced when we were starting out. It wasn't *that* long ago, but the way we worked was substantially different. One of us actually wrote stories on a typewriter, edited film and sent in radio reports via pay phone. Journalists today have more options for telling stories to more people more quickly than ever before, but they need new ways of thinking and new skills if they're going to succeed. At the same time, they must uphold the time-honored standards of good journalism to establish their credibility and earn the public's trust.

This book will take broadcast journalists well beyond the basics, while reinforcing traditional journalistic principles. One is that the story matters more than the medium you tell it in or, to put it more bluntly, "It's the content, stupid." Another is that journalists still have a key role to play in a free society—to provide information that citizens need to govern their lives—a role that matters just as much today as it did when the United States was founded. And it matters just as much as it did more than 100 years ago, when the newspaper publisher Joseph Pulitzer wrote these words: "An able, disinterested, public-spirited press, with trained intelligence to know the right and courage to do it, can preserve that public virtue without which popular government is a sham and a mockery. A cynical, mercenary, demagogic press will produce in time a people as base as itself."

WHERE WE ARE GOING

Between the two of us, we have been teaching and training journalists for more than a quarter century. For even longer than that, we've worked as journalists in TV, radio and print newsrooms, and we've produced online stories, too. Most of what we've learned along the way did not come from a textbook. We sometimes wished we could have read a book to acquire many of the skills we developed through painful trial and error, so we combined our experience with our desire to help you avoid some of the pitfalls we faced, and wrote this book. It's designed to provide the knowledge you'll need to do well from the start, while you perfect your skills with practice.

In our teaching and training efforts, we've often been asked to recommend a good advanced textbook about broadcast or multimedia journalism. What we've found is that there are few, if any, high-quality texts to help broadcast journalists go beyond the basics. And most multimedia texts seem to focus almost exclusively on the theoretical (why multimedia is good or bad) or on the technical (for example, how to use Flash). Those books are useful, but not sufficient. We know this because our friends in newsrooms keep telling us how hard it is to hire journalists who understand both how to do a good TV or print story and how to enhance that story on the Web.

This textbook and companion online workbook will help prepare journalists for jobs in today's newsrooms. They cover the essential topics for any journalist—researching, interviewing, writing, visualizing stories and adding depth, for example—but they begin with a clear message: It's a multimedia world and today's journalists must develop a multimedia mind-set. That means journalists must start thinking from the start about how they will use multiple media outlets to deliver the content they gather. Throughout the book, we discuss how the multimedia approach to storytelling changes the newsgathering and news production process.

Based on that principle, we have divided the book into three sections: newsgathering, news production and multimedia issues. In the newsgathering section, we deal with subjects such as discovering and evaluating diverse sources, capturing great audio and video (even for nonvisual stories), working a beat and computer-assisted reporting. In the news production section, we help journalists focus and structure their stories, write more effectively to sound and video and improve their delivery. This section also includes chapters dedicated to online news writing and Web production, including blogs, interactives and webcasts. Finally, the issues section discusses journalism ethics, including some unique dilemmas created or alleviated through multimedia journalism. It also explores where multimedia journalism may be headed and how journalists can find the best fit for themselves in terms of jobs and careers.

HOW WE GET THERE

We've structured the book so that what you learn in each chapter builds on what you've already read. But we've written it in such a way that you can read individual chapters whenever they seem most useful to you. Our goal is to provide a straightforward guide to what you need to know to practice journalism today. Each chapter includes real-world examples, advice from working journalists and unique elements you won't find in other textbooks.

From the start, we emphasize the importance of understanding the audience. Today's news consumers are more demanding and more distracted than ever before. They want the news they want when they want it, and that's changing the way journalists gather, package and deliver content. Because the audience has access to so much news on so many platforms, however, we also believe that quality matters more than ever. So, Chapter 1 focuses on how a multimedia approach can be used to produce better journalism that takes advantage of the unique strengths of each medium.

We believe any journalist can make an important story interesting by thinking differently during the reporting process. Chapters 2–4 show you where to look for story ideas that work, and take you beyond the basics to improve your newsgathering skills, specifically for multimedia. And because good journalism does much more than scratch the surface, we show you how to make your stories more meaningful by adding depth and detail.

No matter how much information you collect, you can't produce great stories if you can't organize and clearly convey what you've learned. Chapters 5 and 6 will show you how to produce better-quality stories based on the content you've gathered, with an emphasis on story planning and structure. You'll learn how to make the most of sound and visuals—including graphics—in telling stories for any medium.

Writing and producing content specifically for the Web can be intimidating if you haven't studied the characteristics of online reporting. Chapter 7 breaks down the online writing process into a series of manageable steps, and Chapter 8 is designed to spark creative thinking about the storytelling process by exploring what's possible online.

The ability to deliver content effectively is a critical part of any multimedia journalist's tool set, but it's an area left out of many texts. We devote Chapters 9 and 10 to deconstructing what it takes to produce and present television news, including vocal delivery, standups and live shots. We also provide guidance for print or online journalists who appear on TV and a primer to help broadcast writers create print versions of their stories.

While practical skills are essential for journalists, they also need something more—a compass to make sure their actions are in line with their values. In Chapter 11, we explore the new ethical challenges faced by multiplatform journalists, as well as some of the ways a multimedia approach can help resolve ethical dilemmas.

An advanced broadcast and multimedia journalism text would miss the mark if it left out some of the newer forms of content delivery. We touch on podcasts, vodcasts and blogs in various chapters, and in Chapter 12 we discuss user-generated content and producing news for mobile devices. You'll also find a wealth of information and resources for that all-important job search.

Throughout the book, you'll benefit from what other journalists have learned on the job.

Each chapter includes two innovative features: "Know and Tell" and "Trade Tools." The "Know and Tell" reports typically focus on practicing journalists who share firsthand experience with issues discussed in the text. "Trade Tools" help you absorb best practices outlined in the text or provide an easy-to-use guide for tackling a journalistic challenge.

At the end of each chapter, we include "Talking Points" to facilitate discussion, which can also be used as assignments to foster critical thinking about the issues outside the class or training room.

In every chapter, we have tried to be mindful of the need to encourage diversity in newsgathering and delivery. We suggest ways of finding diverse sources and include story examples with a strong diversity component. We've made sure to consult expert journalists from diverse backgrounds and perspectives to emphasize the importance of inclusiveness in high-quality journalism.

AUTHOR BLOG AND INTERACTIVE ONLINE WORKBOOK

One of the biggest challenges in teaching and studying journalism today is staying current. Technology and journalists' use of technology are changing so rapidly that we found ourselves updating some chapters just weeks before publication. That's just one reason we believe our author blog and online workbook (http://college.cqpress.com/advancingthestory) will be of immense value to anyone using this text.

Advancing the Story Blog

The author blog will feature new developments affecting journalists, particularly in the area of multimedia. We'll update it frequently, providing links to the latest research, news reports about multimedia issues as well as examples of great reporting. The most recent posts will be displayed on the workbook's home page. We'll tag them by chapter, so you can easily find the ones that apply to what you're reading in the text. Although you'll want to check the blog frequently, a chapter-by-chapter archive will make sure you don't miss any important developments. Because we believe the best journalism is informed by conversation with the audience, our blog is open for comments. Please don't hesitate to let us know what you think.

Online Workbook

Building on the fundamentals of reporting, writing and producing, we wanted to create a workbook that was both interactive and fully integrated with our text. We think we've created a one-of-a-kind online workbook that offers a self-testing, tutorial package so you can work through exercises and examples as you read chapters. At the same time, the site offers instructors a teaching tool, so the exercises can become assignments, arming them with ready-made materials for class. The workbook's functionality allows students to e-mail solutions and write-ups to their instructors or print and save their work. This gives instructors the built-in ability to assess student work for credit or a grade, but more important, gives students an opportunity to build their portfolios. Also included in the workbook is an instructor's resource area that will provide a wealth of teaching aids, including sample syllabi, teaching tools and more.

The online workbook has five major components, organized by chapter.

Ongoing Story

This unique Web component allows students to report and write a story from beginning to end. Each chapter includes one "Ongoing Story" exercise that draws on the skills you've learned from the text. Starting with a news release, you will plan and conduct virtual interviews, prepare for a one-day shoot, review data to add depth, log sound and video and write a package, as well as a stand-up and Web version. You will then develop a multimedia story plan. Once you complete each step, you can see what the authors did with the same story at each stage.

Skill Building

It's one thing to read about how to do something and another to actually do it. The "Skill Building" section provides exercises that will test what you've learned and your ability to execute the techniques discussed in each chapter. Exercises include honing computer-assisted reporting skills, writing focus statements, developing a blog, creating a newscast line-up, testing ethical decision making and creating your own multimedia portfolio to use as you enter the job market.

Discover

Many people learn best by example. Our "Discover" elements allow you to look at high-quality work produced by other journalists, including their Web projects, slide shows, TV news stories and print articles. We provide explicit guidance on what to look for to help you get the most out of these projects.

Explore

In this section, we provide a guided tour to a vast amount of useful and relevant online material. These "Explore" pages provide annotated links to sites that feature skill-building tutorials, analysis from journalism experts, important research findings and more.

Study

This brief section provides a quick review of each chapter of the text. It includes a summary and a bulleted list of the most important concepts.

ACKNOWLEDGMENTS

"If there's a book you really want to read but it hasn't been written yet, then you must write it."

—Toni Morrison

So we have. Of course, we did it with the help of many, many journalists who took the time to talk with us, to teach us and to share their stories and wisdom. We did it with help from family, friends, colleagues, students, reviewers and editors who believed in the project and worked to make this a better book.

Family members often suffer the most in journalism and in textbook writing, so our deepest thanks go to our spouses and children. Mitch and Jay Wenger seem to have happily forgiven Deb. Bob, Cameron and Evan Witten and Deborah's mother, Louise St. Onge, could not have been more supportive or understanding. And special thanks are in order to Deb's parents, Mike and Avis Halpern, who instilled a love of words in their daughter and who weren't afraid to let her use them.

Colleagues at Virginia Commonwealth University were an invaluable resource, especially June Nicholson, Paula Otto and Jeff South, who freely shared opinions, knowledge and copy editing skills. Sybril Bennett of Belmont University, Don Heider of the University of Maryland, David Kurpius of Louisiana State University, Richard Moore of the University of South Carolina, and Mary Rogus of Ohio University also reviewed the manuscript and offered valuable suggestions.

We are immensely grateful to all the journalists who made much of this text possible. Dan Bradley, Peter Howard and Donna Reed from Media General provided access to the people who work for them and authorized the use of multimedia examples in the text and online. Dan O'Donnell and others at Hearst-Argyle also shared numerous examples, as did Phil O'Connor at Religion & Ethics Newsweekly.

We have quoted liberally from reporters, photojournalists and news managers who have spoken at conferences we've attended over the past decade, including workshops sponsored by the National Press Photographers Association, the Radio-Television News Directors Association and the Online News Association. Many of them also spoke with us in person or on the phone during the writing of the book. We'd specifically like to thank these journalists for their generosity and dedication to improving the profession:

Mary Alvarez	Jason Hanson	Lane Michaelsen
Nancy Amons	Larche Hardy	Kay Miller
Bryan Barr	Byron Harris	Chris Mitchell
Michelle Bearden	Jack Hart	J.J. Murray
Mark Becker	Michele Harvey	Ted Nelson
Kevin Benz	Terry Heaton	Byron Pitts
Bridgette Bornstein	Scott Hedeen	Rod Rassman
Fred Brown	Stan Heist	Juan Renteria
Bob Buckley	Gary Hill	Chet Rhodes
Mark Cardwell	Steve Hooker	Christine Riser
Jennifer Coates	Brad Houston	Les Rose
Candice Combs	Brant Houston	Tom Rosenstiel
Candy Crowley	Cody Howard	Dale Russakoff
David Cullier	Boyd Huppert	Chip Scanlan
Wally Dean	Scott Jensen	Corky Scholl
Bob Dotson	Demetria Kalodimos	Mike Schuh
Mark Douglas	Euan Kerr	Mike Schwartz
Dan Dwyer	Sharon King	Barry Simmons
Mark Fagan	Richard Koci-Hernandez	Sree Srinivasan
Bob Faw	John Larson	Jane Stevens
Celeste Ford	Amy Lehtonen	Steve Sweitzer
Brad Franko	Victoria Lim	Christine Tanaka
Joe Fryer	Scott Livingston	Mackenzie Taylor
Echo Gamel	Caroline Lowe	Julie Templin
Jim Garrott	Chip Mahaney	Al Tompkins
Mark Ginther	Jonathan Malat	Ann Utterback
Seth Gitner	Mike Mather	Stuart Watson
Michele Godard	Regina McCombs	Brian Weister
John Goheen	Josh Meltzer	Dave Wertheimer
Kim Griffis	Preston Mendenhall	Robin Whitmeyer
Tim Griffis	Charlie Meyerson	Amanda Zamora

ADVANCING THE STORY

Marian Pittman of Cox Broadcasting, Deana Reece from KVAL-TV and Bob Witten of NBC News suffered through some early chapter drafts and offered terrific advice for improving the content. We couldn't have produced the "Ongoing Story" exercise of the book's online workbook without the help of Rich Murphy, senior Web producer at WTTG-TV, who shot and edited the video. Mitch Wenger double-checked and clarified our computer-assisted reporting exercises. Any errors are ours alone.

Finally, we would like to thank the people at CQ Press, who were ready to take a chance on a different kind of textbook. In particular, we would like to thank Charisse Kiino, who was the first to get excited about what we had in mind; Mary Marik who copy edited the text and its ancillaries; Kristine Enderle and Lorna Notsch, who worked with us through a hurdle or two along the way; and Jerry Orvedahl, who stretched with us to create our online workbook that we hope instructors and students will actually want to use.

Debora Halpern Wenger
Deborah Potter

1 THE MULTIMEDIA MIND-SET

The way news is gathered and delivered is evolving just as rapidly as audience expectations, techno-logical changes and job descriptions for journalists. In this chapter, we'll take a look at what it means to be a journalist today and why you'll need to quickly develop your own multimedia mind-set.

It's 6:30 a.m. and your alarm is buzzing. You reach out for the remote control to turn on the TV to catch part of your favorite morning newscast. On the drive to work or school, you listen to a little radio news. While sitting at your computer, you get an e-mail alert about an important breaking story, so you check out your favorite news Web site to get more in-formation. On your way to the vending machines, a headline in a newspaper lying on the table catches your eye and you pick it up to glance through the story. Heading back out for an appointment, your cell phone alerts you to the latest developments on a story you've been following.

It's a day in the life of a modern news consumer. But as a journalist, how do you deal with this multitasking, multiplatform, multiple-personality media world?

It's a challenge for many working journalists because they have spent a great deal of time learning how to tell stories to those news consumers using just one form of commu-nication. But it's an incredibly exciting time to begin a career in the field because you now have more ways than ever to tell important stories. Learning to be an effective journalist in a multiplatform world requires an understanding of the ways in which today's news audi-ences are using media, as well as a thorough grounding in the storytelling tools and tech-niques available to you when you're working across platforms.

MULTIMEDIA BASICS

It's hard to spend any time studying journalism without reading or hearing the following terms—multimedia, convergence, cross-platform or multiplatform journalism. Continual advances in communications technology have forced journalists to come up with a new language to describe their storytelling. For the most part, this text will use the terms interchangeably to describe the practice of "communicating complementary information on more than one media platform."

A New Approach

If a television reporter and photographer go out to cover a high school football game, they will shoot far more video of the game and gather a great deal more information than they'll need to tell their story on the 11 o'clock news. If they chose to post online some of the unused video clips and key statistics from the game, they would be practicing multimedia journalism. They would be using more than one media platform—both television and online—and the information they broadcast would be complemented by the unique, additional information posted on the Web. It's this idea that multimedia allows you to communicate more information in new and different ways that gets many journalists jazzed about the concept.

A cross-platform journalist is one who is able to work effectively in more than one medium. For example, some television reporters regularly file separate stories for their stations' Web sites, and some print journalists appear regularly on television news programs because they communicate so well through the broadcast platform. All of these journalists are multimedia journalists.

Audience First

Most news consumers aren't content to get their news and information in one form—the same individual may routinely use television, print and online sources to get information from newscasts, podcasts, articles and vlogs. In fact, according to 2005 research from the Center for Media Design at Ball State University in Muncie, Ind., Americans spend 69 percent of their waking moments using some form of media, from radio to computers to magazines or books. And nearly a third of the time, they're media multitasking, using two or more forms of media at once. For example, many people watch television and surf the Web at the same time, or they work on the computer while listening to music.

FIGURE 1.1 THE MORE THE MERRIER ▬▬▬▬▬▬▬▬▬

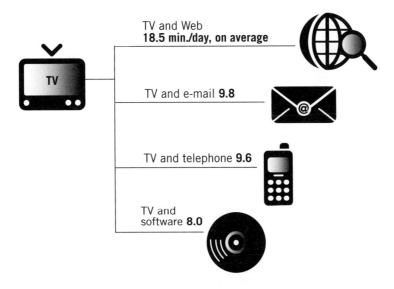

People are multitasking with multimedia these days. Researchers at Ball State University found that people are using television at the same time that they're surfing the Web, answering e-mail, talking on the phone and using other computer programs.

Source: Middletown Media Studies, Ball State University 2005; Scott Wallace.

3

And though it's always been important for journalists to keep the audience top of mind, it's now even more critical than before. As you begin to work on any story, you should be asking yourself what the audience will get out of it, what questions they will have and what answers you can provide. In the world of multimedia journalism, thinking about the audience becomes even more imperative because the platform you use to deliver it will affect what the audience gets out of it.

Let's say there is major flooding in your community. The audience for a television newscast may tune in to see the latest on the impact of the flooding, how some of the worst-hit neighborhoods are being affected, as well as the weather forecast for the next few hours. At the same time, the online audience may be logging on to read and add their own comments to a live blog dealing with issues such as what roads are currently blocked off or which shelters take pets and which don't. The audience for the next day's paper will

A NEW TYPE OF JOURNALIST

"In March of 2004, I was hired by Media General as the first-ever convergence intern and placed in the company's Roanoke/Lynchburg/Danville, Va. market—which includes two daily newspapers and a television station," Crider says. "I was called a guinea pig, a young Frankenstein, an experiment and even a new animal. My official title was 'Convergence Intern/Reporter.'

"My first project began as a daily news story on local homelessness for the newspaper, but it soon mushroomed into a full-blown convergence series, and I found myself writing on all platforms, carrying a video camera, editing a television package and streaming interviews for the Web. My head had become a hat rack, and it filled up fast.

"In the end, the 'experiment' was a success for everyone—including me," Crider says. "I am now a full-time reporter for WSLS in Roanoke—still converging with the company's Web sites and newspapers in Lynchburg and Danville and loving every minute of it."

Jeremy Crider's business cards indicate that he is a reporter for WSLS-TV in Roanoke, Va., but Crider will tell you he's a journalist—the medium he works for may change, but his mission to tell important and compelling stories does not.

likely be looking for the big picture—did emergency preparation pay off or how does this latest flooding compare with previous floods? Multimedia journalists will be thinking about all of these possibilities as they work on their individual stories; they will look for opportunities to use the tools of multimedia to provide many different pieces of information to several different audiences on multiple media platforms.

MEDIA ON DEMAND

In addition to having access to multiple news delivery systems, we are now also living in an "on demand" world. News consumers expect to get information when and how they want it—not on a timetable set by a television station or a newspaper operation. For a journalist, that means getting into a 24/7 mind-set. Instead of focusing all of your attention on one story that will air at 6 p.m. or appear above the fold in tomorrow's newspaper, you need to be thinking about the audience that's out there right now, hungry for information as soon as it's been verified and vetted.

It's quite likely that you will work, or perhaps you already work, for a newsroom that breaks stories on the Web or sends breaking news directly to people using mobile devices first, and then worries about traditional content delivery platforms such as television or print. In the flooding example above, the multimedia journalist may first produce a short vodcast for video-capable cell phones before putting together a more traditional TV story for the 6 o'clock news.

The Multimedia Industry

Several communications companies take a "get the consumers wherever they are" approach to the max. ESPN is truly a multimedia powerhouse—from its cable TV channels to its print magazine to its Web site, the company has become synonymous with sports information by reaching out to sports consumers wherever they can be found.

MTV is another big multimedia player. The music television network has expanded online in a major way through its MTV Overdrive Web site. When Jessica Simpson premiered her latest video on MTV's Total Request Live, the network simultaneously delivered a different version of the show on MTV Overdrive, Broadcasting & Cable magazine reported in 2006. The Web version offered a look at what was going on backstage, as well as a phone interview with the video's director, in which he shared some revealing stories about Simpson. Beyond that, MTV offered on-demand access online to Simpson's most popular videos. "The idea is to give the viewer as much control and access to all things about a particular guest or show," said Dave Sirulnick, executive vice president of multiplatform production at MTV.[1]

Multimedia Journalists

Increasingly, strong news organizations are looking to hire journalists who fully understand this need to give consumers more ways to access information and more control over how they do it. KPNX-TV in Phoenix produces multiple webcasts and periodic "textcasts" for cell phones each day, in addition to its regularly scheduled television newscasts. The producers know that people watching them on the Web want quick updates on the stories, not a lot of depth and detail, so the writers change their styles, depending on whether they are writing the TV or the Web version of the story.

Stations like KPNX want journalists who understand how the gathering and presentation of content change as the distribution of that content differs. In other words, as the medium changes, the best journalists will be versatile enough to know how the message should change as well.

WFLA in Tampa, Florida, is one of many news organizations around the country that are producing content specifically for a Web site. Webcasts typically feature shorter stories that quickly bring viewers up to date on the major stories of the day.

Source: TBO.com.

TECHNOLOGY CHANGES CONTENT

Media are evolving so quickly that within a few years, we'll probably be delivering news and information in ways we haven't even imagined yet. The word "podcast" wasn't in anyone's vocabulary until 2004; within a year, thousands of podcasts were available online.

The concept of considering the best way to present content based on the delivery method goes far beyond the obvious differences, such as the fact that television news uses sound and video and a printed newspaper doesn't. It means that journalists must think about how they can provide useful information to people in all sorts of different ways. The presentation will obviously be different for a podcast, a newspaper article or an online story and so will the content, because consumers using those media want different things. A podcast listener might want a headline summary with sound bites, a newspaper reader might want more details and an online news consumer might want to see the documents that underpin the story. Journalists have to know what elements they have to collect so they can effectively present news and information to consumers in all these media.

In addition, this means that the best multimedia journalists will stay on top of changes in communications technology. For example, the increase in the number of people with high-speed Internet connections is at least partly responsible for changing the thinking about the use of video and elaborate graphics online. Before high-speed connections were common, many news organizations hesitated to post multiple video clips and to create high-level, interactive graphics because the download time for people on dial-up connections made those features nearly impossible to use. Even more recently, the explosion in the number of people with mobile communication devices—from cell phones to BlackBerries to the iPhone—has journalists rethinking the way they handle breaking news. These are just a couple of examples of the ways in which the development and increasing use of new technologies are having an impact on the way journalists do their jobs. We'll talk more about this phenomenon in Chapter 12.

Good Journalism Matters

Journalism is ripe with opportunity for storytellers, and learning how to take a multimedia approach to stories gives you the potential to reach a more diverse group of people with more important news and information.

ON THE MULTIMEDIA HIGHWAY WITH THE READER BEHIND THE WHEEL

By Meg Martin, associate editor, Poynter Online

So the idea of podcasting still makes your skin crawl. And let's not get *started* with blogging . . .

But multimedia storytelling and journalism are forever intertwined.

Acknowledging that fact—and embracing it—not only makes for good cocktail conversation. It's a necessary career move for any journalist, Miami Herald managing editor for multimedia Rick Hirsch [told an audience at the 2006 National Writers Workshop in Ft. Lauderdale, Fla.].

He and Tom Davidson, general manager of Sun-Sentinel.com, gave a presentation on what journalists need to know about "new" media.

But to ride the multimedia wave, not every journalist has to start packing prosumer cameras (although it wouldn't hurt) and learning Flash. You don't even need to get down with the lingo. You just need to start *thinking* like a multimedia journalist.

"You *don't* have to be everything. But you *do* need to know what multimedia elements can do to make your story stronger," he said.

Hirsch recommends:

For reporters: Add one more element to your thought process. *How might this story work on the Web?*

Still, it's important to remember that good journalism skills are universal—they apply to all platforms. As the technology used to manage the content becomes easier to navigate, multimedia journalism is likely to become less about knowing how to post a story or stream a piece of video and more about the skills it takes to gather and present information that is relevant and compelling to an audience—regardless of whether that audience is watching, reading or interacting with the story. As Mike Wendland, who covers technology for

For line editors: Think about the multimedia aspects of the story.

And don't forget the key question. "Who is the reader of your Web site? May be different than the reader of your newspaper," he added.

"If you're a journalist today, I think the idea that, 'Oh, that's not for me,' is a death wish. . . . Survival depends on you."

So teach yourself. Hirsch did. To learn what it took to edit video, he bought himself a MacBook and a camera and edited some footage. He wanted to figure out how much time it took, how much skill was involved and the quality of product he could expect from self-training.

The same thread that kept running through the entire weekend came up in this session, too: "Reporting is the core of what we do," Hirsch reminded his audience. It's just a different kind of delivery platform that he and Davidson preached.

With technology improving constantly, newspapers' multimedia operations are constantly behind the curve, Hirsch said. And they tend to be slow to move. "We are losing ground while we're sitting here talking about whether we should be doing this or not." The beauty—or the bane, depending on which way you look at it, he said—of the Internet, though, is its trial-and-error nature. Staff blogs, for instance. If they work, great. Keep doing them. If readers don't like them? Can 'em.

"The reader drives," he said. *Vroom.*

Source: Meg Martin, "On the Multimedia Highway with the Reader behind the Wheel," Poynter Online, October 2, 2006, www.poynter.org/column.asp?id=86&aid=111476.

both the Detroit Free Press and NBC, puts it, "Our skill set as storytellers will be more in demand than ever."

In addition, adherence to journalism's best practices and ethical codes is also essential. As the speed increases and the methods of dissemination vary, our journalism must be sounder than ever. Your reputation and that of your news organization are only as strong as your credibility, so just because technology allows you to do something does not mean

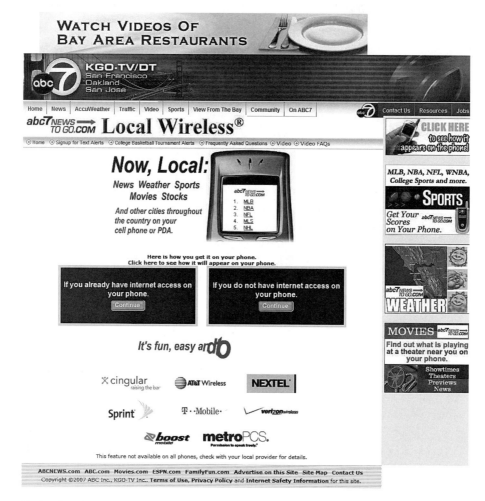

Technology is changing news delivery systems, too. As more people stay informed through mobile devices, journalists like those at ABC7 in San Francisco must adjust to more immediate deadlines and develop new storytelling forms.

Source: KGO-TV/DT, ABC 7 in San Francisco, Oakland and San Jose, Calif.

its something you should do. For example, you may be able to post a horrific 9-1-1 tape on the Web, but you should still ask yourself about the journalistic purpose of posting that audio before taking advantage of the option.

The Power of Multimedia

Never before have journalists had so many storytelling tools with which to work. When you can take advantage of broadcast's powerful sound and imagery, print's depth and detail and online media's interactivity, you have the potential to reach more people with more of an impact. The key for today's journalists is to find a way to report information in the medium that works best for each individual news consumer.

In the most progressive newsrooms, journalists have the potential to do a better job of telling stories because they can now show, tell and invite the audience to interact with the information. For the rest of this chapter, we'll explore what broadcast, print and online media do best to give you the foundation you'll need to develop powerful multimedia stories.

THE BEST OF BROADCAST

Ask most people where they went first to learn about the impact of Hurricane Katrina and they will likely mention watching television news. The same was true immediately following the attacks against America on September 11, 2001, and during the first few days of the war with Iraq. In fact, according to a study done in September 2005 by the Pew Research Center for the People and the Press, 89 percent of the people they polled were following the Hurricane Katrina disaster by watching television news. The numbers for the war in Iraq and the September 11 attacks were almost exactly the same—Pew found that 89 percent of those polled initially kept up with the war in Iraq by watching television and 90 percent got most of their news about the September 11 attacks from TV.[2] So, why were these three huge news events so dominated by television viewing in the beginning? Because technology allows broadcast journalists to present history as it happens.

Even when the events are not nearly as far-reaching or dramatic as Katrina or September 11, television journalists can still combine words, sound and pictures to create a sense of being there for the viewer. A great broadcast storyteller can make you feel like you know the person being interviewed, you've been to the location being showcased or that you were at the event yourself. So, when you begin to plan a multimedia story, you need to keep the strengths of broadcast journalism in mind.

Immediacy

Television news is able to let viewers watch events as they occur or to report on them within minutes, or even seconds, after they happen. Live trucks, satellite uplinks and even Internet connections allow television news crews to broadcast directly from the scene of breaking news events, showing viewers how big a fire is or taking them inside a courtroom to hear a judge read out a verdict in real time.

For example, when the town of Austin, Minn., was inundated with several feet of water, anchor Pete Hjelmstad of KIMT-TV in Mason City, Iowa, donned his hip waders and stood live in the middle of a flooded street to show viewers exactly how serious the situation was in some parts of the city. From that vantage point, he acted as a narrator over live pictures of people trying to break into second floor windows of their own businesses to salvage what little they could.

But this ability to disseminate information instantly or extremely quickly comes with risks. It is always better to be right than first and wrong, so "going live" or "getting on the air with the information" should be secondary to checking the facts.

Some of the best broadcast journalism allows the audience to share in the experience of others. In a story about a home explosion and fire in Baltimore, Md., WBFF-TV viewers could hear and see for themselves how neighbors reacted.

Source: Courtesy of WBFF-TV.

Impact of Visuals and Emotion

Great print journalists are able to convey emotion and create pictures in the reader's mind through their writing, but broadcast journalists have an edge when it comes to this kind of reporting. Through the use of video, broadcasters can actually let viewers hear the mother's plea or see how swollen the river is at flood stage. TV journalists must still use words effectively to explain or supplement the video, but there's no substitute for great pictures combined with strong writing.

At WBBH-TV in Ft. Myers, Fla., vast brush fires were eating up thousands of acres in Collier County, a key part of the station's coverage area. In one story, a reporter-photographer was covering the impact of the fire on a family-owned dog kennel. In his video we saw flames just a few yards away from the dogs and their cages as the owner of the kennel started opening the cage doors and urging the dogs to get out and run. The video of her frantically trying to save the animals and calling out, "Get out of here, go, go!" was one of the most powerful moments in the newscast—one that likely affected viewers in a way that few other stories did that day.

Again, this ability comes with responsibility. There will be pictures that are too graphic to use and sound that's too disturbing to hear. For example, some stations have policies against airing "moment of death" video or audio. If they get pictures of a fatal car crash as it's occurring or if officials release a 9-1-1 recording of a woman being beaten to death, these stations refuse to air the content. They believe the story can still be told without these potentially disturbing elements. Good journalists must always weigh the storytelling benefit against any potential harm the story might cause. We'll talk more about the ethical use of visuals in Chapter 11.

Audience Connection

Part of the reason why broadcast news has been so successful is that it is the medium in which a person is actually "telling" a story to the audience. Viewers make a personal connection with anchors and reporters. That may be one reason why so many newscasts begin or end by saying, "Thank you for watching." Broadcasters realize that many people in the audience do feel as if they are inviting the newscasters into their homes, and that invitation comes with certain expectations.

"When is the last time a newspaper thanked its readers?" asks Michele Godard, news director at KALB-TV in Alexandria, La. "As subtle as this seems, it works its way into viewers' mind[s] and they feel a greater stake in our lives."

Before she became the boss, Godard was one of the station's primary anchors, and her experience convinced her that television stations have an enhanced personal connection with the viewers. "When I was the evening news anchor I was pregnant twice," Godard said. "Do you know people still stop me in the street and sigh when they see how big my kids are? They chart their lives by the ups and downs of ours." For Godard, the connection works both ways. "I can tell you that as a result of the very personal connection I feel with our viewers I tend to take the information we provide more seriously," she said. "When our anchors read a story about a murder, I immediately wonder who the person was. Did that man or woman ever stop me in the store and ask about my children? It drives me to be more vigilant."

Good television newscasts provide the audience with important information presented in a compelling manner. That can include anchors and reporters who are good communicators, graphics that help better explain the stories and even music that helps set the mood or tone of a story.

THE POWER OF PRINT

Newspapers have a long and illustrious history in the United States. When the framers of the U.S. Constitution included the guarantee of press freedom, they understood that the dominant media of the time—newspapers—played a fundamental role in preserving our democracy.

Even today—with the explosion of broadcast and online news outlets—newspapers continue to cover government and politics in far more depth than any other medium.

Newspapers also do much of the great investigative reporting in this country, and some of that may be attributed to the strengths of the medium. As you work on planning your multimedia stories, you'll want to remember the following print attributes.

Depth

In general, most newspaper articles are longer than the broadcast version of the same story. For example, CBS Evening News once did a story about a new treatment for asthma sufferers. The Washington Post reported the same story the next day. The CBS News story was approximately 2:00 long. When, in an experiment, the Washington Post story was read aloud by a local TV news anchor, it was more than 4:40 long. The essential elements of the story were reported by both news organizations, but the Washington Post story included more background on the Food and Drug Administration approval process for the drug, more information about how much the drug might cost and why the drug might not be right for everyone. The added depth would have made the story particularly relevant to someone considering using the drug.

Detail

Though similar to what we've outlined above, detail can also simply mean adding more specifics. For example, many print stories will include the age of a subject, the middle initial of an interviewee and specific numbers instead of a rounded figure. This additional detail can help in terms of ensuring accuracy and understanding. If someone's name is Peter Smith, then reporting on "Peter E. Smith, 52, of Mountain Lake, Va." makes it far less likely that someone will think the story refers to 19-year-old Peter W. Smith who lives in Richmond.

Since newspapers can't rely on video to convey information, television journalists writing print stories story must be sure to incorporate significant details from the video into the text. Using the example of the fire threatening the kennel in Florida, the print version of the story might have included a paragraph like this:

> With the flames less than 10 yards away from the dogs in their kennels, Atwell started unlocking the cage doors one by one. With tears streaming down her face and a voice hoarse from inhaling smoke, Atwell pulled the dogs out, pointed them away from the fire and shouted, "Get out of here, go, go!"

Without video to help set the scene, the writer for print must be more specific about the nearness of the fire and must describe what the subject is doing and how she looks and sounds in order for the reader to fully experience the drama of the moment.

The risk of including too much depth and detail is that you bog the story down or make it boring and unreadable, but most television journalists writing newspaper stories easily avoid that trap.

Permanence and Portability

Ask avid newspaper readers why they like newspapers, and many will mention the fact that you can take the paper with you wherever you go. The portability and permanence of a newspaper allow you to reread something that you didn't get the first time or to save it for later reference. This unique characteristic is important for those planning multimedia stories—anything that you think the audience may want to hold on to for any length of time might best be presented in print.

For example, the Sarasota Herald-Tribune, like many newspapers in the coastal areas of the United States, prints an annual hurricane guide for readers. These guides feature everything from evacuation routes to shelter locations to tips for protecting homes from high wind damage. If the lights go out and the TV and computer fail, readers can refer to their copies of the guide to get vital emergency information.

However, both permanence and portability are becoming part of the online experience—when you can routinely download and save content to a PDA or other device, permanence and portability may no longer be just newspaper strengths.

Seattle is one of the few U.S. cities that still has two major daily newspapers. Commuters there can choose between the Seattle Post-Intelligencer and the Seattle Times newspapers. According to the Newspaper Association of America, the total number of daily newspapers nationwide has been dropping since at least 1980.

THE ORIGINALITY OF ONLINE

All of you have probably already gone online to get news or information at some point. Online news is one of the fastest-growing media sectors. According to the Pew Research Center for the People and the Press, the number of people who go online for news three or more days a week stood at 31 percent in 2006, up from 2 percent in 1996. Looking at Table 2.1, you'll notice it's the only news medium that has a growing audience.[3]

Most likely when you turn to the Web for information, you go in search of something specific. You may choose to get news online because you don't want to wait for the nightly news or for the next day's paper. According to the Pew research, online news is valued most for headlines and convenience, not detailed, in-depth reporting. This "getting the information you want when you want it" is one of three key strengths of online journalism.

TABLE 1.1 THE CHANGING LANDSCAPE OF NEWS ▮▮▮▮▮▮

	1993 %	1996 %	2000 %	2002 %	2004 %	2006 %
Regularly watch...						
Local TV news	77	65	56	57	59	54
Cable TV news	—	—	—	33	38	34
Nightly network news	60	42	30	32	34	28
Network morning news	—	—	20	22	22	23
Listened / read yesterday						
Radio	47*	44	43	41	40	36
Newspaper	58*	50	47	41	42	40
Online news three or more days per week	—	2^	23	25	29	31

*From 1994   ^From 1995

Source: "Online Papers Modestly Boost Newspaper Readership," Pew Research Center for the People and the Press, July 30, 2006, http://people-press.org/reports/display.php3?PageID=1064.

A decade ago, just one-in-fifty Americans got the news with some regularity from what was then a brand-new source: the Internet. Today, nearly one-in-three regularly get news online.

On Demand

With other media, the news consumer is essentially at the mercy of those who select when and what information to air or publish. In the online world, if the information is posted somewhere, the savvy Internet user can usually find it. Even if the information will be included in a broadcast and in the newspaper eventually, if it's also online, the user does not have to wait to access the information on someone else's timetable.

CBS News, for example, streams its nightly newscast on the Web to gain viewers who can't or don't want to watch the broadcast during the time slots it airs on television. Like many other news outlets, CBS is trying to capture audience whenever it is available.

The Web also provides access to more information than could ever be aired in a single television program or published in a single newspaper. The "bottomless news hole" of the Web creates an opportunity to satisfy news consumers who want more than what the traditional media can offer.

Interactivity

Online media give journalists the opportunity to ask the audience to do more than passively read or watch a story—online users can be invited to explore information on their own, add perspectives to the storytelling or literally try something for themselves. This may be the real key to making multimedia stories powerful. For example, you may be working on a story about restaurants that don't meet state health standards. You will only be able include a limited number of restaurants in your broadcast or print story, but if you add an online component, you can give users access to the entire restaurant report database so they can search for their favorite restaurants' ratings on their own. You could ask users to add their own restaurant horror stories to a message board or invite customer reviews of popular restaurants. If you have a creative online production team, you might work with the health department to create an interactive Inspection Game. The game might use a series of photos of a typical kitchen and ask users to spot the violations that health inspectors have set up for the purpose of this teaching tool.

Innovation

As you can see, the online medium allows us to combine the best of print and broadcast in innovative ways. Often journalists who don't understand the technical side of the Web are afraid to brainstorm the online component of a multimedia story because they don't know what's possible. The secret is to think from an audience perspective: How can we present the information in a way that's most helpful to the user's understanding? How can I make exploring this issue fun for the user? How can I find out what the user already knows or wants to know about this story?

When the Richmond Times-Dispatch was working on content to help commemorate the anniversary of the 1965 Selma civil rights march, one of the reporters involved discovered something called the Alabama Literacy Test. Blacks in Alabama had to take the test in order to vote, but the questions were so difficult that almost no one—white or black—would have been able to pass. The Web producers posted a series of the test questions, which helped people understand the type of discrimination that blacks were facing at the time.

Sometimes you will want to create completely unique content but you may not have the technical support to do exactly what you want. Even so, you'll be surprised how much you can accomplish if you can get people excited about a good, interactive idea.

At WGAL in Lancaster, Pa., important stories are routinely enhanced online. In the aftermath of a major storm on Valentine's Day 2007, WGAL posted results of an independent investigation into how the state handled the storm, video of the governor's apology and archive footage from the station's storm coverage; and the station invited viewers to comment on it all.

Source: WGAL in Lancaster, Pa. Retrieved from WGAL.com on August 16, 2007. www.wgal.com/news/11035174/detail.html.

FOCUS ON THE FUTURE

Although the news media are going through a period of rapid change and evolution, change itself is not new and should not be seen as a threat for journalists. It's important to remember that new media seldom, if ever, replace the old. We still read books, we still listen to the radio and we certainly still watch television; however, it's indisputable that most news media are trying to adapt to the changing technologies and a changing news consumer culture that is more fractured than ever. No longer can you count on the fact that a majority of adults in America will read a daily newspaper, and no longer can you be sure that the 6 o'clock newscast will be the most critical broadcast of the day. What you can be sure of is that journalists who are skilled in the journalism basics—researching, interviewing, writing and ethics—will be able to succeed in a changing media environment if they are willing to embrace the idea that it's the story that matters.

Media General, Inc., has been a key player in the area of convergence, especially at its Tampa properties, which include WFLA-TV, the Tampa Tribune and TBO.com. "Journalists have to get over the idea that it's 'their story,' " says Dan Bradley, vice president of news for the Media General Broadcast Group. "The story belongs to the audience and once reporters accept that, it doesn't seem to matter whether the story is published on the air, online or in print."

What Bradley and many other news managers within the field of journalism are looking for are journalists who want to tell stories—regardless of platform. And those journalists who are already adept at telling stories in more than one medium are more likely to get jobs or to move up. Mike McMearty, news director at WTOP Radio in Washington, D.C., says, "If I have two candidates, each with the same skills and experience, but one of them is comfortable writing and working on the Web and one is not, I'm going to hire the one who knows the Web."

And beyond enhancing your ability to get a job in broadcast or print, learning about multimedia journalism may also jump-start a career for you in online journalism itself. Fox Television recently hired Web news producers for all of its owned stations' sites. Web sites like washingtonpost.com are hiring video journalists and calling them VJs—they're one-person storytellers who report what's going on through video on the Web site. As the Web audience grows, it's expected that Web staffs will grow as well, creating new opportunities for online producers, Web-only reporters and editors.

Caroline Little is the chief executive officer and publisher of Washingtonpost. Newsweek Interactive (WPNI), which operates washingtonpost.com, newsweek.com, Slate and Budget Travel Online. Little says newsgathering is still at the heart of what they do within the Washington Post Company. But Little says, "The method, the reach and the scope of how we communicate will never be the same." Today's journalists must remember that though the emphasis on solid newsgathering and storytelling skills remains, the future brings new challenges and new opportunities.

TAKING IT HOME

It is essential for today's journalists to understand how the audience is accessing and using news and information now, as well as the ways in which the message must change as the medium changes. Capitalizing on the strengths of each media platform available to you will make you a more effective storyteller and will help ensure that your audiences get the information they need.

This text is about preparing you for jobs that are changing and jobs that have not yet even been envisioned. "Opportunities to work across platforms will only be limited by the journalists and the organizations they work for," says Mike Schwartz, who heads up editorial training for CoxNet and Cox Newspapers, Inc. He believes that one well-trained and enthusiastic journalist can have a major impact. "The multimedia journalist can be the catalyst to help move a news organization into the multimedia world through his or her multimedia skills." You could be that catalyst, that change agent, that leader; and we hope this text will help you on your way.

TALKING POINTS

1. Log on to the Pew Research Center for the People and the Press (http://people-press.org) and check out the latest research on how people are using news media. What implications does the research have on the way journalists are or should be doing their jobs? Pay particular attention to the demographic breakdowns for media use. What do the data suggest to you in terms of serving a diverse audience?

2. For one 24-hour period, track your news media usage. How much time are you spending with each medium? Are there stories that you saw mentioned on more than one platform? Are there stories that were unique to one platform? Did the news organization involved do anything specific to capitalize on the power of its medium?

3. Find a good multimedia storytelling example. Whether it's a broadcast story with a Web companion piece, or a print article that's enhanced online or a story that uses some other combination of media platforms, analyze how the journalists involved are leveraging the platforms included in the presentation.

eLEARNING OPPORTUNITIES

For chapter exercises, practice tools and additional resources, go to the interactive online workbook at http://college.cqpress.com/advancingthestory. You'll find:

- SKILL BUILDING: Take an interactive quiz to test your knowledge of the strengths of each media platform.

- DISCOVER: Review examples of multimedia reporting and evaluate what worked well and how the storytelling could have been improved.

- ONGOING STORY: Start developing a multimedia mind-set by taking a look at a typical assignment and beginning to think about the reporting you could do for the story.

- EXPLORE: Visit Web sites to learn more about current digital media issues and trends affecting journalists and their newsrooms.

2 REPORTING THE STORY

If you're interested in the news business, you're no doubt curious about the world around you and passionate about learning something new every day. Those traits are essential to generate story ideas, and the ability to find stories is one of the most valuable skills you can bring to any newsroom, no matter what your job. In this chapter, you'll learn how to find and develop better story ideas, gather useful background and research quickly, discover fresh sources and conduct better interviews, with an eye toward producing stories in a variety of media.

Police and fire scanners squawk loudly at the assignment desk. There's a steady stream of incoming phone calls and e-mails with news tips, press releases and announcements of scheduled events. The computer system chimes when the wire services file updates. In a typical broadcast, print or online newsroom, most of the day's stories will come from sources like these. But the scanners, e-mails and wires only provide reporters with a starting point.

Good reporters do much more than just get the facts, check them for accuracy and pass them along. It takes clear thinking and hard work to produce a television story worth watching, a print or online story that's a compelling read or an interactive element that helps the audience understand the story better. And in today's newsrooms, reporters may be asked to do all three.

"It's what's going to be required of them if they stay in the business," says Andy Cole of the Morning News in Florence, S.C. As a business reporter for the newspaper, he frequently appears on his paper's television partner, WBTW-TV. "I really believe that convergence is only going to grow."

It sounds like a lot of work to report for multiple media, but reporter Mark Fagan of the Lawrence Journal-World in Lawrence, Kan., says it's fun and rewarding. He often reports for the newspaper, a co-owned cable TV news operation and their Web sites. "You get a chance to tell your story to more people," he says. Fagan believes all journalists can succeed in any medium if they just know how to report.

FINDING STORIES

You've probably been told that a story's news value is based on such factors as timeliness, impact, proximity, controversy, prominence and oddity. Those are good guidelines, but they don't really help you find newsworthy stories that aren't on the daybook or in the newspaper. To do that, you have to fine-tune your powers of observation and ask new questions to unearth the stories others may miss. The payoff is well worth the investment. "There are so many stories out there, you won't live long enough to do them all," says photojournalist John Goheen, who's done hundreds of stories for CBS and NBC, as well as local stations.

Read, Look and Listen

Go beyond the obvious newspapers, magazines and media Web sites. Bulletin boards, church announcements, zoning notices, club notes, classified ads, community Web sites and school newspapers can be sources of story ideas. One reporter found a great TV feature by following a classified ad that read, "For Sale: Fainting Goats."

Keep your eyes and ears open for what's important or unusual. What are people talking about at the gym, the grocery store or the coffee shop? What do you notice on your way to school or work? Have you tried taking a different route and really looking around? Get outside your comfort zone and visit communities that are different from the one you live in to find stories that other reporters may have missed.

News director Jim Garrott of WEEK-TV in Peoria, Ill., once did a simple exercise to show his staff how to find stories. He took an hour, went home and had dinner and then walked his daughter around the block. In that time he came up with 37 story ideas—including a story about downtown development and another about the growing popularity of home sales "by owner."

Follow Up and Plan Ahead

Journalists are a lot like 4-year-olds, always asking "why?" and "how come?" If something strikes you as interesting, try to learn more about it; you'll often find there's a story just waiting to be told. Here's one example: a Dallas reporter who asked questions about a construction site he passed on the way to work each day turned the answers into a story about the phenomenal growth of megachurches.

Look back and see what's happened since the last report on a particular subject, or look ahead to see what might happen next. Some journalists make a habit of looking back at stories they covered a year ago or five years ago to see if there's a follow-up to be done. Look for a fresh angle on a predictable story that everyone will do, like the tax-filing dead-line or Veterans Day. Find someone in advance to build your story around, perhaps a per-son from a segment of your community that is not often heard from on the news like the poor or racial or ethnic minorities.

Don't give up if your story idea doesn't pan out immediately. If you think you've found a nugget of a story, keep working to develop it further. Good reporters often track ideas for

BRAINSTORMING BASICS

Brainstorming is a time-tested, collaborative way of generating lots of ideas quickly. It works best in groups of no more than a dozen. One person should take on the role of facilitator to establish ground rules, write down ideas and make sure that everyone participates.

- Anything goes and no one can criticize anyone's ideas. Don't even discuss ideas until the brainstorming session is over.

- Keep a record of all ideas, ideally on a flip chart where everyone can see them. Don't edit or elaborate.

- Everyone should participate. If people don't want to speak up, they can write ideas down and hand them in.

- Think fast and work quickly. The more ideas the better.

- Wild and crazy ideas can spark productive ones, so feel free to propose anything and everything.

- Give people time to look over the list and build on what they see. "Hitchhiking" or "piggybacking" on others' ideas should be welcome.

TRADE TOOLS

weeks before their story begins to take shape. We'll talk more about how to do this in Chapter 4.

Develop Stories from Topics

It's important to understand that a story idea is not the same thing as a topic. "Let's take a look at falling gas prices" is a topic. It's a starting point, but it's too broad and general to suggest what direction the story will take, and it fails the "so what?" test. Because you're not asking a specific question about the topic, you're not likely to find any useful answers. "Let's find out if people are driving more now that gas prices have dropped" is an idea. It may not turn out to be true, but it's something worth investigating.

To develop specific story ideas from a broad topic, try brainstorming with a few colleagues to see what questions you might want your story to answer. Or sketch out a story map, as writing coach Don Murray suggests. Put the topic in the center of a piece of paper and see where it leads (see a story map example in Figure 2.1 on the following page). Put the topic in the center of a piece of paper and see where it leads. Each new idea can lead you to a different angle on the story. You might decide to pursue one or two of these ideas for your main piece while you collect information about other angles for use in a graphic, sidebar or a story for another platform.

STORY BUILDING BLOCKS

Every beginning reporter knows the basic questions any story must answer: the five Ws and an H. The reporter needs to know who did what, where and when, and if possible, why and how. But skilled reporters collect more than the essential facts so they can tell a compelling story. They dig deeper for the universal building blocks of great storytelling.

Character

Memorable stories feature people who are directly involved in the issue or situation, directly affected by it or who have a stake in the outcome. Good reporters build stories around strong characters whose experience illustrates a wider truth or the impact of an event or policy. They explore people's motivations in order to develop the characters in their stories. For example, the volunteer serving meals at the soup kitchen might have been homeless once herself. "Great stories begin and end with people," says NBC correspondent John Larson, "not talking heads."

FIGURE 2.1 STORY MAPPING ▰▰▰▰▰▰▰▰▰▰▰▰▰

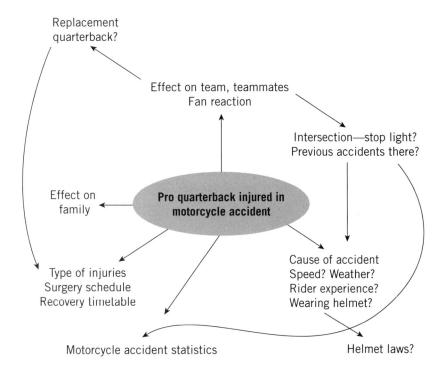

A story map like this one can suggest different angles for reporters to pursue. Start with a news development—in this case, a motorcycle crash that injured a pro football quarterback—and see where it leads you.

27

Place

Great stories transport the audience to give them a sense of what it was like at the scene. Experienced reporters know how to bring a scene to life by using all of their senses—not just looking and listening, but smelling and almost tasting a story so they can use their observations to bring the audience closer to the story. They can tell us what burning rubber smells like after an accident, and how far away you could feel the heat of a fire. In some stories a place can become a kind of central character; in stories about conservation or climate change, for example, the main focus could be on a region like the Everglades or the Arctic.

Emotion

A story that speaks to a human emotion—whether it's anger, joy or empathy—is more engaging to the audience. Al Tompkins, broadcast and online group leader at the Poynter Institute, often says that people remember what they feel longer than what they hear. Good reporters look for the emotion in stories, even when it's not readily apparent. A dry sentencing hearing has significance to someone in the courtroom. You just have to find that person and let him or her talk.

Detail

Well-chosen details help the audience understand a story or character better. Reporters have to be keen observers so they can collect details that will enhance the story, not bog it down. It might be useful to know how long the city council members debated an ordinance, but only if they spent a particularly long or short amount of time doing it. On the other hand, it would be worth knowing that an American Indian doctor is the grandchild of a tribal healer in a story about the use of treatments that blend traditional and modern medicines.

Tension or Surprise

Stories should make the audience want to know what happens next, and how it will all come out in the end. Reporters should look for turning points and moments that illustrate the central theme of a story. A story about immigrants becoming U.S. citizens would likely explore these milestones along the way: deciding to leave their home country, learning English, passing the test and being sworn in.

RESEARCH STRATEGIES

"Knowledge is the precursor of reporting," says reporter Byron Harris of WFAA-TV in Dallas, Texas. "I always felt I had to know more than anyone else to win." Harris is one of those reporters who is always researching. He reads everything he can get his hands on about all kinds of issues, from science to economics, looking for stories and learning as he goes. "The difference between reporters is energy," he says, "intellectual [energy] as well as pursuing the story."

It does take intellectual energy to think about stories in multiple layers, which is what you have to do if you're reporting the same story for different platforms. The need to col-

Imagine that you are covering this event. What might you notice, using all of your senses? Who might you want to interview? What questions would you ask?

Source: Licensed by Creative Commons "Attribute" license. Uploaded by Flickr user Editor B on January 12, 2007, from www.flickr.com/photos/editor/355146869.

lect material that plays to each medium's strengths makes research more important than ever for journalists today. The more you know about a story early on, the more efficient you can be in the field, whether you're shooting a TV story, gathering information for an interactive graphic or both.

Every story requires some research. On a breaking news story, you may not have time to do much more than get directions before you head out to the scene, but you'll probably need some background before you're done. On the other hand, if you're being sent to a news conference, you'll want to do some research in advance so you can ask better questions and identify materials you'll want to bring back. Let's imagine that you're covering the aftermath of a construction site accident that badly injured two workers. Here are just some of the avenues you could follow during the research phase.

Follow the Stakeholders

Find out who has a stake in the story—that is, who is most directly involved or affected. Think as broadly as possible at this point, because there's no way to know what information will turn out to be significant. In this case, you'd obviously want to know what companies were working on the site, who owns them and who owns the land, but you would also want to gather information about neighboring businesses. Learn all you can about the injured workers—were they union members or day laborers, experienced or new on the job? You'd definitely want to contact the workers' families about how the accident has affected them, and you'd follow up with their co-workers and any eyewitnesses who could shed additional light on what happened.

Seek Background and Data

Look into what may have happened in the past to see if you spot a cause or a pattern. You'd want to know whether there had been any safety problems at the site in the past, whether the construction company had been cited for safety violations at any other jobs, which permits the company had obtained and whether anyone had opposed granting those permits. You'd also want to know about any similar accidents that have happened in the past.

Search for related information that can help you put a story in context. How many construction workers are injured in accidents like this every year? Which government regulations—local, state or federal—cover construction sites? How many inspectors does the city have? How often do they inspect each site?

Consult Experts

Once you know some of the questions you need to have answered, find out who and where the subject experts are. In this case, you'd want to look for people who know the construction business and how it's regulated. Look beyond the "usual suspects" for sources who will bring diverse perspectives to your story. For example, if the injured workers were not native English speakers, you might want an expert source who can talk about the particular challenges these workers face on the job.

RESEARCH TOOLS

The good news is that journalists today have more tools available to find the information they need quickly, thanks to computers and the Web. Many modern tools are just high-tech versions of the basic tools of the trade such as almanacs, encyclopedias, directories and maps, but the online versions can provide much more information than the hard copy ever could.

Clips and Scripts

One of the basic research tools journalists use has not changed in a century: previously published or broadcast stories are still a useful starting place. Most news organizations maintain extensive story archives; some make them available online free or for a fee. Thanks to the Internet, it's also easier than it used to be to find and keep track of stories over time. Checking news.google.com or other news aggregators will give you the latest stories for free, and you can easily search for news about specific topics or sign up for an e-alert when new stories about that topic are added to the site.

Many newsrooms subscribe to LexisNexis or Factiva, fee-based services that allow for exhaustive searches of newspaper and magazine archives. Once you've saved electronic copies of stories to your computer, it's easy to find the information again by using a simple keyword search.

Online Sources

Blogs, chat rooms and e-mail lists can help you find the people you need to humanize a difficult story. Let's say you are a reporter in Colorado, doing a story about autism. Because you know that memorable stories are centered around interesting people, you want to find a family willing to talk about their personal experience dealing with the disorder. A quick search on Google's www.blogger.com turns up a series of posts about the issue, including a few from Denver. Reading through them could provide you with a starting point for finding a family to interview.

The Web also makes it much easier to find databases and reports that in the past would have required a personal visit to a library or government building, or that might have been available only in Washington, D.C. If a plane crashes in your area, for example, you can quickly go online to the Federal Aviation Administration's Web site (www.faa.gov) and compare the plane's tail number with tail numbers in a government database of maintenance and repair problems. The information would be used in either a print or TV story, while an online version would include a link to the original data. The Census Bureau's Web site (www.census.gov) is a treasure trove of information that can help you quickly learn about a new community. But beware of depending too much on the Web. As technology reporter Sree Sreenivasan of WNBC-TV in New York puts it, "The Internet does not have all the answers. It has the clues to all the answers."

A reverse phone directory is another type of online database that works like a supercharged phone book. Not only can you find phone numbers and addresses by typing in someone's name, but you can also type in an address and pull up all the names of people or businesses nearby. This is particularly useful in breaking news situations when you are looking for people who might have pertinent information. Sites to try include www.switchboard.com and www.infospace.com.

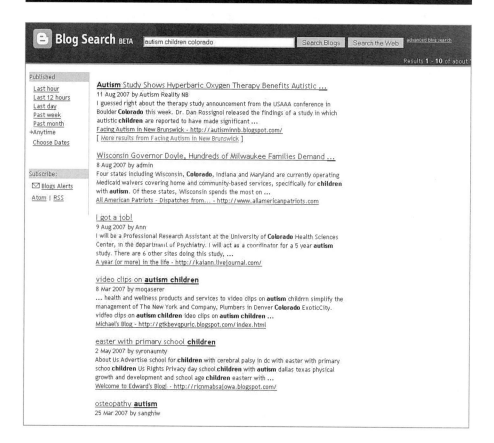

Searching Blogger.com for posts that include the words "autism, children and Colorado," turned up some potential sources for a local story. How would you evaluate these sources?

Source: Captured August 15, 2007, from http://search.blogger.com/?ui=blg&q=autism+children+colorado.

Online maps also provide invaluable data for reporters. Sites such as MapQuest and Yahoo! Maps will generate driving directions to help you get to a story quickly and can give you a feel for the lay of the land. They can also help you locate nearby businesses and provide an instant satellite image. Understanding the geography might help you figure out a better vantage point for reporting or shooting your story or point you to a location where you're likely to be able to go live. And online maps can quickly be converted into graphics.

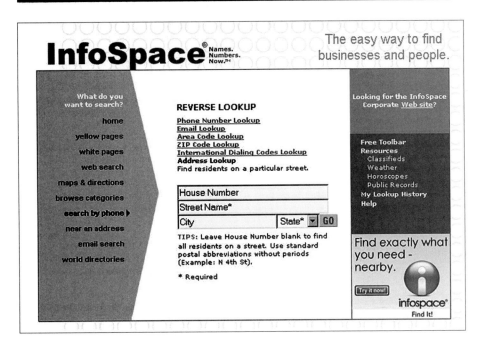

Infospace.com is one of several online directories that include a "reverse lookup" function. You can search by street address to find nearby residences or businesses, or enter a phone number to see what name it matches.

Source: Captured August 15, 2007, from www.infospace.com/home/white-pages/reverse-address.

Phone Calls

No matter how you go about finding background information, you'll probably still do a lot of your research by telephone. "The phone is still the most important tool, where you call as many people as you can," says Joe Fryer, a reporter at KARE-TV in Minneapolis, Minn. One person will refer you to someone else, and eventually you'll find someone you want to interview or learn about an event you would never have heard of that provides great visuals for your story.

Reporting a story or doing an interview without having done any background research is like driving to an unfamiliar place without consulting a map. You might get where you intend to go, but it will take you longer and you'll probably miss a turn or two along the way.

SOURCES

As you already know, reporters use both primary and secondary sources when reporting news stories. A primary source could be an interview with a person who has direct experience of an event or topic, or an original document related to that topic. The journalist as eyewitness is also considered a primary source. Any other source is a secondary source, whether it's someone with knowledge that's relevant to the story or a written report based on the original document.

In the case of a fire, for example, the person whose house burned down would be a primary source. So would a firefighter who had been involved in putting out the fire. But the press release issued by the fire department the next day would be a secondary source, as would a newspaper story about the fire. Reporters always prefer primary sources. "Anything that's in the newspaper I don't report unless I heard it myself from the people who are quoted," says Fryer.

In a perfect world, a reporter would have access to several primary sources when working on a story, but that's not often the case. Secondary sources are most useful as a way of confirming information acquired from primary sources. Writing stories based solely on secondary sources can be risky. When a mine collapsed in West Virginia in 2006, news services reported that 12 of the 13 miners trapped inside had survived. They attributed the information to family members of the trapped miners. Elected officials, including the governor of West Virginia, talked on camera about the "miracle" rescue. But it wasn't true. Only one miner had survived. The journalists had relied on secondary sources (the family members) rather than primary sources (mine officials who were in communication with rescue workers inside the mine). NBC News anchor Brian Williams called it "an awful night for the news media."

New York–based reporter Derek Rose took this photo of the news media encampment near West Virginia's Sago mine, where a collapse killed 12 miners in 2006. Journalists mistakenly reported that all but one miner trapped in the collapse had survived.

Source: Captured from "Media at the Sago Mine," January 5, 2006, from http://flickr.com/photos/derek7272/84524638.

DIVERSE SOURCES

It's not always easy to find diverse sources for your stories, but there are tools available to help. The Society of Professional Journalists has an online resource guide—The Rainbow Source Book at www.spj.org/divsourcebook.asp—that is a database of "qualified experts on key news topics from populations historically underrepresented in the news: people of color, women, gays and lesbians, and people with disabilities."

Another useful starting point is the Source Book of Multicultural Experts, at www.multicultural.com/experts, which lists experts by industry and demographic. You might also consult community directories such as the Hispanic Yellow Pages, www.hispanicyellow.com, to find sources in the Spanish-speaking community.

For more suggestions on how to incorporate diverse perspectives in your stories, take a look at the Diversity Toolkit produced by the Radio-Television News Directors Foundation (www.rtndf.org/diversity/toolkit.shtml).

Multiple, Diverse Sources

One rule of thumb reporters follow when researching a story is that no single source can provide all of the information they might need. Consulting multiple sources allows you to confirm information, add perspective and find new angles on the stories you're covering. As you expand your source list, pay attention to the diversity of your sources to make sure you get a range of opinions and avoid writing stories that rely exclusively on the "usual suspects"—most often white males.

Anyone with access to information can be a useful source for a journalist, including secretaries and clerks. They can provide copies of documents, and they often know who is the most knowledgeable person on a given topic. A reporter who treats them with respect may find that a request for an interview with the secretary's supervisor is accepted more quickly.

Source Credibility

Whatever sources you use, it's critical to consider the validity or credibility of the source. The range of information on the Web is incredible. Unfortunately, so is much of the information. These days, anyone can design a professional looking Web site or arrange to send an e-mail that looks authentic but is really a hoax. Ask anyone who's ever responded to a warning that a personal eBay account was about to expire. Just because you can find something online does not mean that it's true.

Journalists need to verify the source of all information to determine whether it's credible enough to use in a news story. Sometimes, sources contradict each other. To clear up discrepancies, reporters may have to see where the weight of the evidence lies or seek out original sources like documents to determine which version is true.

INTERVIEWS

Interviews are the heart of journalism, and each one is a little different from any other. A reporter might interview a candidate for governor one week and a 5-year-old the next. Obviously, you'd approach those two conversations differently, but there are some basic guidelines that apply to all interviews.

Remember that most adults associate the word "interview" with something stressful, like a job application, so try to avoid describing what you're doing as an interview, even when you're calling ahead to set it up. Instead, tell people you'd like to talk to them on camera or on tape. This may sound like a distinction without a difference, but experienced journalists say that using the right words can help people be themselves and result in a better interview.

Take time to establish rapport with the person you are interviewing before you start asking questions. CBS photojournalist Les Rose suggests leaving the gear in the car when you go to say "hello." When you come back with the camera, he says, "You are a person with a camera, not a camera person. Big difference!" Other suggestions for establishing rapport include putting a microphone on the subject before setting up the camera and lights. This allows the subject to relax and get used to having the mic on.

While setting up, chat with the subject about something unrelated to the topic of your story, like what they had for breakfast or lunch. Get a mic level from what they say while you're chatting. The last thing you want is to remind them that you'll be recording by asking them to do something unnatural like counting to 10. For the same reason, ask

EVALUATING SOURCES

Deciding what sources to use for a story is a large part of a journalist's job. Here are some useful questions for evaluating whether you have chosen the right source or the best source for your story:

- How well informed is this source? Is this person in a position—either personally or professionally—to know these things?
- Can you confirm this information through other sources or through documents?
- How representative is this source's point of view? For example, is this just one person who complains loudly about the landlord because of a personal problem? Or is this the most articulate voice speaking for an entire group with serious, legitimate problems?
- Has this source been reliable and credible in the past?
- Are you using this source only because it's the easy way to go or because you know you'll get a sound bite or quote you can use? Some people are reliably good interviews, but just because they are willing to speak with you doesn't make them the most knowledgeable source on a particular subject.
- What is the source's motive for providing information? Is this person simply trying to look good, or to make someone else look bad? Why is this source talking to you in the first place?

Source: Joann Byrd, "A Guide for Evaluating Sources," PoynterOnline, March 1, 2000, www.poynter.org/column.asp?id=36&aid=4352.

people to spell their names at the end of the interview, not the beginning. And if you're working with a photojournalist, don't turn around to ask, "Are you rolling?" Set up a nonverbal signal in advance—a simple nod of the head will do—so you won't put your subject on edge.

GETTING AN INTERVIEW

Arranging for an interview is not always easy. People may not want to talk with a journalist, especially if the story is controversial. When dealing with public officials, start from the premise that the public has a right to know what those officials are doing. Experienced reporters have found they can persuade even the most reluctant sources to agree to an interview by anticipating their concerns:

- They don't have time. The reporter can offer to meet at the most convenient time or place for the person they want to speak with. Limiting the amount of time requested may also help.

- They are afraid because they think the story will make them look bad. Treating people with respect and telling them precisely why you want to talk with them will help sources be less anxious.

- They don't know what to say. Reporters need to be clear about why the story needs a particular person's point of view.

- They are hard to reach. Reporters often have to go through a secretary or public relations officer to contact the person they want to speak with. If they suspect that their request is not being forwarded, some reporters will write a letter to the source, or call during lunch or after business hours in an effort to get through.

INTERVIEW QUESTIONS

Questions are the backbone of an interview. They're the rudder, keeping the ship going in the right direction. Good questions can reward you with unexpected answers, rich information and surprises. Poor questions can leave you wondering why you bothered to talk to that person anyway. Questions that are too general can let the person you are talking to get away with being unresponsive. Questions that are too specific can lead you down the wrong trail.

Many reporters develop a list of questions or topics for discussion, which they may write down and take along with them but do not consult during the interview. Instead, they'll look at the list only near the end to make sure they haven't forgotten something important. The list also includes other information, documents or visuals they want to obtain from that source so they don't leave the interview without asking for everything they might need for the story. This step is particularly critical to make sure you have all the bases covered when you're planning to produce multimedia stories.

Types of Questions

Most of the time, the best questions are open-ended questions that cannot be answered with yes or no. "Did the fire wake you up?" doesn't get you much. "How did you discover the house was on fire?" might be much more productive. Robert Siegel, senior host of All Things Considered on National Public Radio, tells the story of an interview he did with a Turkish diplomat after Pope John Paul II was shot and wounded by a Turk in Rome. His first question, "Do you know any details about this man, Mehmet Ali Agca—where he lived in Italy, what he did there, what kind of visa the Italians gave him?" The answers were all no. After several more tries, Siegel paused, about to give up. And the diplomat filled the silence with this, ". . . except that he is the most famous convicted murderer in Turkey, who escaped from prison after assassinating the editor of one of our major newspapers." Siegel says he almost lost a good story by asking questions that were too narrow. He acknowledges that a better way to open the interview might have been, "Tell me about this man." [1]

Good questions are also nonjudgmental, in that they do not establish the reporter's point of view. It's the difference between, "What do you think about that?" And "What could you have been thinking!" In most cases, avoid "double barreled" two-part questions because they give the interview subject a chance to answer only half of the question—usually the easy half. We'll discuss one exception to that rule in Chapter 3.

Openers and Closers

The first question in an interview is important because it sets the tone for what follows. A lot of journalists like to begin with an "ice-breaker" question that lets the source relax. It's something they're comfortable answering. It may, in fact, have nothing to do with the reason you are there. But often it helps to establish your credentials with the source, and that can create a sense of trust and openness. If you are interviewing a writer about her latest novel, your opening question could be about her previous book or her family to show you have done your homework and are well prepared for the conversation.

You may want to avoid opening questions that are too broad or too vague. One reporter tells of an interview he started with the question: "Why don't you tell me a little bit about what you have done?" The source just stared back and said, "If you don't know, why are you here?"

Whenever they conduct an interview, reporters usually have some general questions they save for the end. First, they may summarize the conversation to be sure they've understood what was said. Then they will ask if there is anything else the person being interviewed wants to add. They also ask for the best way to get back in touch with the person, especially after hours, and they thank the person for their time. And many journalists have one last question they ask at all interviews: "What else is going on?" It's amazing how many good stories you can find while you're out covering something else.

INTERVIEW QUESTIONS

By Chip Scanlan

The dictionary defines a question as, "a sentence in an interrogative form, addressed to someone in order to get information in reply." Notice that the root of the word is "quest," which is a "search or pursuit made in order to find or obtain something."

"Questions are precise instruments," says John Sawatsky, a Canadian journalist and teacher who knows how to ask questions that get rich answers. Used carefully, questions can make the difference between an answer and obfuscation.

Interviewing isn't an art or a science, he says.

It's something in between, closer to a social science. You can make some predictions about an interview but not absolute ones because interviewing involves human beings who don't always behave in predictable ways. Ask the wrong question, and even a cooperative interview subject may not be able to give you the information you need.

The question is the interviewer's most useful tool, but reporters ask too many questions (one-third to one-half, Sawatsky estimates) that suppress, rather than produce, information.

Sawatsky and other interviewing experts identify two basic categories of questions: questions that encourage conversation and questions that stifle it. Some interviewing experts refer to these types as open-ended and closed-ended.

Tough Questions

Reporters often have to talk with people who have been through some kind of trauma. It's one of the toughest assignments you can get, but the right approach can pay off. KARE's Joe Fryer says his approach is "aggressive, in a nice way." "I hate to lose, but I never ambush someone," he says. "Without ever being intrusive or rude, my goal is still to get something no one else has." Instead of calling repeatedly to request an interview, Fryer will leave just one message for each person who might have something to say. When they are ready to talk, he says, "they remember that, and they talk to me first because I was the most respectful."

The most effective are open-ended, encouraging the person you're interviewing to respond fully. They are the opposite of closed-ended questions, which demand a brief, unequivocal response: "Yes," "No," "I don't know" or "No comment." I prefer the terms "conversation starters" and "conversation stoppers," or "green light" and "red light," because that's what they can do. Whatever you call them, the one you choose to ask may end up suppressing rather than inviting answers.

Reporters are constantly in pursuit of the most timely, compelling and accurate information. Posed by a sincere, curious and open mind, the question is the most important tool you can use to reach that goal. Questions can be keys that open a door to a person's life or beliefs. Or they can act as padlocks, barring you from discovering the information and stories you need to do your job.

Unfortunately, in all too many cases, interviews have become the street theater of news with both sides tacitly accepting their role. The reporters asks questions that may sound tough but provide subjects a variety of exit ramps while the subject pretends that they are responding when in fact they are using the dull question as a launching pad for their own agenda and rhetoric. The biggest loser in these kinds of exchanges, of course, is the public.

Source: Excerpted from Chip Scanlan, "Tools of the Trade: The Question," PoynterOnline, October 23, 2001, www.poynter.org/content/content_view.asp?id=5075.

Fryer also keeps trying to find someone to talk to, long after another reporter might have given up. He once spent 40 minutes talking with the son of a 94-year-old woman who had died in a nursing home fire, hoping he would do an on-camera interview. When the man finally said no, Fryer asked if there was someone else he might talk to. The son put Fryer in touch with the woman's pastor who was planning her funeral service and who turned out to be a terrific interview.

If you have difficult or confrontational questions to ask, it's a good idea to save them for about the last third of the interview. If you ask them first, the interview may be over before it begins. There is an exception to this rule: If you have only a short time for the interview—say the person granted you five minutes only—or if you don't actually have a scheduled interview but you are trying to ask a few questions "on the run." Then you don't have time for pleasantries, and you have to be direct from the start.

It's not always easy to get answers to tough questions, but Larche Hardy, news director at WMBB-TV in Panama City, Fla., suggests this technique: Ask the question three times. "The first time you may get a nonanswer or an 'I'm not prepared to talk about that right now.' The second time, the interviewee will likely get a little huffy and say, 'I told you, I'm not going to talk about that right now.' By the third time you will either get thrown out of the office or you may force the official to justify his answer—a natural reaction to being put on the spot. The answer to the third question is generally the best sound you're going to get."

Silence

While it's important to ask good questions, it's also critically important to be quiet and let the interviewee talk. Good journalists are good listeners, and often learn the most significant information by being silent. People naturally want to fill silences. Give them a chance to do that by responding with nonverbal cues that say, "I'm interested," such as leaning forward in your chair or taking notes in your notebook. What you hear can lead to additional questions that may not have occurred to you. But one word of caution: If you plan to use the audio or video, avoid verbal cues that are used in normal conversation. Saying, "mmm-hmm" or "sure" or making other supportive noises is a good way to ruin a great sound bite. You won't be able to use it, either because the background sound is so distracting or because you can't risk letting anyone think that you were agreeing with the person you were talking to.

NBC national correspondent Bob Dotson is a master of what he calls the "nonquestion question." He often finds that a comment can elicit a more natural response than a direct question. Asking a tornado survivor to describe the damage to his trailer might be less productive than saying simply, "Now that looks like a fine mobile home you used to live in."

TYPES OF INTERVIEWS

Reporters today do interviews in all sorts of different ways—in person, on the phone, by e-mail or even instant messaging. Sometimes the medium dictates the type of interview you'll do. Sometimes your choice will be based on the availability of the source. There are pluses and minuses to each type, so if you have a choice, make an informed decision.

In-Person Interviews

Obviously, interviewing in person is the best way to get on-camera sound bites for television or streaming video and the best quality audio for radio or online news. It's possible to do TV interviews via satellite or to ask questions through a phone and have the answers recorded on site, but there is no substitute for being there. When you are on the scene, you can get a more complete sense of the person you are speaking with. What kinds of photos are on the wall? Is the desk messy or neat? What books are in the bookcase? Meeting in person also gives the reporter the ability to judge the source's credibility based on his demeanor. Does he look nervous or comfortable? Is she willing to look the reporter in the eye?

Interviewing in person also allows you to make adjustments to get the best technical quality for television or the Web. Listen for background noise that could overwhelm your primary sound and relocate if you have to. Make sure the microphone is close enough to the source to capture crisp, clear sound. Avoid chairs that swivel or rock because random movement can be distracting on the air.

On-Camera Interviews

The traditional way to shoot an on-camera interview is to have the reporter facing the subject from a comfortable distance, either sitting or standing. You want to be close enough to have a conversation in a normal tone of voice. The camera is then placed slightly to one side of the reporter, so the subject isn't looking directly into the lens. If you're doing multiple interviews for the same story, change the camera position for each interview so your subjects aren't all facing in the same screen direction. This makes editing easier and the finished product more attractive.

You don't always have to take what CBS correspondent Byron Pitts calls the "Dragnet" approach to interviewing. He likes to sit next to the person he's talking with. "Rarely do I have a 'conversation' with someone standing one foot in front of me," he says. If you're working with a photographer, just make sure he or she knows what you're up to if you decide to try this slightly unorthodox approach.

Some on-camera interviews lend themselves to a different approach that's often called "active interviewing." Instead of sitting or standing while facing the camera, the subject in an active interview is doing something that is relevant to the story while at the same time talking about it. Let's say you're doing a story about a company in your area that has an innovative, on-site child care program. Instead of interviewing the company president in an office and shooting b-roll of the day care center later, you could talk to him or her in the center. As the president describes what makes the center unique, you can get video of those features.

Basically, an active interview involves shooting the conversation and the b-roll at the same time in the same location, which makes editing that much easier. You have to be nimble to make this work, of course. Put a wireless microphone on the subject, and be prepared to move the camera and tripod and even to shoot hand-held to get the video you need. For a two-person crew, shooting an active interview is obviously more challenging than a standard, sit-down interview. The reporter and photographer have to be on the same page throughout. The photojournalist must listen carefully to what's being said and make sure that when the subject says something important it's captured on camera. For the same reason, the reporter must pay close attention to what the photojournalist is shooting, taking care not to ask a crucial question while the camera is off the subject or moving.

Teams that do this well often develop subtle ways of communicating while shooting. Reporter Boyd Huppert and photojournalist Jonathan Malat, who work at KARE-TV in Minneapolis, Minn., have their own verbal shorthand. If Huppert hears a sound bite he knows he'll want on camera while Malat is shooting b-roll, he might interject a comment like, "I'm sorry, what's that?" These apparently offhand remarks are designed to get the subject to repeat himself, and they're a clue to the photographer that he needs to get the subject on camera. You'll notice that Huppert does not directly ask the person to repeat a comment because he's found that people tend to get self-conscious or ruin the sound bite by adding something like, "Well, as I told you before, . . ."

Interviews for the Web

Even experienced television reporters have to think differently about how they do interviews that also may be used on the Web. For the conversation to make sense, the audience has to be able to hear the reporter's questions as well as the answers, so it's a good idea to get in the habit of putting a mic on both the subject and the reporter. If you have only one microphone, move it back and forth to capture the conversation in full. And because your questions may wind up on the Web, approach all recorded interviews as you would a live interview on television. Keep your questions short and to the point. Avoid using acronyms or jargon that your interview subject understands but the general public might not.

Print reporters need to think differently about interviews they do for online use as well. "Print reporters think they can go through and record a two-hour conversation and then go back and transcribe the entire thing and then they can take that, cut it up and put it together," says Seth Gitner, multimedia editor at the Roanoke Times. "They don't understand that they need short, concise sound bites," he says. If you're used to doing print interviews, work on focusing your questions so you get answers that are on point for the online version. Remember, too, that partial quotes don't work on the air or in online audio or video, so one of your goals should be to get your interview subject to answer your questions in complete sentences. Some print reporters find it easier to do two interviews—one for print and a second, shorter one they record for online use—but they have to make sure the interview subject agrees beforehand to answer some of the same questions twice.

Phone or E-Mail Interviews

Interviewing by phone is often convenient for both the reporter and the source. You don't have to spend a lot of time in transit, and it's easier for a source to make time for a phone call than a personal appointment. Phone interviews are great for collecting basic information but less useful for interviewing in depth. Reporters often do "pre-interviews" by phone, getting background and other information before doing an in-person interview. This can be a time-saver but it can also sap spontaneity.

E-mail interviews are useful for reaching people in distant places, but the reporter can't listen to what's being said and follow up in real time. Instant messaging is more akin to a telephone interview. But both online methods raise the question of whether the answers are actually being sent by the person they appear to be from. It's important to confirm the authenticity of the answers before using them in a story.

Reporters using e-mail or other online forms of communication should follow the same professional standards as they would in any other form. They must identify themselves as journalists and tell what information they are seeking and why. And they need to apply the same fact checking and thinking skills they would apply to any other source of information.

REPORT: LIVE INTERVIEWS

Live interviews are more difficult than interviews on tape, and not only because your time is limited. A live interview needs to stand on its own. Your questions have to include enough information for the audience to follow what's being discussed, but not so much that it appears you are showing off your knowledge or dominating the conversation. A good live interview also needs a beginning, middle and end, just like a story does, so you should have a mental road map for the interview before you start.

Former ABC Nightline anchor Ted Koppel is one of the best live interviewers ever. Quality live interviewing, Koppel says, requires adequate time and an ability on the part of the interviewer to mentally edit the interview as it is occurring. "The essence of journalism is editing," he told Columbia Journalism Review.* "And editing while you are on the air is extremely tough. It means sifting out the extraneous from the relevant, the new from the old" in your head, while also listening to what the person is saying and considering what else you want to know.

Koppel says he always tries to consider what the viewer or listener might be thinking and asks questions along those lines. He also believes that the audience should identify with the interviewer and see that person as representing viewers' interests. "You can lose that identification easily by losing control of the interview, or by being too aggressive or rude, or by not asking the right type of questions."

*Tom Rosenstiel, "Yakety-Yak: The Lost Art of Interviewing," *Columbia Journalism Review* (January–February 1995), http://archives.cjr.org/year/95/1/interviewing.asp.

Many newsrooms have policies that require reporters to let the audience know when they use information that's been gathered via e-mail, especially direct quotes. The bottom line: Be aware that these interview methods have their limitations.

INTERVIEW GROUND RULES

Most interviews are conducted "on the record," which means the reporter can use anything that is said and attribute it directly to the person who is speaking. It is important to make sure the source knows this, especially when dealing with ordinary people who are not accustomed to being quoted by name. Even though your notebook, microphone and camera are in plain sight, it may not be obvious to some people that you intend to use their words, voice or image in a news story that everyone can see.

Occasionally, interviews are done under different ground rules. A whistleblower might not want to go on the record with a complaint about the company she works for, out of fear she might lose her job. A lower-level government official might resist going on the record if he's been told not to talk to the media. A Muslim teenager in the United States who wears a veil or a "hijab" headcovering at home but not at school might not want to be identified to avoid angering her parents. If an interview is not on the record, both the reporter and the source must agree in advance to the conditions under which the information can be used.

Background Interviews

An interview "on background" or "not for attribution" generally means the information can be used in a story and the source's words can be quoted directly but the source cannot be named. The source can be identified in a general way, however, for example as "an administration official" or "a company engineer," as long as both the source and the journalist agree on the description to be used.

Reporters should not be too quick to agree to talk on background because sources sometimes try to use it as a cover for a personal or partisan attack, knowing it cannot be traced back to them. And using an unnamed source makes it more difficult for the audience to evaluate the credibility of the information. But there are times when reporters have to get information on background because it's the only way a source will agree to talk. A source who fears for her safety if others learn that she has spoken to a reporter may agree to provide information only on background. Here are some general guidelines for deciding whether to accept and use background information:

- The story is of overwhelming public concern.

- There is no other way to get the information on the record.

- The source is in a position to know the truth.

- You are willing to explain (in your story) why the source could not be named.

Deep Background and Off-the-Record Interviews

Government officials sometimes want to talk to reporters on "deep background," which means the information can be used but not in a direct quote, and the source cannot be identified. For example, a top diplomat might be willing to tell a reporter on deep background that the government is close to reaching an important agreement with another country. The reporter could then write only that observers are "known to believe" an agreement is imminent. When you hear a story that begins, "CBS News has learned . . ." it usually means the information was provided on deep background.

Information that is offered "off the record" cannot be used at all, so most reporters will resist this arrangement unless they are fairly sure that the source is the only possible way they could get the information. Most reporters agree that off-the-record information cannot even be repeated to another source, but it can tip you off to a story that is worth pursuing.

Interview Policies

Many newsrooms require that reporters have the approval of a news manager before accepting off-the-record information or information on deep background. The Media General Broadcast Group, which owns 26 network-affiliated television stations, has a policy that says:

> It is Media General's policy to involve the News Director in any decision to grant anonymity to a source or to report the information from that source. While it is sometimes necessary to quote an unnamed source, it is important to remember that when we do so, we in effect, tell viewers: "Trust us." By not revealing a source, we vouch for the truth of what is said. That puts our own credibility on the line. Before using an unnamed source, you must be convinced that the story is of overwhelming public concern and that there is no other way to get the essential information on the record.

Whatever the arrangement, it's up to the reporter to make sure both sides understand and agree to the ground rules before the interview. Sometimes sources try to change the rules in the middle, by telling the reporter something important and then adding, "But you can't use that, of course." That's why it's a good idea to spell things out at the beginning and not agree to withhold information unless a separate deal is reached before proceeding with the interview. Multimedia reporting raises other issues when it comes to agreements with sources. For example, if a person agrees to be interviewed for print, are they also agreeing to have their story posted online or recorded for television? We'll explore these questions further in Chapter 11.

Journalists also should be clear about how far they will go to protect the identity of a source. As we have seen in some prominent cases involving both print and broadcast journalists, reporters may risk going to jail rather than reveal information about a confidential source in a court of law. In 2004, Rhode Island television reporter Jim Taricani was sentenced to six months under house arrest after he refused to name the source who gave him an FBI surveillance tape that he used in a broadcast. On the tape, an aide to the mayor of Providence, R.I., was seen accepting a bribe from a government informant. After Taricani was found guilty of contempt of court, his source identified himself, but the judge still refused to lift the sentence. Taricani was willing to pay the price to keep his promise not to name his source. If journalists are not willing to face time in prison to protect a source, they should make it clear that their promise of confidentiality only goes so far.

TRADE TOOLS

GROUND RULES

On background: Information can be used in a story, and the source's words can be quoted directly, but the source cannot be named.

Deep background: Information that can be used but not in a direct quote, and the source cannot be identified.

Off the record: Information that is offered off the record cannot be used in a story at all.

Embargo: Information is provided on the condition that it is not to be used until a specific time set by the source.

Embargoes

One other ground rule that is important for journalists to understand is the use of an "embargo" on information provided by a source. That means the information is provided on the condition that it is not to be used until a specific time. A government agency announcing a new policy may provide a written summary several hours in advance or even a day ahead.

That gives reporters time to digest the information before the news conference making the policy official. Reporters who accept information under an embargo are bound to honor it unless the news becomes public somewhere else before the specified time.

NOTE TAKING

Some reporters consider their cameras or audio recorders to be the equivalent of a notebook and pen, but that can be risky. Electronics have been known to fail. If you're asked to go live on television, for example, you may not have time to review the tape of an interview to make sure you have the information straight. And you will probably need more detail for your print or online story than you're likely to get during an on-camera interview. So it's important for all journalists to be skilled note takers.

You won't take notes during an interview the way you would during a lecture because you'll want to maintain eye contact, but you should make a habit of writing down key words and phrases. If you're recording the interview, you should also make a note of the time code or counter time when they were said, or insert a digital marker or index point, to save time finding those sound bites later.

Here are some tips on note taking from experienced reporters:

- Write down important facts and details as well as your own thoughts and ideas, but be sure you can tell them apart. Often, what you are thinking while observing a scene can be turned into a theme that holds your story together. Some journalists put brackets around all notes that reflect their own opinions so they don't confuse what they've written with something a source might have said.

- Draw diagrams of rooms, scenes or items in relationship to each other. This can help you remember and describe exactly what you saw, especially if you don't get it on video or if you need it for a print or online version of the story.

- Always get correctly spelled names and titles in your notebook. And get contact information so you can easily get back in touch if you need more information. Don't depend on business cards alone; the information on them may be out of date, and they're easily lost.

- Spell out interview ground rules in the notebook. Be clear about who said what and under what circumstances, especially if any of it was off the record.

- Don't crowd the notebook. Leave space for adding to your notes later.

Many reporters use their own shorthand for common words so they can take notes more quickly. As soon as the interview is over, they spell out any unusual abbreviations to avoid confusion later. They also will mark the most important information they have learned, anything they need to follow up on or check for accuracy and questions that still need to be answered. Develop your own symbols to distinguish among these notations; you might underline what's most important, mark points to follow up on with an asterisk and insert a question mark wherever information is unclear. Whatever system you devise, use it consistently to avoid confusion.

GETTING IT RIGHT

Credibility is a journalist's most important asset, and accuracy is the best way to protect it. To ensure accuracy, reporters must check and double-check all of the information they collect for a news story. Mistakes will happen, but they should be rare.

Reporters are the news organization's first line of defense against errors. The best way to protect your credibility is to get it right during the reporting process:

- Consult multiple sources to nail down information that may be in doubt.

- Confirm that all numbers you have collected for a story are correct: addresses, telephone numbers, ages, date and time references.

- Check the spelling of every proper name and make sure you have the correct titles for everyone you talked to.

Getting the facts right is just one part of reporting accurately. You also need to make sure you have the facts in the right context, and that's sometimes more difficult. Researchers at Kent State University found that most stories on local TV news in Cleveland were factually accurate, according to people who should know best—people who were interviewed for those stories. But one interviewee in three said that important information was left out of a story; one interviewee in five complained that the interview was taken out of context, and nearly one in five thought the coverage of the particular event was both overblown and sensationalized.[2]

To make sure you can put the facts in context, keep an open mind while you are reporting. Don't assume you know what someone means if there's any doubt at all. This is particularly important when you're reporting across cultures to avoid perpetuating stereotypes based on misunderstandings. Ask for a clarification, or consult another source. If you can't nail something down, it's perfectly acceptable to tell what you don't know as well as what you do. It's much better than going with information you can't confirm.

TAKING IT HOME

All journalists are reporters at heart, whether they have that title or not. They're always looking for good stories and for the opportunity to tell them well. The more broadly you think about what makes a good news story, the more good stories you'll find. Train yourself to be a story hunter, not an "order filler," and you'll succeed in any medium. Stay curious, even if you've lived somewhere for a long time. If you think something's unusual or interesting, look into it even if it doesn't seem newsworthy at first. Ask lots of questions and avoid assumptions as you pursue a story idea. When doing interviews, you'll learn more if you listen more than you talk.

No matter what story you're chasing, find a way to care about it because if you don't, no one else will. Be prepared to be persistent as well. It's hard work to find the stories that others miss, but the opportunity to tell stories that take the audience where they can't go, that give voice to the voiceless or that hold the powerful accountable is always worth the effort.

TALKING POINTS

1. You've been asked to do a story about the increasing use of text messaging while driving. Brainstorm a list of questions you might ask to turn that topic into a story, or create a story map to see what angles you might follow. Write down the one story idea you want to pursue, and summarize it in a single sentence.

2. Look at the local newspaper from two weeks ago, either in print or online. Find as many stories as possible that make you ask: What happened next? Suggest three stories that you think should be followed up and explain why. List three questions you would want answered in each follow-up story.

3. A new study indicates that breast cancer rates are increasing in the United States. The study provides detailed information broken down by race and ethnicity. You've been assigned to localize the story. How might you incorporate diverse sources into the piece? Why would that be important?

eLEARNING OPPORTUNITIES

For chapter exercises, practice tools and additional resources, go to the interactive online workbook at http://college.cqpress.com/advancingthestory. You'll find:

- SKILL BUILDING: Develop a story idea from a broad topic and decide what sources you would consult to begin reporting the story.

- DISCOVER: Watch and read story examples to see how reporters found, pursued and developed stories for different media.

- ONGOING STORY: List people you might want to interview for this story and the top questions you'd want each source to answer.

- EXPLORE: Visit Web sites to learn more about finding stories, evaluating sources and conducting better interviews.

3 MULTIMEDIA NEWSGATHERING

To be successful in multimedia journalism, you have to keep the strengths of each platform in mind as you report. Even if you won't shoot video or build graphics yourself, you need to understand how it's done. In this chapter, we'll explain what it takes to gather the elements you'll need to tell stories well in multiple media, including crisp audio, vivid pictures and more.

You're heading out the door to cover a story for TV and you get this last-minute request: Can you write a version for the Web site? Or—Can you file a version for the newspaper, too? Knowing that in advance will change the way you report the story, because you'll need different elements to do the story justice in each medium.

Approaching every story with a multimedia mind-set is a far better strategy than searching for elements you can use on different platforms after your reporting is done. A television reporter who gathers details and data along the way will be better prepared to write for print as well. A print reporter who thinks about video and sound from the start can more easily produce a TV version. And reporters who collect all of these elements and more, like original documents and graphics, will be all set to file for the Web. It's a good idea to get in the habit of reporting this way because many newsrooms now expect it. "We still have people whose primary focus is TV or print," says news director Cody Howard of 6News, a cable news channel in Lawrence, Kan., that's owned by the same company as the local newspaper, the Lawrence Journal-World. "But we make it clear you're going to be expected to provide video for online and work with our print partner."

THINKING ACROSS PLATFORMS

Multimedia reporters look for the same universal building blocks of great stories that we discussed in Chapter 2: character, place, emotion, detail and tension. But they may concentrate more or less on certain elements depending on the platform they'll be using to tell the story. Let's take a closer look at the strengths and weaknesses of each medium to see how those qualities change the reporting process on one specific story.

Let's say you're reporting on the Census Bureau's announcement that the U.S. population hit 300 million at 4:46 a.m. today. To tell that story on TV, you'd probably want to contact hospitals in your area to find a baby born at about that time whose birth could illustrate the bigger picture and give the viewer a personal connection to the story. Because TV is a visual medium, you'd ask for video of the maternity ward and an interview with the family. You'd also want to talk with a demographer on camera. Your story would include additional information about the population milestone, but not in great detail.

The typical broadcast journalist who is asked to write a print or Web version of a story soon realizes something is missing—namely, enough detail to satisfy the print or online editor. While your TV story about the population milestone would mention that Hispanics are the fastest-growing minority in the country, it wouldn't include a lot of statistics. By contrast, your print or Web version would have to give exact percentages for all minorities, and compare the numbers with where they stood at a previous milestone—say, when the population hit 200 million 39 years ago. It would also explain how the Census Bureau counts the population, and how the U.S. population compares with other countries around the world. Get in the habit of collecting these specifics as you report to save yourself time and frustration later.

To tell the population story online, you might also want to use the data you collected to create interactive graphics. MSNBC, for example, created an interactive map. Different colors indicated which states had the greatest population growth and density. Users could select individual states to get more specific numbers. They could choose a decade on a timeline from 1770 to 2010 to see population estimates and a racial breakdown of the country at that time. Users could also click to listen to audio files of historians or demographers describing what life was like for people born at different times.

Reporters planning to tell a story on the Web need to collect elements like these that clearly go together, says Jonathan Dube, editor of CyberJournalist.net. "Look for words to go with images, audio and video to go with words, data that will lend itself to interactives, etc.," he says. It's a good idea to get as much information as possible in digital form, including data you can use to create graphics. Try to get digital versions of charts, graphs and

MSNBC's interactive population map allowed users to compare states by population change or density. Notice the timeline at the bottom with click-to-listen audio files of demographic experts describing the characteristics of different generations.

Source: "Made in the USA." Retrieved from MSNBC.com on August 16, 2007, www.msnbc.msn.com/id/ 15253291.

documents that you might want to post "as is." You'll also want to collect audio, photos and video for online use. We'll explain how to do this later in this chapter.

Putting It Together

Victoria Lim, senior consumer reporter at WFLA-TV in Tampa, Fla., often reports the same story on multiple platforms. She'll file a story for her station, for the Tampa Tribune newspaper and for the Web site TBO.com, all of which are owned by the same company, Media General. Lim says her television stories are restricted by the amount of time and visuals she has, but she can use much more information online. Because she has that outlet, she reports differently than she used to. "Deeper, wider, longer interviews, much more background," she says. "[Multimedia] requires you to think about more than, well, I only have a minute thirty to give the nuts and bolts because you need more than nuts and bolts."

For a story about insurance companies refusing to write policies for people who own trampolines, Lim interviewed a woman who had been denied coverage, an insurance agent and the trampoline industry association. She also talked to the Consumer Product Safety Commission (CPSC) about trampoline safety and the state Office of Insurance Regulation to find out which insurance companies might cover trampolines. None of the reporting she did was wasted, but she developed each story differently based on the strengths of each medium.

Her television story opened with video of the woman's trampoline piled up in her shed, and we heard from the woman who was furious that her kids couldn't use it anymore. Lim then broadened out the story to explain why trampolines are considered a bad insurance risk, and she included sound bites from the trampoline and insurance industries. Her print story included more statistics about injuries from trampolines and other sports equipment, plus the advice about trampoline safety that didn't fit in her TV story. Both the print and TV versions were posted online, along with a Web-only video segment—a short stand-up with a little b-roll—in which Lim explained how to use a trampoline safely. She also compiled a list of insurance companies in Florida that might cover trampolines and posted that on the Web, along with a link to the CPSC. Lim's stories were built around the universal building blocks of character, emotion and detail, as well as the multimedia building blocks of sound, visuals and interactivity.

Obviously, to tell stories well in multiple media, you'll need clear, crisp sound and compelling visuals. You may have to collect these elements by yourself or you may work as part of a team. Either way, you need to know how it's done.

As we discuss the building blocks of multimedia stories, we'll pay particular attention to the way they're used in television news. But we'll also point out instances when you'd do things differently to accommodate the needs of online or print.

PLATFORM PLUSES

TV news offers:
Immediacy.
Impact of visuals and emotion.
Personal connection.

Print news provides:
Depth.
Detail.
Permanence and portability.

Online journalism is:
On demand.
Interactive.
Innovative.

TRADE TOOLS

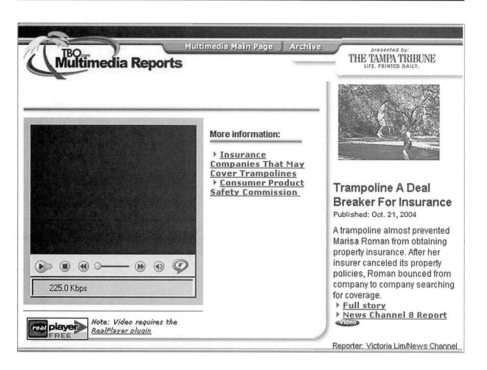

A Web extra report by Victoria Lim, senior consumer reporter at WFLA-TV in Tampa, Fla., demonstrated how to use a trampoline safely. Users could click links for more information, to read Lim's newspaper column or to watch her TV story.

Source: "Trampoline a Deal Breaker for Insurance," captured August 15, 2007, from http://multimedia.tbo.com/multimedia/MGBV6279L0E.html.

SOUND

Sound is an essential element in multimedia journalism, whether you use it to accompany an online slide show, in a podcast or in a television news story. Interview sound should be as clear as possible, so the user or viewer won't have to strain to understand what people are saying. Natural sound, recorded on site, is the other half of almost every picture. Compare a story with lots of natural sound with one that uses almost none and the difference is obvious. "Audio brings the story alive," says photojournalist Stan Heist, who works at WBFF-TV in Baltimore, Md. A story with natural sound lets the viewer experience something

REPORTING CHECKLISTS

Many reporters use mental checklists to make sure they collect the elements they'll need to tell a story in multiple media. They ask the traditional reporting questions a little differently.

Television	Online
Who:	*Who:*
Who can speak most effectively on camera about the story?	Who can give me data or background to flesh out this story?
Whose personal experience will best illustrate the story?	
What:	*What:*
What visuals do I need to support the story?	What interactive elements can I add to this story?
What natural sound can I gather to tell this story?	What information could be told better in a graphic?
Where:	*Where:*
Where can I go to show what happened?	Where did things happen that I could put on a static or clickable map?
Where would it make sense to be on camera in this story?	Where can I refer people for more information?
When:	*When:*
When do I need to be at these locations?	When did things happen that I could put on a static or clickable timeline?

TRADE TOOLS

close to what it was like to be there in person. In television and online videos, sound adds context and information that pictures alone can't convey.

Accomplished photojournalists often say they shoot with their ears. "If something makes noise and it pertains to my story, it draws my attention," says Ted Nelson of WTVF-TV in Nashville, Tenn. He listens carefully when shooting, and makes sure to capture the sound that goes with every picture. Corky Scholl of KUSA-TV in Denver, Colo., is so attuned to sound that he often finds stories by following up on something he's heard while driving around with the car window down. The following tips from professionals will help you record better sound.

Equipment

Do not depend on any camera or recorder's built-in microphone to capture sound. Built-in microphones tend to be of poor quality and are liable to pick up mechanical noise. Use an external microphone and make sure you put it as close to the source of the sound as possible while keeping it out of the shot if you're shooting video. "If you want to hear the picture, you have to get the mics close," says longtime photojournalist Dave Wertheimer, former president of the National Press Photographers Association (NPPA). Mic the bird feeder and you can hear the beating of the hummingbirds' wings. For a story about National Guard troops in training, Ted Nelson taped a small wireless lavalier mic to the soldiers' cell phones to record both ends of their conversations with their families back home.

Never record audio or shoot any video without listening to the output of the recorder or camera. Wear headphones and use both earpieces to be sure that what you're hearing is actually being captured. "Your mic hears differently from your ears," says Euan Kerr, an editor at Minnesota Public Radio (MPR). "Headphones can alert you to a loose connector, a bad mic, and/or dying batteries," he says, not to mention the buzz of fluorescent lights and distracting background noise like traffic and air conditioners.

Ambience

Whenever possible, record ambient sound or "room tone" for about a minute in every location. You may need it during editing to make smooth audio transitions. For example, you might want to cut from a sound bite from an interview conducted in a quiet room to a bite from a second interview conducted near a busy highway. If you sneak in the sound of the highway a few frames before you cut to the video, the change of sound quality won't be so distracting.

When KSTP-TV reporter Bridgette Bornstein reported live on a brutal Minnesota snowstorm, she wore a wireless microphone on her boot (right) to pick up the sound of ice crunching underfoot.

Source: KSTP-TV video courtesy of Bridgette Bornstein.

It can also be useful to carry and use a separate audio recorder to pick up "wild sound" while you are shooting video. If you're shooting a musical performance, you can capture entire songs on a separate recorder, leaving you free to stop and start your camera while shooting cutaways. TV photojournalist John Goheen often leaves a recorder rolling on the announcer or emcee of an event while he shoots the action. This play-by-play sound can help in the edit.

Online Use

If you are recording audio to use with an online slide show, you can shoot pictures first and record sound later, but make sure you don't leave a scene until you have captured the sound that goes with it. You'll also want to ask specific questions about each person, object, activity and setting you've already shot. "If I have a really nice moment in a photo, I have to ask the person about that later, asking them how that happened or how they felt when it happened," says Josh Meltzer, a staff photographer at the Roanoke Times.

CAPTURING SOUND

As a young child, Stan Heist listened to old-time radio shows like The Shadow that engaged his imagination. As a professional photojournalist at WBFF-TV in Baltimore, Md., Heist preaches the gospel of great audio. "It's the audio that's a huge part of TV news that sometimes gets overlooked," he says. "Watching a story on TV is a passive act, but listening is how you get involved. Think about how many viewers watch our stories and they're making dinner or putting their pajamas on. Not everybody is going to be as engaged in our stories as we are. Audio brings the story alive."

Heist is one of those photographers who shoots with his ears, looking for "what's making interesting noise and who's making interesting noise. I don't waste a lot of time trying to find that perfect sound bite or convince anybody to talk. I shoot and move and move the mic to things that make sound, and to people who are doing something that makes sound. Maximize your moments with simple sounds. It doesn't have to be a siren. Be mindful of the natural sound you hear every day. The whiz-bang stuff is great but don't forget about the sound that is all around us."

Heist uses a wireless lavalier microphone most of the time. "A lavalier mic doesn't have to be pinned to a person. Put it on a rake, inside a port-a-potty or a Dumpster. Where there's a lot of movement and action, it's tough without a wireless, but you can still get a long cord and put a lavalier somewhere. You can zoom with your feet. Just being closer will make it sound better. [When I worked] in Richmond, I had a 50-foot cord and a lavalier mic. I wouldn't use it in high traffic areas, but you have to think about ways to get around the problem."

VIDEO

Whatever you shoot should be up to broadcast standards, whenever possible, whether you intend to use it on the air or online. Here are some tips from the pros on how to shoot top-quality video.

Photojournalist Stan Heist of WBFF-TV in Baltimore, Md., uses a detachable shotgun microphone to get close when he's capturing audio.

Source: Photo courtesy of Mike Buscher, www.buscherphotography.com.

Framing

Pay close attention to the location of objects and people in each shot. Leave just a little space or "head room" between the top of a person's head and the top edge of the frame. Too little space and the person looks cramped; too much and the person looks lost. Frame your shots so there is space or "looking room" in front of people who are facing either screen right or left. The closer people are to being in profile, the more space you need to leave in the shot. As a rule of thumb, don't center a person in the frame unless he or she is looking directly at the camera.

Watch out for distracting background objects that can draw attention away from the foreground. Position the camera so that trees and lamps do not appear to be growing out of people's heads. Be careful that horizontal lines like doorjambs or window frames don't slice across the top of people's heads.

Steady Shots

If your camera isn't steady, your video will be shaky and hard to watch. Use a tripod whenever possible, and make sure it's level. You can also use a solid platform like a chair or railing to steady the camera. "When you frame a shot and you like it, take your hands off the camera for a couple of seconds," says photojournalist Jason Hanson of KSTP-TV in Minneapolis, Minn. If you absolutely must shoot handheld or with the camera on your shoulder,

Photojournalist Jason Hanson of KSTP-TV in Minneapolis, Minn., insists on rock steady shots, and gets them by shooting from a tripod.

Source: Photo courtesy of Jason Hanson.

get close to the subject and zoom out wide for steadier video. Keep your arms close to your body while holding the camera gently. If you grip it too tightly, the tension in your hands and arms may cause the camera to shake. On rare occasions, you may want to move the camera while shooting but only if you have a specific purpose in mind. For example, you might run along behind an athlete in training to give the viewer a sense of what that person goes through to get in shape.

Hold each shot for at least 10 seconds. You can't edit if you don't have enough steady video to work with. When shooting action, position yourself so the action moves into and out of the frame; hit "record" several seconds before the action enters the frame and keep rolling for several seconds after it moves out of frame. If you plan to pan or tilt the camera to follow action, be sure to roll for several seconds on a static shot before and after the camera move. Let's say you're covering a parade. Roll on the empty street just ahead of the marching band and hold the camera steady as the band enters the frame. You can stay on a static shot or pan with the action, but once you've completed the pan be sure to hold another steady shot as the band exits the frame in the other direction. Always shoot more than you think you need. It's not unusual to shoot 20 minutes or more to produce a one-minute story.

Get in the habit of zooming with your feet, not with the lens. "The human eye cannot pan, zoom or tilt," says photojournalist Dave Wertheimer, explaining why he avoids these camera moves. Using the zoom to get wide, medium and tight shots from the same location is acceptable, but it's not sufficient. Once you have captured a sequence, move to a different location and shoot it again. Not only will your story be more visually interesting, it will be easier to watch. "If all of your shots come from the same spot, you get a 'vertigo effect'" similar to a jump cut when you edit them together, says award-winning editor Brian Weister, formerly of KMGH-TV in Denver.

Sequences, Action and Reaction

A sequence is a series of shots of the same action taken from different perspectives or focal lengths. The most basic sequence consists of wide, medium and tight (or close-up) shots. You won't necessarily use them in that order, but you need to have them all: wide shots to establish the scene, medium shots to introduce characters and bring the viewer closer to the action and tight shots to show details. For example, let's say you're shooting a story about a freight train derailment. The wide shot might show most of the train, with several cars off the track. The medium shot would show just the jackknifed cars. Tight and supertight shots would show a crumpled section of rail and a leak from one of the tanker cars. Those shots also can be lifesavers in the edit room. "Tight shots, really tight shots, can help you get from here to there," says Brad Houston, a two-time NPPA editor of the year. To make it easier to find those shots when you start editing, Houston suggests shooting a lot of close-ups back-to-back.

Make sure you get the action, especially if it's developing quickly. Try to anticipate action so you can be in the right place at the right time. Covering an apartment fire, KUSA's Scholl noticed a piece of the roof fall in but missed getting it on tape. He figured it would happen again, set his camera up on the tripod and let it roll for five minutes until he captured "the money shot." But always remember that action is more meaningful to the viewer when it's connected to a reaction. "Reaction validates the action," says Scott Livingston, a former chief photographer who is now news director at WBFF-TV in Baltimore. The clowns in the parade may be funny in person, but what makes them hilarious on video is the reaction of the wide-eyed kids along the parade route.

Opens, Closes and Introductions

Look for shots that will draw attention to the beginning of your story and shots you can use at the end to reinforce the central point of the story. An opening shot can set the scene, introduce a main character or establish a tone. A closing shot wraps up the story. It should be the image that sticks in the viewer's mind once the story is over. A good closing shot often includes "negative action"—movement away from the camera as someone leaves the room or drives out of the shot. Keep shooting until you are sure that you have an opening and closing shot "in the can."

Make sure you have a head-on medium shot of any major characters you plan to introduce in your story. Boyd Huppert, a reporter for KARE-TV in Minneapolis, calls it a "handshake shot." "When I'm meeting someone, I'm going to look at them," he says. "Unless the subject of your story is in the witness protection program, there's no reason to introduce a character without looking him in the eye. I don't want to see the side of the head or back of the head or the person in a shot with other characters so I don't know who I'm supposed to be looking at."

Online Issues

If you're shooting video or stills specifically for use online, a few additional considerations apply. Although technology is evolving quickly, the experience of watching video on a computer screen or handheld device still isn't quite the same as watching it on television.

It's even more important to keep the camera steady when shooting video for online use because shaky shots and shots with a lot of movement look blurry on the Web. "Every change in pixels makes the encoder work harder and makes your picture fuzzier," says Regina McCombs, multimedia producer-photographer for StarTribune.com, the Web site of the Minneapolis newspaper. McCombs also says that when shooting video for use online, "remember your image will be quite small. This means you need to fill up your frame." [1] As a result, close-ups and medium shots work better online than wide, establishing shots.

You also want to minimize background elements that may be distracting to the online user. A study by the Nielsen Norman Group found that Web users' attention was diverted from a "talking head" at the center of an online video segment to a sign behind the person being interviewed.[2] Try to keep your framing clean and simple for online video. The foreground or background elements you might include to give TV video some depth just don't work as well online.

Even for experienced news photographers, shooting stills for the Web is a little different. Roanoke Times photographer Josh Meltzer says that instead of looking for a lead photo and two or three detail shots for the newspaper, he's now thinking about capturing 40 shots or more that he can use in a slide show. "I have to be conscious while I'm working of what audio have I got, what pictures do I have," he says. In addition, he has to think about tran-

The red on this "heat map" shows where people looked the longest when they watched a video story on CNN.com. Notice how they seemed to be distracted by the video controls and the signs in the background.

Source: "Eyetracking Study of Web Video," Jakob Nielsen's Alertbox. Retrieved December 5, 2005, from www.useit.com/alertbox/video.html.

Notice how these photographs were framed using the "rule of thirds." The elements in the photo that should draw your attention are located at the intersections of the grid.

Source: Photos courtesy of the authors.

sition shots that he would never use in the newspaper, like a shot of a sign to establish a location in a slide show.

If you're not used to working with stills, you may need a refresher on the importance of composition and the role of captions. A well-composed still frame has a clear center of interest that draws the eye. According to the "rule of thirds," that center of interest should fall at the intersection of those imaginary lines that split the frame into thirds, horizontally and vertically. And just as you do in video, make sure subjects in close-up shots have enough headroom and "looking room" in the frame.

A text caption should convey basic information that helps viewers understand what they are looking at. It almost always tells the "who" and "where" of the image. Make sure you have this information for each photo before you leave a location. It's very difficult to play catch-up afterward.

LIGHTING

Cameras today are more sensitive in low light than previous models, so it's possible to shoot much of your work using available light and the camera's automatic iris. But the key to making video look really good is to manage the available light. "Control the canvas," says Steve Hooker, chief photojournalist at WIS-TV in Columbia, S.C. Knowing the basics of good lighting will improve your photography.

Technical Issues

Most digital cameras today can automatically adjust for color temperature so that white objects actually come out white, but the auto white balance function isn't always dependable. Test your camera under different lighting conditions (sunlight, clouds, incandescent-tungsten and fluorescent bulbs), and you're likely to see that the auto setting leaves something to be desired. Learn how to set the white balance manually to produce the best possible image. Fill the frame with a white object like a sheet of paper, set the white balance and be sure to reset it for each lighting situation.

A simple lens hood—a collar that surrounds and extends the lens—helps to exclude light you don't want in the frame, especially sunlight. Light coming in at an angle can distort or wash out part of the image, resulting in what is called "lens flare." A lens hood can prevent that. Even when your subject isn't backlit, you can get lens flare from sunlight that's coming from the side, especially when the sun is low in the sky. If you don't have a hood, you can shade the lens with your hand, but be careful to keep your fingers out of the picture.

Photojournalist Steve Hooker of WIS-TV in Columbia, S.C., augments the available light from a lamp (bottom right) by adding a key light. Notice how he uses barn doors to target the light.

Source: Photo courtesy of Steve Hooker.

Placement

Whenever possible, position your subject so the main light source is facing that person and slightly to the side, not behind the subject. For example, you don't want to interview a person who's standing in front of a window. That kind of strong backlight will leave your subject in the dark. If you or the subject can't move, or if you need a particular object in the background, you can always adjust your exposure for the subject but then the background will wash out. A better approach is to expose for the background, and then use an external light to illuminate the subject so its exposure matches the background.

If you do add light to a scene, make it motivated. That simply means adding light to supplement an existing source, whenever possible. For example, if you're shooting in a room with a window or a lamp, place your light source so that the light in the frame appears to be coming from the window or lamp.

NONVISUAL STORIES

Not all stories are "made for TV," with eye-catching pictures and sizzling sound, but you can still tell those stories in a visual way if you think creatively. A metaphor or simile might help you convey the central point of the story. For example, in a story about hearing loss for WCCO-TV in Minneapolis, Minn., reporter David Schechter explained the damage that loud sounds cause to tiny hairs inside the ear by comparing it with the effect a crowd of playful children would have on a small field. The video of kids trampling the grass made the point quite clearly. Ask experts to compare complicated concepts to something simpler and more concrete, and you may be surprised by the visual possibilities. Comparing the electric grid to a row of falling dominoes might help explain how a power outage spreads and could give you a much better visual than static shots of electric meters.

Stories with lots of numbers are often challenging to tell on TV, but they can be made more engaging, too. Consider the government's monthly unemployment report. KOMO-TV reporter John Sharifi made the dry statistics compelling by visiting a food bank in Seattle, Wash. Photojournalist Tim Griffis shot a long tracking shot of the people waiting in line. As he moved along, he focused in on a few individuals. After Griffis was done shooting, Sharifi asked those people about their employment status and told their stories to bring the statistics to life.

Just because there's nothing happening in front of your camera doesn't mean there are no visuals for your story. Home video, photo albums and yearbooks can yield great images. Government agencies routinely shoot video to document their work, and they may be willing to share it with you. When reporter Nancy Amons at WSMV-TV in Nashville, Tenn., was covering a story about a government dam project that failed, she realized that showing the dam just sitting there wouldn't be compelling. But it turned out the government had video of trial runs showing exactly why it didn't work, and officials gave her a copy to use on the air. Even documents can be brought to life for use on the air, if you shoot them with care.

SHOOTING DOCUMENTS FOR TV

Why would you want to shoot documents for a television story? Because showing the audience documentary evidence that supports what you're talking about can build credibility. The trick is to find a way to bring the documents to life.

- Instead of creating full-screen graphics, shoot the page, tight. Use highlights or lighting techniques to make the words stand out.

- Capture and use natural sound as you move pages or flip through documents.

- Be sure your narration repeats the words on the paper to reinforce their significance.

- If the volume of the documentation is part of the story, use it in a stand-up. For example, one reporter took a computer printout of DUI convicts who had never served their sentences and unrolled it along the jail's hallways. The sheer length of the list made the point that the city wasn't holding violators accountable.

- Have someone directly involved in the story read the documents aloud. This provides an opportunity for b-roll, and brings the documents to life, sometimes with emotion that would be inappropriate in a reporter's narration.

Graphics

Charts, diagrams and maps can convey significant information visually in news stories in all media. As we've already mentioned, you'll want to collect any graphics you run across that you can use "as is" on the air or online. For example, a developer holding a news conference about a building project would likely have renderings to show what the development will look like once it's completed. If you can get a digital version, so much the better, but a good-quality paper version can be scanned and posted almost as quickly. Just make sure you're not violating any copyright protection.

While pre-made graphics are a time-saver, it's important to fact-check them just as you would a press release so you'll still need the data that was used to build them. You'll also need raw data to construct interactive graphics for the Web. It's often easier to do that by starting from a data set than by extracting the data from an existing graphic. Instead of trying to decipher the color code on a complex world population map, for example, you could build your own map from a simple list of countries and their populations.

Get in the habit of asking for data whenever you cover a "numbers" story—whether it's the city budget or election returns—and get the data in a digital form if you possibly can. Make it easy for people to give it to you by providing a CD or a USB flash drive so they can burn you a copy on the spot. A promise to e-mail it to you later is often forgotten, but it's worth asking if all else fails. If you have a choice, ask for raw data in a format that's easy to work with, like Microsoft Excel or Access. We'll talk more about graphics in Chapter 6.

Natural Sound Stories

Some stories rely exclusively on pictures and sound, with no reporter narration (also called "track"). These natural sound stories or "nat sound" pieces aren't easy to produce. If the result is to be more than just a photo essay, you have to create a coherent narrative with the sound you collect. That can require more planning and just as much reporting as any other story. But the results can be powerful. Having a clear focus helps you decide what kind of sound and pictures you need to tell the story. "The sounds you record and the interviews you conduct are your only tools when you hit the edit bay," says photojournalist Tim King. Think story structure from the start. Your sound needs to introduce the issue and the people involved, explain it and demonstrate its resolution. Listen for sound that will give you a strong ending to tie up your story.

For a nat sound story, you'll conduct interviews differently than you would for other kinds of stories. As we've noted, in a traditional interview, it's advisable to avoid two-part questions because the subject may just answer one part. But for nat sound stories, double-barreled questions actually work well. For example, instead of asking someone to identify themselves, you might ask who they are and what they're doing. "It's an easy way to introduce the subject and the story," says chief photojournalist Bryan Barr of WBFF-TV in Baltimore. It's also a good way to get responses in complete sentences, containing complete thoughts, which photographer John Goheen believes are essential for nat sound stories.

Because the people you interview will serve as your narrators, seek active sound in multiple locations. Talk to people while they're doing something, and repeat your questions at several locations. "This gives me more options later in the edit room," says Goheen. Get more sound than you think you need. Goheen often conducts a more formal sit-down interview at the end of the shoot in a quiet location, just for audio purposes. This gives him additional sound he can use over the video he's already shot.

Don't be afraid that asking the same question several times will make you look stupid. "If you ask someone to re-explain something, they will usually be a lot more descriptive," says Barr. Playing dumb also can elicit sound you'll need to construct your narrative. Go ahead and ask what the score is and how much time is left in a game, even when the answer is obvious, because you may need that information on tape.

TEAMWORK

While journalists today do more and more of their work independently, television and multimedia news are still team sports. Reporters and photojournalists work together to collect the visual and audio elements they need to tell a complete and memorable story. Reporters, producers and graphic artists work together to develop charts, maps and other illustrations that will make the story more understandable.

Teamwork means sharing responsibility for what goes on the air or the Web. Photographers help reporters write, suggesting lines that go with the video or still photos they've shot. In the field, reporters help photographers spot great visuals to illustrate the main points of the story. Even when working in pairs, reporters and photographers must both be visual journalists, committed to understanding and telling a story together.

Story Planning

Reporters and photographers should suggest story ideas and touch base with each other as soon as they know they're working on a story together. A reporter making calls on a story can benefit from a photographer's perspective. Before the team leaves the newsroom, photographers can help reporters think about the video they might need. An early conversation about the story could tip the photographer to bring special equipment for the shoot. Don't wait until you are in the car!

In the Field

Longtime photojournalist Lane Michaelsen, now a news executive at Gannett Broadcasting, likes to joke that the root word in reporter is "porter." Reporters should volunteer to carry equipment, put microphones in place and hold lights. Unless they're writing on deadline, they should not sit in the car while the photographer gets b-roll. By the same token, photographers shouldn't hang back while the reporter gathers information. Unless they've decided to split up in the field for efficiency's sake, reporter-photographer teams work side by side so they both know what elements they've collected and what they still need. And on breaking news, they stay together so they can watch each other's backs.

Mind reading only works in the movies, so teams need to communicate and collaborate from start to finish. Photographers need to tell reporters when they've captured a great shot, and if they have a line in mind to go with it, they should share that too. Reporters need to tell photographers whether there's a shot they definitely need in order to get a point across. Talk about what you'll use for opening and closing video while you're still at the scene. On breaking news, when there's no time to screen the video, photographers should make sure reporters know exactly what they have to work with before they write.

When concluding an interview, the reporter should routinely ask whether the photographer has any questions. Some photojournalists have a knack for rephrasing a question that was asked earlier so you get a better response. Photographers also should have the confidence to ask questions during a shoot. "A simple 'What's up?' may yield a good two-second bite," says KARE-TV's Jonathan Malat. Photographer Juan Renteria of WFAA-TV in Dallas, Texas, says he tries to think like a reporter as well as a photographer. "I ask, 'What lines would I use here, if I use this image? What other shots do I need for a sequence?' Everybody should think like each other, and like a producer, to make the best story."

WORKING ALONE

For a long time, it's been common at small-market television stations for journalists to work as "one-man bands" to report and shoot their own stories. But in recent years the practice has spread to larger stations and even to some networks. Whether you call them video journalists (VJs), solo journalists (sojos) or backpack journalists, the concept is the same: one person is responsible for reporting the story, shooting and editing the video and producing the final product for television or the Web, or both.

VJs and Backpackers

Young Broadcasting Inc. made headlines in 2005 when it converted all of the reporters and photographers at two of its stations, in San Francisco and Nashville, to VJs. The British Broadcasting Corporation (BBC) took a similar step at its local newsrooms. Other companies have introduced the concept more slowly. Gannett, for example, had backpack journalists at about half of its stations in 2006, but most stations had only one or two people working as "backpackers." CNN had a half dozen of what it calls "video correspondents," which the company describes them as journalists "equipped with CNN's specially designed digital newsgather-

Backpack journalist Kevin Sites carried both a video and a still camera when reporting from Nepal in 2006.

Source: Photo courtesy of Dinesh Wagle, Kantipur Daily Newspaper, Kathmandu, Nepal.

ing kit to enable a single correspondent to shoot, edit and transmit reports from anywhere in the world."

As we've already noted, technological improvements have made it more feasible for one person to do it all. Cameras are lighter and more foolproof than ever, so it's not as difficult as it once was to produce acceptable pictures and sound. Digital editing software is widely available and fairly easy to master. But that doesn't mean it's easy to be a sojo.

Pros and Cons

"You learn very quickly that, while aiming to be a jack-of-all-trades, it's hard to be a master of one," says Preston Mendenhall, a pioneering sojo who reported extensively from Iraq and other hot spots for NBC News. "It's tough to conduct interviews and concentrate on keeping a camera steady at the same time, so never forget a tripod," he says. "Take the time to set it up, and if you see your interview subject moving around a lot, stop the interview and fix things."

Kevin Sites, who covered the Iraq war for CNN, later spent a year as a sojo covering "hot zones" around the world for Yahoo (http://hotzone.yahoo.com). He told the Online News Association conference in 2006 that he often felt he was stretched too thin. "When I first started this job it was really confusing because I was carrying a video camera, a still camera and a notebook and I wasn't sure which one I was going to use first," Sites says. "It took me three African countries to figure out, what do I need to focus on?" Eventually, he adopted a strategy of focusing on the text story first to get the details, then shooting video to document action and still photos to put a human face on conflict.

Mendenhall believes the sojo concept works best on feature stories. "Breaking news breaks the back of a solo journalist, and dampens quality," he says. But the BBC's Lisa Lambden says an all-VJ newsroom can outperform a traditional one on breaking news by not asking one VJ to do it all. "When the bad weather hits and homes and businesses are flooded we can field five or six times as many cameras as our opposition. We are able to get really close to the people affected and our stories are more powerful as a result," Lambden says.

"VJs can also outperform in terms of access. We've had many examples of where a VJ with a small camera can get access on a story where a conventional two-person crew can't."[3]

If you do work alone on breaking news, you have to establish some priorities. "Your video is the most important content you bring back from the field, so concentrate on your shooting," Mendenhall advises. His point is that if you miss a shot you may not get another opportunity to capture it. The old adage "shoot first, ask questions later" is good advice for sojos and photojournalists in breaking news situations.

TOOLS OF THE TRADE

In addition to a notebook and pen, today's journalists may carry a gear bag filled with an audio recorder, cameras (still and video) and computer media like a USB flash drive or recordable CD to capture all the elements they need to tell a story on different platforms. They're also likely to have a cell phone or a BlackBerry-type handheld or laptop computer so they can file reports from the field.

Audio gear and camera equipment gets smaller, lighter and more sophisticated all the time. It may take a while to learn what your equipment can do, but it's worth the investment. "Read the manual," says Minnesota Public Radio's Kerr. "It could be some of those buttons on your machine could help you in gathering sound. Just as likely they could really mess you up." Trying to figure that out in the middle of a breaking news situation is foolhardy. Practice ahead of time so you know what to do when it counts.

Whatever you carry, it's important to be sure that your tools are in working order every day. There's nothing more embarrassing than arriving on the scene only to discover there is no tape in the camera or that the batteries are dead. It's a good idea to have an equipment checklist to make sure your gear is always ready to go, and to carry extra batteries and spares whenever possible.

Cameras

These days it seems that every person on the planet carries a camera at all times. Pocket-sized point-and-shoot cameras and even cell phones can capture digital video. The quality is uneven to say the least, but in breaking news situations it's proved to be more than acceptable for use online and even on TV. When a small plane piloted by Yankees pitcher Cory Lidle crashed into a high-rise in New York City in 2006, Fox News Channel streamed video from a Palm Treo smartphone on the air, live, until a better quality feed became available.

Thanks to the latest advances in technology, the mantra for at least some profes-

TRADE TOOLS

GEAR LIST

Most news organizations provide their journalists with gear, but if you decide to build your own kit, here's very a basic list:

Digital video camera.
Digital still camera.
Digital audio recorder.
Headphones.
At least two good quality lavalier mics.
Handheld mic (may be a shotgun mic).
Lightweight tripod.
Portable, battery-powered light.
Laptop with editing software.
A wireless card so you can file from the field (overseas, you'll want a broadband global area network [BGAN] satellite Internet connection).

sional photojournalists is "one tool, many platforms," as they can now use the same camera to capture both stills and video. At the San Jose Mercury News, every photographer has been outfitted with a high-definition Sony video camera. Instead of shooting separate still photos, Richard Koci-Hernandez, deputy director of photography-multimedia, says they can simply grab still frames from the video they shoot and publish the pictures in the newspaper. Because the video is high-definition, Koci-Hernandez says, the quality of the stills is plenty good enough to print, even in fairly large formats. Not all photojournalists are convinced, however, and many who now shoot for both print and online outlets continue to carry a digital still camera as well as a video camera. The problem, of course, is that they can't use both at once, which means they may miss the "money shot" in one format or another.

Audio Recorders

While a digital camera of any size can usually capture audio, the result is often muddy sounding at best. If you don't have a decent camera with a separate mic input, you're far better off recording audio separately if you hope to post it online. Digital audio recorders come in a variety of shapes and sizes. The earliest digital format adopted by professionals was the DAT or digital audio tape recorder, but it's been replaced in many newsrooms by the smaller and less expensive minidisc recorder. Today, some journalists carry recorders that use flash memory instead of replaceable media, making it quick and easy to drag and drop the recorded audio files to a computer for storage and editing. Ideally, you want a recorder that lets you control the recording level manually and that has a separate microphone input.

With an audio recorder, you can begin experimenting with multimedia journalism without jumping straight into shooting video. Rather than trying to take pictures and record audio at the same time, the Roanoke Times' Meltzer started out by carrying a minidisc recorder and shotgun microphone in a waist pack in addition to his standard still camera. After shooting a story, he'd take out the recorder and ask people to talk about the moments he'd documented with his pictures. Or he'd go back to the paper, sit down in a quiet room and record his comments about the story. He'd then use the stills and audio to create a slide show for the newspaper's Web site.

Microphones

As we've discussed, built-in microphones are mostly worthless for recording clear, crisp audio. A professional gear bag usually includes at least two kinds of external microphones: lav (short for lavalier) and handheld, either a stick mic or shotgun. Lavs and stick mics are most commonly used for interviews and shotguns for picking up natural sound, but the roles may be reversed on occasion.

If you're recording sound while also shooting video, wireless microphones offer the most flexibility but they're expensive and their transmitter-receiver system can be tricky to work with. If you're using wired mics, make sure you have plenty of audio cable so you can move the camera and still get good sound. All mics are sensitive to wind noise, so it's a good idea to use a windscreen whenever you're shooting outdoors.

TAKING IT HOME

Reporting for multimedia requires much more than the basic facts of a story. You need a lot of different elements to help you tell that story in a way that takes advantage of the strengths of multimedia. To construct a strong TV news story, you need to capture top-quality video, clear sound bites and crisp natural sound. An online story might also call for still photos, audio and interactive graphics. In today's multimedia newsrooms, journalists must think differently about every story in order to collect all the different elements they will need to tell it in print, on the air and online.

Chad Lawhorn, who covers city hall for the Lawrence Journal-World in Kansas, says multimedia journalism is more work, but it's also liberating. "I feel I have more freedom to tell more of the story because I have the online edition," he says. "I have an outlet that can give more detail."

TALKING POINTS

1. A national report on drinking and drug use by college students has just been released and you are assigned to do a local version of the story. What images and sounds would you want to capture to tell this story in video form for broadcast or online? Tell specifically how you would go about collecting those images and sounds.

2. Do you think VJs or sojos will be the standard in broadcast newsrooms within five years? Why or why not? What difference do you think this will make to the range and quality of broadcast journalism?

eLEARNING OPPORTUNITIES

For chapter exercises, practice tools and additional resources, go to the interactive online workbook at http://college.cqpress.com/advancingthestory. You'll find:

- SKILL BUILDING: Decide how you would shoot a follow-up TV story based on newly available information.

- DISCOVER: Take a video tour of a professional TV photojournalist's light kit.

- ONGOING STORY: Develop a shooting plan for this story, including times, locations and the elements you want to collect.

- EXPLORE: Visit Web sites to learn more about photojournalism and multimedia skills.

4 REPORTING IN DEPTH

Journalists who report in multiple media need to know how to do more than scratch the surface and meet a deadline. They must be able to report in depth, so they can produce meaty stories in any medium. In this chapter, we'll take a look at how you can go about digging deeper to report more fully on a community or a topic.

CBS's Jeff Greenfield once compared news reporting to dry cleaning: In both cases, he said, it's often "in by 9, out by 5." But not all stories are one-day wonders, and even a "quick turn" can lead you to another story down the line if you keep track of the information you discover and the contacts you make along the way.

Following stories over a period of time and digging for information to put the news in context can add depth to your reporting in any medium. Journalists who can do this well are highly valued in their newsrooms. They're the beat reporters who break news on a regular basis and the investigative reporters who hold the powerful accountable. They're the multimedia reporters who always have enough information to build graphics or interactive elements online.

One way to report in depth is to do it in "3D," with data, documents and diverse sources, says Randy Reddick, a pioneer in the field of computer-assisted reporting. Data and statistics allow reporters to make comparisons over time or between groups, which adds perspective to their stories. Documents can add background or validate or refute a claim, and diverse sources can add texture and authenticity. Data sets and original documents can be posted online to supplement your stories or can be used to create graphics to illustrate them. To acquire all this extra information and master the 3D approach, you'll need more than basic reporting skills.

MAPPING THE COMMUNITY

To report the news in depth you have to really know the community you cover. But journalism these days can be a transient business, so you may find yourself working in an area you know little or nothing about. It's incumbent upon you to learn your way around and figure out what makes the community tick. The military motto, "Time spent in reconnaissance is seldom wasted," applies just as well to journalists; the payoff in story ideas and sources is well worth the investment.

Research and Explore

Get to know the area you'll cover by doing some research. Look at government data on local demographics and the economy (www.usa.gov is a good starting point). Find out who the largest employers are and whether they're thriving or hurting. Check with the local Chambers of Commerce and historical societies to get a sense of the area's past as well as its present. Drop by local libraries and talk to a veteran librarian. Browse the classified section of the telephone book. Are there more restaurants than churches? More movie theaters than massage parlors?

As you build your background knowledge, buy a good map and spend some time exploring on your own. Don't be afraid to get lost—you never know what you'll discover. Walk around the downtown areas and drive through the neighborhoods. If it's available, ride public transit and listen to other riders. Take cabs and talk to the drivers. Make a special effort to visit places where people who are different from you live and congregate. Eat out at ethnic restaurants and chat with the owners and customers. What do the people you meet have in common? What divides them?

Read, Listen and Connect

It may seem obvious that you need to read the local newspaper, but don't forget to pick up smaller community newspapers that cover neighborhoods or the suburbs, or that serve different ethnic or minority groups. Be sure to scan the letters to the editor—they often provide a glimpse into the community's values. Listen to local radio DJs and talk show hosts to see what the hot topics are. They often have a finger on the pulse of what matters most to the subset of the community they cater to. Watch as much local news on television as you can, too. But don't stop there. See what local bloggers are writing about and scan community Web sites for people you might want to get to know.

Attend a few public meetings on your own time and introduce yourself to the people who seem most informed and involved. Arrange to meet community leaders for coffee and conversation or ask them to give you a tour of their favorite places. Seek out places where people gather to talk—places like churches, synagogues, mosques and temples, community centers and parks, barbershops, diners or the sidelines at soccer or Little League games. Don't do any formal interviews; just listen to what different kinds of people are talking about and chat with them about what's important in their lives. Get contact information for the people who seem most plugged in and follow up with them. Ask them for the names of two other people they think you should know. In a few weeks, you'll be well on your way to building a diverse group of sources that will help you tell deeper, richer stories.

BEAT REPORTING

When Springfield, Mo., was searching for a new school superintendent, one reporter got the scoop everyone wanted: The leading candidate for the job had turned the offer down. John Shields broke the story on KYTV and sat back to watch the other stations and the local paper scramble to catch up. How did he do it? As the station's education reporter, Shields had developed sources who were in the know and who gave him the story first because they trusted him to get it right.

Many newsrooms assign reporters to beats or specialties, usually a geographic area or a specific topic. Beat system advocates believe there's no better way to encourage original reporting that has substance and depth. That's because reporters who specialize become experts in the subject they cover, so they know which questions to ask and where to look for answers. They are constantly expanding their knowledge of the issues and their sources, and they're persistent and organized enough to follow developments over time.

You may not have the opportunity to focus exclusively on one beat, especially when you're first starting out, but you can use the tactics and strategies beat reporters use to enhance your stories on any subject. Choose a topic that interests you and dig right in.

Getting Started

Beat reporters need the same basic reporting skills we discussed in Chapter 2, and more. They need the ability to develop sources and track information efficiently for months or even years. They often need to master a specialized vocabulary to decipher documents and data on the beat. And they need to really understand the institutions that dominate the beats they cover. Learning how the system works takes time and effort, but it pays off in stories that non-beat reporters can't match.

To develop these skills, you need to put in some study time. Read everything you can about the topic and subscribe to specialized publications that cover your beat. Look for mentions of government agencies, nonprofit groups and experts you can contact for more information. Most important, get up and go. Beat reporters have to spend time on the beat, meeting and talking with people. "No one ever got a story sitting around the newsroom," says veteran reporter Mike Mather at WTKR-TV in Norfolk, Va.

Get to know everyone who could be helpful—from officials to clerks—and pass out your business card to everyone you meet on the beat. Ask them to put you on the mailing list (e-mail or paper) for news releases and reports. Reporter Ann Notarangelo of KRON-TV in San Francisco makes a point of handing out business cards and telling everyone she talks to that she'd love to hear from them again. "Most of those cards, I'm sure, get thrown out," she says. "But somctimes I get a call, even weeks or months later, about a story idea."

Collect budgets, organizational charts, directories, schedules and agendas from all the agencies and groups that touch on your beat. Attend public meetings even if you don't plan to report on them; it's a great way to get to know the players. Listen for any mentions of data or statistics, and ask for copies of documents. You goal is to learn how the institution is supposed to work, how it really does work and who makes the decisions.

Understanding the institutions and collecting data and documents are just the first steps to covering a beat well. Once you know your way around, look for the bigger picture. What are the most important issues these institutions deal with, and how do their decisions affect people in your community? Sometimes the best sources aren't official or even immediately obvious, says Jim Detjen, director of the Knight Center for Environmental Journalism at Michigan State University and a long-time environmental reporter. "When I've written about water pollution being discharged into a river by a chemical company, I've sometimes found it useful to interview anglers, swimmers or water skiers who utilize the river to get their views on the situation," he says. "When I've written about air pollution, I've interviewed window washers, city foresters and pilots." [1]

Covering a beat means getting to know people well enough so they will trust you, while still maintaining a professional distance. That can be a tricky balancing act. To serve the public, you need to be careful not to "go native"—that is, to identify more with the people you cover than with the audience you're supposed to serve. For example, all beats have their own specialized vocabulary, and you'll want to learn the terms used by the people you cover so you can talk with them knowledgeably. But you also need to remember that most of the audience might not be familiar with those terms, so you won't want to use them in your

BREAKING AND ENTERING

"If our best stories are told through people, our toughest reporting tasks often involve cracking the associations they form," says Eric Nalder, an investigative reporter at the Seattle Post-Intelligencer. He uses these questions to begin learning his way around an organization or institution:

- Who are the players? Get staff directories and newsletters; contact professional associations; check for government contracts, permits, complaints and lawsuits.

- Who is in charge? Check Dun & Bradstreet (www.dnb.com) for private companies, Edgar (www.sec.gov/edgar.shtml) for public companies and Guidestar.org for IRS 990 forms of nonprofits (www.guidestar.org).

- Who are the regulators? Most federal agencies have an inspector general (www.ignet.gov); contact state auditors, legislative oversight committees and watchdog groups.

- What are the rules? For government agencies, use the index to federal regulations; for private companies, ask federal regulators which laws apply.

- How are things done? Follow the paper trail; get internal memos; talk to insiders.

- Where are the mistakes recorded? Learn how the organization monitors and tracks errors and ask for the documents.

- Where is the spending recorded? Obtain a budget, which outlines spending plans, and a balance sheet, which documents how money was actually spent.

- Who knows the story and how can I get it? Work your sources to gain access to significant events. Firsthand knowledge is always best. "Be there, and you will be aware."

Source: Adapted from Eric Nalder, "Breaking and Entering, How to Dissect an Organization," http://home. earthlink.net/~cassidyny/breaking.htm.

KNOW AND TELL

stories. For example, a hospital spokesperson might tell you that the victim of a mugging suffered "lacerations and contusions," but you'd want to use the phrase "cuts and bruises." Always define or translate insider language to make sure your stories make sense.

Language isn't the only challenge beat reporters face. The hardest part of being a beat reporter, says the Poynter Institute's Chip Scanlan, is "dealing with sources you have to return to every day even if you've written a story they don't like." However, beat reporters who know their subject matter, and who tell accurate and fair stories, find that even sources who may dislike their stories will often respect them. As Celeste Ford, who covers education for WABC-TV in New York, says, "School officials know my stories may criticize them but they'd rather have the critical story come from me, because they know I do my homework."

Tracking the Beat

To cover a beat or to follow stories over time it's essential to be well organized. To keep track of developments, you'll need a basic calendar, a source list and a future file. Use the calendar to note meetings, hearings, anniversaries and due dates for reports or action. Check it daily, and make sure to look several days ahead so you can confirm details and get a jump on upcoming stories. Maintain a reliable, portable system for filing and retrieving contact information. And keep a file of future story ideas, with daily lists of things to follow up on.

Many reporters use computer programs for each of these tasks to make it easy to search for people, dates and information. They'll synchronize their files between an office computer and a laptop, personal digital assistant (PDA) or "smart phone" like a BlackBerry or Treo so they can access the information in the field. Because technology can be unreliable, though, it's critically important to back up the information frequently.

Some people still prefer to track information on paper, using a pocket planner or even a wall calendar. Choose whatever system works for you—just be sure to use it and to update it regularly, at least once a week. If possible, try to set aside a few minutes every morning or evening to sort and save the information you've been collecting all day long. Yes, it takes time to get organized and stay that way, but it's a habit that can save you on deadline.

If you're like most people, you'll probably have some manila folders for hard copy and computer "folders" for electronic documents, data, digital voice recordings and e-mails. Use the same labels for each to avoid confusion. Don't let things build up in a general file; sort them regularly by subtopic or you'll never find what you want. For example, you might begin with a file labeled "City Budget," but as you follow the story you'll probably create separate folders for the biggest budget categories. Don't keep entire newspapers or documents in a stack. Clip and select what you want to keep and file it by topic. Or find the online version of the article and store it in a digital file. Keep copies of stories, scripts and tape logs in the same places as your background information so you can quickly find file tape or bites for follow-up stories.

Get as much contact information as possible for every source—not just an office address and telephone number but also cell phone and home numbers, and e-mail and instant message addresses as well. Move names and numbers out of your notebook, off press releases and business cards and into your database daily. And don't stop at just names and numbers. Enter keywords so you can find that person again: Story topic, type of business, general location—anything that might help you find someone if you've forgotten the person's name or where they work. You may also want to note a source's race, ethnicity or languages spoken to help you build a "rainbow Rolodex" of experts in all sorts of fields. If you're working on a story over several days or weeks, you may want to make a master list of contacts and keep a copy in the story file.

Working the Beat

Once you discover a helpful source of information for one story, stay in touch with that person over the long term. Good reporters "work" their sources regularly, contacting them to see what's going on. Reporter Bob Buckley of WGHP-TV in High Point, N.C., makes what he calls a "five and three list" on Sundays—five people to visit during the week and three people to call each day. "People give information and stories to those they're comfortable with," he says. "And they'll get that way when you visit them some time other than when you need something from them."

When you make routine "beat checks" by telephone, don't just ask whether there's anything new and then hang up. Take time to get to know your sources and demonstrate your interest in the subject, and it will pay off over time. "I know that when I have seven calls on my voice mail about the same crime, I return the calls of reporters who make regular beat checks," says Susan Rossi Medina, public information officer for the Arvada (Colo.) Police Department.[2]

CBS News national correspondent Byron Pitts is an expert at keeping track of good sources. Every time he interviews someone, he makes a note of things he has learned about that person. Maybe the person likes to fish or has a daughter who plays basketball. Mentioning that the next time he calls can help him resume contact or give him a lead on a related story. Say, for example, that when he interviews a military expert about defense spending, they happen to have discussed the pictures of horses he noticed in her office. Pitts will make a note of that in his handheld computer or PDA. Then, let's imagine he's assigned to do a story about equine virus. He would run a search for "horses" in his electronic contact list and pull up the military expert's name. Even if she is not an expert on equine virus, she might be able to help him find the right person to talk to for his story.

TOPICAL BEATS

Topical beat assignments are common at newspapers and even in many broadcast newsrooms, despite their relatively small staffs and high turnover rates. According to a national survey by the Project for Excellence in Journalism, almost two-thirds of local television stations assign at least some reporters full-time to covering beats. Stations where all reporters are on general assignment were the exception, not the rule. Less than a quarter of the stations surveyed said they don't use beats at all. But it's not unusual for TV reporters to be responsible for tracking news on a beat in addition to covering everyday news.[3]

Many newsrooms assign reporters to cover issues that are of particular interest or importance in the local community, so you won't find the same beats everywhere. In Orlando, Fla., for example, a beat reporter may cover transportation and tourism; in South Dakota, you might be assigned to cover issues involving the state's large American Indian population; and in communities with big defense installations reporters often track the military beat. That said, the following beats are among the most common in newsrooms today: crime and justice, government and politics, education, business and health and medicine.

Crime and Justice

Few reporters have any training in criminal justice, but veterans on the police beat recommend taking at least one course in the subject. Police officials are notoriously reluctant to provide information to journalists, says veteran crime reporter Caroline Lowe of WCCO-TV in Minneapolis, Minn., but if you know their rules, regulations and procedures, she says, you can ask better questions and improve your chances of learning what you want to know. Lowe herself didn't take just one criminal justice course; she has a graduate degree in law enforcement and says her studies gave her insights that helped her build relationships with police sources and tell stories that make a difference. "Nothing is more satisfying than doing a story that helps a victim or leads to positive change in the system," says Lowe.

Spending time on the crime beat means hanging out at police stations, firehouses and with emergency medical technicians, getting to know their problems and procedures. Reporters who cover crime make it a habit to listen to the scanner and read the "blotter" or daily log as well as any incident reports they can get their hands on to get a sense of what's happening in the community. To learn your way around the beat, arrange for a ride-along or ask a homicide detective to walk you through an unsolved case.

Police reporters need to know exactly how crimes are defined. A burglary and a robbery are not the same thing, for example. Developing a glossary of essential terms can prevent embarrassing mistakes.

A police news release may provide the basic facts about a crime, but good reporters dig deeper. Whenever possible they go to the scene to look for details and to talk with neighbors or eyewitnesses. They connect not only with the official police community but also with Neighborhood Watch captains and activist groups, such as those that oppose drunk driving or domestic violence. Covering crime and public safety is not just a matter of reporting on incidents as they occur; to do it well, you have to look for patterns and trends, and always look for the impact of crime on individuals and communities.

Reporters who cover crime also need to pay attention to the potential impact of the coverage itself. Research has found that news reports tend to feature more minorities as perpetrators of crime and fewer as victims of crime than the actual data would support. According to several studies, the disparity is greatest when it comes to violent crime. "The absence of Black victims, coupled with the repeated presence of Black suspects across different sources of news, reinforces stereotypes about African Americans as a group audiences should fear," say researchers Lori Dorfman and Vincent Schiraldi.[4] They suggest that reporters broaden their sources, provide more context in crime stories and conduct periodic content audits to make sure their coverage reflects reality.

Crime reporters also dig for data they can use to develop stories and supplement their coverage online. One of the most innovative uses of crime data is the mash-up created by

THE COP BEAT

Covering cops is both hard work and a lot of fun, says Kathryn Sosbe, assistant managing editor at the Idaho Statesman. "Your performance on the street will be evaluated and tested by every officer you meet," she says. "They will tell you something in secret just to see if you can keep your mouth shut. Once you've passed their trust test, maintain that trust. But don't ever cross the line and become their pal. Get them to respect you for the work you do: be fair in your stories, accurate in your facts and professional in your conduct."

Nancy Weil of IDG News Service in Boston advises reporters to play by police rules when covering cops. "Don't be rude to them, especially at crime scenes. If they tell you to move back, do it," she says. Avoid at all costs getting them angry at you for any reason, Weil advises. "I have found that cops can hold grudges for all eternity. If one of them gets it in for you, that can infect others and you can be hosed when it comes to trying to build other relationships. If you treat them with respect and handle the stories you write with respect and let them know that you think what they are doing is important you'll do a lot to earn their respect in turn and their trust."

Source: Deborah Potter, "Tracking the Police Beat," NewsLab, n.d., www.newslab.org/resources/cops.htm.

online journalist Adrian Holovaty at Chicagocrime.org. Mash-ups are Web sites or software applications that combine data from other sources. Holovaty's project merged a database of all crimes reported to the Chicago police department with a Google map of the city. Users can search and sort the data by type of crime, date or location and then pinpoint the information on a map.

To cover courts, reporters must understand the judicial process from beginning to end. They should know what happens when a suspect is arrested, charged, arraigned, tried and sentenced or released. Experienced reporters say the best way to learn the process is to spend time at the courthouse. Begin with the court clerks, who keep track of the docket (the list of cases) and the calendar. Find out how to get copies of the court record, filings and testimony. Read the case files, including motions and pleadings before trial, and keep

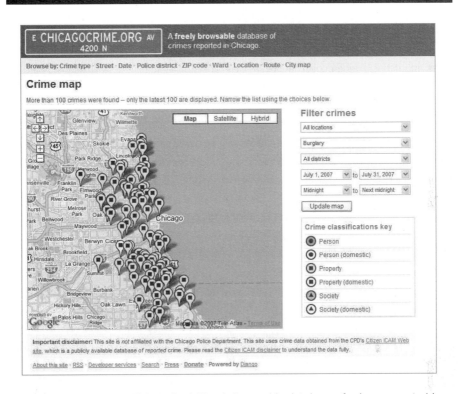

Chicagocrime.org is a self-described "freely browsable database of crimes reported in Chicago." Searching this mash-up for burglaries in all locations for the month of July 2007 turned up more than 100 incidents, plotted on a city map.

Source: Captured August 26, 2007, from www.chicagocrime.org.

track of what's reported about the case if you can't be in court every day, which is more typical than not.

Some of the best sources of information on the justice beat are defense attorneys, who are often more willing than prosecutors to talk with reporters about cases they are working on. Do your best to understand legal jargon, but avoid using it in your stories. "Lawyers are counseled to use big words to confuse journalists," says S. L. Alexander, author of Covering the Courts: A Handbook for Journalists. "If you don't know what something means, ask the person you're interviewing to explain it," she advises.

Government and Politics

Reporters who cover government need to understand its inner workings and keep a close eye on the impact of government actions. Reporters who ask the basic question, "Who cares about this?" when covering government are able to find people whose lives are affected by what government does; stories that feature those people are much more interesting to the audience.

Much of the business of government is conducted in meetings, so reporters on the city hall or state or national capitol beat can expect to cover plenty of them. Just remember, a dull meeting does not justify a dull story. The audience depends on the journalist to tell them only what's important, not everything that happened in chronological order. And the

TRADE TOOLS

REPORTING ON POLLS

Public opinion surveys are a staple of campaign coverage, but journalists need to look closely before deciding whether a poll's results are worth reporting. The National Council on Public Polls suggests asking these 20 questions:

Who did the poll?
Who paid for the poll and why was it done?
How many people were interviewed for the survey?
How were those people chosen?
What area (nation, state or region) or what group (teachers, lawyers, Democratic voters, etc.) were these people chosen from?
Are the results based on the answers of all the people interviewed?
Who should have been interviewed and was not? Or do response rates matter?
When was the poll done?
How were the interviews conducted?
What about polls on the Internet or World Wide Web?
What is the sampling error for the poll results?
Who's on first?
What other kinds of factors can skew poll results?

best stories about meetings focus not on what happened in the room but on the results of the decisions that were made.

On the government beat, it's critically important for journalists to know how to read and interpret a budget and other financial statements. "Follow the money" is good advice for all journalists, but particularly for those covering government and politics. Stories about government funding may seem dry, but taxes and spending affect the audience directly and people need to know where their money is going. Documents in general are the lifeblood of government, so beat reporters must be able to obtain them, understand them and interpret them for the audience.

Political reporters basically have one central mission: to provide citizens with the information they need to make an informed choice among the candidates for elective office.

What questions were asked?

In what order were the questions asked?

What about "push polls"?

What other polls have been done on this topic? Do they say the same thing? If they are different, why are they different?

What about exit polls?

What else needs to be included in the report of the poll?

So I've asked all the questions. The answers sound good. Should we report the results?

"Horse-race" polls that tell what percentage of voters support each candidate are of limited value as a snapshot of the race on any given day. Some journalists believe these polls may actually bias voters in favor of the leading candidate because people want to be on the winning side. But researchers have discovered that voters who pay attention to polls also learn more about the issues involved in the campaign. The study suggests that journalists should continue to report the results of legitimate "tracking" polls throughout the campaign, but not make them a major focus of the coverage.

Sources: List is excerpted from Sheldon R. Gaweiser and G. Evans Witt, "20 Questions a Journalist Should Ask about Poll Results," National Council on Public Polls, n.d., www.ncpp.org/?q=node/4; the concluding paragraph is from Philip Meyer and Deborah Potter, "Making a Difference: Covering Campaign '96," University of North Carolina at Chapel Hill, School of Journalism and Mass Communication, 1997, www.unc.edu/~pmeyer/meyrpot1.htm.

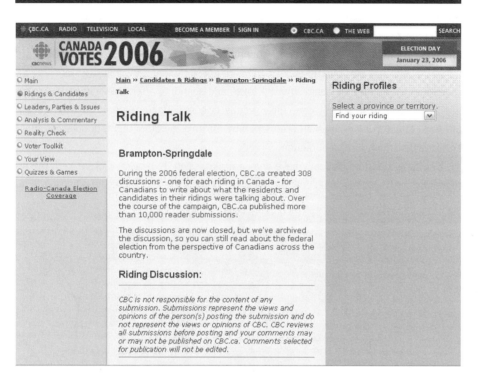

The CBC created 308 discussion boards during Canada's national election campaign in 2006—one for each "riding," or precinct in the country, and published more than 10,000 comments from readers.

Source: "Riding Talk," CBC. Captured December 15, 2006, from www.cbc.ca/canadavotes/ridingtalk/2005/11/114.html.

To do that, journalists need to examine the candidates' backgrounds and qualifications, their positions on the key issues and what they're saying in campaign appearances and advertising. Reporters who cover politics also look at the candidates' supporters, because their interests can often shed light on what a politician will do if elected.

Good political reporters do not simply tell where the candidates stand on the issues; they also ask what the candidates have done about those issues in any previous elected office they have held. And to bring the issues to life, reporters look for people whose individual stories can illustrate why the issues matter and what difference it would make to them if one candidate or the other wins the election.

When it comes to campaign issues, journalists should pay attention not only to what the candidates say but also to what the voters want to know. Many news organizations conduct "issue polls" or focus groups to see which topics are of greatest interest to the public during an election year. Online forums can serve much the same purpose, although it's important to remember that they're not statistically reliable and they may not fairly represent the views of diverse groups in the community. The Canadian Broadcasting Company (CBC) hosted more than 300 moderated forums on its Web site during the 2006 national election campaign, one for each "riding" or precinct in the country. The online conversations focused on political issues that mattered to people in each district, and the journalists monitoring the chats found ideas for stories that hadn't been covered.

Education

The education beat is a wide umbrella, covering everything from preschool through higher education, and from school funding to learning outcomes. The beat has become even broader and more complex in recent years in part because of the expansion of charter schools, the increasing popularity of homeschooling and new federal requirements under the No Child Left Behind Act. These days, education stories are often political stories as well, and reporters on the beat frequently have to navigate overlapping layers of authority to get the information they need to understand what's really happening in the schools.

If you're on the education beat, you'll probably spend time attending school board and PTA meetings, not so much to report on them as to look for sources and story ideas. WABC's Celeste Ford once found a story by scanning the agenda for an upcoming meeting and noticing a proposed city resolution that would ask the state to tighten beeper requirements on school buses. At the time, the state required back-up beepers only on buses built after 1990, but thousands of city school buses were older than that. Ford located statistics through the Board of Education and the Department of Motor Vehicles. She did the math, determined how much it would cost to install beepers on the buses that lacked them and then took that number to a city official for comment. Her story included the voices of schoolchildren, parents, a deputy chancellor of city schools, a school bus company executive and a representative of a school where a student was killed when a bus without a beeper backed over her.

Reporters covering education need to understand the structure, staffing and economics of the school systems they cover, which may vary widely. They should be prepared to decipher statistics and to compare budgets over time to see where the money goes and what happens as a result. Covering education also means tracking statistical data such as dropout and graduation rates, teacher retention and vacancy rates, principal turnover and

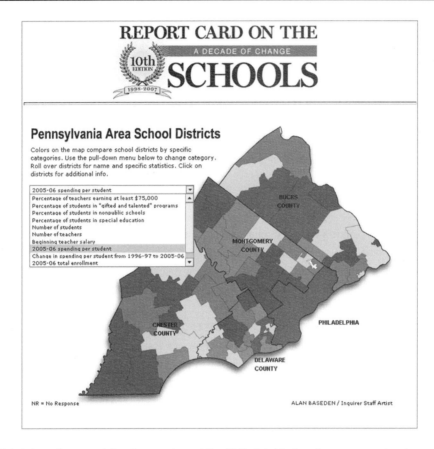

This interactive map let online readers of the Philadelphia Inquirer compare local school districts by a variety of measurements, including teacher salaries and spending per student.

Source: Philadelphia Inquirer. Captured August 20, 2007, from http://inquirer.philly.com/specials/2007/report_card/schools_pa.

the results of high-stakes testing. Many news organizations post this kind of data online. The Philadelphia Inquirer, for example, developed a school report card using data on spending, teacher salaries, student diversity and test scores and created a clickable online map so users could easily compare their district with others in the area.

Some news organizations use education data to create their own measurements, like the Washington Post's "challenge index" that ranks high schools based on the percentage of students who take Advanced Placement, International Baccalaureate or other college-level tests.

When education reporters cover policy issues like the certification process for teachers or efforts to end social promotion, they need to know how these issues have been handled in the past or in similar school districts, and what research has shown about the effectiveness of these policies. When they cover test results, they need to examine the details behind the data. Ranking schools' performance without considering demographics like race, income or parents' education, for example, will produce a misleading story.

One of the toughest challenges many education reporters face is a lack of access to schools and students; superintendents often cite privacy concerns to keep reporters out. It's difficult to put a human face on education stories if you can't shoot pictures in classrooms or talk to students and teachers on school grounds. Reporters who invest time in developing relationships with individual students, parents, teachers and administrators can eventually earn their trust and gain the access they need to tell compelling stories on the education beat.

As an education reporter, you should read school newspapers and Web sites, subscribe to parent newsletters and e-mail discussion lists and check local university alumni reviews to see which issues are bubbling up. To stay abreast of national developments so you can put local stories in context, make a habit of reading Education Week (www.edweek.org) and the Chronicle of Higher Education (http://chronicle.com).

Business and Economics

The business beat may sound as dull as can be, but when you think about it, stories about business and economics touch almost everyone's life. Unemployment, the cost of food and gasoline, personal savings and investment—all of these topics matter not just to business leaders but also to workers and consumers. Covering the local business beat means reporting on jobs, construction and property sales, as well as the business sectors that keep the local economy going, whether it's farming, manufacturing, mining or health care.

Reporters covering business and economics have to make their stories accessible to a general audience. They must understand economic concepts and terms and be able to define them or restate them in plain language. This is good practice even for reporters working for specialized publications, Web sites or broadcasts, whose audience might be expected to be familiar with business jargon. The Wall Street Journal, for example, is aimed

COVERING EDUCATION

Long-time education reporter Dave Marcus says the best stories are found in classrooms. "They have to do with the way teachers teach; with the way students soar and struggle; with the way some parents pressure their kids while others ignore their kids," he wrote in a column for the Casey Journalism Center on Children and Families. Here are some of his tips for education reporters:

- Cover what the kids and the best teachers are talking about—avoid the agenda of the district's public relations office.

- Spend a few days in a school, even volunteering as a mentor or writing teacher (but be honest and constantly remind everyone you're really a reporter).

- Follow the money. "Plenty of education software, test-prep tools and other gimmicks impress taxpayers, but much of it is junk," Marcus says. Keep an eye on the soaring costs of basics as well. At budget time, ask what a district spends on heating and health insurance. Then ask what special education services must be provided because of federal laws and pressure from parents' lawyers.

- Don't be hemmed in by artificial constraints like county lines. Why not look at innovative programs in middle schools throughout your readership or viewership area?

- Write about parents, parents, parents. You can usually judge a school by its parents. If they're involved, the school probably will have higher standards. What can poorly performing schools do to draw in parents?

Source: Dave Marcus, "The Secret of the Education Beat," Casey Journalism Center on Children and Families, November 14, 2005, www.cjc.umd.edu/jcommunity/articles/Marcus_11.14.htm.

at business-savvy readers, but it still spells out the meaning of common terms like gross national product—the total value of a nation's output of goods and services. Over time, business reporters develop their own list of concise definitions they can plug into their stories. They also become skilled at explaining why all of this matters to individuals, not just to corporations and governments.

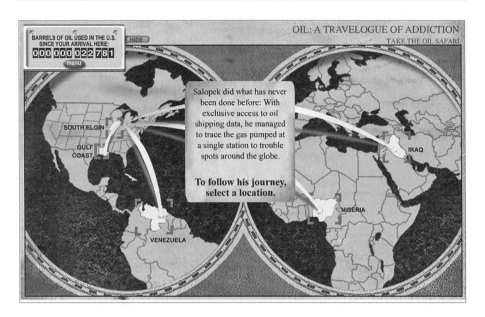

BARRELS OF OIL USED IN THE U.S. SINCE YOUR ARRIVAL HERE:

000 000 022 781

menu

HIDE

SOUTH ELGIN

GULF COAST

VENEZUELA

IRAQ

NIGERIA

Salopek did what has never been done before: With exclusive access to oil shipping data, he managed to trace the gas pumped at a single station to trouble spots around the globe.

To follow his journey, select a location.

To supplement a four-part newspaper series on America's "mighty thirst for gasoline," the Chicago Tribune invited online users to take an "oil safari." This Flash animation let users follow reporter Paul Salopek's journey to trace the source of the gasoline at one suburban gas station.

Source: Paul Salopek, "A Tank of Gas, A World of Trouble," Chicago Tribune. Captured August 23, 2007, from www.chicagotribune.com/news/specials/broadband/chi-oilsafari-html,0,7894741.htmlstory.

Multimedia features are a great way to make business stories more accessible to a general audience. For example, when Chicago Tribune reporter Paul Salopek decided to track the flow of crude oil from producers around the globe to one suburban gas station, his online story included a "Travelogue of Addiction" that allowed users to follow his reporting journey to the sources of the oil.

Business reporters need to be able to read and understand financial statements, balance sheets and annual reports. They often find stories by looking at year-to-year changes in income or spending that seem unusual. They compare companies with others in the same industry or the same region. For example, when a business closes, reporters want to know how many people have lost their jobs and what impact the shutdown will have on the community. To answer that question, they need to know whether the company was one of the largest employers in the area, whether other local companies provide the same product or service, what the local unemployment rate is and so on.

The business beat requires a deeper knowledge of math and statistics than most other topic areas. But business reporters should use numbers sparingly in their stories because too many figures make a story dry and dull. The most compelling business stories show the significance of developments by putting them in human terms, telling how individuals have been or will be affected.

Health, Science and the Environment

Stories about health and the environment have a direct impact on people's lives. Reporters who cover AIDS know that ignorance is almost as big a killer as the disease itself; their stories can educate people so they can protect themselves. Journalists on the health, science and environment beat may report about everything from avian flu to the mapping of the human genome and the effects of damming rivers.

In large newsrooms, reporters may specialize in only one of these three areas. But in all cases, the underlying issues are complicated and the journalist's job is to explain them clearly. Multimedia features can convey complex information in an interactive form. For example, MSNBC created simple Flash animations to explain how illegal street drugs affect the human body.

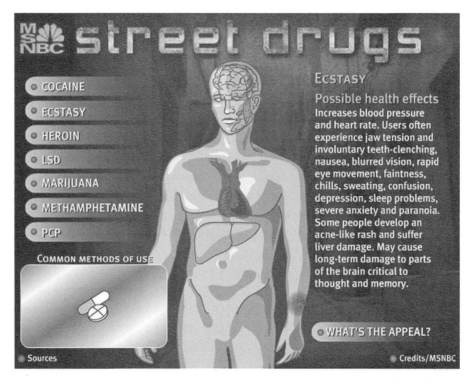

This screen shot is from a Flash animation created by MSNBC. When the user selects a drug—in this case, ecstasy—a pop-up graphic shows the specific parts of the body the drug affects.

Source: "How Drugs Affect the Body," MSNBC.com. Captured June 23, 2007, from www.msnbc.msn.com/id/12423004.

When dealing with these kinds of stories, journalists need to be familiar with the language of scientists and medical researchers, which can be confusing to say the least. Like business reporters, science writers develop their own list of definitions and explanations for complicated terms so they can write stories that make sense to the general public.

Reporters who cover scientific subjects need to understand the scientific method as well as basic math and statistics so they can double check the results of research studies. They should always ask for and compare results for different demographic groups. If the study looked only at white patients, for example, the findings might not apply to other groups. At the same time, reporters should resist the urge to turn every development into a breakthrough, or to press for yes or no answers instead of accepting probabilities. Their stories may not seem as dramatic, but they will certainly be more accurate.

Journalists who are trained to report all sides of a story often fall into a trap when covering science. Giving equal coverage to differing scientific opinions can actually mislead the audience. For example, the overwhelming majority of scientists believe that exposure to lead can harm children's intelligence levels; only a few researchers dispute the connection. You could mention both viewpoints in a story about lead exposure, but you'd have to be careful not to suggest that the science is really in dispute.

Carol Rogers, editor of the journal Science Communication, has two useful tips for health and science beat reporters. First: identification matters. Journalists often don't identify the experts they quote in a meaningful way. For example, a story about an international conference on climate change quoted the head of the White House's Office of Science and Technology but never mentioned that he was a respected climate scientist. Leaving that out made his comments seem politically motivated.

Second, Rogers says, audiences don't bring anywhere near the background journalists do to any kind of story, much less to complicated ones. That means if you're covering a science conference, for example, you can't assume your audience has heard or read yesterday's story, or that they'll hear tomorrow's. Give them the background they need to understand a story as if that will be the only information they will ever read or hear on the subject. It may well be.

INVESTIGATIVE REPORTING

Investigative reporting is by definition in-depth reporting, requiring extensive research and interviewing. But investigative stories often begin the way ordinary stories do, with a phone call or a conversation. In 2003, a waitress at a diner in Charlotte, N.C., mentioned her

ENVIRONMENTAL REPORTING

Demetria Kalodimos is a full-time anchor at WSMV-TV in Nashville, Tenn., who reports in her "spare time." She won an award from the Society of Environmental Journalists in 2006 for an investigation into tricholoroethylene (TCE) pollution in a rural Tennessee county. The contamination had been reported before, she says, but officials insisted the levels were considered "safe." "To be honest, hearing that phrase parroted over and over just caused my journalistic senses to tingle," Kalodimos says. "I decided to look a little closer."

What she found were stories of human suffering: "a family's dream home lost to contamination they should have been told about, the almost cavalier attitude of a summer church camp that continued to fill its swimming pool with contaminated spring water because it was cheap, the heartbreak of 19 families whose children were born with cleft lip/palate, defying the epidemiological odds."

Her advice to other reporters wanting to tackle a similar story?

- Do not be afraid of what seems like a technical issue, or something "out of your league." Chances are very good that an expert is willing to give you a thorough science tutorial. And, believe it or not, starting with a mere layman's understanding can help you explain the difficult material more effectively to viewers who are in the same boat.

- Go back [and] look at property deeds, old hearings, old minutes. It was fascinating to learn how concerned people were with one of the contaminated springs 30 years before the TCE problem surfaced. This context helped me build a stronger story.

- Be ready and prepared to get no official comment or cooperation. These days municipalities, even the feds, seem to have no qualms about just not playing ball at all on an issue. It's difficult for us to imagine telling a story without the traditional balance we are used to, but there are ways to be fair and skeptical without interviewing folks in suits.

Source: Mike Dunne, "Top TV Reporters Say Don't Fear the Technical," *SE Journal*, Fall 2006, 1, http://notes. sej.org/sej/sejourna.nsf/21fd4c7bbafa1be5862568a50017a819/183a8a1cd7b2f6f7862571f60017662f/ $FILE/sej_fa06.pdf.

KNOW AND TELL

grandson's unpleasant experience at a local dental clinic to WCNC-TV photojournalist Doug Stacker. He passed her name along to reporter Stuart Watson, one of the station's investigative journalists, who decided to check out the story.

The first step was to talk to the child's mother and get her son's dental records. The records showed that 4-year-old Brandon Dillbeck had had 16 of his baby teeth drilled and capped with stainless steel crowns—all in one three-hour session. Watson knew he was on the trail of a good story, but his reporting had only just begun. To find out whether the boy's treatment was typical or excessive, Watson needed a dentist to review the dental records. He needed background on the clinic where the work was done, and he needed pictures to tell Brandon's story on television. He also had to try to get a response from the dentists who treated the boy.

"We put that story on the air," Watson says, "and then, as is the case when you find systemic problems, the phone starts ringing." More than six months later, one woman's complaint had led to a series of 13 reports about dental treatment for children on Medicaid. The station's investigative team obtained and analyzed thousands of dental records, Medicaid billing records and corporate and property records for the series that eventually won both a Peabody and a duPont-Columbia Award—two of broadcast journalism's most prestigious prizes.

So what makes a story "investigative"? It's not just the time that's spent developing a story nor the length of the finished product, although investigative reporters usually do get more time to research and write, and more air time or space than general assignment reporters. And it's not just that investigative reporting is enterprising—that is, it requires original work and effort. Lots of daily stories do, too. What sets investigative reporting apart is its focus on mistakes or wrongdoing that affect the public. True investigative stories are about corruption, mismanagement, dysfunction, dishonesty, system failures or fraud, and they hold the powerful accountable. Because of that, investigative reports require more stringent verification and more disclosure about the sources of information. Investigative reporters often use specific techniques to obtain and decipher the information they need for their stories, such as using Freedom of Information (FOI) laws, computer analysis or going undercover.

Using FOI

The federal Freedom of Information Act (FOIA) and state open records laws are tools that reporters can use to find stories that won't show up in a news release. These laws basically protect the public's right to know what the government is doing by providing access to records, data and documents. Beat reporters and investigative reporters use FOI laws routinely to search for stories and to document what they hear from their sources.

Brant Houston, former executive director of Investigative Reporters and Editors, Inc. (IRE), urges reporters to collect public documents and databases so they can investigate what goes on behind the scenes. For example, a local government reporter would want to have a list of public employees and their salaries, contracts and disciplinary records; disclosure forms for elected officials; accident and inspection reports for businesses regulated by local government agencies; and any audits and investigations conducted by and of those agencies. Most of that information is public, so Houston says your first step should be to check the Internet to see whether it's been posted online. If you can't find it, then just ask for it. Only if that doesn't work, Houston says, should you file a formal FOI request.

Planning and follow-up are critical to a successful FOIA request, Houston says. Begin by asking what information is really needed for the story. Keeping your requests reasonable and targeted will improve your chances of success. Then figure out who has the record you're looking for. It's not always obvious, so find out who tracks the specific data you want before you make a request. It's also a good idea to determine who else might have the information, so you know where to go if the first agency says no. Local crime statistics, for example, are usually shared with state and federal agencies, including the FBI. "The farther away you go from the 'official custodian,' the more likely the record will be released," says Houston.

It's useful to know if the kind of record you're after has ever been released before. Knowing whether there's a precedent can help you make a case that you should be allowed to have the information you're requesting. You should also know what exemptions might apply to the records; under the law, exemptions may keep some information from being released to protect national security, individual privacy, business interests and efficient government operations. But the FOI law says that even if part of a document is exempt, the government still has to let you have the rest of it. Take what you can get, Houston advises. If you're looking for trends in Medicaid spending, for example, you may not need to know the names of individual patients.

Computer-Assisted Reporting

The term "computer-assisted reporting" or CAR has been used to refer to everything from creating multimedia to gathering databases. For the purposes of this text, we'll confine our discussion of CAR to the use of computer programs to analyze information, especially data. CAR isn't just useful for major reporting projects; it can also be used to add depth to daily stories and even to uncover quirky features, like the fact that on the 13th of every month, the number of marriage ceremonies performed in North Carolina drops by 40 percent. The (Raleigh) News & Observer discovered that little gem about love and luck in the state's marriage database.[5]

Government data is a journalist's gold mine. Police incidents, highway patrol citations, medical examiner reports, state university payrolls, political contributions—reporters have used all of these records and more to develop stories they would never have discovered any other way. In North Carolina, for example, the state's official death database includes a field that describes the type of burial. A reporter at the News & Observer spent an hour or so sorting and comparing the data and discovered that cremation had become increasingly popular across the state. "Good reporting and good writing turned that into a business-front story," says the N&O's veteran investigative reporter Pat Stith.[6]

Nancy Amons of WSMV-TV in Nashville, Tenn., is a skilled database reporter who describes herself as a pack rat, always fighting for more file space. "I save data longer than the city does," she says. She's uncovered dozens of stories by crunching the data. One of her favorite stories involved a 20-year-old man who had killed a woman in a traffic accident and had never been prosecuted. "I stumbled on the story by looking at speeding ticket records, hoping to profile the driver with the most tickets," she says. It turned out that driver had a vehicular homicide on his record and had never gone to court. After her story aired, the young man went to prison. That same data set of speeding records had a field showing whether violators' tickets had been erased after they attended traffic school. Amons crunched the numbers again and reported that some people were getting away with going to traffic school half a dozen times a year.

Amons advises reporters to find out how the data is kept before requesting it. "If you want court information, for example, start by asking for the form that the clerks use to do data entry from." Knowing the fields and the record layout will help you formulate a request that's easy to fulfill. Then ask for the data in a form you can use. Microsoft Excel, for example, uses .xls files, while Access files have the extensions .mdb or .dbf. It's sometimes safer to ask for a text file or ASCII file,[7] delimited by comma, space or tab, which allows you to import the data into almost any spreadsheet or database program. Obviously, your best bet is to get data in digital form, but if the information is available only on paper, you'll need to enter it into a program by hand so you can sort and compare the information efficiently.

Once you have the data in your computer, make sure it's "clean" and complete. Check for inconsistencies in spelling and see if any pieces of data are missing. After that, it takes only a few clicks to perform the most basic analysis, such as sorting the numbers in ascending or descending order. That's how Amons determined who had the most speeding tickets in Nashville.

If you're working with budgets, you can program Excel to perform calculations, like the difference between last year's spending and this year's and the percent change from one year to the next. Then, by sorting the numbers, you can easily see which budget categories increased, which were cut, and by how much. As you become more experienced at using CAR, you can begin to compare data sets using a "relational" database program like Access. Just by asking the right questions, you could learn how many convicted felons have hunting permits, for example, or how many sex offenders live near day care centers.

Microsoft Excel - arrests.xls				
File Edit View Insert Format Tools Data Financial Manager Window Help Acrobat				
A1 = Arrests - Liquor Law Violations				

	A	B	C	D	E
1	Arrests - Liquor Law Violations				
2					
3	Reporting Location	Sector of Institution			
4	On Campus		**2002**	**2003**	**2004**
5		Public, 4-year or above	23,864	24,568	26,539
6		Private nonprofit, 4-year or above	4,673	4,821	5,822
7		Private for profit, 4-year or above	5	5	19
8		Public, 2-year	1,728	1,700	1,797
9		Private nonprofit, 2-year	29	8	33
10		Private for profit, 2-year	58	33	79
11		Public, less-than-2-year	45	83	61
12		Private nonprofit, less-than-2-year	1	1	9
13		Private for profit, less-than-2-year	3	15	35
14		Total	30,406	31,234	34,394
15	Residence Halls (included in on-campus)		**2002**	**2003**	**2004**
16		Public, 4-year or above	11,660	11,756	12,445
17		Private nonprofit, 4-year or above	2,594	2,957	3,433
18		Private for profit, 4-year or above	0	2	9
19		Public, 2-year	927	951	1,025
20		Private nonprofit, 2-year	20	3	22
21		Private for profit, 2-year	52	23	26
22		Public, less-than-2-year	0	2	0
23		Private nonprofit, less-than-2-year	0	0	4
24		Private for profit, less-than-2-year	0	0	0
25		Total	15,253	15,694	16,964

Data from the U.S. Department of Education's report on campus crime was downloaded into this Excel spreadsheet, making it easy to work with. You can sort the data to determine what kinds of institutions report the fewest liquor law violations, or calculate the rate of change over time to see where and when the sharpest increases occurred.

Source: "Arrests—Liquor Law Violations, 2002–2004." Downloaded March 17, 2007, from www.ed.gov/admins/lead/safety/crime/arrestreferrals/arrests.xls.

The key to good computer-assisted reporting, says Amons, is to remember that the data is not the story. The people and the problems you uncover are the story. The data is evidence, which you will refer to in your story for print or television and then post online so the audience can check the facts for themselves.

Undercover Reporting

Investigative journalists sometimes go undercover to report stories that would be difficult or almost impossible to confirm any other way. Reporting undercover is a controversial practice that should be considered only as a last resort. That's because going undercover almost always involves some deception and raises ethical concerns, so it should not be undertaken lightly. "Hidden cameras are not unlike weapons and power tools that should be kept away from the unskilled and the reckless," says the Poynter Institute's Bob Steele, a leading expert in journalism ethics.[8] News organizations have strict rules governing the use of undercover techniques, and reporters should always have management approval before using them.

To decide whether going undercover or using a hidden camera is justified, reporters and news managers should consider whether the story they're covering is of vital public importance. Will it prevent substantial harm or expose a major system failure? By that standard, the stereotypical TV sweeps story about valet parking attendants stealing loose change simply doesn't measure up.

Pam Zekman, a longtime investigative reporter at WBBM-TV in Chicago, has broken some of her biggest stories by going undercover. As a reporter for the Chicago Tribune and later the Sun-Times, she shared in two Pulitzer prizes for local reporting. She urges reporters to think and plan carefully before attempting an undercover assignment. Make sure your superiors are on board and are willing to commit the personnel and money it will cost. Undercover reporting is not a shortcut and can require weeks or months of extra work. "Remember that going undercover is just an additional tool; it shouldn't serve as an alternative to good old-fashioned digging," Zekman says. "The best undercover reports are bolstered by public records research, human sources, and interviews with experts before and after anyone goes undercover." [9]

The Multimedia Advantage

The ability to tell a story in multiple media is a huge advantage for investigative reporters. They can use information in print or online that would never fit in a TV story because of time limitations or the need for visuals. Print and online graphics can be more detailed than the television versions, and additional video and supporting documents can be posted online to bolster a story's credibility. And reporters say that because stories told in multiple media reach more people, they can pay off in new leads and additional sources.

WFLA-TV reporter Mark Douglas put the multimedia advantage to work when he learned that parts of the Tampa Bay Sunshine Skyway Bridge were corroding just 10 years after it was built. Over a period of months, Douglas accumulated thousands of pages of technical and engineering records for the stories he eventually reported on television, in the Tampa Tribune newspaper and for tbo.com online. "It was quite a relief to have different ways of telling it to make optimum use of all of that research," he says.

The online story became an outlet for raw video of the corrosion and for documents that that didn't work in either the newspaper or TV version. The print version allowed Douglas to explain some of the technical details of the corrosion problem that he couldn't get into on television. "I also had the ability to develop a narrative style of storytelling about events in the corrosion investigation that I couldn't discuss in such detail on TV because I didn't have the pictures and it was just too lengthy," he says.

Telling the story in three dimensions made the topic hard to ignore, held state officials accountable and gave news consumers choices of how they wanted to digest the information, Douglas says. The print story had a wider impact, as well. "Quite frankly, writing a story or two for the Tampa Tribune opened some doors in state government that probably would have remained shut if this had 'just' been a fleeting story in the six o'clock news," Douglas says. "Newspapers get the attention of the high and mighty in [the state capital in] Tallahassee in a way local TV can't compete with sometimes."

TAKING IT HOME

Reporting in depth is hard work. It's time consuming and labor intensive, but it can be enormously rewarding. One of the criticisms of daily journalism is that it barely scratches the surface. Covering events and incidents in isolation doesn't help the audience make sense of the world around them. Reporters who dig deeper are able to connect the dots and tell stories that have an impact, by focusing attention on problems that might have been overlooked and forcing action to remedy those problems.

Some journalists say there's not much room for this kind of reporting in today's news media. They point to budget cuts at news organizations and a society that seems to value immediacy over quality. But journalists who bring passion, persistence and skill to work every day are able to report in depth, even if they have to do it in between other assignments. And reporters who do this kind of work in multiple media can use more of the information they uncover and make it available to a wider audience by presenting that information in different and more engaging ways.

TALKING POINTS

1. This chapter discusses some typical beats that journalists serve. You also read that some newsrooms have additional beats, determined by the makeup of the community they cover. Think about your community and suggest several specific, nontraditional beats for a local newsroom to consider. What sources would you need to connect with to cover those beats? What stories might you find?

2. Imagine that you have acquired the following data sets for your community:

   Public school bus drivers.
   Registered handgun owners.
   Drunk-driving violations.
   Vehicle recalls.
   Campus liquor law violations.

What questions might you ask to analyze and compare these data sets in search of possible stories?

eLEARNING OPPORTUNITIES

For chapter exercises, practice tools and additional resources, go to the interactive online workbook at http://college.cqpress.com/advancingthestory. You'll find:

- SKILL BUILDING: Practice basic computer assisted reporting skills to analyze a data set and develop story ideas.

- DISCOVER: Watch one of Stuart Watson's award-winning investigative stories.

- ONGOING STORY: Decide how you would add context and depth to this story with data, documents or details.

- EXPLORE: Visit Web sites to learn more about reporting in depth and how to use freedom of information laws.

5 WRITING THE STORY

No matter what medium you're writing for, stories that are overstuffed with information are harder to understand. In this chapter, we'll discuss how to take your writing to the next level by sharpening your focus, organizing your material before you write and choosing your words with care. We'll also show how you can improve your work by using time-tested strategies to revise your writing, quickly and effectively.

For many journalists, the most difficult part of telling a story is deciding what to leave out. All news stories are created from a mass of facts, observations, comments and details. Reporters work hard to collect all of that information, so their natural impulse is to use as much of it as possible in their stories. But airtime and print space are limited, and even online, there's a limit to the audience's attention.

Good journalism involves selection, not compression. Cramming in all the facts that will fit rarely results in a well-told story that will engage the audience. What the painter Georgia O'Keefe said about art applies just as well to writing: "It is only by selection, by elimination, by emphasis that we get at the real meaning of things."

A reporter who tries to explain everything in one dense story may succeed only in confusing the audience. Multimedia reporters can put additional elements online that won't fit in a print or broadcast version, but they're still selective about what they use. Good reporters use their news judgment and experience to decide what is most important to include in a story and what order to put it in. They also take a systematic approach to writing, whether they call it that or not. Their first step is to choose a central point or a theme for the story, also called a focus.

FINDING THE FOCUS

The focus of a story is basically the answer to the question, "What is this story really all about?" That sounds simple, but it's not. To decide on a focus, you have to sort through the information you've collected and figure out what's at the heart of it. You need to know what the news is, of course, but often that's not enough. For a story to be memorable, it also needs to have a central point. The news might be that a woman was arrested for robbing a bank. The point might be that police had no trouble finding her, because the note she passed to the teller had her home address on the back.

Experienced reporters don't wait until the end of the day, after they've done all their research, interviews and observation, before finding a focus for their stories, especially if they're working on tight deadlines. As we've discussed, they may actually start the reporting process with a focus in mind, which helps them decide where to go and whom to interview. Reporter Joe Fryer of KARE-TV in Minneapolis, Minn., compares it to a grocery shopping trip when you have some idea of what you'll be serving before you go to the store. "You can't buy apples, lemons, pears and kiwis, and when you get back decide your story is about peaches," he says.

Of course, the focus can change as you collect more information, and it often does. Victoria Lim, the consumer reporter from WFLA-TV in Tampa, Fla., says she tries to keep an open mind in the field. "Sometimes I think that when you go in thinking you know what the story is all about you don't leave yourself open to other possibilities that could come out of it," she says. KARE-TV reporter Boyd Huppert says he looks for a focus from the moment he starts reporting, which he defines as "a concept, a character or emotion that can tie the disconnected pieces of a story together." What's most important is to decide on a focus before you start writing your story. That may seem obvious, but it's astounding how many reporters skip this step and start scribbling as soon as they're done reporting. Small wonder they often turn in stories that are boring, confusing or both.

Focus Questions

One way to find a focus is to ask yourself why you care about the story, and why the audience should bother to watch or read it. After all, if you don't care, there's no reason anyone else should. Your story ought to answer the question, "So what?" To focus a complicated story, ask the question several times. Let's say you are reporting on standardized testing in your state's high schools. So what? Students will have to pass tests in five subjects in order to graduate. So what? Last year, almost 40 percent of seniors who took

WRITING WISDOM

Reporter Boyd Huppert of KARE-TV in Minneapolis has won dozens of awards for his writing, including four national Edward R. Murrow Awards from the Radio-Television News Directors Association. Huppert works hard to focus his stories while he's still out reporting. "Writing a focus statement often gives me an opening or a closing line," he says. "If I don't know what the open is going to be when I'm heading back, I start to panic. I'm always asking, 'Where should this start?' "

Many of Huppert's most memorable stories are built around unusual characters, and he pays special attention to the way he introduces them to the audience. "I try to find at least one meaningful detail I can tell you about that person right away," he says. For an amusing story about a man who can play three trumpets at once, Huppert introduced Wally Pickal as "a man who shares his name with a gherkin." "I went to the grocery aisle to find a word that sounded funny," he says. "A meaningful detail."

Stories have layers, Huppert says, and he makes it his job to find them. "Even the best story can be better if you look for the other layers," he says. Take his story about the high school janitor who for 14 years has manned the public address system at the prom, introducing each couple as they arrive. Cute story, right? But much more meaningful when you learn that Duane Ammann already knows almost every kid in the school by name, and that the kids love him for it. After he had a heart attack a few years back, students pooled their money to buy him an exercise bike. Huppert carefully structures his stories so each layer builds on the one before. "I map out the things we're going to reveal. What are my moments, what are my layers?" Once he's made a plan, he says, the rest comes easily. "My job is writing transitions."

Huppert honed his writing skills by reading voraciously and listening to other good TV writers. "There are certain things that good writers do," he says. "Putting the most important part of the sentence at the end. That way, when you slow down as you're reading, at the end of a thought, you slow down and stop at the most important word."

How to get better? "Go to seminars, study good writers, read a good novel, go to a good movie. Get people to critique your work. Make relationships. I'm still learning."

practice tests failed at least one of them. So what? Schools aren't preparing students for a test that will shape their futures. Now you have a focus.

Bruce DeSilva of the Associated Press sometimes gives reporters what he calls the bus stop test for focus. "Suppose you are at a bus stop and someone leans out the bus window and shouts, 'What is that story you are working on?' The bus engine starts and begins to pull away from the curb. What are you going to shout?" [1] This forces reporters to break down the action in the story by stating it in a simple sentence: subject-verb-object. Who is doing what to whom? See if you can do it in three to six words. For example, the focus of the testing story might become: "Schools fail students."

Let's take it one step further. Imagine that you're covering a fast-moving wildfire. You've been out talking to people and observing the damage all day. Now, you need to focus your story before you begin writing.

- What's the news?
A fire destroyed two houses in the mountains east of the city, but no one was injured and the city business district was spared.

- What's the point?
Two families are homeless but grateful to be alive.

- How can I tell it in three to six words?
Fire destroys homes, not spirits.

- So what?
Property damage from a dangerous fire was limited.

This is not meant to suggest that every story has only one acceptable focus. On the contrary, reporters for different news organizations may take the same basic facts and write their stories quite differently because they have decided on a different focus. In the case of the wildfire story, a reporter could use the same questions to come up with a different focus.

- What's the news?
Businesses in our city escaped damage from a wildfire that destroyed two houses in the mountains east of downtown.

- What's the point?
Business owners are grateful the fire spared them this time.

- How can I tell it in three to six words?
Fire doesn't stop business.

- So what?

Economic impact of a dangerous fire was limited.

The first story would concentrate on the families who lost their homes in the fire and use sound bites from the people directly affected. The second would pay more attention to the businesses that were spared, including the reactions of business owners. Both stories would contain the same basic information—that two houses were destroyed while businesses were unaffected—but their emphases would be different.

Focus for Multiple Media

We've said it before, but it bears repeating—if you're reporting for multiple platforms, keep the strength of each medium in mind as you decide on a focus. As we've discussed, a TV story is well suited to sharing experience and emotion, while a print story can provide more depth and context, and an online story can offer elements of both.

Let's say you're covering a protest march in your city. Everything is peaceful until the marchers close in on City Hall and police decide to use tear gas to break up the crowd. On television, you might choose to tell what happened and why through the eyes of a demonstrator and a police officer. Your focus statement might be something as simple as this: "Chaos and confusion at City Hall." The focus of your print and online stories would likely be broader and include the impact of the march and its aftermath on demonstrators, bystanders, government workers and downtown businesses. The focus statement in this case could be something along these lines: "Protest paralyzes city."

For a television story, your focus statement also helps you decide what to shoot, which can be a huge time saver both in the field and in the edit room. You don't have to run from place to place, shooting video you won't end up using. And you don't have to sort through all that excess material when it comes time to edit. Take a KARE-TV story about the aftermath of a tornado that's focused on the loss of trees in one community. Photojournalist Jonathan Malat framed every interview for that story with a damaged tree in the shot.

You may not think you have time to focus your story before writing. It seems like an unnecessary extra step when you're already in a rush to make deadline. But that's when it's most critical to have a focus. Knowing what to emphasize before beginning to write helps the reporter decide which facts, images and sounds to include and which to leave out. "The less time you have to write, the more time you should take to think about it," says CNN senior political correspondent Candy Crowley. Thinking time helps you make sense of all that stuff you have collected, which saves time when you start to write. You wouldn't shoot video without making sure it's in focus. You shouldn't write stories without focusing first.

PLANNING YOUR STORY

Having a focus in mind is just the first step in preparing to write a story. You now know what you are trying to say, but you still have to decide how you are going to say it. That means you need to get organized. Here is a step-by-step guide to planning your story.

Review

Flip through your notes and look over any background material you've collected. Mark the key points that fit your focus—information that absolutely must be in the story for it to make sense. Use any system that works for you. Some writers like to use colored high-lighters; others use a mix of stars, asterisks, underlining and brackets to isolate the good stuff. If you do this as you go along, you can quickly home in on the best material.

If you've piled up a lot of notes and documents, make a list of all the facts and details you expect to use. Obviously, when planning a report for multiple media, you'll need to consider the audio, video and graphic elements you've collected that you might include in different versions of the story. We'll talk in detail about how to do this in Chapter 6.

Don't worry about putting any of your elements in order yet; you'll get to that soon enough. At this point, you just need to get a handle on what you've collected during the reporting process, and tease out anything that will help you deliver on your focus statement.

Select

Choose quotes or sound bites that fit your focus, and follow this basic rule: Don't plan to use a bite or quote if you can say it better. The best quotes and bites are subjective, offering opinion, reaction, experience or emotion. They add insight and perspective to stories, not just facts. Too many news stories are stuffed full of quotes and sound bites that fail this test; often they come out of the mouths of officials. There's no need to let the mayor say, "We expect to have a decision at the council meeting later this week on contingency plans for the distribution of funds to low-income residents in the Brentwood area." That kind of information would be much better stated in clear, concise language by the reporter. In this case, the reporter might have written, "According to the mayor, people in Brentwood won't find out if they'll get any money from the city until later this week." Then he could use the mayor's words explaining why it's taking so long or reacting to complaints about the delay.

THE ROSENBAUM METHOD

Great reporters often cover the same stories everyone else does, but somehow they do it better. David Rosenbaum of the New York Times was one of those reporters whose stories left competitors muttering to themselves, "Why didn't I see that?"

"David beat all of us by noticing things that were in plain sight, but that we somehow missed," said Dale Russakoff of the Washington Post at Rosenbaum's memorial service. "He'd look at the same documents and talk to the same people. But where we saw trees, David saw a forest."

Russakoff had always wondered how Rosenbaum could be so efficient, how he managed to stay on top of things while everyone else was running around. On a slow news day in the Senate press gallery some 20 years ago, she asked him to show her how he organized his notes before writing. "I tried it the next time I wrote a story and was stunned at how much easier it was," Russakoff said. "His system doesn't just organize your notes; it organizes your mind."

Here's the Rosenbaum method:

Number every page of your notes.

Go through each page and mark every fact, quote or detail you want to use in your story.

Create an index of this information on a separate page—just a couple of words for each element and the number of the page where it's found in your notes.

That's all there is to it. "The process of thinking about the things that matter, and boiling them down to a word or two, allows you to store information better," Russakoff says. Colleagues sometimes wonder why she spends all that time reading over her notes, she says. "The truth is it makes the rest of it go faster."

Russakoff says she uses the Rosenbaum method on every long story, and sometimes on daily ones too, because it helps her feel organized when she starts writing.

Rosenbaum was murdered in January 2006, just weeks after he retired from the Times. Sharing his note-taking strategy will help keep his memory alive.

When you've narrowed the list of possible bites and quotes, get them down on paper word for word. If you left space in your notebook as we suggested in Chapter 2, you can simply insert any missing words. At this point in the planning process, many reporters choose to type the quotes or bites into a document so they can easily cut and paste them into their stories. You need to know exactly what a person says in order to write what goes before and after. Remember that while sound bites for TV will be short, you may be able to use a longer segment in an audio clip or as streaming video online. You may want the exact or verbatim text of those clips as well, so you can post it online.

Organize

Once you have the key points, quotes or sound bites, details and scenes isolated, group them by topic and put them in a rough order and see if one point or scene leads logically to the next. Jack Hart, a managing editor at Portland's Oregonian newspaper, recommends what he calls a "jot outline"—four or five words or phrases that summarize the main points of your story. Here's what your initial jottings might look like for the protest march story:

Focus: Protest paralyzes city

—Protesters demand hike in minimum wage.

—Marchers converge on City Hall.

—Police spray tear gas.

—Businesses close.

—Traffic is jammed.

Once you have all the main topics on paper, rearrange them until the order makes sense. You may have to do this several times before you start writing, but it's worth the trouble. Your finished outline will serve as a kind of road map for your story. You can consult it as you go along to make sure you haven't skipped anything important.

Consider the Extras

You may use the same information in stories for different media, but the way you use it may change. You'll usually include more information in a print or online story than you will in a TV piece, but that additional information doesn't have to be folded into the narrative. Now is the time to consider what you can break out into graphics, bullet points or timelines.

Think about interactive elements you could add to the online story in the form of links, searchable databases or surveys.

Let's go back to that protest at City Hall again. Your TV story is going to be tightly focused on the experience of one protestor and one police officer. But you may want a more detailed map of the protest route for your print and online versions, highlighting businesses that had to close as a result of the chaos. You might also include a list or timeline of previous downtown demonstrations, a link to the city ordinance regulating police use of tear gas and another link to public health information about the potential effects of "riot control agents."

STORY PLANNING

- Review your notes.
- Select the best parts of your interviews.
- Organize your information.
- Consider the extras.

Deborah Potter made this jot outline for a story she reported in 2005 about the aftermath of Hurricane Katrina. Notice how she rearranged some of the elements to produce a road map to consult as she wrote the story for the PBS program Religion & Ethics NewsWeekly.

PRESB. CHURCH   CHOPPER
CARROLLTON FLOOD   CHURCH
                           WATER
ST. GEORGE TILES – CRUNCH
not worried not occupied INTERIOR MOLD (NAT)
                                  DRYING
BISHOP ARRIVES @ CHURCH
   NOT TOO BAD
   DEAN STRIPS ALTAR
STAND-UP – TO BATON ROUGE
DEVOTIONAL → RIVER CENTER
AT FIRST BAPTIST
   NEWBORNS.
   JACOB + MOM
   (SHALITA)
   PASTOR – ~~LEARNING~~
   V/O GOD'S GRACE – REUNITED

PASTOR – LEARNING
IN NO. BISH. LEARNS
   IT'S OK –
WATERS DEATH
ETERNAL LIFE
IT'LL COME BACK
   NOT TAKING ADVENT
VESTMENTS   ↓ 10 WKS
              2½ MOS

SCHOOL KIDS

TRADE TOOLS

119

THE STORY "QUEST"

Dateline NBC's John Larson likes to structure stories by thinking about them as quests, in which someone is trying to do something. This helps him choose a central character to build his story around as well as an action to illustrate the story. It also provides some tension, because the viewer doesn't know whether the character will succeed in his quest.

For a National Press Photographers Association workshop, Larson wrote this story about growing fears of an economic recession.

BOB TAYLOR HASN'T SLEPT WELL FOR WEEKS.

FOR ONE THING, HE HAS TO GET UP AT ONE IN THE MORNING JUST TO BAKE TOMORROW'S PASTRIES.

BUT HE WORRIES THAT NO MATTER HOW HARD HE WORKS, NO MATTER HOW CAREFULLY HE MIXES THE BATTER, THE RESULT MAY NOT BE SWEET.

BECAUSE SOMETHING HAS CHANGED.

LAST YEAR, BUSINESS WAS SO GOOD, HE BOUGHT NEW OVENS. THIS YEAR, HE IS DIPPING INTO SAVINGS JUST TO KEEP HIS BAKERY OPEN.

STORY STRUCTURE

All stories have a structure in the same way that people have a spine—or at least they should. Without a structure, stories would be a jumble of facts with nothing to hold them together. Structure is essential for stories to be understandable and meaningful. Choosing a structure before you write can help you decide what goes where—the logical next step in the planning process that makes the actual writing go more smoothly.

Good writers choose the most suitable shape for the story they are telling and the medium they are using. As you'll see, some structures are more appropriate for breaking news or features, and some work better on television than in print or online. The last thing you want to do is to follow a formula that makes your stories all seem alike. "Approach every

THE PROBLEM?

THE WAREHOUSE ACROSS THE STREET HAS LAID OFF 20 PEOPLE. THEY'RE NO LONGER BUYING HIS PASTRIES. AND HIS COSTS HAVE RISEN.

SO NOW, WHEN BOB TAYLOR'S ALARM GOES OFF, HE FINDS HE IS ALREADY AWAKE. AND HE IS WORRYING.

OFFICIALS IN WASHINGTON SAY WE ARE NOT IN A RECESSION. THEY SAY THERE IS NOTHING TO WORRY ABOUT, YET.

BOB SAYS HE DOESN'T HAVE TIME TO LISTEN TO THE NEWS. AND HE WONDERS, WOULD WE LIKE TO BUY A DOZEN PASTRIES? OR EVEN ONE?

JOHN LARSON, FOR THE WORKSHOP.

You can see how Larson was able to focus his story by centering it around Bob the baker, whose personal experience reflects that of many Americans. Bob's quest was to bake his doughnuts, and that action became the visual narrative for the story. But the point of the story is that Bob's experience illustrated the bigger topic of people fearing recession. Larson built his simple story out of three elements that are a storyteller's grail: Character, action and tension.

story differently," says KARE-TV's Joe Fryer, who says he got into a rut of beginning every television story the same way, with short voice tracks and lots of natural sound. "It's not bad to start a story with a longer track if it's well written," he says. "You don't always have to have that same pattern."

Inverted Pyramid

Many stories begin with the most newsworthy information, following the classic "inverted pyramid" structure you are already familiar with. This form puts the most important information at the top, followed by additional information in descending order of importance. A report on a massive storm, for example, would likely begin with the death toll and the lo-

FIGURE 5.1 INVERTED PYRAMID

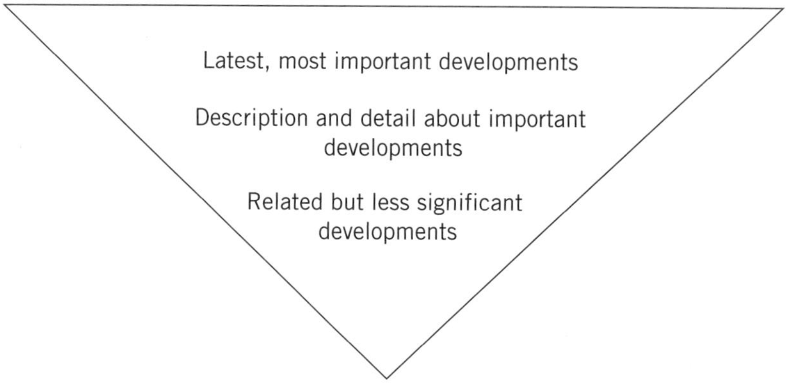

Latest, most important developments

Description and detail about important developments

Related but less significant developments

The "inverted pyramid" story structure is commonly used when time is of the essence. If you start with what's most important, the audience knows immediately what your story is about.

cation of the heaviest damage. Next, the reporter might describe the scene of the worst devastation, and then include a sound bite or quote from a survivor or a rescue worker. Supporting paragraphs would fill in details and provide background on the storm.

Some journalists argue that this structure is outdated and dull, because it requires writers to tell stories backwards. Using this structure, they say, is tantamount to telling a joke by starting with the punch line, because the audience knows how the story will end from the very beginning. But the inverted pyramid survives because it makes sense in some circumstances, especially when reporting important or breaking news when timeliness is of the essence. If you are the first to report a significant development, you'll want to tell the audience what has happened right at the top. Reporters who resist using this structure when it is called for may be accused of "burying the lead," making it more difficult for the audience to determine the importance of the story.

Hourglass

A modified form of the inverted pyramid, frequently used in broadcast, is known as the "hourglass" structure. It begins in a similar fashion with the latest and most important information, but after a few paragraphs it takes a turn and becomes a narrative told in chronological order.

FIGURE 5.2 HOURGLASS

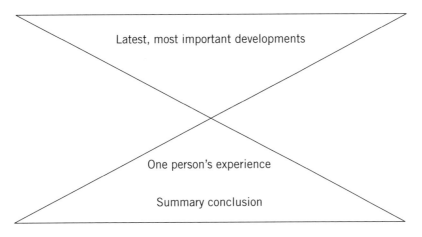

Latest, most important developments

One person's experience

Summary conclusion

This "hourglass" story structure is a modified form of the inverted pyramid. It still begins with a summary lead, but then becomes a more focused narrative before broadening out to a summary conclusion. In broadcast, the lead and conclusion may be read by the anchor, leaving the reporter to tell the story in narrative form.

When you're on deadline on a breaking story, chronology can be a lifesaver. Just start at the beginning and write until you've told everything that happened, putting the most recent information last. Sticking with the example of the story about the massive storm, a television reporter could provide the anchor with a hard lead, and then tell the story of the storm as witnessed by one survivor. This structure allows for a summary ending, either by the reporter or the anchor in a tag. On the Web, this structure can be used to create a story timeline, either static or interactive. In print, the summary information could be placed in a box or subhead, so the story itself could stay focused on the survivor's experience, told in chronological order.

Diamond

A reporter using the "diamond" structure would begin with an anecdote, introducing a character whose experience illustrates what the story is all about. This small story would then broaden out to show its wider significance. Toward the end, the reporter would

FIGURE 5.3 DIAMOND

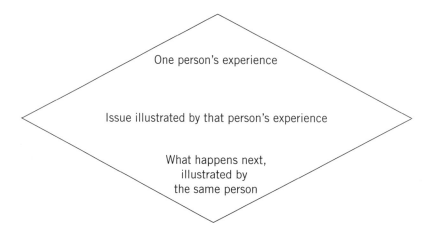

A story told in a "diamond" shape begins with an individual's story and weaves that person's experience throughout. It's a useful way of approaching "issue" stories, since issues are just personal problems on a bigger scale.

return to the individual character's story as a way of concluding the narrative. These stories are most effective if you don't abandon your character in the middle.

For example, a reporter might begin a story about a new AIDS treatment by introducing a patient who desperately needs the treatment, then describe the person's experience with an experimental drug, explain how it works, and conclude by noting that doctors give the patient we met at the beginning only a limited time to live if the new treatment is not effective. This story form "hooks" the audience by presenting an individual's dilemma first. The important information that follows is more interesting because it's clearly relevant to that individual. The diamond structure is often used for stories that might otherwise seem dull. You can apply it by remembering that every "policy issue" is really someone's personal problem, writ large.

Christmas Tree

This story shape might suggest a kind of random approach, considering the haphazard way many people stick decorations on Christmas trees. But "Christmas tree" is really a struc-

FIGURE 5.4 CHRISTMAS TREE

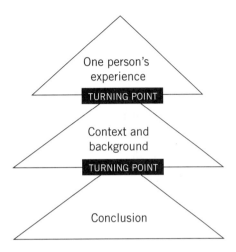

A story in the shape of a "Christmas tree" has multiple turning points. This structure is useful for longer-form stories because it makes sure there are "moments" or surprises all along the way to keep the audience engaged.

ture that helps the writer build tension and release it several times as the story moves along. KARE-TV's Boyd Huppert says he uses this structure in many of his longer-form stories. He focuses tightly at the top, introducing a character or a place, then broadens out to provide more context. Each time the tree narrows before widening again represents a turning point or unexpected moment in the story. Keeping the tree shape in mind, Huppert says, helps him construct a story that keeps the audience engaged. "Let them catch a breath," he says, "then build to the next surprise."

You could apply this structure to the AIDS story by introducing the patient right at the top, then revealing that he's fighting the disease. He's tried many treatments that have worked for others but (turning point) not for him. Now he's looking desperately for a new approach and (turning point) his doctor learns there's an experimental drug that could help. The patient has signed up for a study of the drug but (turning point) nobody knows if it will really work. If it doesn't, (conclusion) the patient's future looks grim.

BEGINNINGS AND ENDINGS

Knowing what your structure is helps you decide where to begin your story and how to end it, which just happen to be two of the most difficult decisions any writer has to make. Experienced reporters are able to decide on a beginning and end while they are still in the field, but this takes lots of practice. Your opening needs to make the audience sit up and take notice. Your conclusion needs to button things up. Once you've settled on a beginning and an end, the middle is much easier to write. Think of each story as a journey that you're inviting the audience to take with you. The opening should make them want to go along. The ending should make them glad they did.

"When I sit down to write, I sit down like a lover planning a seduction," Robert Krulwich, who reports for ABC News and National Public Radio, told Current magazine. "My job is to make them notice me—find me interesting, tantalizing. Like any lover, I want their attention first, I want to get them comfortable. I want to get them in the mood—not prone, not right away—just relaxed, willing to let me go further, and then I want to put my hands on their minds—and get 'em excited, bit by bit, so they want a little more." [2]

Leads

You're no doubt familiar with the various types of leads most often used in news stories—hard or soft, anecdotal or delayed, for example. We're not going to review them all here. Check the box on page 127 for a quick summary. What's important is to write a lead that fits the structure you've chosen for your story. Inverted pyramid? You'd probably write a summary lead. Diamond? You could choose to write an anecdotal or a narrative lead. Sometimes the idea for a lead comes to your mind first and the structure follows. Just be sure to keep that structure in mind as you put the rest of the story together or you could end up with a mushy mess that's either repetitious or missing significant information.

The style of lead you write also depends in part on the subject matter. A story about five pets being rescued alive from a burning building wouldn't need to begin with the same hard news angle or gravity as a story about a fire that killed three people.

Another way to decide on a lead is to think about what your story is trying to accomplish. You'd begin a story that's designed to share an experience with the audience differently than you would a story that's aimed at explaining why something happened. For example, let's say it's Election Day, and you're doing a story about voter turnout. Election officials have told you the turnout is the lightest they've ever seen, about 23 percent. You've talked to people who didn't vote today, asking them why, so your lead might say: "Less than a quarter of the registered voters in our county voted in today's election. What kept the rest of them away?" You're providing the hard news in the lead, and explaining it in the story. But if your story is focused on what happened at one polling place, where only three voters showed up during a two-hour period, you might write a lead along these lines: "The noisy and expensive campaign for governor has ended with a whimper." In this lead, you have introduced the topic, but you'll give the facts about voter turnout in the story.

Whatever type of lead you choose, make sure it's honest. Don't bait the hook with a promise on which the story can't deliver. For example, a story about a woman who found a paper clip in her breakfast cereal should not begin with a warning that breakfast cereals can be deadly. If you pump up the lead just to draw attention and the story doesn't measure up, you may simply annoy the audience, leaving them feeling like they've been victims of a bait-and-switch sales pitch.

One last important point about leads for television: Remember that the lead to

TYPES OF LEADS

- *Anecdotal (or narrative):* Introduces a person as well as the individual's experience, which illustrates what the story is about.

- *Delayed (or blind):* Establishes the central facts of the story, without immediately identifying the person or event at its center.

- *Descriptive:* A type of delayed lead that sets the scene for the story by describing a situation, setting or event before revealing its significance.

- *Summary:* General synopsis of the most important facts of the story.

- *Umbrella:* A listing of several equally important elements, each of which will be elaborated in turn.

your story is whatever comes first, whether you read it or the anchor does. The anchor lead-in should set up what comes next, not repeat it. Make a habit of writing your lead-in and then your package so your entire story holds together. A good lead grabs the viewer's attention and gives a sense of what the story is about but leaves the audience wanting more. You can't do that if your lead is an afterthought.

Endings

It's a good idea to have an ending in mind when you begin writing, much as it's helpful to have a destination in mind when you set out on a journey. As Yogi Berra famously said,

"If you don't know where you're going, you might wind up someplace else." This is particularly important for television stories, because of the linear nature of the broadcast media. Viewers can't jump ahead in a TV story to find the parts they're most interested in the way they can in a print or online version. Besides, research has found that viewers tend to remember best what they hear last. For that reason, many broadcast stories conclude with a kind of summary ending, reinforcing the story's main point. Print stories often achieve that same goal by ending with a "wrap-up" quote—something for the reader to ponder. This technique is less successful on TV because each story is followed by something else—either another story or a commercial—so there's no time for a final sound bite to sink in.

Endings often echo beginnings in that they return to an important place, person or theme. KARE-TV reporter Boyd Huppert began a flood story that aired on a Sunday night with this line: "On the Lord's Day in Granite Falls, life along the river went to hell." He concluded by echoing the same theme, referring to people in that town "not knowing what will be left when the unholy waters recede."

In a chronological narrative, the ending is what happens last. If a story has raised a problem, the ending might offer a solution. Endings frequently look to the future, to what might happen next. These approaches work equally well in all media, presuming that you've written a story compelling enough for the audience to make it all the way to the end.

WATCH YOUR WORDS

No matter which medium you're using to tell a story, the words you choose matter. As Tom Stoppard put it in his play, The Real Thing, "Words are sacred. They deserve respect. If you get the right ones in the right order, you can nudge the world a little." Choosing the right words and putting them in the right order is the basic task of any writer. There are some universal keys to writing stronger stories in all media.

Keep It Simple

You've heard this advice a million times, but if you read or watch a lot of news you'll notice that it's frequently violated. A story about a house fire might call it an "inferno" or a "conflagration" or describe "firefighters battling the blaze." There's nothing wrong with using a simple word—fire—more than once. In fact, it's better because it's so much easier to understand. Charles Osgood of CBS News put it this way: "Bloated words and phrases don't penetrate. Well-chosen, well-ordered ones do."

Simple writing means avoiding jargon—specialized language or technical terms unfamiliar to the general public. If a technical term must be used for accuracy, it's a good idea to include a definition as well. For example, the term "fossil fuels" in a story about global energy issues should include a short list of what those fuels are: coal, oil and natural gas. Steer clear of bureaucratic euphemisms—words or phrases that may confuse or mislead the audience. If the city council votes to approve a new interment facility, your story should tell residents that the city plans to build a new cemetery.

Stay Active

Write simple, declarative sentences in the active voice: subject, verb, object. In the active voice, the person doing the action comes first. "Police found the body," for example, is written in active voice. Who (police) did what (found) what (body). Using the passive voice means putting the object first: "Shots were fired," for example, or "Mistakes were made." This kind of structure often begs the question: Who did it? When you spot the passive voice, it may be a clue that you need to do more reporting to fill in the blanks.

That doesn't mean you should never use the passive voice. You may want to begin a sentence by naming the most important person in the story. For example, you'd probably write, "Michael Jackson was found not guilty by a jury of eight men and four women," because the defendant's name is an attention grabber. On television, you'd also use this construction to make your words match your pictures. Just be sure that when you do use the passive voice, you're doing it on purpose.

Use Powerful Words

Nouns and verbs give writing power. Adjectives don't, especially empty adjectives that tell people what to feel. A murder is always "brutal" or "horrifying." A fire could be "shocking" or "devastating." Broadcast writers fall into this trap all the time. In a 15-minute span one morning, reporters and anchors on one channel promised "stunning new developments" that weren't in the least bit astonishing, described a Vatican gathering of visibly delighted members of the College of Cardinals as a "solemn ceremony," and discussed the possible punishment for a "heinous crime" without ever mentioning what had actually happened.

Great writers seek and use specific details, not shopworn generalities, to convey information and emotion. Instead of telling the audience that there has been a tragic accident, provide the facts: Six members of one family were killed. The only survivor is a six-month-old boy, now in critical condition. And it happened on Christmas morning. Let the audience

WRITING TIPS FROM CNN'S CANDY CROWLEY

1. If you don't understand it, don't write it.

2. The less time you have to write, the more time you should take to think about it.

3. Stories should have a beginning, an end and a middle. Not necessarily in that order.

4. The way you would tell a story to your Mom is probably the way you should write it.

5. Write seamless stories—woven so tightly there is no place to cut.

6. Sound bites are not production techniques to break up the sound of your voice. Think of them as part of your narrative.

7. It is important to remember that grammar counts.

8. The harder you try to be clever, the less likely your writing will be.

9. Et tu, Brutus?
   I think therefore I am.
   I have nothing to offer but blood, sweat and tears.
   I have a dream.
   I am not a crook.
   The Eagle has landed.
   Take adjectives and adverbs out of your story.

10. Style is not something you seek. It is something that happens when you write it right by following the rules.

11. Break the rules.

12. Good writers read. Superb writers read more.

13. When you are finished, stop.

decide if that's tragic. KARE-TV's Boyd Huppert put this principle into practice in a story about a spreading grass fire. Instead of telling viewers that the situation was terrifying, Huppert described the scene through the eyes of the fire chief: "He had men out there, and he couldn't see them."

Sometimes adjectives are simply redundant. Close proximity. Shower activity. That kind of writing makes a journalist sound ignorant. It undermines credibility and wastes time besides. Does this mean all adjectives must go? Of course not. Just the ones that add no meaning, or worse yet, distort the truth. If you habitually describe all victims as "innocent," for example, you'll be wrong when it turns out one particular victim was wanted for armed robbery in four states. Don't waste time on worthless adjectives. Think of words like this as fat, and put your writing on a diet.

Be Conversational

In broadcast writing especially, tell the story to the audience the way you would tell it to a friend or family member. That doesn't mean it's OK to use slang or bad grammar. But it does mean writing copy that is conversational, as opposed to the stilted journalese that reporters often use. If the victims were taken to a hospital far away, that might be news and worth mentioning, but why bother telling us they went to a "nearby hospital"? And where is this "area" that "area-man" comes from, anyway?

Surely you wouldn't call home and describe your dinner at a "60-year-old family-owned eatery," but that's what a local reporter said on the air one night. If a person or an institution's age is important, by all means include it, but put it in a separate sentence. Instead of referring to "the ailing 82-year-old prime minister," break out the information this way: "The prime minister is 82." By the way, it's perfectly fine to use a pronoun on second reference. Martin Luther King Jr. could be referred to as "he" instead of "the slain civil rights leader." Wouldn't that be more conversational? If your words are so stilted they call attention to themselves, you've failed as a writer. As the English author George Orwell put it, "Good prose is like a windowpane. It does not draw attention to itself. It makes the reader see the story, not the words."

Preserve Surprise

The late BBC reporter Alistair Cooke once said: "To write a dull sentence, a sentence without suspense, a sentence that doesn't make you want to know what is coming next—that is the only gross incompetence in broadcasting." That's a tough standard but a welcome reminder of the importance of surprise in storytelling.

People remember what surprises them. Before you write any story, think about what you learned that surprised or moved you. It could be the most memorable part of the story. Make sure to include it, but be careful not to spoil the surprise by announcing it. Let the audience discover the surprise for themselves through quotes, sound bites or images, and your story will have a lasting impact.

ACCURACY

As you already know, there's nothing more important in journalism than getting it right. In Chapter 2, we talked about the importance of accuracy in reporting. But even if you've captured everything accurately in your notes, errors can slip in during the writing process.

Sometimes mistakes happen when you translate complicated information, especially numbers, into simpler terms the audience can understand more easily. Make sure that when you round off a number you're not making too big a leap. For example, $1.6 billion is not "almost $2 billion," but rather "just over $1.5 billion." You may also raise doubts about the accuracy of your information if you don't let the audience know as much as possible about where you got it. When you're writing, pay close attention to calculations and attribution to avoid questions about accuracy.

Attribution

Attribution is critically important in news stories in all media, because it answers the question, "Who says?" Identifying the source of the information allows audiences to judge its credibility for themselves, particularly when it comes to controversial statements. For example, a report that North Korea has decided to suspend its nuclear program could be seen as more or less credible depending on who is quoted as saying so: a visiting Chinese scientist or a team of United Nations officials.

Another reason for attribution is to place responsibility for a controversial statement where it belongs: with the person who said it, not with the reporter or the news organization. This does not imply immunity from lawsuits, of course. But it is good journalistic practice to make clear who is making allegations or taking a particular stand.

Attribution can be explicit or implied. Print stories typically use explicit or direct attribution, for both direct and indirect quotes. For example, a newspaper reporter might write: "The man was arrested and charged with murder, Montgomery County police sergeant

Robert Perez said." For broadcast and online, the sentence would be rewritten using implied or indirect attribution to read, "Montgomery County police arrested the man and charged him with murder." In both cases, the audience can tell that the source of the information is the police.

Not all information in a news story needs to be attributed, however. Naming the source of every bit of information would make stories almost incomprehensible. Information that a reporter observed directly can be stated without attribution. Indisputable or well-accepted facts do not need to be attributed, either. For example, a reporter could say which team won a football game without attribution because the final score would not be in doubt. But writing that one candidate won a political debate would need to be attributed; without attribution, it would cross the line from fact into opinion.

Numbers

A journalism teacher once described her students as "do-gooders who hate math." Most journalists will never come to love math, but they need it. Numbers may look solid and factual, but they are not infallible. Journalists need numerical competence in order to tell the difference between a meaningless number and a significant one. If they can't, they risk writing stories that are misleading and confusing at best, and at worst flat out wrong. Just ask any reporter who's ever been fooled by the numbers in a city budget or a federal spending bill.

Journalists need math intuition so they can tell when the numbers they're looking at just don't add up. They need math mechanics to find the meaning behind figures and data. They need math concepts so they can understand banking and business, bankruptcy and boom times. Simply put, journalists need math skills to make sense of numbers the way they need language skills to make sense of words.

Competent journalists are both capable and careful with numbers. They're quick to spot an implausible number, and they have a basic working knowledge of arithmetic and statistics so they can confirm their suspicions. They know how to calculate percentages, ratios, rates of change and other relationships between numbers that tell far better stories than raw data can. They can and should translate numbers into terms that readers and viewers can relate to.

Steve Daniels, now an anchor at WTVD-TV in Durham, N.C., says that when he's out reporting he carries a calculator wherever he goes. "I use it to check out what sources are telling me," he says. He has also found it essential for translating information into terms familiar to viewers. Once, covering a plane crash, he learned how many tons of fuel the aircraft had on board. Out came the calculator, and into the script went the number of gallons of fuel, a measurement anyone could understand. In television news, when it comes to writing with numbers, the rule of thumb is the fewer the better. Numbers that are used should be rounded off for simplicity's sake, and put in context for clarity.

Remember the election turnout story we mentioned earlier in this chapter? We didn't use the specific number, 23 percent, but instead referred to a turnout of "less than a quarter" of registered voters. A story about a $13 million increase in school spending would be more understandable to viewers if the reporter translated the raw numbers into the additional amount that will be spent per child—$500. If that amount is 95 percent more than it was 10 years ago, you could write that it's almost doubled in 10 years. As we mentioned in Chapter 1, print and online stories usually provide more exact numbers but not always in the story itself. You can keep the text clear and relevant by rounding off numbers and using the specific data to create a graphic or interactive element.

Journalists with numerical competence are more important than ever in today's highly technical world. They are the writers and editors who can assess and explain scientific, medical, technological and economic developments. They are the journalists who can find stories in databases by crunching numbers themselves, instead of waiting for someone with a vested interest to do it for them.

Journalists who fail to master math lack a basic skill needed to decipher much of the information in the world around them, such as crime statistics, pollution standards, real estate taxes and unemployment figures. Without math skills, journalists are bound to fall short in their quest for accuracy. The good news is that there are tons of online tools to make math easier for journalists, and you can find links to them on the companion Web site for this book.

REVISING YOUR STORY

Revising is a lost art in many newsrooms. Reporters say they don't have time to revise their stories because they work right up to deadline every day, and besides, isn't it the supervisor's job to make any changes that need to be made? Don't bet on it. The story approval process in many broadcast and online newsrooms amounts to a quick read to make sure the facts are right. There really isn't time for supervisors to improve reporters' writing on deadline. That's something a reporter needs to do before submitting the story.

Building in just a little time for revision will make your writing stronger. Set yourself a deadline that's a little earlier than it needs to be, so you can spot problems and fix them before submitting a final story or going on the air. As little as five extra minutes will help.

Don't start revising as soon as you get to the end of your first draft. If you start revising immediately, you may see what you meant to write, rather than what you actually put on the page. Take a short break, walk away from your desk, clear your mind. When you come back, read the story from start to finish as if you know nothing about it. Does it make sense? Are the elements in the right order? Is any crucial information missing?

Read Aloud

Spot jargon and journalese by reading your story out loud. Not under your breath, but really out loud. If you're writing for broadcast, it's the only way you will notice things that look fine on paper but sound silly when you hear them. When Lynn Swann, a former pro football player, announced that he was running for governor of Pennsylvania in 2006, one reporter referred to him as the 53-year-old Swann. Not good if you're writing for the ear. As you read aloud, try adding an extra phrase to the beginning of each sentence: "Hey, Mom . . . guess what?" Or "You won't believe this but . . ." If what follows that opening line is stilted or convoluted, you'll notice it right away and you can revise your copy to make it more conversational.

Reading aloud also gives you a good sense of a story's rhythms. You don't want every sentence and paragraph to be the same length. Variety maintains interest. But you also want to avoid using long strings of modifiers. "Allegheny College sophomore and budding electronic musician Paniya Ly . . ." is hard to read without picking up speed like a freight train. Derail those phrases by breaking them up. "When she's not in class at Allegheny College, Paniya Ly writes electronic music . . ."

Nuke Wasted Words

Well-written news stories are not vague, ambiguous or repetitious, because every word counts. As E. B. White notes in his classic book, The Elements of Style, one of the basic rules of writing is simply, "Omit needless words." A "marathon seven-hour operation" is redundant. Here's another example from a local TV script: "In Mecca, Saudi Arabia, thousands are gathering in the city for the annual Muslim pilgrimage there." The sentence has three references to the location: Mecca, city and there. One would do. Unless you are repeating something for emphasis or clarity, don't do it.

Look closely at any use of superlatives, and when in doubt, leave them out. They're red flags, says Alice Main, former executive producer at WLS-TV in Chicago, Ill. "Just think of the potential for error when you declare something is the best/worst/most/largest/smallest thing." Her advice: If you're going to say it, make sure you can prove it.

Bob Faw 4/9/2007 13:33:17   page 1

SLUG	SHOW	WRITER	MODIFIED	TIMING
big rig woes - draft		bfaw	4/9/2007 13:17:43	1:19
			MODIFIED BY bfaw	

#1

(vo) big rigs can be deadly:

500 people killed, 114-thousand injured
in truck crashes in 2005

last month, on the capital beltway
outside washington

jose portillo villalto was killed when
his honda accord was slammed into

by a tractor trailer driven by roger
scofield.

----- sot---family relative -----

"...he wasn't supposed to be driving; and he
had a suspended license..."

(vo) not only that -- but as the washington
post documents:

scofield had traffic citations in 7
different states, with convictions in two --
56 violations, his license suspended 7
times in delware alone

(for, among other things, speeding and
reckless driving)

ronald karp represents the victim's
family

----- sot---ron karp -----

(atty karp says this guy should never have been
allowed to be
on the road)

----- sot---faw on camera -----

there outta be a law -- and there is: a federal
law, infact, requiring
states to keep traffic of violations like
scofields
data the fed govt is supposed to collect --
and distribute
(to make sure drivers like him aren't on the
road)

(vo) but states do poor job, critics content
--

data often incomplete and untimely;

result: of 2.8 million truckers on the
road -- carrying 43 million

*NBC correspondent Bob Faw is a meticulous writer. He revised this draft of a story
about truck safety four times before it aired on April 9, 2007.*

Wasted words often show up at the ends of sentences, oddly enough in three-word phrases. A story about a chrysanthemum show said it featured "51 varieties of the flower." Another story talked about people living "miles apart from each other." Those last three words aren't necessary, are they? Try to end your sentences with a strong word, not a weak phrase. Look again at how KARE-TV reporter Boyd Huppert did it in his flood story: "On the Lord's Day in Granite Falls, life along the river went to hell." That's a sentence that ends with punch.

Revise your entire story by going over it backwards. Take your script, cover up the final sentence and work back to the beginning, sentence by sentence. You may find that your story actually ended long before you finished writing. Cutting back makes a story stronger, just as it does a rose bush.

REVISE AND CONQUER

Make time to revise.

Read aloud.

Nuke wasted words.

Derail freight-train phrases.

Edit backwards.

Beware of superlatives.

Check for errors.

Check for context.

Check for Errors and Accuracy

Look closely at dates, addresses, quantities and all the other details. Getting someone's name or age wrong is the kind of error that can erode a journalist's credibility. Make sure your story is grammatically correct. Pay particularly close attention to subject-verb agreement and misplaced modifiers. And check for spelling errors, too. Broadcast journalists used to joke that spelling didn't count on the air, but it certainly does now, with scripts being used for closed-captioning and adapted for posting online.

An accurate story tells a complete story, not just one side or another. That doesn't mean that any single story can include everything there is to say about a topic, but it does mean that reporters must not leave out key information that could distort the story's meaning. For example, writing that a new test makes it easier to detect oral cancer suggests that the old test was unreliable. If the new test is merely faster, the reporter should say so.

TAKING IT HOME

Journalists today have more tools and options for telling stories than ever before, but the words they use still matter. As the late CBS News correspondent Eric Sevareid once said, "One good word is worth a thousand pictures." A big part of the job is choosing the right words to tell a clear and meaningful story, whether you're doing it on television, online or in print.

Good writing is not magic. It's a skill that can be learned and improved with discipline and practice. To become a better writer, read, watch and listen to great writers in all media. Take their stories apart and figure out what makes them work. Challenge yourself to find a clear focus for every story you write. Be ruthless about leaving things out that don't fit your focus. And if you choose to do only one thing to improve your writing, make time for revision.

TALKING POINTS

1. Take a script or story you've written and look for wasted words. How many words can you remove without losing the meaning or power of the story? Is the story better after you've taken those words out? Why or why not?

2. Choose a script or story and review it for attribution. List all the statements that include either direct or indirect attribution. Are there elements of the story that should have been attributed but that weren't? What questions would you need to have answered in order to include more attribution in the story?

3. Watch and record a local newscast, paying close attention to the writing. Make note of what you would have changed if you'd been in charge of editing copy before airing.

eLEARNING OPPORTUNITIES

For chapter exercises, practice tools and additional resources, go to the interactive online workbook at http://college.cqpress.com/advancingthestory. You'll find:

• SKILL BUILDING: Practice writing focus statements of six words or less for some well-known movies or stories.

• DISCOVER: Read and watch two versions of the same story to see how conversational writing can add power and meaning.

• ONGOING STORY: Write a focus statement and "jot outline" for this story.

• EXPLORE: Visit Web sites for grammar help, writing checklists and math tools.

6 VISUAL STORYTELLING

Multimedia journalists tell stories with video, photos, audio, text, graphics, data and documents that complement rather than repeat each other. They choose these elements carefully and combine them to present information in the most appropriate way for the medium and the audience. In this chapter, we'll describe how to select and write to the sound and pictures you've gathered, and how to add other elements to create stories that are both informative and engaging.

Once you've captured all the elements you need to create a compelling TV or multimedia story, you still need to choose the best of those elements and decide how to use them. If the foundation of great writing is selection not compression, great visual storytelling depends on your choice of pictures, sound, graphics and interactives, and the way you put those elements together with the words you write, either text or narration.

Every element you choose to include should enhance the story's impact and credibility. Do it well online, and you can offer the audience multiple ways to experience and explore a story.

Travis Fox, a video journalist at washingtonpost.com, says the key is finding the right balance among the different media. For example, in an online report about the fence Israel is building in the West Bank, Fox used video stories, panorama still photos and a Flash graphic showing the route of the fence. Fox says his successful projects all have some things in common. "Those would probably be ones where you took the various media and combined them in a way that was logical," he told the Online Journalism Review, "using a blog for user feedback and conversation; using the panoramas to give you a sense of place; and using videos to give you a sense of people, the character, the location, and then combining [them] to give you a full picture of the story." [1]

Defining the Barrier

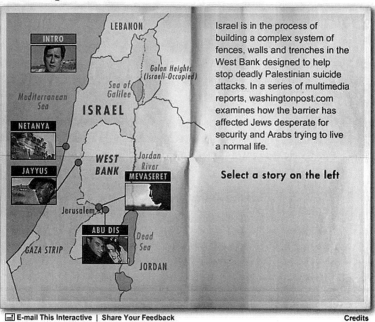

The Washington Post gave online users multiple ways of experiencing a story about Israel's security barrier. Each hot spot on the map led to a Flash animation showing the barrier's path and a video essay featuring local residents; some also had 360° panorama still photos of the area.

Source: "Defining the Barrier," washingtonpost.com, 2005. Retrieved August 15, 2007, from www.washingtonpost.com/wp-srv/world/interactives/israel/israelFence.html.

PLANNING

As we made clear in Chapter 5, you can't construct a story without knowing exactly what you have to work with. For a multimedia story, you need detailed notes on all the video, still photos and audio you think you might use on the air, online or in print. You also need to decide what information you want to convey in graphic form in each medium.

Screening and Logging

Even if you recorded all the audio and video for your story yourself, you should still review it to make sure you captured exactly what you think you did. Don't fall into the trap of writing a script based solely on your recollection of what you observed at the scene, or you may have to rewrite or re-edit when you discover you don't have the pictures or sound to make it work. If you've taken good notes in the field, you can quickly find and screen just those segments you think you'll use. It takes a little time, but investing it at the front end will pay off in a quicker edit.

As you screen, create a detailed log of your material. If you've captured digital video or audio clips, note the name and location of each file or bin and what's in it. If you're working with linear video or audio, note the exact time-code or counter time so you can cue it up for digitizing or editing. You'll also need a description of the pictures and a word-for-word transcript of the audio, both sound bites and natural sound "pops."

Not everyone does this the same way, but good writers tend to be meticulous loggers. Reporter Mike Schuh of WJZ-TV in Baltimore, Md., logs in two columns—visuals on the left and audio on the right. He uses his own shorthand to describe the video: EW-2 means an extreme wide two-shot, for example, and OOF stands for "out of focus." KOMP tells him the shot was taken with a long lens, so the video is compressed. He uses the symbols < and > to note the direction people are facing on the screen, so when he writes he doesn't call for back-to-back sound bites in which everyone is looking in the same direction.

Schuh logs all the audio he might use "up full," whether it's nat sound or a bite from an interview. If the sound is off-camera and he plans to use it as a V/O (voice over), he draws a squiggly line—his symbol for "radio."

Timing

If you've interviewed a slow talker, what looks short on paper may actually take them a long time to say out loud. You definitely need to know the total running time (TRT) of each bite before you write a television story, and before you decide which clips to post online. The Internet may not have any built-in time limits, but most users do. "One of the hardest things to learn in editing video or audio is discipline," says Regina McCombs, a multimedia producer with the Minneapolis Star-Tribune. "Sometimes—many times—shorter is better." [2]

If you're doing an online or print version of your story and you have enough time, transcribe segments of sound that are longer than the bites you'd use on television. You can

```
    schuhm              Tue Dec  3 16:03  page    3
                                     TAPE ONE 9:14
                                     RUNS:01

T/1  9:45 CU MANHOLE COVER MOVE


T/1  9:57 DRIVE DOWN STOPPED CARS <

ENG/SOT                              ENG/SOT
                                     BUSINESSMAN
                                     DAVID COHEN
                                     TAPE ONE 10:24
                                     "WELL THE WAY THEY..... MIDDLE OF
                                     DAY... IMPOSSIBLE TO GET AROUND
                                     RUNS:08


ENG/SOT                              ENG/SOT
                                     BUSINESSMAN
                                     DAVID COHEN
                                     TAPE ONE 10:57
                                     AND I DON'T KNOW WHY THEY CAN'T DO IT
                                     AT NIGHT
                                     RUNS:04


T/1  11:23 LO EW STAND AROUND PAVERS

T/1  BBBB :04 KOMP WORKER NAT WIPE

ENG/SOT                              ENG/SOT
                                     NATS
                                     JACKHAMMER ECU W/ NAT WIPE
                                     TAPE ONE BBB :47
                                     RUNS:01


T/1  BBB 1:24 EW TRUCKS BACKHOE

T/1  BBB 1:35 BACKHOE OPERATOR

T/1  BBB 2:24 NO PARKING ECU MACRO

T/1  BBB 2:36 BARREL

ENG/SOT                              ENG/SOT
                                     RIDE ALONG
                                     TAPE ONE BBB 2:42
                                     WE'RE GOING TO BE AT THEIS LIGHT FOR A
                                     WHILE
                                     RUNS:02


ENG/SOT                              ENG/SOT
                                     RIDE ALONG
                                     TAPE ONE BBB 3:03
                                     OH IT'S HORRIBLE REALLY....
```

WJZ-TV reporter Mike Schuh's log notes for a story about construction in downtown Baltimore, Md. Notice how detailed his log is, with tape number and time-codes, a short-hand description of each shot and the exact running time of sound bites and "nats."

Source: Courtesy of Mike Schuh.

use the transcript to select quotes for print, to post online in its entirety, or to help you create short natural-sound videos or slide shows with audio for the Web. We'll talk more about how to do that later in this chapter.

CHOOSING SOUND

You probably have a good idea of what bites or quotes you might use in a story as soon as you complete each interview. You may even do as we suggest and highlight in your notebook the sections you like best, making it easier for you to find them on tape and transcribe them. But you can't make a final decision about what to use by looking at a transcript. And you still have to consider all the other sound you might want to include to bring your story to life.

Sound Bite Content

Choosing good sound bites is a little trickier than choosing quotes. Something that looks great on paper may not work on the air or online. Too many stories include bites that are off mic, muffled or so thickly accented that they're hard to decipher. A good sound bite has to be perfectly clear and understandable, whether the person is on camera or not. To make sure of that, listen to each bite with your eyes closed, and if you have any doubt, ask someone who wasn't involved in the story to listen for you. Reporters and photographers who hear a bite on the scene and then hear it again in the edit room may think it's easier to understand than it really is.

Sometimes a bite that's hard to decipher is still essential to the story you're telling. For example, you might have emotional sound from a person who is not a native English speaker but who was the only eyewitness you could find to a natural disaster. Don't reject the bite out of hand. Instead, consider using the bite with subtitles or a translation so your

TRADE TOOLS

LOGGING SHORTHAND

CU:	Close-up.
XCU:	Extreme close-up.
MCU:	Medium close-up.
MS:	Medium shot.
WS:	Wide shot.
LS:	Long shot.
>:	Screen direction right.
<:	Screen direction left.
INT:	Interior.
EXT:	Exterior.
RF:	Rack focus.

audience can both experience the emotion and understand the content. At the same time, make sure you discuss whether doing so could be seen as disrespectful.

Bites should not only be clear, they should sound authentic. Avoid using bites in which people sound like they're robots reading from a script. As we've discussed, the best sound bites are subjective and provide insight, not just facts. Great sound bites have passion, says reporter Tony Kovaleski of KMGH-TV in Denver, Colo. "During interviews, try and capture the passion," he says. "During writing, make sure not to miss it."

Sound Bite Number and Length

There's no rule about how many sound bites you need for any given story, nor how long or short each bite should be. Some terrific stories have been told without a single bite; others are told almost entirely in sound bites with very little track. "Not every package needs three sound bites," says assistant news director Mark Ginther of WFAA-TV in Dallas, Texas. "Every package needs to make sense."

Even so, most beginning reporters tend to let their bites run too long, especially when they think everything being said is important. It's often more effective to paraphrase a portion of a long bite and use the information to set up a shorter bite. When three climbers were stranded on Oregon's Mt. Hood in December 2006, the local sheriff talked to the media about the ongoing search. "We've been searching all week—but when an opportunity opened up because of the weather, [it] gave us a break to be up there this morning," said Sheriff Joe Wampler.

> What's going on—what our strategy is today, and it's going to continue through the weekend, is we've got teams on the mountain right now that basically started at 4:00 this morning—and our strategy is to get a summit team from the south side of the mountain, from Timberline, and this is totally dependent upon avalanche conditions, which are extreme on the mountain right now. As you can see, even from right here, we have some wind on the mountain now to the east and there's a lot of fresh snow and there's blowing snow up there. But that's OK, we're able to operate in that environment today.[3]

There's a lot of good information in that sound bite but it runs 35 seconds. In a case like this, you might want to apply the "12 second rule"—if the bite runs longer than 12 seconds, it had better be riveting. In this case, it isn't. The first part of the bite is just factual information you can summarize, so the last part of the bite where the sheriff shares a personal opinion works best: "As you can see, even from right here, we have some wind on the mountain now to the east and there's a lot of fresh snow and there's blowing snow up there. But that's OK, we're able to operate in that environment today."

Generally speaking, a sound bite should convey a complete thought, be easily understood and keep the audience's attention. If it's too short, it may be hard to absorb. Keep in mind that the human brain takes a few seconds to adjust to a change in voice before it can process what's being said. Bites that run only a few seconds can't really convey much useful information, but they can reinforce what's in your narration or video. Long bites can be boring, but they can also be compelling. The best advice on how to make good decisions about sound bites is to focus primarily on content, not length.

That same advice can help you avoid feeling obliged to use a bite for the wrong reasons. Maybe it took a lot of effort to set up the interview, or it was a long drive to the location. That's no excuse for using a worthless bite. Viewers don't know or care how hard you had to work to get it. If it's bad or it doesn't fit the focus of your story, leave it out. And resist the temptation to include a bite just to avoid upsetting the interviewee. If you think they've called every living relative to tell them to watch your TV story, let them know before air that they're not in it. Better yet, make parts of the interview available online and point them there.

Natural Sound

In addition to choosing sound bites from interviews, review your material for other sound you can use in your stories or as supplementary material online. Some audio may have been captured on the fly while you were shooting b-roll of an activity. For example, when covering a flood you might put a microphone on a volunteer while he's stacking sandbags to keep a river from overflowing. Your mic could pick up the comments he makes to the man next to him, including this one: "These things are getting mighty heavy." Using that comment in your story would bring the audience closer to understanding the experience of those volunteers. "Nat pops" like these will likely be short, but they can still play an important role in your narrative. If you intend to use this kind of sound "up full," apply the same standards you would for an interview bite and make sure the words are clear and understandable.

Listen as well for other sound you can use to reinforce the theme of your story or move it forward. In the flood story, for example, you'd probably want to include the sound of the river rushing by, water pumps chugging to keep the river from overflowing its banks, the hiss of sand being poured into bags and so forth. As you log, make a note of where these sounds occur.

You also may have audio from other sources that will help the audience better understand your story. Mark Bowden, who wrote the Philadelphia Inquirer series that turned into the book and movie Black Hawk Down about U.S. forces fighting in Somalia, obtained radio transmissions of soldiers during the battle. He posted that audio as part of the online version of his story, "sounds that captured the frenzy and terror of the fight," he said.[4]

CHOOSING VIDEO

Selecting the best video or photos to tell your story isn't as easy as it sounds. Sure, there are some stories where the choice of pictures is obvious. You wouldn't tell a breaking news story about a warehouse fire without shots of flames and smoke. But remember to log the establishing shots and reaction shots we talked about in Chapter 3, and make sure the video you planned to use to begin and end the story is as good as you think it is. "The opening needs to say, 'watch me' and the close needs to say, 'the end,' " says Sharon Levy Freed, director of the NPPA Television NewsVideo Workshop.

Moments

Make note of what many photojournalists call "moments" in the video—images or sequences that capture the real impact of the story. Scott Jensen, director of photography at KTUU-TV in Anchorage, Alaska, says the best moments are spontaneous, and typically symbolize joy or struggle. "What moves you will probably move your audience," he says. "What you remember from a shot is likely going to be what your audience remembers."

Sometimes you won't even be aware of these moments until you review what you've shot. As he screened video for a story about a house being moved across a frozen lake, photojournalist Jonathan Malat of KARE-TV in Minneapolis was surprised to discover a shot of the ice almost breaking under the house trailer's wheel. He'd shot a close-up of the wheel to use as a cutaway, but didn't notice the movement of the ice until he was in the edit room. Using that shot allowed him to prove just how dangerous the move really was.

Say It, Prove It

The audio you've chosen will dictate some of the video you'll use to tell your story. If you've selected a sound bite from an active interview, you'll probably want some b-roll shot in the

The "moment" in this WTVF-TV story about the dedication of a new statue in Nashville wasn't the predictable unveiling (left) but the unexpected (right)—when the cable used to remove the tarp broke.

Source: Courtesy of WTVF-TV.

same location. Look for pictures that prove the point of the sound bites. When the volunteer in your flood story says the sandbags are getting heavy, you'll want to cut to video that proves he's right—for example, a shot where he accidentally drops a sandbag while trying to hand it to the next person in line.

WRITING TO SOUND

Now that you've chosen your best audio, decide which bites you'll definitely use. Eliminate sound bites that duplicate information unless you're using them on purpose to emphasize a statement or fact. NBC's Bob Dotson warns, "Don't use sound bites as substitutes for more effective storytelling." Reporters who simply string bites together are often taking the lazy way out. On the other hand, don't write your script first and then look for sound to plug in. Remember what CNN's Candy Crowley said: "Sound bites are not production techniques to break up the sound of your voice." Your goal is to create a seamless narrative, to keep the audience's attention from beginning to end, and your success depends to a large degree on the way you write in and out of each sound bite.

Leading In

Look closely at the beginning of each bite you've decided to use. Your goal is to write a line just before the bite that prepares the audience for what they're about to hear. Because the best sound bites express opinion or emotion, they often don't make sense without a good setup line, and a bad setup line can leave the viewer confused.

Let's say you're reporting on a candidate for political office who has promised not to take money from lobbyists. You could write: "He signed a pledge not to accept gifts from lobbyists," but if you follow it with this sound bite—"We should be able to expect that they're going to enrich us and not themselves"—you'll leave viewers wondering why anyone should expect that lobbyists would "enrich us." That's because the pronoun "they" in the sound bite appears to refer back to the noun in your script that's closest to the bite, "lobbyists." What the candidate meant was that elected officials should not enrich themselves. You'd have served the audience better by writing, "He signed a pledge not to accept gifts from lobbyists, saying it's wrong for politicians to line their own pockets." Write so that the ear gets the information needed to decode what's coming next as late as possible.

You also don't want to write lead-in lines to sound bites that echo or repeat what the person says. You'll bore the audience and steal the thunder from the characters in your story. Let them say how they feel or what they learned. You don't have to say it for them. There's nothing more annoying than a story full of lines like this: "Many women were upset they weren't notified," followed by sound bites from women saying, "I was upset" and "It made me angry." One way to avoid this is to think of sound bites as reaction to the action in your script or video, or as punch lines that you set up in your script. Use your narration to tell what happened—"Many women weren't notified"—and leave it to the women themselves to describe how they reacted.

Leading Out

Repetition may not be the best way to set up a bite, but it's often effective to repeat words from a bite in the line that follows it. Let's say you have a bite from a hurricane survivor who says, "Insurance isn't going to do me any good, so I'm in big trouble here." You might be tempted to write out of the bite this way, "That's because it only covers flooding, not wind damage." But you'd be better served to repeat the word insurance in your narration to avoid any confusion as to what "it" stands for, so you'd write, "That's because her insurance only covers flooding, not wind damage."

You can also repeat the very last words in a sound bite for emphasis or clarity, as former ABC correspondent Jim Wooten did in a story about integration. A person he spoke to in Oxford, Miss., described adults in the community this way: "They're not used to being around the other color, the other races, and they want their kids to grow up that way too." His next line said, "That way meant that when integration began, the annual prom ended."

Some sound bites may convey complete thoughts, but the person speaking may not come to an obvious stop at the end. Some people seem to end every sentence with an upward inflection so their statements sound almost like questions. You can still use these bites if you're careful about how you write out of them, so your line completes the person's unfinished thought. For example, let's say your hurricane survivor says something that sounds like this: "The cops came through with a bullhorn. They wanted us to leave?" Her inflection makes her sound uncertain, even though she's making a statement of fact. Your line coming out of the bite can make that clear to the audience. The simplest solution is to begin with a conjunction like "and" or "but." In this case, you could write, "And they left immediately," or "But they decided to stay."

One more point about using sound bites: they usually need company. "When you use a sound bite to either open or close a piece, pair it with a line of track," says reporter Wayne Freedman of KGO-TV in San Francisco, Calif. "If you close with a sound bite, it should be stronger than any other words you might write." That's a high standard most sound bites just don't meet.

Using "Nat Pops"

Natural sound should be used just as deliberately as sound bites. Decide where it works best—whether it's a quick pop of someone talking or a sound you've recorded on scene. Like every other element in your story, nat sound should move it forward and not interrupt the flow. Use nat sound to glue your story together, like "mortar between bricks," says photojournalist Tim Griffis, not to "break up" your narration.

You've probably seen stories that overdo the use of nat, bringing it up almost at random in the middle of lines of track and making it harder for the audience to follow the story. KARE-TV reporter Boyd Huppert says that thinking of nat as punctuation helps him put it in where it makes sense. A very short nat could be used where you'd pause for a comma. Longer nat works as a period at the end of a sentence. Put a longer nat where a short one belongs and you create what Huppert calls a "Knievel," named for the stuntman known for his daring motorcycle jumps. "If it's too long," Huppert says, "you can't get to the other side."

MAKE IT MEMORABLE

NBC national correspondent Bob Dotson is a brilliant visual storyteller who regularly shares his insights at the annual TV workshop of the National Press Photographers Association. He uses the term "commitment" to describe a story's focus. "The commitment should be stated as a complete sentence with subject, verb, and object," Dotson says. "Prove the commitment visually."

His story checklist includes these additional tips:

- Write your pictures first. Give them a strong lead, preferably visual, that instantly telegraphs the story to come. Ideally, the ending is also visual.

- Write loose. Be hard on yourself. Say nothing in script your viewers would already know or that the visuals say more eloquently.

- Build your report around sequences. Two or three shots of a guy buying basketball tickets; two or three shots of a husband and wife drinking coffee at a kitchen table, etc. Sequences demand matched action.

- Strong natural sound. Some reports merely let you watch what happened. The best reports let you experience what happened.

- Short sound bites. Short bites prove the story you are showing. Don't use sound bites as substitutes for more effective storytelling.

Source: Adapted from Bob Dotson, "Story Checklist" workshop for National Press Photographers Association.

WRITING TO VIDEO

As you write your multimedia story, think video first. It's a simple rule, but that doesn't mean it's easy to follow. Thinking video first means you have to consider what the audience will be looking at before you decide what audio or narration should go along with the pictures. That's because pictures are powerful—so powerful they can trump words. Studies have found that when the video and audio in a television news story are not in sync, people remember what they see much better than what they hear.[5]

CBS News correspondent Lesley Stahl says she learned that lesson when covering the White House in the 1980s. She used video of President Ronald Reagan visiting nursing homes and speaking at the Special Olympics in a story that detailed the administration's plans to cut benefits for the elderly and handicapped. Far from being unhappy, the White House loved the story. In her book, Reporting Live, Stahl says an official told her why. "Nobody heard what you said," he explained. "When the pictures are powerful and emotional, they override if not completely drown out the sound."

Sequence Your Story

Put the video for your story in order, scene by scene, and see if you can let each sequence play out before you move on to the next. Jumping back and forth between locations and going backward and forward in time makes a story choppy, not seamless.

For example, let's say you're doing a story about those missing mountain climbers. You have shots of the search team heading out of base camp before dawn, a midmorning news conference by the sheriff, daytime video of the mountain with helicopters overhead and two interviews with family members of the missing men. You'd probably start with the search team video because everything else was shot in daylight and you wouldn't want to go from day to night and back to day again. Bring the family members into your story to have their say, and then say goodbye to them. And once you've introduced a main character like the sheriff, don't feel obliged to use a shot of him on camera every time you refer to something he's said—especially not a silent shot of him talking. Lip flap is almost always a bad idea. If you want to mention the sheriff's plan to keep the helicopters flying all weekend, stick with the video of the choppers and keep your story moving smoothly along.

Show, Don't Tell

One key principle of news writing is to show the audience what happened rather than tell about it. For example, instead of saying that family members attending a funeral were grief-stricken, a well-written story would show their grief by describing or using video of them hugging and sobbing. "You can say she's a devoted mother, or you can show a child jumping into her lap," says Mike Mather, a reporter at WTKR-TV in Norfolk, Va. "Which is more effective?"

That sounds obvious enough, but it gets tricky when reporters try to write something to go along with the video. Too many take the old TV news maxim, "See dog, say dog," literally, and what they write just repeats what the viewer can already see. Words should enhance the visual elements in stories by adding context or meaning. For example, in a story for WTVF-TV in Nashville, Tenn., about National Guard troops preparing to head for Iraq, reporter Barry Simmons used video of soldiers in their barracks and in tanks, but he didn't talk about their training routine over those pictures. Instead, he referred to what the soldiers had left behind: "Just six weeks ago, they had careers, woke up in their own beds, and drove to work on wheels." Some reporters call this technique "writing to the corners of the picture," because their words convey what the viewer can't see.

Draw Attention

On rare occasions, you may want to refer directly to what the viewer is looking at to avoid confusion. If you're writing to a shot of two people but you're referring to just one of them, it's a good idea to identify that person as being on the left or right.

You might also want to explain video that could raise questions in the viewer's mind. Years ago, the only video of accused serial killer John Wayne Gacy showed him dressed in a clown costume doing charity work. Using that video without explanation would have been puzzling to say the least. You may also want to use words to draw attention to the significance of something on the screen that otherwise might be missed. For example, "You can just see the bear's nose poking out of those bushes."

Parallel Parking

Another way to create a seamless narrative is to "parallel park" part of your narration between sound bites that occur in one continuous shot. Instead of removing a relatively long pause or stumble in a sound bite you want to use and covering the edit with a cutaway, let the video roll and insert a short line of narration during the pause.

For example, when reporter Barry Simmons talked to a woman near a huge sinkhole in front of a day care center, she stumbled and paused while saying, "We ride on this street every day, every single day and um, er, ah, you know . . . my first thing was oh, my God, what if I had been driving or fell in or something." Instead of "cleaning up" her bite as he might have in a print story, or covering the stumbles with a cutaway, Simmons simply parked a line of narration in the pause. "We ride on this street every day, every single day. [SIMMONS: Frightening to parents.] My first thing was oh, my God, what if I had been driving or fell in or something. [SIMMONS: Fascinating to their kids.]" Obviously, if you're not editing your own story, you need to clearly communicate what you have in mind to the person doing the edit so the narration winds up precisely where you want it.

WORDS AND PICTURES

When words and pictures work well together, the result is a stronger, more memorable story.

- Pictures should illustrate the story, not dictate the story. Great pictures don't make a story newsworthy. A lack of pictures doesn't mean the story shouldn't be told.

- Use words to add a further dimension to pictures. Don't describe the obvious. Explain the significance of what the audience is seeing or the implications of the pictures.

- Use words to draw attention to pictures. Words can tell the audience: "This matters," or "Look at this."

- Understand the value of silence and natural sound. Let the audience see and hear what it was like to be there. Give them time to feel something.

- Let the pictures reveal surprises. Use words to set them up. Don't steal the thunder from your pictures.

EDITING

As an editor, you have a lot of power over the way a story will be received. You can change the order of events, shrink or expand the time it took for them to unfold and increase or reduce their impact, just by the way you put the elements together. When editing news video, take care to follow the same ethical guidelines you would when reporting or shooting in the field. Staging is a cardinal sin in journalism. You wouldn't ask someone to do something just so you could shoot it, unless you plan to explain that in your story. So you shouldn't manipulate video or audio in the edit room unless you plan to explain that too. We'll talk more about the issues raised by digital manipulation in Chapter 11.

The editing process varies widely from place to place, but there are some general principles most video editors follow to produce a story that will keep the audience's attention from start to finish.

Video Edits

Always open with strong video, but avoid the trap of using all your best video off the top. "If you do, what's left?" asks KARE-TV reporter Joe Fryer, "and will the viewer have enough background to care about it?" Instead of starting your story with people weeping at a funeral, for example, you'd serve the audience better by setting the stage for that scene, offering some details about the person being buried or how he or she died. By the time you use the video of people crying, the audience will understand why.

Rather than using all the best video and sound at the top, skilled editors often put together a sequence that pulls the viewer into the story. Quick edits and nat sound can create a sense of urgency for a breaking news story, for example, while a static "beauty shot" sets the tone for a feature.

By combining careful editing with adept writing, you can let the audience discover surprises in your stories. A story about a wheelchair basketball team could open with a wide shot of the court, but that would give away the surprise that the players are in wheelchairs. Instead, you could begin with tight shots of dribbling, a ball going through the hoop and players' faces, to establish that your story is about basketball. Then you can let the video reveal what makes this game different from others.

As you build video sequences, let shots last as long as they have "energy," says award-winning editor Jon Menell. For example, if you have a shot of a girl yawning, cut to the next shot when her mouth is opened the widest. One of Menell's watchwords is to avoid pointless cutaways. "A cutaway is the right name for it," he says, "because it cuts the viewer's attention away from the story. You want to take their attention to the next thing." So don't feel that you have to cover part of every sound bite with b-roll. The long-term success of CBS News' 60 Minutes proves that viewers are more than willing to watch "talking heads" if they're saying something interesting.

Don't forget the basics when editing video. Remember the rule not to cross the axis, the imaginary line that divides a scene in two. If the video has been shot from one side of the axis, you won't have a problem in the edit. But if you have shots taken from both sides of the line, be careful how you edit them together or you can wind up with moving objects that appear to reverse direction.

When editing video for use online, it's often advisable to split your story into chapters

WBFF-TV photojournalist Stan Heist opened a breaking news story about an explosion in a Baltimore neighborhood with a quick montage of pictures and sound that set the scene and established an urgent pace.

Source: Courtesy of WBFF-TV.

or topics. You might want to post a short video segment on each of the main characters in your story, or construct segments around different themes. For example, a crime story might be broken into segments on the details of the crime, the investigation, the trial and the sentencing. Angela Grant, a multimedia producer with the San Antonio Express-News says she edits video segments that run only two or three minutes to make her video presentations more interactive. "The user gets to choose which topic interests them, and only watch that video if they want," she says. "Also, if they choose one and then think it's boring, they don't have to just drop my story like a hot potato. They may choose another video instead." [6]

Audio Edits

When working with natural sound, let the type of sound determine how you should edit it into the story. Award-winning editor Brian Weister says he'll cut directly to a sharp, crisp sound like a hammer hitting a nail, but he'll bring up a droning sound like a circular saw about 20 frames ahead of where he wants it up full, and then will fade it back down. Weaving this kind of audio in and out of the story helps to create a seamless narrative.

Audio can help you make transitions from inside to outside, or from location to location. WBFF-TV photojournalist Stan Heist uses a foreshadowing technique, sometimes called an "L-cut," which involves bringing audio in before making a video edit. "You hear the sound before you're there," he says. For example, he might use audio of a door creaking open under video of the exterior of a house, then cut to an interior shot of the door closing. "Dissolve with your audio, not your pictures," Heist says, "and your story will feel smoother and have more energy."

GRAPHICS

Multimedia journalists use graphics of all sorts to enhance their reporting, in print, on the air and online. Graphics can make relationships clear and illustrate complex information to make it more understandable. On the Web, interactive graphics allow users to explore

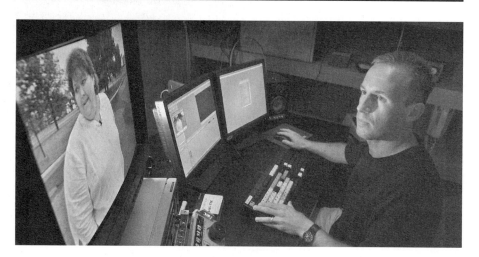

KSTP-TV photojournalist Jason Hanson works in a nonlinear edit suite that can easily produce effects like dissolves, but he rarely uses them in daily news stories.

Source: Courtesy of Jason Hanson.

ONE EDITOR'S WISDOM

Shooting video is hard work, says photojournalist Jason Hanson of KSTP-TV in Minneapolis, Minn., kind of like cutting down trees. But editing is like woodcarving, he says; that's where you can truly be creative. "Watch raw footage and you'll be blown away at how dull it is," he says. "We shoot hours of stuff that we whittle down to nothing. Editing can save the day almost any time."

Hanson's editing skills earned him the National Press Photographers Association 2006 Editor of the Year award. He says the key to excellent editing is to assume ownership of the story. "If you think of something that might work, try it," he says. "It's only TV news. If you're editing nonlinear you can always change it."

For Hanson, pacing is king. The best stories vary the pace, he says. "Give the audience one shot where they can see what's going on," he suggests. "Sit on a wide shot. If it's all fast, you lose the sense that it feels fast." He also advises against using all the best shots right out of the gate because "you'll run out of steam. People remember endings. If you want to dazzle the audience, save it for the big finish."

Hanson is not a big believer in visual effects. "Dissolves waste time," he says. He almost never uses them in spot news. In features, he'll use dissolves for effect, and in long-form, in-depth stories he uses them for pacing. On the other hand, Hanson's stories are packed with sound. He'll even add sound to graphics, just to keep stories moving. "Graphics are made-up anyway," he says. "Find creative ways to add sound."

When there's an emotional reaction to a story, Hanson says, the sense of time goes away. So he never tells producers how long a story is before they see it. He'd rather show them a finished story and ask what they want to cut. "The kudos don't happen until the editing is done," he says. "I don't show a rough cut. They always go for the weak spot. I make it a point to finish, even if they want to see it 15 minutes before air."

information at their own pace and in as much or as little detail as they wish. "The hardest job is getting information into a recognizable form," says John Sculley, the former chairman of Apple Computer, who believes it is well worth the trouble. "In an age of quick information, reading is knowing, but seeing is believing," Sculley says.[7]

While many journalists aren't expected to have the technical skills to build elaborate graphics, they may be asked to create simple graphics for both television and the Web. And even if that's not part of their job description, they should know what it takes to create graphics that will draw a user's attention and provide information in the most useful way.

Why Use Graphics?

The first question any journalist should ask before suggesting a graphic is, "Why do we need it?" Far too often, graphics are a reporter's first recourse when faced with a complex or picture-poor story, but the weakest possible reason for using a graphic is to fill space or cover a black hole you don't have video for.

Make sure you fully understand the story before you develop a graphic. Sort through any data or premade graphics you've collected during the reporting process and make sure you have material in a form you can use—complete data sets to build a graphic from or legible documents if you plan to scan them.

Decide if you want the graphic to convey basic facts or to illustrate a process. The answer will determine the type of graphic you should use. To illustrate a process—showing how air pollution affects the lungs, for example—you might want animation with no words on the screen. To illustrate the fact that the air is unhealthy in some parts of your community, you might want to use a map. Make sure you pinpoint a "locator" on the map—a main city or highway, for example—to give people an easy reference point. Online sites like Google Maps (www.maps.google.com) take only seconds to create satellite images that can easily be embedded into Web pages, published in the paper or even used as a full-screen graphic on the air.

Simple Is Better

Avoid graphics that are crammed with too much information. The audience should be able to look at the graphic and take away one or two basic ideas. This rule applies especially to TV graphics, because viewers don't have time to study them. A television graphic is a lot like a highway sign—the driver has to get the key points quickly because in a few seconds the sign is out of view. Let's say you're doing a story about the state budget. It's now twice

FIGURE 6.1 CITY SPENDING

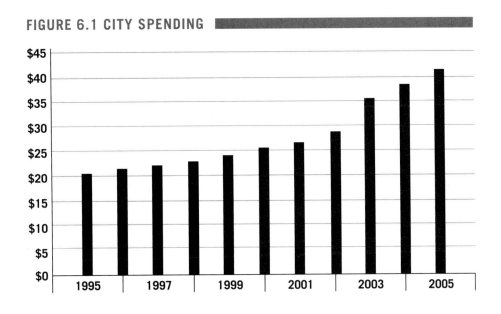

FIGURE 6.2 CITY SPENDING

Complex information can be grasped more easily in graphic form. The simple bar graph (top) shows that a city's budget more than doubled over 10 years. The line graph (bottom) includes a visual cue of $100 bills to reinforce the point.

as big as it was 10 years ago, and most of the growth has been in the last three years. A simple bar chart could make those two facts clear, and you could add more interest to the graphic and reinforce the content by creating the bars out of coins or dollar bills.

Keep the visual look simple as well. A multilayered graphic may look terrific when you design it full-screen, but it may just look cluttered on a small home television set or computer screen.

Shapes and Movement

It's easier for the audience to absorb information that's presented with shapes rather than raw numbers. Instead of listing the number of apartments and office buildings in the area, for example, you could create a pie chart that shows the relationship between the two. Compare rates or percentages whenever possible, not raw numbers. It is misleading to show that one town has twice as many robberies as another, when the first town has 10 times as many inhabitants. Calculate the rate of robberies per inhabitant so you can make a fair comparison.

Animated graphics that build or shrink can illustrate change over time. Be sure that you match the rate of growth on screen to the actual rate. For instance, if the crime rate in a neighborhood has doubled, but it did so over 15 years, it would not be accurate to put an arrow on screen going straight up. Too much movement, however, can be distracting and counterproductive. Avoid movement just for the sake of movement.

Writing to Graphics

A graphic can serve as a roadblock in a television story if it comes up without warning. Lead the viewer in and out of the graphic by what you say in your track. Make a clear transition from the moving video to the fact-based graphic: "As city budget records show . . ." or "You can see how the budget has grown. . . ."

If you have words in your television graphics, be sure that what you say in the track matches what's on the screen. If possible, write your script before the graphic is created and revise it if necessary before tracking. Some producers make an exception for numbers, so that the graphic might read "5,431 but the narration would say "more than 54-hundred." But when words appear on the screen, people read them. It's human nature. If you don't want the audience to read the screen, don't use words. If you do, make sure the words are large enough and on the screen long enough for people to read them. And don't let the graphic get ahead of your track. If you're listing information—perhaps the items found in a suspect's home—build a graphic that puts the information on the screen, one line at a time, as you say it.

Online Graphics

Interactive graphics for the Web can be challenging to design, and producers are still learning how to create and use them for best effect. While many of the same principles that apply to still and TV graphics also apply online, the potential for interactivity adds another layer of complexity. Again, you may not be expected to design interactive graphics on your own, but it's helpful to understand the principles and concepts behind them.

One way to build interactivity into online graphics is to think broadly about what a graphic can be. When gasoline prices spiked during the summer of 2005, Business Week decided to compare the price of a gallon of gas to what other liquids cost by the gallon. Instead of putting the information in a table or graph, the magazine created an interactive

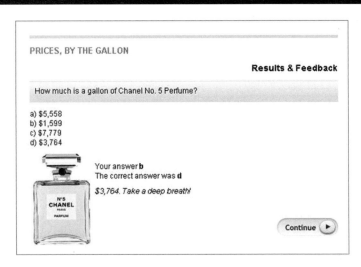

Business Week created an interactive quiz to let users compare the rising cost of gasoline with other items that might be sold by the gallon. Notice how the comment, "Take a deep breath!" next to the cost of Chanel No. 5 perfume, heightens the user's sense of interactivity.

Source: "Prices, by the Gallon," Business Week, 2005. Retrieved August 15, 2007, from http://bwnt.businessweek.com/quiz/galloncosts/quiz.asp.

quiz, letting users guess how much they'd pay for a gallon of spring water or Chanel No. 5 perfume (correct answer: $3,764).

Research conducted by the department of Media Studies at the University of Trier, Germany, suggests these guidelines for producers of interactive graphics:[8]

- Avoid information overload: If you put too much information into a single graphic, users are unlikely to find it all.

- Keep users' expectations in mind: There's no one standard for embedding links in online graphics, so users tend to expect everything to be clickable. Don't include buttons, legends, keys or points on a map just as decoration or to fill space.

- Be careful with animation: Animation can attract or distract users. Blinking, flashing or fading arrows, dots and circles are guaranteed click magnets. "If there is text competing with animation, the text will lose," says Trier's Peter Schumacher.

- Let users control the interaction: Give users clearly marked buttons to start, stop and restart interactive graphics.

NATURAL SOUND STORIES

As we discussed in Chapter 3, you can tell powerful stories on television or online without a reporter track if you've collected the necessary elements with that kind of story in mind. These "natural sound" stories can be constructed with video, sound bites and natural sound recorded on scene or with still photos combined with audio and a limited amount of text on the Web. In either case, your story should be structured with a beginning, middle and end, using the building blocks of strong characters, tension and emotion.

Whether you're working with video or stills, begin by creating a story outline, with sound bites in a logical order from start to finish. Because the nat sound approach is particularly suited to stories that unfold in chronological order, identify the high points in the story and select the sound bites and nat sound that go with them. Remember that you can't depend on narration to fill in the blanks or clear up confusion; the sound you have must tell a complete story. Photojournalist Brian Barr of WBFF-TV in Baltimore, Md., says he usually asks a reporter or producer to screen his nat sound stories before air to make sure he's accomplished his goal. "They weren't [at the scene], and if the story makes sense to them, you did it," says Barr.

Opening sound is critically important in a nat sound story. It has to get the story started by setting the scene or introducing a central character. A nat sound story about a Christmas program at a local mall that Brian Weister produced for KMGH-TV in Denver began with a woman saying, "This is our first ever holiday challenge," one line that explained what the story was about. A piece Tom Aviles shot for WCCO-TV in Minneapolis started with this sound bite: "I'm just one voice. I've never really been a man of many words. I never thought I could make a difference." The story was about a man named Tom, who waved an American flag near a highway after the 9/11 terrorist attacks in 2001 and stirred a patriotic response from everyone passing by.

Your final sound should leave the viewer in no doubt that the story has come to a close. Tom's flag story ends with him saying simply, "God bless America." A story John Goheen shot about the annual wedding dress sale at Filene's Basement, a department store in Boston, ends with the main character saying, "I almost get teary-eyed because we took this completely chaotic consumer event and somebody actually won, actually got exactly what they wanted."

SLIDE SHOWS

A slide show is a way of showcasing multiple still photographs online. Instead of just posting photos and captions on a Web page, you can use a slide show to display pictures in a specific order, with or without an audio track and text captions. A slide show at its best is an animated photo essay telling a coherent story, not just a collection of interesting pictures in some random order. Some slide shows are presented with narration; others just use sound from the people featured in the photos along with natural sound captured on scene and are essentially nat sound stories designed for the Web instead of TV.

It's relatively easy to build a simple slide show, using drag-and-drop software that's built in to most computers: Macs come preloaded with iMovie, and PCs have Movie Maker. Many professional photographers swear by Soundslides, an inexpensive program developed by photojournalist and interactive producer Joe Weiss. Basically, these programs create a video file that plays automatically; the producer decides how long each photo should stay on screen and what audio should accompany each picture. But the user can still pause and restart the slide show, turn the audio on or off and control whether or not to display text captions.

Captions and hyperlinks can give slide shows depth and context that nat sound stories on TV often lack. Good slide show captions convey more information than newspaper photo captions, which typically are little more than labels to help the audience understand what they're looking at. A slide show caption could do only that too, but additional background can be added, as the Washington Post did in its "Being a Black Man" series. In a slide show

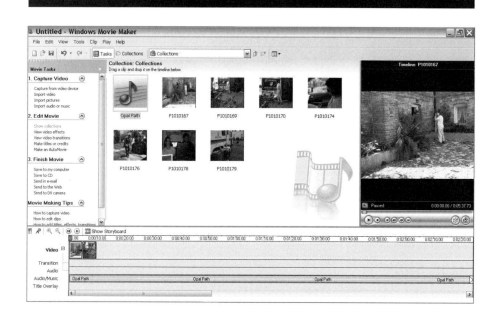

Windows Movie Maker has easy-to-follow instructions (left) for building a slide show with an audio track. You simply drag and drop images and audio files into the timeline (bottom).

Source: Courtesy of the authors.

profiling Eric Motley, a special assistant to President Bush, one photo was captioned: "Motley wraps up a day at the State Department. While a student at Samford University, a highly regarded conservative Baptist school in Birmingham, Motley headed up the school's speakers program, bringing in officials such as Supreme Court Justice Clarence Thomas."

Be aware that writing and fact checking extended captions like these can take a lot of time.

When using captions in a slide show that also includes audio, be mindful of how the user will absorb the information. You might want to pause the audio track as captions are revealed so the users' attention isn't divided between what they're hearing and what they're trying to read. Or you might choose to show captions only when the user mutes the audio, or when the user decides to navigate the slide show one frame at a time rather than let it play automatically.

Motley wraps up a day at the State Department. While a student at Samford University, a highly-regarded conservative Baptist school in Birmingham, Motley headed up the school's speakers program, bringing in officials such as Supreme Court Justice Clarence Thomas. *Photo by Jahi Chikwendiu - The Washington Post*

Well-written slide show captions often add background that would not typically fit in a newspaper caption. The caption for this image from the Washington Post series "Being a Black Man" tells not just what Eric Motley is doing, but also where he went to school and his connection to U.S. Supreme Court Justice Clarence Thomas.

Source: "Being a Black Man," washingtonpost.com, 2006. Retrieved August 15, 2007, from www.washingtonpost.com/wp-srv/metro/interactives/blackmen/blackmen.html.

TAKING IT HOME

The combination of words, pictures and sounds can add up to powerful and memorable stories in all media, but only if the elements are put together with skill and care. Words and pictures should reinforce but not repeat each other; sound should glue a story together; and graphics should make complicated information clear.

The ability to do this in print, on television and on the Web gives today's journalists more avenues to reach a wider audience. Stories can have more layers and more depth. They can be more engaging, using video and audio to help viewers see and hear a story as well as using interactive elements that let the audience participate in discovering information for themselves. Stories told in multiple media have many entry points, allowing the audience to choose what information they want and the order they want it in. But as exciting as these presentation options can seem to you, don't forget this basic truth: It's all about the story.

TALKING POINTS

1. Watch a network television newscast with the sound off. Can you tell what each story is really about? Listen to a television newscast without watching it. Are you missing anything? If not, does that suggest that video is not being used to the fullest?

2. Watch another newscast to see how reporters write to their video. Are they describing what you're looking at, or using their narration to add context and meaning? What difference does that make to your appreciation or understanding of the story?

3. Find a graphic on a news Web site. Does it make good use of interactivity? How could you build a different graphic for the same story with more interactive features?

eLEARNING OPPORTUNITIES

For chapter exercises, practice tools and additional resources, go to the interactive online workbook at http://college.cqpress.com/advancingthestory. You'll find:

- SKILL BUILDING: Consider whether using a graphic would help you tell specific stories better, and if so, decide what kind of graphic you would use.

- DISCOVER: Watch a nat sound story and a slide show to learn how to use these storytelling methods to best advantage.

- ONGOING STORY: Log raw video and audio for this story, and write a TV package. Learn more about shooting and editing from the photojournalist behind the lens.

- EXPLORE: Visit Web sites for tutorials on working with audio, video, still photos and graphics.

7 WRITING FOR THE WEB

The fundamentals of good reporting, writing and ethics apply to news in all media, but to disseminate information most effectively online, additional considerations and skills are needed. This chapter will outline some of the best practices for writing and presenting content on the Web, as well as discuss current standards for adapting broadcast and print styles to meet the needs of the online audience.

Brad Franko gets it. As a journalist in Charleston, S.C., he gets up long before the sunrise to anchor the morning show at WCBD-TV and routinely spends the second half of his day reporting stories for later newscasts. In his relatively small newsroom, Franko also gets the fact that he works for his station online as well as on the air. If a story breaks during his morning shift, he's one of the people who quickly gets the information to the station's Web site. He posts Web versions of his TV stories, too, and routinely updates his blog.

What Franko gets is that, while the audience has been shrinking for both broadcast and print journalism, the online audience has been growing. According to the Pew Research Center for the People and the Press, nearly one in three Americans regularly went online for news in 2006 compared to just one in 50 a decade ago. Serving this growing news audience is forcing many traditional news organizations to rethink the way they gather and present the news and to retrain their people to work more effectively on the Web.

Obviously, to do a good job in any medium a journalist must understand the audience. For example, in television, it's understood that most people don't really watch morning news programs; instead, they listen to them. So, broadcast journalists working on morning shows have been advised to write in a way that puts less emphasis on the visual elements of a story. Since the writer can't count on the audience seeing what is on the screen, the story has to make sense without any visual support.

In the newspaper world, more people read the paper on Sunday than on any other day of the week, so when journalists do special stories that they hope will get lots of attention, those stories will often run first in the Sunday edition.

Because people have been using print and television as sources of news and information for a lot longer than they have the Internet, our understanding of the online news audience is still evolving. But current research offers insights into what people want from a news organization's Web site, and you can use that information to tell your stories more effectively by producing online content that will satisfy their needs.

HOW PEOPLE USE THE WEB

Since Web-based news sites first appeared on the scene in the 1990s, a myriad of studies have been done on Web usability, in other words, how people use Web sites. Though each study may say something slightly different, there are some universal principles for Web use. Typical Web readers:

- Skim content. Online users are often skimming or scanning the content of a site, particularly when they first log on. That doesn't mean they won't read every word of an article that deeply interests them, but initially they're most often looking for information that grabs their attention. That's why headlines, for example, become so important on the Web.

- Look for points of entry. With the Web's bottomless news hole, it's tempting to go wild and write long when you're writing for online. As a general rule of thumb, an 800-word online story is plenty long enough. But users tend to look for entry points in your story—places to jump in and start reading—rather than starting at the top and going through to the end. Think about using multiple headlines or breaking up your text with bullets and frequent paragraph breaks. The technique will help long stories seem less daunting and will help users find what interests them most, even in shorter stories.

- Look for more. In addition to readers who skim the content of a site, the online audience includes people who are actively seeking information about a particular topic that interests them. For example, let's say your station airs a story about a tuberculosis outbreak at a local school. At the end of the story, the news anchor could encourage viewers to go online for a list of the disease warning signs and preventive measures. At other times, you might be giving online users access to additional information through links to other useful Web sites or reminders of previously posted, relevant stories that are still available on your own site.

The Eyetrack07 study involved 600 readers in four U.S. cities. Their eye movements were tracked in 15-minute online reading sessions. The results revealed how long readers spend with the stories they pick, as well as a host of other details about reading patterns.

Source: Courtesy of the Poynter Institute.

One ongoing Web usability study has focused specifically on the use of news Web sites. Since 2003, the Poynter Institute, the Estlow International Center for Journalism and New Media and a company called Eyetools Inc. have been studying Internet users and literally looking through their eyes at various news Web sites—using "eyetracking" technology. Each test subject spends time reading news sites and multimedia news content while being observed. Here are two key findings from the 2007 study:

- When people click on a story, they read most of it. In fact, users read to completion 63 percent of the stories they selected.

- Online readers can either be methodical in their reading or simply scan the copy. About half read the stories in a more linear way, from top to bottom, while the other half jumped around—reading parts of the story and looking at photos—in no particular order. In both cases, users read about the same amount of the text.

One of the most interesting new findings had to do with story form. The study found that alternative story forms like Q&As, timelines, short sidebars and lists helped users better understand the content of a story. During a follow-up interview, participants who accessed these alternative forms were able to correctly answer more questions about the content than their colleagues who didn't have those alternatives.[1] Keep this finding in mind as we talk about the production and presentation of Web content in the next two chapters.

WHEN NEWS ON THE WEB FALLS SHORT

Despite what we know about Web usability, not every Web site takes advantage of the research. Many news organizations publish what's commonly known as "shovelware" on their sites. They essentially take the stories that were published in that day's paper or aired on that day's newscasts and post a text version online. What type of problems do you think might arise when a site simply repurposes content produced for another medium? As you can imagine, what works in one medium might not in another.

Broadcast Shovelware

As you know, most television stories are written with video references. The script might say, "You can see how the flames ate away at the building for most of the night." The problem is, when a Web user simply reads the script, the video references don't make sense. In addition, video also provides important information for the viewer. For example, a TV reporter covering a story about the effect of an overnight freeze on the Florida orange crop wouldn't have to describe the rows and rows of trees laden with ice-covered fruit because the viewers could see that for themselves. But in the Web version, an important element of the story might be lost if the reporter doesn't write in the description of how the trees looked in the video. Of course, the Web allows you to post video clips online, but you can't be sure that someone will take the time to view them. That means your text must provide enough information for the online reader to fully understand your story without screening the video.

Simply posting a text version of your broadcast script can also lead to confusion when time references, such as the words "today" or "tonight," are included. A story might refer to a meeting that happened "tonight," and thereby confuse users who might be reading the story on the day after the meeting.

Part of the problem is that few television news sites have large Web staffs and a good number rely on producers and reporters to add Web postings to an already long list of job duties. Sometimes the Web work just doesn't get done or sites are left with outdated or incomplete versions of stories and little unique content.

Print Rehash

Newspapers have their own online problems as well. Researchers at the School of Journalism of the University of Texas at Austin examined how some of the largest newspapers in the country were using the Web in 2004. They looked at 30 newspapers and found that five of them made virtually no updates during the day while 13 added only a few breaking news stories. Just 12 of the newspapers studied updated their sites constantly. Considering that these were some of the country's largest newspapers, with ostensibly the most resources, it's probably fair to assume that a survey of smaller papers would find even less updating on the Web.[2]

Many newspapers have computer systems that automatically feed the paper's content onto the Web, but these systems have limitations. For example, automatic feeds can sometimes create version control problems. Let's say a Web producer updates a story on the site with new information after the paper's deadlines have passed. That's great, but when the automation kicks in overnight, the more current copy can often be blown out by the older version of the story.

Shovelware can create other problems, too. A headline in the printed publication may be too long for the Web format, so some systems will just lop off the end of it. Because of that you can get headlines that simply don't make sense, for example, "Mayor Heads to Buffalo to Compare" instead of "Mayor Heads to Buffalo to Compare City Costs."

Many news organizations are coming to realize what you probably already know from reading this text; online users want something on the Web that is a little different from what they are getting on the air or in the newspaper.

WRITING FOR THE WEB

It's almost certain that all journalists will need to know how to write for the Web in the future. Mary Alvarez, news director for WCNC-TV, the NBC affiliate in Charlotte, N.C., says that every future journalist should be learning everything possible about working with the

Web. "Our reporters are required to write a Web version of every story they work on for the day," Alvarez said. "We're breaking stories on the Web, we're not waiting until 11 o'clock to run a story that we know about at 8 p.m., so reporters have to get used to putting the Web first."

Fortunately, many of the techniques you've learned as a broadcast or print journalist will help you succeed online; however, there are some additional things you need to know.

Grab Their Attention!

People often come to the Web to see what's new in a breaking or ongoing story—the immediacy of online attracts them to the Web much as it does to broadcast news. That means the opening of your online story has to be much like a good broadcast lead. A good online lead jumps out at users and makes them want to read more. Check out this example:

> Omaha State University is canceling classes for an entire week. The school's computer room flooded yesterday, shutting down the network and making it impossible for the university to operate.

If you're a student at Omaha State, that lead sentence will clearly capture your attention. Even if you don't attend the school, canceling classes for a week is unusual enough that it's likely a user will read on. When you write a lead sentence, you need to tell us what the news is and present it in a way that will encourage as many people as possible to read more.

Use Time and Tense

Whenever possible, tell users what's happening right now or what's expected to happen in the future. Web stories can and should be updated whenever information changes. For example, the flooding mentioned above happened yesterday, but the news is that Omaha State has decided to cancel class for a week.

This sounds simplistic, but to write in present tense, you have to know what is happening right now. To write in future tense, you have to think about what's expected to happen soon. So, in the example above—a future tense lead might look something like this:

> Omaha State students won't be sitting in classrooms as usual next week. The University's computer room flooded yesterday, shutting down the network and making it impossible for the university to operate.

Specific time references can also add to a sense of urgency online:

Omaha State University is canceling classes next week. The school's computer room flooded yesterday, shutting down the network and making it impossible for the university to operate. At 2 p.m. today, school administrators will meet to figure out how to make up the instructional time lost. They are considering a shorter December holiday break. That could disrupt vacation plans and leave some businesses without part-time workers.

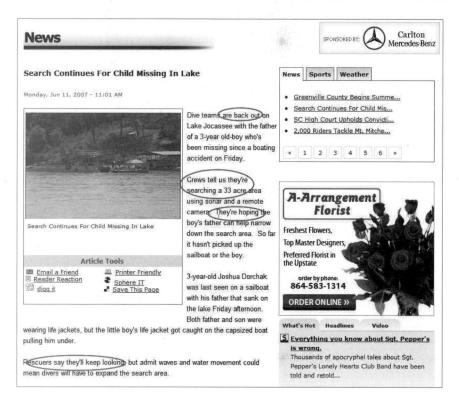

At WSPA-TV in Spartanburg, S.C., the goal is to capitalize on the Web's immediacy. Note the multiple uses of present and future tense in the story about a search for a missing child.

Source: Courtesy of WSPA-TV.

One word of caution here: If you are using specific time references and even present or future tense, it is critically important that you stay on top of the story and remove those references when they become outdated. For example, at 8 p.m., you don't want a story online that looks ahead to a 2 p.m. meeting that has already occurred.

Be Relevant

After the lead, it's important to explain why the story matters. Sticking with the flood example, the next lines might read like this:

> Omaha State University is canceling classes next week. The school's computer room flooded yesterday, shutting down the network and making it impossible for the university to operate. At 2 p.m. today, school administrators will meet to figure out how to make up the instructional time lost. They are considering a shorter December holiday break. That could disrupt vacation plans and leave some businesses without part-time workers.
>
> The school's decision will have an impact on many people, including students and university personnel and their families who may be planning celebrations or vacations. Even businesses counting on holiday help may be affected.

In this situation, the first paragraph gives the user the basic facts of the story, and the second paragraph explains why this story might be relevant to more than just the students.

Be Concise and Conversational

For both the lead and the body of the story you want to use the same kinds of writing techniques we discussed in Chapter 5. It's particularly important for Web stories to use short declarative sentences. This technique should help you be clear and concise. It's also a good practice to stick to one idea per sentence, so that means avoiding long clauses and passive writing. Remember, readers are often scanning your copy, so this short and declarative style of writing may help hold their attention.

Also keep in mind that you're not writing to impress your audience, you're writing to inform your audience. You can be even more informal online than you might be on the air. "Write like you're dashing off an e-mail note to a friend," says Scott Atkinson, news director at WWNY-TV in Watertown, N.Y. For example, Atkinson's Web story about a predicted snowstorm that never came opened with this line: "OK. We were wrong." Write clearly and with context, he says, but use an intimate style, which seems well suited to the Internet. Here's another example:

Don't say: "The state Department of Health has added 172 rivers and lakes to the list of Florida water bodies that contain fish with harmful levels of mercury."

Do say: "The state says 172 more rivers and lakes in Florida are full of fish with too much mercury."

Web users want to get the news quickly, and conversational writing makes content easier to absorb.

Conversational does not mean sloppy. It's absolutely essential that your online copy follow all the rules of good journalism. You need to be accurate, you need to attribute information, and you need to be grammatically correct and so on. Online readers are no different from TV audiences or newspaper readers; they expect their sources of news to be credible, no matter what the medium.

Write for the Scanners

Remember what we said earlier about the way people use the Web? You need to make things easier for the skimmers. Whenever possible you should break up the text.

- Use subheads. Smaller headlines in the body of the story describe for the reader what that section of the story is about.

- Try bullet points. If you have a series of ideas you need to communicate, try laying them all out in a list for the reader.

- Keep paragraphs short. We've already described the need for short, declarative sentences, but even the paragraphs should be brief in an online story, with no more than three to five short sentences in each.

Most of what we've just described about writing for the Web should be somewhat familiar to you, but you probably decide which of these techniques and stylistic approaches to apply depending on which medium you're writing for. Multimedia journalists, on the other hand, use all of them in almost every story they tell online.

WEB WRITING STYLE

For broadcast writers in particular, the online writing style has a lot of similarities to the way you already produce copy. But don't forget that writing for the Web involves thinking about the unique characteristics of the medium:

- Grab attention with your first line of copy.
- Be sure to use present or future tense in the opening line whenever possible.
- Make sure you're explaining why the story is relevant to a general audience.
- Use short, declarative sentences to make the copy easier to read and absorb.
- Use a conversational style that capitalizes on the intimacy of the Internet.
- Keep the fundamentals in mind—good grammar and punctuation, accuracy and ethics.
- Write for the scanners; use subheads, bullets and short paragraphs.

PRINT TO ONLINE STORY

So, let's put all of this into practice. The following story was published online after it was adapted and modified from a print piece.

VCU Gets Out the Vote

By Melissa Lynch

Virginia Commonwealth University political organizations are pushing to register student voters by the deadline of Oct. 4. They are responding to the fervor of the presidential election that has captivated young voters.

Omar Yacoubi, a member of the VCU Young Democrats, has manned a table every other day for two and a half weeks to register students. Yacoubi, a sophomore double major in mass communications and international studies, said, "I stay overtime because I think it's so fun."

Yacoubi said the Young Democrats register students regardless of their political affiliation. He has given VCU's College Republicans' e-mail address to interested students.

"I think it's more important to get their voice heard," he said. "Being involved is more important."

Aaron Larrimore, president of the Young Democrats said the Democrats have registered approximately 300 people by setting up a table at the University Student Commons for 12 days at nine hours a day. The Young Democrats organization has seen a 325-member increase in membership this year, peaking at around 450, Larrimore said.

The College Republicans and Students for Bush, two new organizations on campus, have also successfully gained members in their first two weeks of recruitment.

Students for Bush has about 30 members. Justin Rose, president of Students for Bush, said students have been waiting for a Republican organization on campus. For the past few years VCU has been without an active Republican organization.

"Students have come and said, 'Finally. Thank you.' What concerned me was there wasn't this intellectual diversity," he said, noting a friend who was the "token Republican" in a class.

Focus on the Issues

Both Rose and Larrimore said the candidates are talking about issues that students care about in this election.

"This is the first election in 40 years that hasn't focused on swing voters," Rose said. "The issues that are being discussed have more relevancy to young people." Specifically, he said that jobs, national security and Social Security are being addressed.

"Students as they become young adults are reading their paychecks and asking critical questions," Rose said. "This is the most important election of our lifetime."

Larrimore, a fourth-year political science major, said this election is important specifically because the next president will probably get to nominate several justices for the Supreme Court of the United States in the next few years. "[This election] is really about the next 20 to 30 years," he said. "It's really going to set the tone for our lives."

New Voters

According to a July 2004 study conducted nationally by students at Harvard University's Institute of Politics, 75 percent of college students polled said they will definitely vote in the upcoming election. Holly Teresi, communications director of the Washington, D.C.–based Youth Vote Coalition, said in the past presidential election about 60 percent of students, 15 percent less than the current number, said they would definitely vote.

Teresi said in the past young people weren't as invested as they seem to be this year.

"[Last election] young people weren't watching the media that politicians use to get their message across," she said.

How to Register

Getting registered is the first step. To vote in the Nov. 2 general election, you must register to vote by 5 p.m. Oct. 4. Richmond voters may register at the Office of the Registrar in City Hall. Mailing or faxing an application is another option.

Ramona Taylor, assistant city registrar, advised students to be cautious when registering.

"If they register in Richmond they're declaring that their legal residence is here," she said. This could cause complications concerning taxes if a student's parents have him or her as a dependant or scholarships if legal residence is a factor.

For students using a VCU campus address for voter registration, here's a look at where you'll go to vote on Nov. 2.

• Residents of all dormitories on the Medical Campus, which are Bear Hall, Cabaniss Hall, McRae Hall, Rudd Hall and Warner Hall, vote at the City Hall lobby, 900 E. Broad St.

- Residents of Gladding Residence Center vote at William Byrd Community Center, 224 S. Cherry St.

- Residents of Johnson and Rhoads Halls vote at the Richmond Main Library, 101 E. Franklin St.

- Residents of West Grace Student Housing vote at Dominion Place, 1025 W. Grace St.

For Virginia students interested in more information on voter registration and voting:

- Find your <u>registrar</u>.
- Download a <u>registration form</u>. (This file requires Adobe Acrobat Reader.)
- Find your <u>polling place</u>.
- Download an <u>absentee ballot</u>. (This file requires Adobe Acrobat Reader.)[3]

As you can see, the writer added subheads to help readers scan the story for relevant information. The story includes bullet points with important details and links to additional content. The opening line is present tense and in active voice, the writing is conversational and the sentences and paragraphs are concise. The story is packed with good information, but it's broken down in a way that makes it easy for the online user to follow.

CONVERTING BROADCAST TO ONLINE

The most basic kind of convergence requires cleaning up or revising copy for the Web, whether it's a newspaper story or a broadcast script. TV scripts, in particular, require special attention. Try these tips from Cory Bergman, the founder of LostRemote.com, a Web site about television news and new media:

- Combine copy. If you're modifying a package script, combine the lead-in, body of the package and tag all on the same page. Delete redundancies. Make sure the story starts off with a strong sentence, not a tease line.

- Remove extraneous information. Strip out computer coding, including director, editing and graphics notations.

- Fix capitalization. If you use all upper case for your scripts, convert to upper and lower case, correctly capitalizing as you go along.

- Add quotes. Change the sound bites to quotes, adding the correct attribution.

ONLINE WRITING TIPS

Jonathan Dube, publisher of CyberJournalist.net, says Web writers must keep the needs and habits of online readers in mind. Here are some of his tips to improve your online stories:

- Write lively and tight. Writing for the Web should be a cross between broadcast and print—tighter and punchier than print, but more literate and detailed than broadcast writing. Inject your writing with a distinctive voice to help differentiate it from the multitude of content on the Web. Conversational styles work particularly well on the Web. At the same time, don't forget that the traditional rules of writing apply online. Readers notice sloppy writing and they don't forgive. They'll stop reading a story and they won't come back for more.

- Explain. Don't think that all that matters is that you have the latest news as fast as possible. Speed is important online. But people want to know not just what happened, but why it matters. And with all the information sources out there now, in the end it will be the sites that explain the news the best that succeed.

- Never bury the lead. You can't afford to bury the lead online because if you do, few readers will get to it. When writing online, it's essential to tell the reader quickly what the story is about and why they should keep reading—or else they won't. One

- Form complete sentences. Drop unnecessary punctuation like ellipses and hyphens, and convert sentence fragments into complete sentences.

- Remove video references. Delete any language that makes a direct reference to video and audio, but add appropriate description to bring a visual element to your copy.

- Beef up the story. Add important details. Web copy should deliver more information than 20-second TV stories (with the possible exception of breaking news).

- Bring it all together. Make sure the story reads well from beginning to end.

- Add interactivity. Finally, add links to any relevant materials.[4]

solution is to use a "Model T" story structure. In this model, a story's lead—the horizontal line of the T—summarizes the story and, ideally, tells why it matters. The lead doesn't need to give away the ending, just give someone a reason to read on. Then, the rest of the story—the vertical line of the T—can take the form of just about any structure: the writer can tell the story narratively, provide an anecdote and then follow with the rest of the story, jump from one idea to another in a "stack of blocks" form or simply continue into an inverted pyramid. This enables the writer to quickly telegraph the most important information—and a reason to keep reading—and yet still retain the freedom to write the story in the way he or she wants to.

- Break it up. Larger blocks of text make reading on screens difficult, and you're more likely to lose readers. Using more subheads and bullets to separate text and ideas helps. Writing should be snappy and fast to read. Keep paragraphs and sentences short. Like this. Try reading sentences aloud to see if they're too long. You should be able to read an entire sentence without pausing for a breath. It also helps to display information in charts, tables, bulleted lists and interactive graphics.

Source: Adapted from Jonathan Dube, "A Dozen Online Writing Tips," CyberJournalist.net, November 10, 2000, www.cyberjournalist.net/news/000118_print.php.

The script below is an example of a standard broadcast package script. After you read it, we'll use the steps outlined above to convert the copy to a Web story.

Anchor introduction:

NEIGHBORS SAY IT HAPPENS ALL THE TIME. THIS AFTERNOON PHOENIX POLICE DISCOVERED A HORSE TRAILER PACKED WITH 79 ILLEGAL IMMIGRANTS, ONE JUST FOUR MONTHS OLD. (Map showing location.) AN OFFICER PATROLLING NEAR 14TH STREET AND POLK AVENUE SPOTTED THE TRAILER AND SAW THE DRIVER TAKE OFF. JAMMED INSIDE—68 ADULTS AND 11 CHILDREN.

Anchor Package Script:

(Bob Brunelle/Business Owner) "It's weekly like I said. You see vans pull in here, drop 'em off, and then the guy drives off and the people just disperse in the neighborhood."

BOB BRUNELLE SAYS HE'S OWNED A DISCOUNT AUTO BUSINESS IN THIS PHOENIX NEIGHBORHOOD FOR 30 YEARS. JUST RECENTLY, HE SAYS HE'S SEEN THIS COMMUNITY BECOME A DUMPING GROUND FOR ILLEGAL IMMIGRANTS.

(Brunelle) "I've called before and told them there was a van in the alley here with a lot of people in it, well, you'll have to contact so-and-so, and by the time they get contacted, the van's gone!"

THIS TIME BRUNELLE DID NOT HAVE TO MAKE A CALL. A PHOENIX POLICE OFFICER SPOTTED THE HORSE TRAILER, INVESTIGATED AND FOUND 79 PEOPLE INSIDE. AFTER TWO DAYS IN AN UN-AIRCONDITIONED TRAILER, EVERYONE WAS THIRSTY AND HUNGRY, BUT NO ONE WAS SERIOUSLY ILL.

(Brunelle) "I'm glad they did something about this. It's too bad there were those two babies in there, they took a hell of a chance."

IMMIGRATION CUSTOMS ENFORCEMENT LOADED EVERYONE ON A BUS, HAULING THEM TO THE TEMPORARY HOLDING FACILITY IN DOWNTOWN PHOENIX. BRUNELLE SAYS HE'S GLAD TO SEE IT.

(Brunelle) "I don't think they'll drop them off in this neighborhood again for awhile."

Anchor tag: AN IMMIGRATIONS CUSTOMS ENFORCEMENT SPOKESPERSON SAYS HE EXPECTS MOST OF THE ILLEGAL IMMIGRANTS TO BE SENT BACK HOME TONIGHT.

Now, let's follow the guidelines set out by Bergman to see what kind of Web story we can create from our package script.

Immigration bust: 79 people packed in horse trailer

An Immigrations Customs Enforcement spokesperson says he expects dozens of illegal immigrants to soon be on their way back home. This afternoon, Phoenix police discovered a horse trailer packed with 79 illegal immigrants, one just four months old. An officer patrolling near 14th Street and Polk Avenue spotted the trailer and saw the driver take off. He found 68 adults and 11 children jammed inside.

Bob Brunelle is a business owner in the neighborhood. He says this incident is nothing really new. "It's weekly like I said. You see vans pull in here, drop 'em off, and then the guy drives off and the people just disperse in the neighborhood," said Brunelle.

Brunelle says he's owned a discount auto business in the neighborhood for 30 years, but just recently, he says the community has become a dumping ground for illegal immigrants.

"I've called before and told them there was a van in the alley here with a lot of people in it, well, you'll have to contact so-and-so, and by the time they get contacted, the van's gone," said Brunelle.

This time Brunelle did not have to make a call. A Phoenix police officer spotted the horse trailer, investigated and found the 79 people inside. After two days in an un-air-conditioned trailer, everyone was thirsty and hungry, but no one was seriously ill.

"I'm glad they did something about this. It's too bad there were those two babies in there, they took a hell of a chance," said Brunelle.

Immigration Customs Enforcement loaded everyone on a bus, hauling them to the temporary holding facility in downtown Phoenix. Brunelle said he was glad to see it, "I don't think they'll drop them off in this neighborhood again for awhile."

That actually took about 12 minutes to rewrite and spell check, but we're left with a credible story that pulls together the anchor intro, package script and tag into a solid textual presentation.

Even so, Lost Remote's Bergman says he now believes it's better to start from scratch every time you write a Web story. He thinks it's easier to write a more effective Web story if you start with a fresh page and do a complete rewrite. Whichever approach you use, these text versions of your TV stories should be a point of pride for you as a journalist—if your name is on it, you'll want it to be as good as it can be.

WEB HEADLINE WRITERS WANTED

Now that you've learned how to prepare text versions of your stories for the Web, you need to make sure that people are actually going to read them! Headlines play a critically im-

WEB HEADLINES

Charlie Meyerson is a senior Web producer for ChicagoTribune.com. He and his colleagues have come up with a list of recommendations for creating what they believe are effective Web headlines.

1. Place the most interesting word or phrase as close as possible to the start of the headline.

2. Avoid use of proper names except for the very famous and well-known.

3. Don't rule out simple, direct headlines that say exactly what the story is about.

4. Questions can work, for example, "Who Was Deep Throat?"

5. "How-to" or "Why" headlines may be effective.

6. Directly address the user, for example, "Check state's list for your name."

portant role on the Web. Just as in newspapers, people often make decisions on whether or not to read an online story on the basis of the headline. But headlines do function in a slightly different way online than they do in a newspaper. A clever layout that includes a photo with a caption, a headline and a subhead may work just fine in print, but this arrangement may fall flat on the Web. For broadcast journalists, writing headlines may be something you learned a little about in a print reporting class, but you probably don't feel like you're much of an expert. This next section looks at how to write effective online headlines and summaries.

The best headlines are straightforward, using action verbs and indicating exactly what the story is about. Remember, Web users are often skimming for information, and they want to know what they're getting into before clicking on a headline to read the complete story.

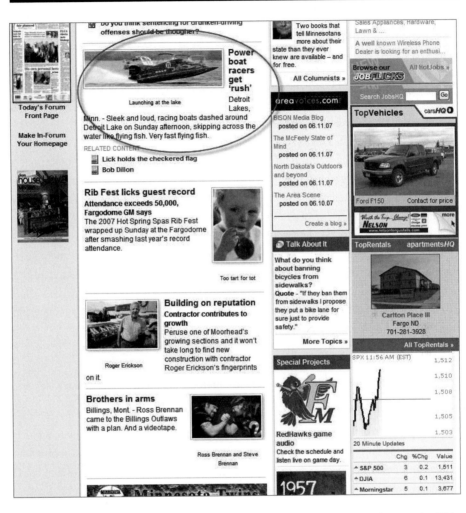

What's the "news" in this story? Is it simply a feature story about powerboat racing? We can't really tell from what was posted here on the Fargo Forum newspaper site.

Source: Courtesy of IN-FORUM.com.

In addition to being the founder and editor of LostRemote.com, Cory Bergman is the director of digital media at KING-TV in Seattle, Wash. To give you an idea of how important a headline can be, Bergman says he's seen the number of people clicking on a story double when a poor headline was replaced with something more specifically designed for the Web.

Online producers at the Richmond Times-Dispatch are well aware that headlines matter. The newspaper headline over a story about a football game that Virginia Tech lost to Auburn read, "Maroon & Blue." It was meant to be a clever reference to Tech's team color (maroon) and the fans' feelings (blue), but it wouldn't have worked online. So the newspaper's Web producers changed the headline to "Va. Tech falls to Auburn despite 4th-quarter burst." The more literal headline tells the online reader exactly what this story is about.

For that same reason, you'll need to be careful using the first sentence or two of your story as a summary below the headline. What might work well as an anecdotal lead in your print or broadcast story may very well fail as a story summary on the Web. As a good multimedia journalist, you will need to make sure that you've written a headline and a summary that will help Web users to know exactly what your story is about, rather than risk confusing them and losing them.

For the powerboat race story discussed on the previous page, your Web summary and headline might look something like this:

Headline: Powerboat Races Return to Detroit Lakes

Summary: For the first time in more than 10 years, powerboat racers hit the water in the Detroit Lakes "Quake the Lake" event.

The real issue here is that sites that simply republish content from one medium to another are missing the unique characteristics of the Web and failing to take advantage of online journalism's power. Amanda Zamora, world editor for washingtonpost.com, says that headlines and summary blurbs "serve as a gateway between readers and your content. Whether they see the headlines and introductory text on a homepage, a page of search results or a headline only in RSS—if that text isn't relevant to what you are trying to convey or to what they seek, they will move on. Your first objective should be to entice them to open that gate and read your content with accurate, concise and inviting copy."

WEB EXTRAS

In addition to simply rewriting or changing the presentation of information you've gathered for another medium, working with the Web gives you an opportunity to add more or unique

Once you've clicked on the headline, you learn that this is a story about the first power-boat race in Detroit Lakes in more than a decade. A good Web headline and summary would have made that clear.

Source: Courtesy of IN-FORUM.com.

information that will enhance what's been aired or published. We call this additional or unique information "Web extras," and we break them down into three broad categories.

Provide Additional Content

As we discussed in Chapter 1, in a strong multimedia story, each platform supplements the others with unique information. These Web extras offer a way for journalists to include content that they had to cut from a broadcast or print story to save time or space or to keep their story tightly focused. For example, you might interview four or five people for a story and wind up using quotes or sound bites from only three. The Web allows and, in fact, encourages you to use the content that wound up on the cutting-room floor. You can simply rewrite your story to include the fresh voices or use clips from the interviews that didn't appear in your original piece. You can even produce a sidebar element for the Web to supplement your print or broadcast story.

Let's say you have written a piece on the opening day of the state fair. Your story is supposed to be an overview of the event, but while you're at the fairground, you meet a fascinating corn dog vendor. He's been coming to your state fair for 60 years with no plans to retire. Since you can't do the story justice in your overview, you choose to write a profile piece for the Web instead. You have now taken advantage of the power of convergence—you are providing unique but related content on more than one platform.

As we mentioned earlier in this chapter, providing additional content can also be as simple as including links to relevant Web sites or documents or even to your past stories on related topics.

Produce Original Web Content

This is where the true multimedia journalist shines. In more and more news organizations, reporters or photojournalists are encouraged to produce content exclusively for the Web—creating additional types of Web extras. For example, Bill Ward is a print reporter who covered the 2006 Olympics for the Tampa Tribune. He took a small video camera with him so he could capture some of the sights and sounds of the hoopla surrounding the event. He ended up producing a series of short vignettes for the paper's Web partner, Tampa Bay Online (www.tbo.com). The online stories featured content such as a tour of Turin, the Olympic host city, some particularly wacky Dutch fans, a behind-the-scenes look at the Olympic Village and other details that were not included in his more traditional print stories. The online content gave avid Olympics fans access to information they were not getting anywhere else.

There are many instances in which photojournalists have used the Web to tell powerful stories though slide shows of still photos on subjects that were not included in the paper or on a newscast.

We'll talk more about producing original multimedia content, including blogs, maps and webcasts, in Chapter 8.

Produce Web Interactives

Journalists with few or no Web technical skills can create much of what is posted on the Web. However, some of the most creative news content being produced for the Web does require technical knowledge. We've mentioned the tremendous potential of interactivity on the Web and some of the most sophisticated Web extra content is called just that—an interactive. Interactives allow users to enter or select information and receive customized responses. For example, during the 2004 hurricane season, the Orlando Sun-Sentinel newspaper site created an interactive that allowed users to create their own hurricanes. Users made choices concerning location of the storm, water temperature and wind speed, and with each decision the storm took on different characteristics. The hurricane interactive provided an entertaining way for people to learn critical information about these storms, how they form and what makes some so powerful. The average online journalist might not be able to create such an elaborate interactive after coming up with the idea, but partnering with an expert or a team of experts could make it happen!

The goal for you as a multimedia journalist should be to stay current with what's going on with the Web and interactivity. Stay on top of the technology and the techniques being used to create a valuable user experience on the best Web sites. You can do that by checking out award-winning Web sites, such as those honored by the Online News Association, the Radio-Television News Directors Association, Editor & Publisher magazine and several others. In addition, there are Web sites devoted to online journalism, such as www.cyberjournalist.net, which links to some of the best work in the industry. In Chapter 8, we'll explore various types of interactive content and how they can be applied to enhance your multimedia storytelling.

TAKING IT HOME

For several years, as the online news audience grew, there was a lot of hand wringing in newsrooms. Some experts asserted that print would soon be dead, and that traditional over-the-air news broadcasts might not be too far behind. While that may eventually be true, traditional news outlets now expect to ensure their survival by building new audiences and finding new sources of revenue online.

Research indicates they're making some progress. According to the State of the News Media 2007 by the Project for Excellence in Journalism, the Internet is the only part of the mainstream news business that is not losing audience, and newspaper sites are growing faster than others.[5] The RTNDA/Ball State University survey in 2007 found that 97.1 percent of television stations had Web sites and many are hiring people specifically to staff them. On average, television stations have 1.99 full-time and 1.78 part-time employees identified as Web staff.[6]

For those embarking on a career in journalism today, all this likely means there will be job opportunities in online news. So today's journalists must have a solid understanding of the Web and how people are using it for news consumption, and they must apply that knowledge to their writing and storytelling online. It's no longer enough to simply cut and paste content from another medium onto a Web site and expect users to accept what's there. At a minimum, your Web stories should be formatted to fit online users' expectations when it comes to style—from language, to paragraph length to headlines. Writing for the Web is different from writing for broadcast or print, and good multimedia journalists embrace the online style.

TALKING POINTS

1. Think about your favorite news Web site. What do you like best about it? Log on to it to see if you can find any evidence that the site's producers are trying to take advantage of the ways in which people use Web sites. List at least three things the site is doing well and three things the site could do better to capitalize on Web site usability.

2. Go online to your favorite news Web site. Find a headline that looks intriguing enough for you to click on it and read the story. Was the headline true to the story's content? What was it about the headline that enticed you to click through? Is the sub-

ject matter inherently interesting to you? How did the headline writer make sure that someone interested in this topic would click on it? Can you suggest a better headline that might invite more people to read the story?

3. Brainstorm a list of three Web extras for a story about your school system's plan to do away with recess in the elementary schools. Your TV story includes interviews with the superintendent, a teacher, a parent and some kids outside playing during recess. What could you do to enhance this story online?

eLEARNING OPPORTUNITIES

For chapter exercises, practice tools and additional resources, go to the interactive online workbook at http://college.cqpress.com/advancingthestory. You'll find:

- SKILL BUILDING: Convert a standard television story script into a Web version and then review what the reporter for the story actually published online.

- DISCOVER: Examine expert analysis of what makes a good Web headline and summary. Learn more about how to create successful headlines and summaries on your own.

- ONGOING STORY: Write a Web version of this story, using the techniques outlined in the chapter you've just read. See one approach to telling this story online.

- EXPLORE: Visit Web sites for new research on the way people use the Web for news information and more great Web writing advice.

8 PRODUCING FOR THE WEB

Whether you plan to work as a Web producer or as a broadcast or print journalist who also produces content for the Web, it will be essential for you to understand what it takes to produce a compelling online news site. This chapter introduces you to some of the interactive tools available and the critical skill of planning for a multiplatform package, especially one that might involve a partnership with journalists from more than one medium.

Very few of today's online journalists will tell you that they've always dreamed of working with the Web. Fewer still will likely tell you that they specifically went to school to learn how to work as an online journalist. Just as in the early days of television news when many radio journalists made the switch into an exciting new world of words, sound and pictures, online news sites have been staffed primarily by people trained as journalists in another medium or by those who understand the technical side of the production process.

Even today when journalism practitioners and educators talk about preparing future journalists for jobs in the online arena, they still make some distinction between the skills needed to be a good multimedia journalist and the skills needed to work as a Web producer. Throughout this text, we've been sharing tools and strategies that any journalist might use to produce strong content across media platforms. But those of you who are excited about the possibilities of working more specifically as online journalists need to have a slightly different skill set based on all of the fundamentals you've been learning.

THE SKILL SET

What does it take to be a successful online journalist? In November 2006, the Online News Association released the results of a study on the skills needed in online news organizations. It's one of the first quantitative studies done regarding the skills needed to do the job.

Survey respondents included both managers and producers for online news sites who were asked to rate the importance of 35 job skills. According to the report, managers were defined as those who manage operations or content production, or both. Managers were asked to rate each skill based on whether they believed it was an essential requirement for a job applicant. Producers were defined as those who "create, edit or package online content," and they were specifically asked to rank the skills based on how often they use them on the job.

Four skills topped the list for both managers and producers, though not in the same order.

The need to multitask, communicate, work under pressure and pay attention to detail is fairly universal—in fact, there aren't many jobs in journalism that would not require these skills. However, the survey revealed other skills that are clearly important for online journalists, including editing and copyediting skills. Web producers stated that they used the skills of headline writing, story combining and shortening and caption writing for the Web frequently or every day. In earlier chapters we've highlighted some of these skills, par-

TABLE 8.1 SKILLS FOR ONLINE JOURNALISTS

Managers	Percent considering it requirement for job	Producers	Percent using this skill frequently/ every day
Multitasking ability	91.9	Attention to detail	94.9
Attention to detail	90.7	Ability to work under pressure	94.9
Communication skills	85.2	Communication skills	94.9
Ability to work under time pressure	84.3	Multitasking ability	94.4

Source: C. Max Magee, "The Roles of Journalists in Online Newsrooms," Medill School of Journalism, released by Online News Association, November 1, 2006, http://journalist.org/news/archives/MedillOnlineJobSurvey-final.pdf.

ticularly headline and caption writing. Both producers and news managers emphasized the importance for online journalists of news judgment and an understanding of grammar and style, skills that are critically important for any journalist, of course.

One of the most interesting findings of the survey dealt with online production tools. With so many software programs and a variety of standards and tools that journalists could learn, it's difficult to determine which are essential. The Web producers who responded to the survey said the emphasis should be on three skills:

- Use of a content management system

- HTML

- Photoshop

A content management system (CMS), according to Webopedia, is "software that enables you to add and/or manipulate content on a Web site."[1] Many of you have probably logged on to or sent e-mail via Blackboard, a content management system common at many universities. When instructors post an announcement or a link to an assignment, they are using a content management tool whether they know it or not. A software package called Adobe Contribute is another commonly used CMS, and many news organizations develop their own content management systems for their Web sites. All of these systems are generally quite similar and designed to be user friendly, making it easy for people to post simple text, video or audio files and to create links to additional content. Web producers obviously learn how to use the software to a much fuller extent, but every multimedia journalist should have some familiarity with what a CMS is and how to use it.

You've probably at least heard the term HTML at some point, even if you're not entirely sure what it means. HTML is an acronym for hypertext markup language. At its most basic level, Web producers use HTML to create documents that can be accessed, viewed and used on the Web. HTML also allows Web producers to create simple links to other Web pages, and it's one of the tools used to develop more complicated interactive features, such as games, polls and quizzes. A typical multimedia journalist probably won't need to know HTML, at least for now. Content management systems make it possible for a broadcast or print journalist to use simple cut-and-paste templates to post Web content. But anyone considering a career as an online journalist should make the effort to learn HTML.

Finally, the Web producers surveyed said that Adobe Photoshop is another essential online production tool. Web producers use HTML at its most basic level to create documents, still pictures and graphics. There are other software packages available, but Photoshop is the most common in the industry. Again, it certainly would not hurt the average multimedia journalist to learn Photoshop, but right now it probably isn't essential to the job; however, most online journalists will tell you the program has become an integral part of their work. Journalists who have made the transition from print or broadcast to working primarily online say it's important that you don't let the technical aspects of the job scare you.

Online producer Candice Combs is a good example. In 1999, Combs graduated from college and started working as a print reporter. By 2006, she had moved into online journalism at TriCities.com, the Web partner for WJHL-TV in Johnson City, Tenn., and the Bristol Herald Courier in Bristol, Va. "They brought me on solely as a content generator, knowing that I had minimal Web experience," said Combs.

Combs said she's learning the technology as she goes, but it's her journalism background that's helping her succeed. When live ammunition caught fire at a local firing range, Combs knew exactly what to do. "I grabbed a Web production person who can shoot video and we headed out to the scene," she said. "He started taking video of the blaze, and I grabbed three people who had been inside when the fire started and began interviewing them on paper. A photographer from the TV station showed up and asked me to do on-camera interviews as well. I did a brief story for the 6 o'clock news and then sat down to write my story for the Web. The next day the paper ran the story with my information, too."

Combs said she's seen the Web go from an afterthought to something that's at the forefront of journalism. She encourages young journalists to learn as much as they can about online journalism. "It's the only medium that's growing," said Combs.

ONLINE TUTORIALS

W3C is an international consortium working to develop standards, protocols and guidelines "to ensure long-term growth of the web." Check out World Wide Web Consortium's 10-minute guide for newcomers to HTML at www.w3.org/markup/guide.

Dozens of tutorials are available to help guide you through the use of Photoshop. Some of the best come from the software maker at www.adobe.com/designcenter/tutorials/.

There are also Web sites that aggregate tutorials for a variety of multimedia tasks. MediaCollege.com is one free resource providing tips and tutorials for working with video, audio, graphics and more. You can find the site at www.mediacollege.com.

CONTINUOUS PRODUCTION MODE

Whether your primary job is to produce your news organization's Web site or you are a TV or print journalist who must produce multimedia stories, too, you need to realize that the Web is changing the news production cycle in many newsrooms around the country.

Most local newspapers publish just one print edition a day. Most local television newsrooms produce an average of about 3.5 hours of news each weekday, at specific times. But an online news site is more like an all-news radio station that's staffed around the clock—always on, with the potential to operate in what could be called a continuous production mode.

What does that mean for you as a multimedia journalist or someone hoping to become a Web producer? It means changing the way you think about presenting the information you gather.

Breaking News versus Developing Stories

A significant amount of research indicates that breaking news is one of the major motivators for people to log on to a news Web site. During the day, when most people are at work or school, it's often easier to access a computer than a television set to find out what's going on.

Many news organizations have written plans for how to cover breaking news, and at least some of them include a section on how to get important breaking news stories posted on the news organization's Web site. Many sites have special banners and sections of the home page that direct users to these breaking stories.

What is breaking news, anyway? According to researcher Andrea Miller of Louisiana State University, traditionally, "breaking or non-routine news is defined as hard, unplanned news that takes the newsroom by surprise, such as a plane crash or earthquake. Breaking news cannot be predicted." [2] But most television news organizations have expanded (some say distorted) that definition to include stories that simply contain new or recently obtained information.

On the Web, it's essential to provide new information and constant updates on developing stories, however you label them. Amanda Zamora, world editor for washingtonpost.com, says that multimedia journalists and Web producers should "recognize that if people are reading the Web, it generally means they expect the latest information available."

What that means for you is that even a predictable story update may have value on the Web. For example, let's say you're attending a regularly scheduled transportation board meeting where you know they plan to release a list of the roads slated for repair in the next six months. For your television news story, you plan to talk to some of the people affected by the announcement, including those who are getting their streets repaired and those who are not. If you wait until you have done all of that reporting before you post a brief story with the list of roads on your station's Web site, you've missed a great opportunity to keep your audience informed about a developing story.

Strategies for Constant Updates

Though the Web is always on, most news sites get most of their traffic during the day, and specifically during working hours. But most reporters tend to produce Web content after they've completed their TV stories or filed their print articles—generally after Web traffic has died down for the day. So, some news organizations and individuals have developed strategies to provide more frequent postings to the Web.

Amy Lehtonen, managing editor for WCNC.com, says they had to set some new deadlines for the reporters at WCNC-TV. "Reporters are now Web journalists as well, so they are filing their stories for the Web site, and we are setting Web deadlines for them based on our hit traffic. The majority of the users log on at 8 o'clock in the morning and they leave shortly after 4 o'clock in the afternoon, so we're definitely serving at-work users," said Lehtonen.

WCNC has set Web deadlines for the morning at 7:30 and 11:30, then there's an afternoon deadline and an evening deadline as well. At these points during the day, reporters working on stories are asked to file a Web version based on the information they've gathered so far. In some newsrooms, reporters don't file directly to the Web, but they're expected to call in a new story or a story update and have a Web producer or another newsroom employee post the content.

Web producers themselves have developed updating strategies as well. Andrew Pulskamp, the Web producer at WGAL-TV in Lancaster, Pa., seldom waits for a reporter to come to him with information. He listens to what he's hearing from the assignment desk and the producers as reporters call in to update them on their stories. He reads scripts and watches the station's own broadcasts, particularly the noon newscast, and writes updates from what he sees on the air. He even watches as crews feed in video and sound bites from the field and then posts content based on what he pulls from the feeds.

These strategies might not work in every newsroom, but news organizations are looking for journalists who know how to keep the Web top of mind and how to incorporate frequent Web updating into their workdays.

Accuracy Matters

One of the things that worries some journalists about the continuous production mode is that it gives them less time to double-check information, so the chance of reporting an error is greater. That's an important concern. If you don't have enough verified information to write or call in a Web story, you absolutely need to make that clear to your news managers. They're likely to agree that missing a Web update in order to make sure you have your facts straight is a worthwhile trade-off.

A great deal of Web work is done by a single individual. A reporter on a weekend shift might post a story without anyone else reviewing it. A Web producer might watch a feed coming in and not realize that it's file video. If your newsroom doesn't have an approval process for Web content, it's imperative that you develop one on your own. Ask someone whose news judgment you trust to double-check your story for you. One more set of eyes should significantly reduce your risk of getting the story wrong.

Producing Webcasts and Podcasts

The continuous production mode means you might also be asked to produce short audio or video newscasts for the Web—often called podcasts and vodcasts or webcasts. These online mini-newscasts allow TV stations to continue "broadcasting" even when they aren't on the air with a regular full-length newscast. A fair number of newspapers have also begun producing podcasts and webcasts as well, giving them a chance to compete with traditional broadcast outlets.

WSOC-TV in Charlotte, N.C., produces a brief Web update called Eyewitness News On Demand at least four times a day. News director Robin Whitmeyer says the webcasts are put together by newscast producers who write the copy and edit the video for one of the station's anchors.

When preparing copy for these online newscasts, a series of several short stories tends to work best. Remember, your online audience is using these primarily as an update on the news of the day, so including packages will be rare.

Remember, you also need to think about the way that video works online. As we indicated in Chapter 3, researchers in the area of Web usability have studied the presentation of video online. In general, they've found that video clips work best when they're short, and they also say it would be wrong to assume that an online story with video is always better than one without.[3]

BLOGGING

The online medium gives journalists many new ways of telling stories and providing information to the audience. One of the most popular new story tools is the blog.

The word blog is short for Web log, traditionally defined as an online diary that is frequently updated and often includes links to additional material and interactivity. The Web site Technorati.com measures the popularity of blogs based on the number of unique links to a blog over the previous six months. In June 2007, "Boing Boing: A Directory of Wonderful Things," was one of the most popular blogs in the world with more than 20,000 sites linking to it. On the Technorati Web site, Boing Boing is described as "a weblog of cultural curiosities and interesting technologies."

Blog use and creation by the public has been growing. Technorati is now tracking more than 50 million blogs worldwide, and the site's founder, David Sifry, says the blogosphere in 2006 was more than 100 times bigger than it had been just three years earlier. He reports that on average there are more than two new blogs created each second of every day.[4]

However, creating a blog is just part of the process. There is no accurate way to determine how many of Technorati's 50 million blogs are active blogs. (An active blog can be defined as a blog that has been updated in the past six months.) Blogs are sometimes created in conjunction with specific events but remain posted long after the event and the updates are over. Sometimes people create blogs and then lose interest in them. There are many reasons why the blogosphere's numbers may be inflated, but you can be sure that blogging is an important phenomenon for a multimedia journalist to understand.

In terms of blog use in the United States, a survey by the Pew Internet & American Life Project provides some perspective. In 2005, Pew reported that blog readership stood at 27 percent of Internet users; and 12 percent of Internet users had posted comments or other material on blogs. Still, in 2005, 62 percent of Internet users did not know what a blog was.[5]

Though many blogs include nothing more than opinion or a rehash of what others are reporting, journalists can use blogs to provide news and information to the audience in a variety of ways. On a news Web site, one reporter might be writing about a political campaign and including additional information like fundraising totals that did not make it into the TV or print story, as WHO-TV's Dave Price did during the 2006 elections. On the same site, a popular news anchor might decide to share what it's like to live with cancer and invite viewers to share their own stories.

Blogs can be used in breaking news situations as a way to allow multiple users to post information quickly. For example, during hurricane coverage, WVEC-TV in Norfolk, Va., used its Web site to disseminate information from reporters and citizens alike.

boingboing
A DIRECTORY OF WONDERFUL THINGS

suggest a link | defeat censorware | rss | archives | t-shirts | digital emporium | podcast feed | mark | cory | david | xeni | john

Search Boing Boing

VIEW A RECENT DAY: AUGUST 17 | AUGUST 16 | AUGUST 15 | PREVIOUS DAYS | BY MONTH AND YEAR

Wednesday, August 15, 2007

Liveblogging court hearings: NSA's spying, AT&T's alleged complicity

Over at Wired News Threat Level blog today, Ryan Singel and David Kravets have been liveblogging the U.S. 9th Circuit hearing in San Francisco on the NSA's domestic surveillance program, and AT&T's alleged assistance.

Here's a blow-by-blow from earlier today: Link. The money quote:

> Judge McKeown: "I feel like I'm in Alice and Wonderland."

And here's a snip from Singel's analysis, posted after the hearings:

> While the same three 9th Circuit Appeals Court judges heard arguments in two different spying cases today, they seemed to be two entirely different sets of judges.
>
> When listening to the government attempt to bury, on the grounds of national security, a lawsuit against AT&T for allegedly helping the government engage in a dragnet surveillance program aimed at Americans, the judges expressed dismay that the government and AT&T could not simply show documents proving the surveillance did not exist.
>
> That case relies heavily on company documents provided to the Electronic Frontier Foundation by former AT&T technician

Blogs like Boing Boing can have tremendous impact on traditional media. For example, if a link to a journalist's story is posted here, thousands of people have been known to click through and read that story on a site they might have never visited otherwise.

Source: Retrieved August 19, 2007, from http://boingboing.net/2007/08/15/index.html.

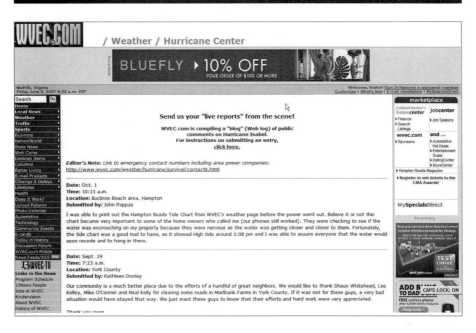

In this example, WVEC was using the blog as a content management system—a way for multiple people to easily share information on a particular topic.

Source: Courtesy of WVEC.com. Retrieved June 11, 2007, from www.wvec.com/blog/isabel.

Obviously, blogs can be a useful coverage tool and a way to engage the audience in a conversation, but they don't usually work well if they are written in the same style as a traditional news story. The washingtonpost.com's Amanda Zamora says that the best blogs have an "authentic and engaging voice." She recommends that reporters think differently when they write a blog: "Instead of writing for someone sitting at a breakfast table, a reporter is catering to someone more immediate—someone who can directly offer feedback, agree or disagree, praise or criticize in a moment."

Some news organizations that do post blogs do not allow users to comment because users might post inappropriate material. Others will post comments, but only after those comments have been reviewed by someone in the news organization. But the primary purpose of reporting in a blog form is to allow for interactivity, so when you are writing a blog, you should expect to keep the conversation going. Be prepared to check for reader comments and respond to them when appropriate.

11 TIPS FOR BETTER BLOGGING

More and more journalists (pro and amateur) are catching on to ways that blogging can enhance their work.

Vince Maher, a lecturer in new media studies at Rhodes University in South Africa, has these 11 tips for managing a good blog entry:

1. A blog entry is a stub [or starter] for conversation.

2. Think about the perspectives of your audience.

3. Write tight headlines that encourage interest.

4. Make points or lists and make them scan-friendly.

5. Link to the context.

6. Quote indirectly and link.

7. Format long documents for print.

8. Never delete anything.

9. Troll the blogosphere for secondary conversation.

10. Be active in your own conversations.

11. Create buzz everywhere.

Source: Vincent Maher, "11 Tips for Managing a Good Blog Entry," vincentmaher.com, October 12, 2006, http://vincentmaher.com/mit/?p=174.

Another important element of blogging is transparency. If you are commenting on something in your blog, make it easy for the reader to see what you're talking about. For example, if you're writing about something reported in the local newspaper, try to link to the article directly. Or, let's say you're covering a story about a new dress code for the local school system. While you're interviewing school staff, the superintendent says something about the need to revitalize local parent-teacher organizations because most of them have few members. You probably wouldn't use that information in your TV story because

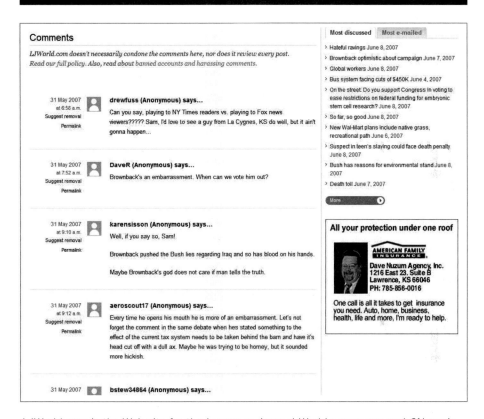

Comments

LJWorld.com doesn't necessarily condone the comments here, nor does it review every post. Read our full policy. Also, read about banned accounts and harassing comments.

31 May 2007
at 6:58 a.m.
Suggest removal
Permalink

drewfuss (Anonymous) says...

Can you say, playing to NY Times readers vs. playing to Fox news viewers????? Sam, I'd love to see a guy from La Cygnes, KS do well, but it ain't gonna happen...

31 May 2007
at 7:52 a.m.
Suggest removal
Permalink

DaveR (Anonymous) says...

Brownback's an embarrassment. When can we vote him out?

31 May 2007
at 9:10 a.m.
Suggest removal
Permalink

karensisson (Anonymous) says...

Well, if you say so, Sam!

Brownback pushed the Bush lies regarding Iraq and so has blood on his hands.

Maybe Brownback's god does not care if man tells the truth.

31 May 2007
at 9:12 a.m.
Suggest removal
Permalink

aeroscout17 (Anonymous) says...

Every time he opens his mouth he is more of an embarrassment. Let's not forget the comment in the same debate when hes stated something to the effect of the current tax system needs to be taken behind the barn and have it's head cut off with a dull ax. Maybe he was trying to be homey, but it sounded more hickish.

31 May 2007

bstew34864 (Anonymous) says...

Most discussed | Most e-mailed

> Hateful ravings June 8, 2007
> Brownback optimistic about campaign June 7, 2007
> Global workers June 8, 2007
> Bus system facing cuts of $450K June 4, 2007
> On the street: Do you support Congress in voting to ease restrictions on federal funding for embryonic stem cell research? June 8, 2007
> So far, so good June 8, 2007
> New Wal-Mart plans include native grass, recreational path June 6, 2007
> Suspect in teen's slaying could face death penalty June 8, 2007
> Bush has reasons for environmental stand June 8, 2007
> Death toll June 7, 2007

More

LJWorld.com is the Web site for the Lawrence Journal-World newspaper and 6News in Lawrence, Kan. In May 2007, a blog entry describing Kansas senator Sam Brownback's views on evolution generated 106 comments.

Source: Courtesy of LJWorld.com. Retrieved June 8, 2007, from http://24.124.1.183/blogs/brownback_report/2007/may/31/brownback.

it doesn't fit your focus. But on your blog, if your newsroom's systems will allow it, you could post that sound bite along with a brief overview of the situation and then ask the blog's readers to comment on the issue.

If you're going to start writing a blog for your news organization, it's a good idea to spend some time reading blogs to get a feel for how they're written. Some large news organizations host dozens of blogs on their sites—often replacing outdated topics with new high-interest content or allowing one reporter to take a break while another gives blogging a shot.

When you're getting a feel for successful blogs, be sure to look at the number and type of comments left by readers. Those posts with a high number of comments obviously caught the readers' attention.

To do a blog well takes time and effort, but it does give you an opportunity to interact with your audience and can potentially make your reporting better. Sometimes the comments can be a good source of story ideas or offer perspectives that you may not have considered previously.

INTERACTIVE TOOLS

Blogging is just one way to create interactivity on a news site. Earlier in the text we talked about creating "clickable" maps or timelines that allow users to click on or scroll over a graphic to get more information about a given topic or location. To create those and other kinds of Web "interactives," you need some specialized skills, such as knowing how to use software programs like Flash or JavaScript. To learn those skills, you might take a course or teach yourself through online tutorials, some of which are included as links on the Web site accompanying this text. Whether you plan to be a Web producer or not, you will want to know a little bit about what's possible in terms of interactivity online.

Searchable Data Sets

Because space on the Web is almost unlimited, news organizations can offer users access to complete sets of data behind the news, like the restaurant inspections list we mentioned in Chapter 1. But data sets are most useful when they're searchable or sortable, which usually requires some work. Even if the data is available electronically, journalists still have to decide how to let users manipulate the data. Should they be able to sort that list of restaurants from cleanest to dirtiest? Or should they be able to search the list by name, location, food type or quality rating?

This type of searchable data set has been used successfully by a number of news organizations. In Spokane, Wash., the Spokesman-Review newspaper created a searchable data set of U.S. fatalities in the Iraq war. For example, if you want a list of all the women who have died serving in the Marines, you simply enter the relevant key words into the search boxes provided, and click enter to see the results. The Web page also includes links to a related blog, current Iraq headlines, a photo gallery and profiles of local servicemen and women.

Blogs allow MSNBC.com to report more fully on certain topics. For example, in June 2007, the site featured the Cosmic Log—a blog written by MSNBC.com science editor Alan Boyle, with daily links about science and space news.

Source: Courtesy of MSNBC.com. Retrieved August 19, 2007, from www.msnbc.msn.com/id/3032105.

ADVANCING THE STORY

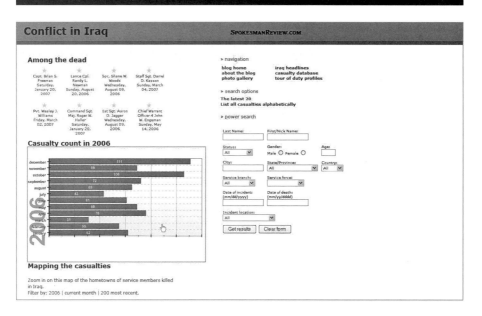

Searchable data sets like this one created by the Spokesman-Review are particularly valuable for stories that will have a long shelf life, something users can access over time and use repeatedly.

Source: Courtesy of Spokesman-Review.com. Retrieved April 20, 2007, from www.spokesmanreview.com/iraq/database/casualties_search.asp.

Creating and updating this kind of database is time-consuming, but once you've created a template you can provide a valuable tool for the audience and you can use it over and over again for a variety of stories.

Clickable Maps and Interactive Timelines

Clickable maps and interactive timelines allow you to put information in perspective. WCNC.com, for example, created a timeline and clickable map for a story about a series of armed robberies in Charlotte, N.C. Because the story involved seven different locations, it was difficult to give WCNC-TV viewers a good sense of the criminals' path in the TV version of the story. On the station's Web site, however, producers were able to post a timeline on which each incident was linked to an icon on a map. Viewers could get a good sense of the progression of the crime spree by clicking on each link.

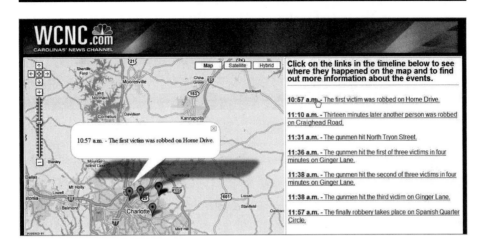

WCNC-TV in Charlotte, N.C., routinely uses maps on its Web site (WCNC.com) to help viewers see the big picture in a complicated story.

Source: Courtesy of WCNC.com. Retrieved April 20, 2007, from www.wcnc.com/includes/googlemaps/022007/ 022007-robbery.html.

Online Calculators

Creating an online calculator for a story can take a mundane discussion of a new tax rate and turn it into a fun, interactive learning process. Several news organizations have used calculators as a way of explaining stories about money in a more personal way. For example, WISH-TV in Indianapolis, Ind., posted a "College Planning Calculator" to help students and parents figure out exactly how much money it will take to pay for school.

When a user enters numbers into the boxes provided, the online calculator begins tabulating and comes up with a personalized, estimated cost.

Polls, Questionnaires and Quizzes

You've likely seen Web polls that ask you to answer a question or series of questions and then allow you to click to see the current poll results. This works well for stories about topics on which people have strong opinions. For example, you might ask people whether school uniforms are a good idea for students or not. This is one of the easiest types of Web

Creating online calculators for important stories can help people learn more about the way a particular story will affect them directly. Often these types of Web extras will be used by people long after the original stories on the topic are forgotten.

Source: Courtesy of WISH-TV.com. Retrieved April 20, 2007, from www.wishtv.com/Global/link.asp?L=212103.

interactives to create, but beware: The information should not be used as a scientific representation of how people feel on a given topic. So, if the Web poll shows most of the respondents are opposed to school uniforms, you can't be sure that most people in the community are opposed to the uniforms without doing a more scientific survey. It's a good idea to include a disclaimer about the validity of any poll you report to be sure that people know how to evaluate the information.

Questionnaires and quizzes are also fairly self-explanatory. If you're doing a story about anorexia, for example, you might post a quiz that would help people determine if they're at risk for an eating disorder. The National Association of Anorexia Nervosa and Associated Disorders provides just such a quiz online. News organizations often pull quizzes or questionnaires from expert sources like this one. If you use a quiz or a questionnaire from another source, be sure to provide appropriate credit.

Interactive Storytelling

Creating games and other complicated interactive online content takes a great deal of expertise and time, but the results can be impressive. In July 2006, the San Jose Mercury News ran a series on the conflicts of interest between medical companies and Stanford University School of Medicine researchers. To help tell that story online, the paper built a "you be the researcher" game. The game allows you to pretend you are a medical researcher and forces you to make the kinds of choices they have to make in order to get funding to explore an idea.

This type of interactive storytelling is generally used only on major projects for which a news organization commits a great deal of time and resources.

PLANNING THE MULTIMEDIA STORY

All of the skills and elements we've described so far come together in multimedia stories, whether you are working on your own or with others. Good multimedia stories require an understanding of what each medium does best. You need to gather more and different content for your stories than you would for a single medium, and you need to think about how the execution of the story will be different on each platform.

News organizations are always looking for ways to make important news more relevant and engaging. By creating this online game, the San Jose Mercury News hoped to entice readers into learning more about the subject of conflicts of interest in medical research.

Source: Courtesy of MercuryNews.com. Retrieved April 20, 2007, from http://mercurynewsphoto.com/conflict/main.html.

Jane Stevens, who teaches multimedia journalism at the University of California–Berkeley Graduate School of Journalism, divides multimedia stories into two categories: reporter-driven and producer- or editor-driven.[6]

According to Stevens, a reporter-driven story is "usually a daily beat story, a feature or part of an investigative series or special project." The reporter or reporter-photographer team gathers all the elements of the multimedia story—everything from video and audio to the information that will go into text and graphics. The story is in the reporter's head and that's who "makes the basic decisions on how to assemble the pieces that make up the whole."

In contrast, the editor- or producer-driven story is generally breaking news or a special project. The editor or producer assigns individuals to produce pieces of the story and may ask a photojournalist for stills and video, send one reporter to do interviews in the field and another to gather information by phone and assign a graphic artist to produce maps or illustrations.

In either situation, you'll want to make sure you have an idea of what you want your finished multimedia story to look like as you proceed with reporting and producing it.

Review Your Plan

There are few stories that don't evolve and change over the course of your reporting. You may have started out doing a story about rising home prices and then discovered a bigger story—that the city was backing out of a plan to build a number of subsidized apartments for low-income families. Your reporting on home prices might be saved for another day or used as a Web element if you've already collected enough material to create one.

You will want to review the information you've gathered in your reporting to be sure you have what you need to produce unique content for each medium involved. We've said it before—multimedia will not be as effective as it could be if you are simply doing the exact same story on more than one media platform. In our housing story example, you may have just what you need—both a solid story on the city's decision to drop its plan to build the low-income apartments and a Web-only element on housing prices in your area.

Storyboards

In Chapter 6, we talked about making a list of all the video, audio, still photos and other multimedia elements you've gathered as part of your story plan, but some multimedia journalists also like to use storyboards to help them plan their stories. They draw sketches to illustrate what their content will look like online.

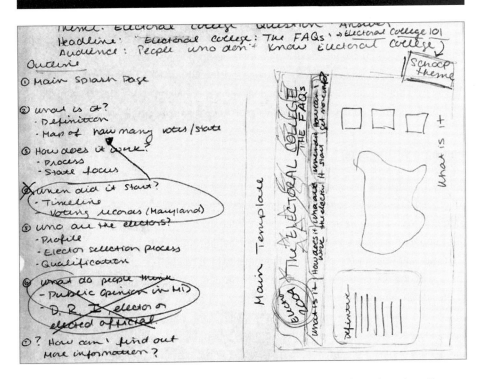

The storyboard above was used to rough out a plan for a Web project about how the Electoral College works. It includes an outline of the content as well as a sketch of how that content might appear on the page.

Source: Courtesy of Lauren Eshkenazi, BaltimoreSun.com.

Storyboards help you think through the pieces of your story and can make it easier for you to decide how to use the information, video, audio and stills you've gathered most effectively. You should start by listing every element you want to include in your multimedia package, and then think about how to present the information in a way that will engage your audience.

For example, some pictures have much greater impact when you have more time to study them. For the fifth anniversary of September 11, the Atlanta Journal-Constitution created a slide show that rotated between photos shot on September 11, 2001, and present-day images from the same scene. The comparison was much more striking in still photos than it would have been in moving video.

Ashley Wells, senior interactive producer at MSNBC.com, believes too many online news sites forget the importance of storytelling and don't engage users in a way that helps them relate to the story. "Interactive stories that incessantly nag the user to 'click to continue' become cumbersome," said Wells. Instead, he said he wants to "make them forget the mouse is there. When I want them to use it, I'll tell them why and show them where."[7] As you are thinking about what content you will use online, keep in mind that the goal is storytelling here as well, just as it is in your broadcast or print piece.

Putting It All Together

As you might imagine, storyboards are used most often for major multimedia projects, which can take days or sometimes even weeks or months to plan and execute. But many of the same concepts we've just discussed can be used to plan the content you would produce online in conjunction with a daily broadcast or print story. Once you've listed all the elements you want to report and have decided which medium is the best fit for the content, you continue on to produce your TV or print story and to post your own Web content or provide the online content to a Web producer.

At the Lawrence Journal-World in Lawrence, Kan., reporter Chad Lawhorn, included several examples of multimedia enhancements when his story about access to health care was posted online. The story featured links to a relevant study on health insurance in the United States and a report prepared by a local hospital regarding its efforts to provide more health care access. The online version also provided a place for readers to post comments, and it included an audio interview with one of the key players in the story. In this example, use of the Web allowed the reporter to provide far more information and interactivity than ever would have been possible in the newspaper alone.

THE MULTIMEDIA TEAM

Teamwork is another important skill for online journalists. Teamwork is considered essential by more than 80 percent of both online news site managers and producers, according to the Online News Association study.[8] Some multimedia projects are developed across platforms by teams of journalists from different media. For example, a television station might work in partnership with a newspaper and a jointly operated Web site to produce stories for all three. In this situation, the team members would each have expertise in broadcast, print or online, and the group would go through a three-step process of determining content, sharing resources and developing a presentation to arrive at the finished products for each platform.

TRADE TOOLS

STORYBOARDING QUESTIONS

The following tips are excerpted from the Multimedia Reporting and Convergence Web site created by Jane Stevens:

- Decide what pieces of the story work best in video. Video is the best medium to depict action, to take a reader to a place central to the story or to hear and see a person central to the story.

- Decide what pieces of the story work best in still photos. Still photos are the best medium for emphasizing a strong emotion, for staying with an important point in a story or to create a particular mood. They're often more dramatic and don't go by as quickly as video.

- Does the audio work best with video, or will it be combined with still photos? Good audio makes still photos and video seem more intense and real. Avoid using audio alone.

- What part of the story works best in graphics? Animated graphics show how things work. Graphics go where cameras can't go, into human cells or millions of miles into space.

- What part of the story belongs in text? Text can be used to describe the history of a story (sometimes in combination with photos), to describe a process (sometimes in combination with graphics) or to provide first-person accounts of an event.

Source: Jane Stevens, "Storyboarding," University of California–Berkeley Graduate School of Journalism, n.d., http://journalism.berkeley.edu/multimedia/course/storyboarding.

Determine Unique Content

The first step in a cross-platform project is to decide what kind of content works best in each medium. Let's use coverage of the first day of school as an illustration. A typical story might feature a child going to school for the very first time. The TV reporter might arrange to be at the child's home as soon as she wakes up in the morning, then follow her as she puts on her new school clothes and chatters excitedly about her new adventure and then watch as the child's mother gets tears in her eyes as the little girl walks off to the bus stop.

Using that same content to create excellent profiles for both a TV and a print story would not be the strongest use of multimedia—remember, the best multimedia offers the audience complementary information on multiple platforms. So, consider this alternative. Let's say the print reporter also talked to a longtime elementary school teacher about the funniest things that have ever happened on the first day of school and then included some statistics on the number of new students in the system. On the online front, the Web producer featured a discussion board with a local child psychiatrist about easing first-day jitters. Now, you have a multimedia project in which each individual medium offers something unique to the story—the content plays to each medium's strengths. The broadcast piece elicits emotion, the print piece adds depth and online offers interactivity.

Communicate and Share Resources

To ensure the success of any multimedia project, it's obvious that there must be a great deal of communication among the multimedia partners. The reporters and editors for each medium must define for one another the content that each platform will include. Because most stories evolve and change during the reporting process, it's important that the communication be ongoing.

Members of the broadcast team might, for example, decide they need to add some hard news information into the anchor introduction to the student profile package. They may want to add information about the number of new students entering the school system. At that point, the print team needs to be alerted. Why? The enrollment information was going to be a point of differentiation for the print story. There will now have to be additional discussion among the partners to determine whether it makes sense for the print reporter to share enrollment data and to decide on other unique content elements to be featured in the print story.

When a multimedia team works together well, it maximizes resources. The broadcast reporter will no longer have to dig up the data on school enrollments because the print reporter has already done it, or vice versa. This approach gives each journalist involved in reporting for the project the chance to help the others and save time. In another example, the broadcast reporter may have worked with an excellent child psychiatrist in the past and is willing to pass along that doctor's name to the online editor, saving that editor time in trying to track down someone for the online chat component of the project. This sharing of resources is an extremely important part of successful multimedia teamwork.

Develop a Presentation Plan

Our first-day-of-school multimedia project provides a good illustration of why it's so important to think through the timing for publication of each portion of the project. In our scenario, the television station is doing a student profile, the newspaper is focusing on a teacher and our online partner is giving the audience a chance to ask questions of a child psychiatrist. It's only logical that the online partner take the lead by publishing the first installment of the project—the feedback from the psychiatrist is only useful if you're offering it before parents and children have to deal with those first-day jitters. However, it won't always be that easy. Sometimes when a group of convergence partners are working on an important investigative piece or breaking an important story, every medium wants to go first. That's when the real negotiations begin!

Because the Web is "always on," it may make sense to get a brief version of the story online right off the bat and then promote the additional content coming on TV or in print. Can you grab viewers' attention with television and drive them to the depth in the paper the next day? Or do you publish first in print and show people what you're talking about that night on the TV news? The answer will likely be different for every project, but more and more, news organizations are thinking Web first to leverage the immediacy of this important platform.

Sometimes, despite all your efforts, a multimedia project falls flat for one reason or another. Most often, it's because the content didn't lend itself to execution across multiple platforms. One pitfall you want to avoid is letting one medium succeed at the expense of another. For example, you don't want to delegate all the emotional, people stories to television and leave only the dry facts and figures to print and online. On the flip side, you don't want the broadcast journalist to report only fluff and let the print and online partners get all the meaty parts of the story. Unless a multimedia approach makes the storytelling better across ALL platforms, a project is probably not the right project for full-scale multiplatform storytelling.

In the end, it doesn't matter whether you are practicing full-blown convergence with a multimedia team or simply trying to supplement your own story by reporting in another medium. It's important to remember that successful multimedia storytelling involves planning, communication and creativity on the part of everyone involved.

CITIZEN JOURNALISM

A citizen journalist is someone who actively participates in the newsgathering and reporting of content. At the very start of this text we talked about interactivity as one of the key strengths of online journalism, and on one level, citizen journalism is about inviting the audience to interact with you through the newsgathering process.

When people in the Norfolk, Va., area were posting comments on WVEC.com about the gas stations in the area that still had power in the aftermath of a hurricane, they were acting as citizen journalists—gathering and reporting information.

When a Harrier jet crashed in the Arizona mountains near Yuma one summer, the only pictures of the jet going down were shot by a bystander with a cell phone camera. When she shared that video with local news stations, she became a citizen journalist.

From these examples, you can see the benefits of citizen journalism. In these situations, citizens were providing valuable information that news organizations would have otherwise been unable to report.

But citizen journalism has its messy side, too. For example, some news organizations are resistant to the idea of allowing citizens to post photos on their news sites because of a concern over whether citizens know enough about journalistic standards. Let's say a local high school student died in a drive-by shooting and a makeshift memorial was set up outside her home. A trained photojournalist would know that it's inappropriate to move some of the flowers closer to the young woman's photo to create a better picture, but a citizen journalist might not understand why that shouldn't be done, that it distorts the truth of the situation. Similarly, most trained journalists understand that it's important to keep one's own opinion out of a story, but most citizen journalists are only motivated to report on issues or events that matter deeply to them, so they may find it difficult to keep biases in check.

Fact checking is also an issue. Jay Rosen of New York University has been a leader in the area of public journalism for more than a decade. Answering questions for a Slashdot.org forum in October 2006, Rosen said, "To simply pass along unchecked reports received from strangers over the Net would be fantastically dumb." [9] The difficulty is that many newsrooms don't have the staff to do extensive fact checking on the work of citizen journalists.

Another reason why some news organizations are resisting citizen journalism is less altruistic. Some traditional journalists are concerned that citizen journalism dilutes the power and influence of the mainstream media and potentially puts their jobs at risk. For example, the South Korean news site OhmyNews is produced largely by citizen journalists who are paid only a small fee for their work—between $2 and $20 per story, according to online news expert Steve Outing. [10] Business Week magazine reports that in 2006 the site had about 90 full-time staffers—just 65 of them journalists—and about 44,000 citizen contributors. [11] In addition, much of today's citizen media involves analysis and criticism of what's being reported by traditional media outlets, and few people appreciate having their work reviewed in a negative way.

Still, understanding citizen journalism and how it can be valuable to a newsroom is important for today's journalists. Technology will only make citizen reporting easier and the most progressive newsrooms will find a way to incorporate the best of citizen work into its own reporting.

TAKING IT HOME

One of the most exciting things about online journalism is its possibilities. Whether you choose to work exclusively as an online journalist or you are simply using the online medium as another vehicle for your storytelling, today's journalists have the opportunity to innovate like never before. For every broadcast journalist who wanted another minute of time, for every print journalist who wanted to show the readers what happened, and for every online journalist who needed more resources, multimedia reporting can be an extremely powerful tool.

By reporting online we are engaging our audiences in a two-way conversation; we are allowing them to explore the information we've gathered to help them make sense of the news on a personal level; and we have been given the opportunity to provide more depth and detail, more context and perspective than we have in the past.

But the Web's potential is still largely untapped by many of today's newsrooms. You are in a unique position to discover new ways of storytelling and to help reinvigorate the importance of journalism in public life. Be creative.

TALKING POINTS

1. People in your community have been arguing over a plan to build a new stadium for the local football team. At 8:30 a.m., you get word that at 1 p.m. today city leaders will be making an announcement on what they've decided to do. Create a story plan for the Web. When will you post your first story and what will it include? How will you keep the story updated throughout the day and with what information?

2. Go online and find a blog entry from a news organization that has received 25 or more comments. What is it about the entry that promoted so much feedback? Do the comments give you any ideas about future stories you might do on this issue? How would you respond to these comments if you were the reporter who wrote the original post?

3. Choose a story you've produced recently for a single medium. Now you're being asked to take a multimedia approach to the content and to develop a presentation plan across platforms. What unique elements would each platform have to offer? Would the print, TV or Web story be published first and why?

eLEARNING OPPORTUNITIES

For chapter exercises, practice tools and additional resources, go to the interactive online workbook at http://college.cqpress.com/advancingthestory. You'll find:

- SKILL BUILDING: Create you own individual or class blog to get a feel for how the technology works. Discuss what stories or content would work best in the blog form.

- DISCOVER: Check out how one news organization covered an important ongoing story online. Analyze the project to determine what else might have been done.

- ONGOING STORY: Develop a multimedia plan for this story and create a storyboard for the project. Review the authors' multimedia approach to the content.

- EXPLORE: Visit Web sites for examples of award-winning multimedia journalism and tutorials on developing your HTML or photo editing skills.

9 PRODUCING FOR TV

In this chapter, we'll share what multimedia journalists need to know about the job of producing for TV and offer some advice about working effectively with producers. In addition, we'll take a look at a newscast producer's work online and the ways in which multimedia may change TV newscasts in the future.

Few people are more important to the success of a television newsroom than its producers. The best producers are organized, they love to write and they always want to be the first to know everything. Toss in some great journalistic instincts, managerial skills, tease writing and graphic design and you have a great producer.

In most newsrooms, producers are truly at the center of the action. They work with the assignment editors to make sure the best stories of the day get covered, they work with reporters and photographers to discuss what elements of the story should be included, and they work with the production team to determine how to present the entire newsroom's work to the viewers.

From a multimedia perspective, many television newscast producers play a vital role in funneling and posting content to their stations' Web sites, especially in breaking news situations when reporters and photographers are out in the field, sending information back to the producers in the newsroom. In addition, producers are involved in promoting the online elements that enhance the stories airing in their newscasts.

Reporters and photographers who understand the producer's job and work to make it easier will generally see a payoff in the way their stories are showcased and promoted. Print reporters who are asked to go on television may also have a better experience if they understand the way broadcasts are put together and can speak the producer's language.

THE JOURNALIST PRODUCER

It's important to remember that a producer is first and foremost a journalist. Although producers may not often go out into the field to report, they play a major role in determining which stories will be included in a station's newscasts each day.

Producers, like all journalists, need to be informed, and not just about what's happening locally, nationally and even internationally. In this highly competitive news environment, it's critical for producers to know a great deal about the station's goals as a news organization. This knowledge will help you evaluate which are the most newsworthy stories of the day. You'll make better choices if you educate yourself on the following issues:

- Know the news philosophy. No matter what job you do for the newsroom, it's important to know your station's news philosophy, but it's critically important for producers. Is your newsroom committed to covering education better than anyone else in town? Is breaking news the number one priority? Does your station brand itself as a viewer advocate? Unless you know what your news organization is trying to achieve each day, it's difficult for you to help decide which stories should be covered and with what emphasis.

- Know the research. Ask if your station does audience research and if the news managers will make some or all of it available to you. It's important to know what the audience is saying about your newscasts and what kinds of stories viewers would like to see on the air. Research should not be used as a substitute for good news judgment, but it can help guide some of your decisions.

At the same time, don't be afraid to throw out all the rules. If you know in your heart of hearts that an important or interesting story needs to be told, champion that story idea. Write up a story proposal, including the people to interview, the visual elements and the relevance to your audience. Some of the best stories ever told on television got on the air because someone was passionate about the story idea.

SHOW CHOREOGRAPHY

After producers, reporters and photographers leave the morning meeting, they naturally become very focused on the individual jobs they have to do. But no one in a newsroom works in a vacuum, and understanding what it takes to produce a newscast can help reporters and photographers do a better job of executing their stories.

PITCHING STORIES

Many great ideas never survive the morning meeting. It's not just that they're overridden by breaking news. Sometimes story ideas die because no one can figure out how to make them into television. We've all heard it said about a complex issue story: "That's a great one for the newspaper." It's the kiss of death. So what can you do to keep a story idea alive? Try these strategies:

- Plan ahead. Have a clear focus in mind for your story. Be prepared to explain it clearly and briefly. If you can't, it's going to be difficult to persuade anyone that it's worth doing. Know who the main characters are, and what the main locations will be. Know why the story matters to your audience. This means you must have done some advance reporting before you even bring up the idea.

- Think visually. Describe what the story might look like on the air. Give examples of ways you would illustrate the story if it's not naturally visual. Be specific and concrete: Tell what the viewer will see and whom the viewer will meet along the way. If the story has appeared elsewhere, give credit but explain how your piece, with its visual elements, will provide a different look at the story and move the issue forward.

- Include others. Consult with a photographer early on about ways of making the story more visual. Talk to the desk about logistics, to see how you can make your story plan work. If you have enlisted an ally before the meeting, your chances of success improve dramatically. If you expect to need graphics, get everyone thinking about them early.

Once producers have a good idea of what stories are available for the day's newscasts, they begin the process of crafting their shows. You will most often hear this referred to as "show stacking," but the term "show choreography" seems to reflect the more thoughtful, creative approach that good producers take when they are putting their newscasts together. When WNCT-TV's Jennifer Coates sits down to produce her newscast each day, she says she focuses on the audience first. "I think about what story or stories will affect the most people," says Coates.

Right out of college, Jennifer Coates took a producing job at WNCT-TV in Greenville, N.C. She says she learned early what was essential to success on the job—keeping viewers at the top of her mind.

Source: Photo courtesy of Jennifer Coates.

Keeping your viewers top of mind throughout the process is essential to good producing, but there are other important factors to consider.

The Lead

As you might expect, the lead story is generally considered the most important story in the newscast. But here's the tricky part—often the lead is whatever you say it is. On many days, there's no obvious story that must air first in the newscast. On those days, a producer's showcasing and writing skills really come into play. Producers are essentially "selling" the viewers on their story choice.

Unless the news breaks very late, a reporter will usually have been assigned to the lead story earlier in the day. That means the producer should spend a fair share of time working with the reporter, photojournalist, graphic artist, director and others to make sure that the story is executed as well as possible.

Echo Gamel, who produces the 6 o'clock show for WTVQ-TV in Lexington, Ky., says the show's lead story is her top priority. "The first thing I think about is my lead—how can I really make this sing? What elements do I need to tell this story?" Gamel says. "I work closely with the reporters to find out how I can best showcase and tell their story with graphics, video and breakouts. I stay in contact with them throughout the day in case things change and I need to adjust."

Producers need to know everything they can about the story—why it deserves to be the lead, what are the best pictures, the most emotional sound, why the viewer should care. Armed with that information, they need to make decisions like these:

TRADE TOOLS

PRODUCER SKILLS

Jennifer Coates' list of the "Top 7 Skills" for producers:

1. Is well-organized.
2. Is able to multi-multi-multi-task.
3. Is able to communicate well.
4. Stays cool under pressure.
5. Is open-minded.
6. Enjoys writing.
7. Is able to be a leader.

• Should the reporter be live or is the story better told as a straight package? If the live shot won't add important information to the story, it may be better to go without a live element.

• Can the story be developed beyond a single package? The best lead stories often include breakouts or sidebar information for the anchor to read. Those additional elements can add depth and perspective to the important lead package.

• How can this story be written and showcased to help the viewer understand its importance? Is there great video or a powerful sound bite that could be used right off the top in what's called a "cold open"? Does the station have any special graphics that can be used to showcase the story, or should some be created? Does the writing grab viewers' attention immediately and leave them wanting to know more about the story?

A NEWS DIRECTOR'S EXPECTATIONS FOR PRODUCERS

Angie Kucharski is a former producer who moved up to become a news director in Denver and is now station manager at WBZ-TV/WSBK-TV in Boston, Mass. She thinks producers are the heart and soul of a newsroom. She calls them the coaches, the compasses, the glue, the leaders and the future.

High praise—and it comes with high expectations. At a Poynter Institute seminar in 2002, Kucharski said producers have to be focused. This means, above all, being selective. Know what you want and how to get there. Of your many story options, know which one should play today. Know when to use graphics and video—and when not to. When resources are limited, decide what to do well, and leave the rest alone.

Kucharski wants a producer who can delegate. You aren't expected to write the entire newscast yourself. News directors understand that producers are responsible for all the details—not just the journalism, but the technical stuff, too. So ask for help from managers, anchors, photojournalists, anyone with a spare moment. Let them write. Trust them to pull their weight.

When you're in the booth, Kucharski wants you to focus on the anchors, the director and the viewers. Give your full attention to the people who matter most to what's going on the air right now.

Focus early, Kucharski says. Decide during your drive to work what you'll do well that day. Stake your claim early and marshal the resources you need to do good work.

Kucharski wants you to walk in and say, "This is what I wanna do with my newscast today!" She wants you to generate story ideas—lots of them. She wants you to disagree with her—and then convince her that you're right. She wants you to stop by her office—accost her if necessary—to tally the day's successes and review the opportunities for improvement. She wants you to take risks.

Above all, she wants you to be a "doer." Enlist aid, line up resources and set up deals with other producers to make things happen without her supervision. Start conversations about ethics. Produce surprising stories. Put your signature on your newscast.

Source: Adapted from Robin Sloan, "Being the Brightest and Best: A News Director's Expectations for Producers," PoynterOnline, September 6, 2002, www.poynter.org/content/content_view.asp?id=9500.

Reporters and photographers can help the producer think through the answers to these questions and, in the process, help themselves do their own jobs better. For example, the focus of a reporter's package is often sharpened when part of a story is turned into a break-out element for the anchor to read. The payoff for all is that a good lead story, properly executed, may keep the viewer engaged.

Flow

This is one of the most controversial aspects of producing. For the most part, producers are taught to create "flow" in their newscasts by placing stories on similar topics together in the show. For example, on a day when a local school system releases new numbers on student test scores, many producers would also place stories concerning a new study about dropout rates and new ways to get college scholarship money immediately adjacent to the test-score story. The argument is that it's easier for an anchor to transition between those stories. Here's what a rundown with those stories might look like:

TABLE 9.1 STORY FLOW

Page #	Anchor	Story name	Story form	Length	Backtime
		SHOW OPEN		:20	
1	Bill	Test Scores	PKG	1:45	
2	Meg	Dropout Rates	V/O	:35	
3	Meg	College Cash	PKG	1:50	
4	Bill	Animal Abuse	V/O-SOT	:45	
5	Bill	Previous Charges	RDR/FS	:25	
6	Meg	Toss to WX	—	:10	
7	Paul	1st WX	—	1:00	
8	Meg	State Fair	V/O	:25	
9	Bill/Meg	Tease 1	V/O	:20	

Note: The stories on student test scores, dropout rates and college scholarship money are airing one after another. This is an example of creating flow within a newscast.

To make the stories flow, the producer might write copy like this to transition between the end of the test score story and the beginning of the dropout story:

Meg: "With great test scores like those, it's hard to understand why so many students continue to drop out of high schools around the state . . ."

And then the transition to the scholarship story might be written this way:

Meg: "If you do stay in school, it might now be easier for you to get to college. The state has just created a new scholarship fund . . ."

The goal is to help the viewer see the connections among these three stories, all of which are education related. However, some research has shown that grouping like stories together can end up confusing the viewer. The researchers say that information can get jumbled when a series of stories with a similar theme are run back to back.[1] For example, the viewers might walk away from the newscast we just described thinking the new scholarship fund is for dropouts or that the test scores are down when they're actually up.

Some newsrooms speak in terms of "clustering" instead of flow. It probably seems logical to cluster stories on similar themes—so that one airs right after the other. But additional problems can occur when you air too many similar stories together—more important stories may be pushed later in the newscast, and you risk losing those in the audience who aren't interested in the cluster topic. For example, you might have a strong lead story about crime, followed by a series of four other crime-related stories. But if your newsroom has produced an important package about a huge issue facing local schools, airing the school story second and moving the other crime stories down to air later in the newscast will better serve your audience.

No matter how your newsroom approaches flow or clustering, you will be expected to write good transitions between stories that allow the show to move seamlessly from one element to another. Reporters must also be sensitive to this issue; they should be cognizant of where their stories appear within a news block and should be able to write an anchor intro that helps move the newscast along.

When creating transitions, writers will want to be sensitive to both the anchors and the viewers. You don't want to create content transitions that are difficult for them to handle. Take another look at the rundown in Figure 9.1 on page 232. Our anchor, Meg, is reading a story about college scholarship money, so it makes sense to have Bill read the next story about animal abuse. If Meg were reading both, you might get stuck with an awkward transition like this one:

Meg: "The school superintendent expects next year's test scores to be even higher, thanks to the new teacher initiative at area high schools.

Tonight investigators are at the scene of what some call one of the worst cases of animal cruelty in Macon history!"

That's a tough read—the anchor has to go from delivering a positive to telling people about animal abuse. Abrupt topic changes are sometimes unavoidable, however, especially in newscasts that rely on a single anchor. In those situations, an over-the-shoulder graphic, or OTS, can help a single anchor shift from one story to another. Turning to a different camera, with or without a graphic, can also add separation that makes it more comfortable for anchor and viewer. At other times, your writing will help the anchor make a smooth transition between unrelated stories:

Meg: "The school superintendent expects next year's test scores to be even higher, thanks to the new teacher initiative at area high schools.

In tonight's Crime Tracker report, investigators are at the scene of what some call one of the worst cases of animal cruelty in Macon history."

There are certainly other transitions that would work just as well, if not better, but you get the idea. You want to ease the anchor and viewer from one topic to the next. Some producers like to think in terms of emotional shifts for both the anchor and viewer. Are you asking them to make too large an emotional change? If so, you may want to put your stories in a different order, making them easier for the anchor to deliver and for the audience to understand.

Pacing

Another slightly less controversial producing technique involves pacing. Many producers believe it's important that a show has a rhythm, and those rhythms may change from newscast to newscast. For example, some 5 o'clock newscasts are faster paced—they include shorter stories and more of them—than 6 o'clock newscasts. In contrast, a more traditional "newscast of record" at 6 o'clock would include longer stories with a great deal of depth and detail on the most important events and issues of the day.

Whether a show is fast paced or a little more deliberate, many producers believe that you shouldn't air multiple packages back-to-back because it slows down the show. In our sample newscast rundown on page 225, we created pacing by varying the story format often—we didn't run any packages back-to-back. But other producers will tell you that compelling content and energetic anchor delivery will keep a newscast moving even if a show includes a series of packages in a row. Suffice it to say that, in general, content is more important than either pacing or flow. If you have urgent, important information that directly affects your viewers, they'll watch!

Newscast Blocks

Newscasts are divided into segments, often called "blocks," of news. Between each block of news, you will typically find a commercial break. In the past, the lead and the other first-block stories could be compared with the front page of a newspaper. The most important or attention-grabbing stories were included in the first block.

But as competition grew along with understanding of how viewership patterns work, producers had to adjust their thinking to create highly interesting segments throughout the show. The second, third, fourth and perhaps even fifth block had to include compelling content as well, to give viewers a reason to keep watching.

Now there is no block of the show that's considered unimportant. As producers work to keep the audience involved from one segment of the show to the next and from one news program on the station to another, every block must be produced to keep the audience watching. Reporters will sometimes argue to get a good story placed higher in the newscast, but they should know that great stories are often more valuable to a news organization if they can be used to pull viewers deeper into a newscast.

Tease writing is another essential tool that helps producers achieve the goal of keeping the audience watching. We'll explore tease-writing strategies in detail a little later in this chapter.

Timing

You've probably heard the expression, "Timing is everything," but you may not have known that the person who coined the phrase was talking about producers. All kidding aside, timing a show is an important part of the producer's responsibility.

Producers need to keep track of how long every story and tease, every weather and sports segment and every commercial break will take. That's called a running time. Before the newscast begins, those running times are simply estimates, so part of a producer's job will involve copyediting stories to make sure they aren't too long or too short, or negotiating with weather and sports anchors to reach an agreement on how long those segments will last. Reporters and photographers will often argue with producers over running times for their stories. There's nothing wrong with fighting for a few extra seconds to help tell a compelling story, but understand that producers are responsible for the big picture. If three reporters beg for more time, that may force a producer to drop another important story from the newscast.

Because commercial breaks are generally NOT negotiable except in extreme circumstances, producers must develop strategies for filling or cutting time when the unexpected happens once the show is on the air. Many producers will identify stories that can be dropped from the show if another segment runs long, and some will even write an extra story or two to add into the newscast if something runs shorter than expected or has to be dropped because it isn't ready.

AUDIENCE AND RATINGS

The need to keep viewers watching throughout the entire newscast is driven by the fundamental way that television news makes money. As you already know, advertising supports the news departments at commercial television stations. Advertisers buy commercial time on stations based on the number of people or the specific types of people watching a particular station's programs.

For example, politicians often buy time during programs like Wheel of Fortune or Jeopardy because they know that many older viewers are watching those shows. Because the elderly vote in much greater numbers than any other demographic, those programs deliver an important audience for political ads.

News producers don't have to worry about selling ads, of course, but they do have to worry about creating newscasts that viewers will want to watch. If enough viewers are watching, advertisers will want to buy time during the newscasts. There are several things producers need to know about how newscast audiences are measured and the producing strategies used to maximize audience.

Demographics

Advertisers target different groups depending on which audience they feel will be most receptive to their product, whether it's a candidate or a car. Advertisers look for television programming that provides a significant number of people in that targeted group. For example, many newscasts have traditionally targeted women aged 25 to 54 because that's a demographic traditionally coveted by many advertisers. Women in that age group are believed to make many of the buying decisions within a household. Producers at stations targeting these women try to include stories that will make them want to watch the newscast. In turn, the hope is that advertisers interested in targeting these women will buy time in the newscast. Other stations have different demographic targets, so knowing who your station is trying to reach is an important part of producing.

Diaries and Meters

There are more than 200 television news markets around the country—each ranked by size, based on population. In about three-quarters of those markets, the audience is measured solely through the use of "diaries." A diary is simply a written record of what the people in a particular household were watching over a particular period of time. Diaries are only as accurate as the people filling them out, and they are collected just four times a year during what are called "sweeps months." Sweeps or ratings periods include the months of February, May, July and November, but in some of the largest television markets, the measurement is year-round.

That's because in most big markets a combination of diaries and electronic meters is used to measure audience. The meters track television viewing all year, but the results do not usually include the kind of demographic information that the diaries provide. Meters tell you that a television set was tuned to your newscast, but they don't tell you anything about the person who's watching.

That has already changed with the advent of the Nielsen People Meter, in use in the 10 largest markets as of mid-2006. People Meters measure both what is being watched and who is watching. According to Nielsen, each family member in the sample household is assigned a personal viewing button on the People Meter. Whenever the TV is turned on, a red light flashes reminding viewers to press their assigned button, which records the viewer's age and gender. This more advanced kind of meter is likely to become widespread in local news markets as the cost of the technology behind it decreases, giving producers more detailed information, more often, about who's really watching their newscasts.

Ratings and Share

Producers strive to produce highly rated shows with as large a share of the audience as possible. According to Nielsen, a rating is a percentage of all the homes that have television sets in a given market. So, if you have a 10 rating for your newscast, 10 percent of all the homes with television sets in your market are presumed to be watching your show.

A share is the percentage of people watching a program in households using television at the time the program airs. Therefore, if your show has a 20 share, that means 20 percent of the homes that actually had their television sets on at the time of your newscast chose to watch your show. Take a look at Figure 9.2 on page 232 to help understand the differences between rating and share.

STRATEGIC PRODUCING AND SPECIAL REPORTS

Producers employ many different strategies to keep people watching. We've already described how story selection may be geared to target certain demographics. In a metered market, the newscast may also be choreographed to take advantage of the way most meters record viewership. The relatively new People Meters track what viewers are watching minute-by-minute, but most meters track the audience in 15-minute increments beginning at the top of the hour. That means you have a chance to beat your competition every 15 minutes. If you can get people to watch your show for the first seven-and-a-half minutes of the quarter hour before switching to another station, your show is credited with a "win" for that particular quarter hour. Even if the viewer switches to watch six minutes of another newscast, you get the credit for the quarter hour of viewing.

Producing "for the demos" or "for the meters" is a controversial practice because it can lead to story decisions that have less to do with journalism and more to do with making money. The best producers are able to do both—take important stories and present them in a way that attracts and keeps viewers watching.

In addition to developing specific newscast strategies, producers are also heavily involved in most stations' overall strategies for success, including any sweeps month or ratings period plan.

During the traditional sweeps months of February, May, July and November, most stations around the country air special stories in their newscasts. These stories are designed to boost the ratings by bringing in viewers who might not otherwise watch the newscast.

Some news directors dislike this approach because it seems artificial to produce special content just to drive the ratings. They believe that their journalists should be producing important content throughout the year and should air those stories whenever they're ready, instead of holding them for sweeps months. Whichever approach your station takes, producers and anyone else involved in creating these special reports need to know a few general things about them.

First, they tend to be a little longer than the typical news story. Depending on your station's tolerance for length and the significance of the information, some stories might run

FIGURE 9.1 TV RATINGS/SHARES

Rating = The percentage of ALL persons or homes tuned to your station. For example . . .

Household rating

Total TV
households: 10

Households
tuning in: 3

Share = The percent of homes or persons USING TV who are watching your station. For example . . .

Household Rating

Total TV
households: 10

Households tuning
in to the same source
(black dot): 3

Share: HHs tuning in
HHs using television $= \dfrac{3}{6} = .50$ or 50%   SHARE = 50

Understanding how newscasts are measured—including the concepts of ratings and share—is critically important for any multimedia journalist, especially newscast producers.

four to five minutes and even longer, but it's more common to see a sweeps package come in at 1:45–2:30 in length. Stations also determine in advance which newscast these stories will air in, and many even predetermine which newscast block contains the series piece.

Producers must factor in all of this as they choreograph their shows—keeping in mind any timing, pacing and blocking issues created. Reporters and photographers must understand that their content should merit the extra time allowed. They should also realize that knowing the newscast they're shooting for in advance gives them a chance to think more specifically about the audience for their stories. For example, the video and sound bites you use for a story about drug dealing might be a little different for an 11 o'clock audience than for a 6 o'clock show when children might be watching.

In addition, special reports lend themselves easily to being enhanced online. Reporter-photographer teams are typically given a little extra time to produce these stories and often gather far more information than they can use in the TV piece. These stories are often completed well in advance of the broadcast as well, giving a Web producer or the reporter-photographer team time to create a comprehensive Web package.

TEASES

Another major tool in your producing arsenal is the newscast tease. Teases alert viewers to what would be airing later in the program and to encourage them to continue watching through the commercial breaks.

A newscast tease is essentially a mini-advertisement for an upcoming story. It's different from a headline because it doesn't summarize the story; it generally leaves some intriguing questions unanswered or promises a payoff to the viewer who sticks around to see the story.

Tease copy is some of the most important and the most difficult broadcast writing to do well. Many producers hate to write teases, so they may delegate that job to an associate producer or the anchors. If you are assigned to write a newscast tease, here's the number one rule: Don't wait until the last minute to write it! Give yourself time to play with the copy and make it as compelling as possible.

Know the Story

Too often tease writers will rely on a cursory glance at the reporter intro or the first few lines of the story before they begin to write. To effectively promote content, you have to thoroughly understand what you are writing about.

Knowing the story includes knowing the video. The best thing to do is to watch the video for the story you're teasing. If you can't do that, at the very least, talk to someone else who has seen the video—preferably a video editor or photojournalist. There may be times when the video for a story is so poor that you decide not to tease the story rather than risk losing viewers with boring or irrelevant video. On the flip side, great video can help convince a viewer to stick around to watch.

Armed with all this information, you must still keep copy concise. "Still to come," "More on that when we come back," "Right after this"—all these phrases send one signal to the viewer: "Commercial coming! Commercial coming!" Commercials are one big reason why viewers change channels, so avoid using those phrases. You also don't want to give the whole story away, so writing tight can help you focus on "teasing" the viewer with what's to come.

At the same time, you can't assume that the viewer knows as much about the story as you do. Be sure that someone tuning into your broadcast for the very first time will be able to understand the story you are promoting. For example, check out this tease:

> Air Tran's heading east, but what about those flying west? See how the Fair Fares search for a discount carrier's going, coming up.

The problem with that tease is that it assumes people know what the "Fair Fares" program is all about. Consider this alternative:

> Half of the country is already covered—now see what the airport is doing to help you get cheap air fares nationwide.

The second version is short and to the point, and you don't have to have as much background on the story to understand the tease.

Viewer Benefit and Station Brand

The concept of viewer benefit is popular in many newsrooms around the country. The idea is to tease stories that can provide viewers with a personal reason to keep watching—stories that provide a direct benefit to the viewer. In other words, what's the payoff if someone watches this story? Here is an example of a tease for the same two stories, written with and without viewer benefit:

WITHOUT VIEWER BENEFIT:

Still to come on the news at 6, Barksdale Air Force Base suffered millions worth of damage last month, but repairs are on the way. More on that when we come back.

And we'll visit Peabody Magnet High School where teachers and students are getting set for a brand new facility. Allison Braxton has that story right after this.

WITH VIEWER BENEFIT:

The Pentagon is doing more than fighting a war on terror right now—hear why top brass are sending millions to Barksdale Air Force Base.

Plus News 5 is On Your Side with a look at what your tax dollars are doing at the new Peabody High School. We check up on the spending, next.

The viewer benefit includes a promise to look out for the viewers' interests, showing them how their tax money is being spent at an important local military installation and in local schools.

In the example we just used, the station's brand was "On Your Side." Since "you are what you tease" you want to make sure that the stories you're promoting are consistent with the station image you hope to project. Teases are an opportunity to remind viewers of who you are.

Weather Teases

Although weather is consistently considered a number one reason why people watch local TV news, many producers never speak to their meteorologists or weathercasters before writing teases for the weather segments. That's why we too often hear teases like this: "How long will today's severe weather last? Paul has the forecast next." That's just plain lazy. The tease writer needs to get a handle on the day's weather story. Here's an example:

The thunderstorms are moving out, but there's more trouble behind them. Paul's up next with an important change in the forecast.

The story was that skies would be clearing, but high winds were expected for the following day. Your station's weather expert prepares two to three minutes of weather content for the newscast every day and can help with writing an effective weather tease.

Sports Teases

If weather teases are bad, sports teases are generally even worse. They often give the story away and leave little for those who aren't sports fans to care about at all. Here's an example of a typical sports tease:

TYPICAL TEASE:

Coming up in sports, our Athlete of the Week Award goes to a local high school softball team that has been one of the big surprises in the Class 4A playoffs.

Also tonight, the Pineville Lady Rebels gear up to face the team that eliminated them last season in the playoffs. We'll have that story and much more coming up in sports.

That wasn't so much a tease as a menu of what was to come. Here's one way you might have given this tease some pizzazz:

ALTERNATIVE TEASE:

It's Ladies Night in sports.

The Athlete of the Week Award goes to an entire team of women who are surprising everyone in the 4A playoffs.

Plus the Lady Rebels are gearing up for a grudge match.

The second version also has the advantage of being much less wordy (:12 vs. the original :18). To write an effective sports tease, you'll probably need to take the time to talk to the sports anchor about what's in the show that night or, at the very least, check the sports rundown—there may be a story with wide appeal that will make a better tease element.

Plenty of producers love to write teases. They see promoting the content in their shows as a challenge, and they like the idea of convincing viewers to keep watching. The ability to write a well-crafted tease can set you apart as a valuable newsroom employee.

Stand-Up and Live Teases

In some news organizations, reporters are asked to do live or taped on-camera teases. Most reporters look at this assignment as an annoyance rather than an opportunity. They produce teases that are little more than headlines for the story.

At WLOS-TV in Asheville, N.C., a reporter once recorded this stand-up tease:

A Spindale woman fights off an attack by a fox and is now getting tested for rabies.

Now that all the viewers know the most important facts of the story, the reporter has given them little reason to keep watching. Consider this alternative:

For the first time in 20 years, health officials are worried about rabies in Ruther-
ford County.

The second version is based on another element of the reporter's package—the fact that
county health officials say they haven't had a rabies investigation there for two decades.

It's also important for reporters and producers to communicate about teases. For this
same fox attack story, the reporter produced a second stand-up tease. This time, she asked
her photographer to start out by shooting the porch of the house involved and then to zoom
out to show the reporter in the shot as she said the following words:

You won't believe what ran across this lady's porch and forced her to get treatment
at the hospital.

This version is a little better tease, but unfortunately, the producer chose to add the words
"Fox Attack" as a super on the bottom of the screen—so much for that tease! Producers
can also spoil the surprise of a story with a careless tease. For example, a reporter and
photographer might be trying to create suspense in a story about a dog trapped in a sewer
pipe. Their story might be told chronologically, showing the rescue from start to finish,
leaving the question of whether the dog survived unanswered until the very end. If the tease
shows a happy tail-wagging pup, the story will lose its punch.

Reporters and producers, working together to create compelling teases, should keep
in mind all of the principles of tease writing that we've outlined in this chapter.

Teasing Pitfalls

In addition to the missteps mentioned above, you should be aware of a few other pitfalls
to avoid when promoting the stories in a newscast.

One of the most common mistakes is teasing a story that doesn't deliver. The producer
may have written a compelling promotion for the story, but viewers will feel cheated if the
story doesn't live up to the tease's promise. This happens often when you promote a story
that's little more than a :20 voice over. There's usually not enough information in a story
that short to make viewers feel that sticking around was worthwhile.

Another common problem is the tease that uses the exact same sequence of video
that we see at the start of the actual story—especially if that story airs in the block immediately following the tease. That's generally the result of lazy editing; whoever's cutting the
video is just pulling the first few shots from the story rather than looking for a way to make
the tease video different.

Producers and reporters will also want to avoid tease clichés. For example, some writers love to start teases with a question such as: "Would you like to find an easy way to get your kids to study more?" The problem with a question tease is that too often the viewer's answer is No! What about all those people who don't have children in school? You've basically told them the upcoming story is not going to be of interest to them.

Other clichés involve using phrases such as: "You won't believe . . ." or referencing the "shocking video." Yes, you are "selling" these stories, but good tease writers find a way to make their copy relevant through content rather than hype.

Working with Promotion Producers

Producers, reporters and photographers may all find themselves in situations where they are working with promotion producers. Promotion producers are generally employed by a station's marketing department, and their job is to get viewers to watch the station's programming, especially the newscasts.

Promotion producers use some of the station's commercial time to create advertisements for particular stories within the newscasts. These promos, as they're often called, are different from newscast teases because they usually air during non-news programming. For example, if your station is a CBS affiliate, a promo produced for your station's late newscast might air during an episode of CSI.

At WFLA-TV in Tampa, Fla., Julie Templin and Sharon King each have 14 years of news promotion experience behind them. They say they love it when a reporter comes to them with information about a story. King says one reporter likes to start out by saying, "Here's why you should care about this story," something both King and Templin find very helpful in the promotion process.

What many promotion producers find frustrating is having to track down a reporter and photographer to get what they need. "I can remember some nights, trying to write a promo. Our station announcer [records] at 6:30 p.m. on the dot. It was already 6 o'clock, and I was desperately trying to get information from the reporter to find out if there was a story and the angle of it in time," said Templin. "We both have deadlines, but ours comes first."

Templin says reporters and photographers should make the assumption that their story will be promoted, and they should try to anticipate the promotion producer's needs whenever possible:

- If it's a story that every other station is covering, tell the promotion producer what is different about your story.

TEASES "Я" US

Teases seem to live longer than almost any other part of a newscast script. Communicator magazine, published by the Radio-Television News Directors Association, recently resurrected a few teases that the producers who wrote them no doubt would like to forget.

Years ago, at WSVN-TV in Miami, Fla., the first line of a tease went something like, "Food poisoning sends dozens to local hospitals." The second line really brought the story home: "It's all coming up at eleven," reports Kim Nolan.

A tape playback error at WVLT-TV in Knoxville, Tenn., had the anchor teasing a story on the latest fashions, while the audience watched the Pope in full regalia.

In a preshow tease, the producer wrote about a new crackdown on people who write bad checks. Five minutes to air, editing said they couldn't find any video of people writing checks so the producer said to run Crimestoppers video instead. Unfortunately, the copy never got changed. The tease said: "Police have a new way of dealing with people who bounce checks." The video showed a man firing several shots at someone in a car. Now that's a tough policy!

Source: Excerpted from Bob Papper, "The Lighter Side of News," *Communicator* [online], n.d., www.rtnda.org/members/communicator/53_oct.asp.

• If you have a great, short sound bite or particularly compelling video, make sure the promotion producer gets it.

• Some stations will want to include good, active video of the reporter in the field or brief reporter stand-up teases in the promos.

For a big breaking story or a special report that everyone knows will get promoted, Templin suggests that those involved might actually ask the promotion producers what they need. Templin says it's essential for everyone to remember one thing: "You can do a compelling story, but if it doesn't get any promotion, that's so many more viewers you're losing out on."

Promoting Multimedia

Newscast producers and anyone else involved in promoting multimedia content need to keep one important point in mind: The audience—whether you're talking about viewers, readers or users—will only see the benefit of a multimedia approach if it truly offers unique content on each platform. Many converged news operations have learned the hard way that news consumers don't like and seldom respond to news promotions that look or sound like this:

> For more information on the baby food recall, log on to our Web site at KDUH.com.

Even worse are the online or print promotions with copy like this:

> Watch Eyewitness News 6 tonight at 10 for more on the first day of school in our area.

Both of these examples are typical of the way multimedia has often been promoted in the past—vague references to additional content on another platform with no clear indication of what the viewer, reader or user will actually get. Consider these alternatives to the convergence promotions above:

> For a complete list of the lot numbers for the baby food jars affected and a reminder of which stores are offering refunds for the contaminated food, log on to KDUH.com.

AND

> Tonight at 10, Eyewitness News 6 takes you on a tour of the most overcrowded school in Peoria. See what students are up against when it comes to getting a good education.

Both of these alternative teases give the news consumer a specific reason to turn to another platform. Simply promoting that there's more information in the newspaper or online or that another version of the story is on television will generally not be enough to get people to seek it out. Writing effective multimedia promotions means you must know exactly what each medium has to offer that's unique to that medium, as well as how that additional information is relevant to the audience. You don't want to promote something they've just seen or read, and you don't want to tell them to get more information on something they care nothing about.

WORKING WITH NEWSCAST PRODUCERS

Even if you have absolutely no interest in ever becoming a producer yourself, as a multimedia journalist you will probably find yourself working with one someday. By now, we hope you have a better appreciation of the tough job they have to do, and you can probably anticipate their needs a little better as well.

Producers are important to reporters and photographers because they often have a strong voice when it comes to deciding what stories go into their newscasts, which means they have a big say-so in the stories that reporters and photographers are assigned to each day.

Lane Michaelsen, former director of photography at KARE-TV in Minneapolis, Minn., is now vice president and news executive at Gannett Broadcasting. When he was working as a photojournalist, he used what he called the "pennies in a jar" approach to working with producers. Basically, he believed that if you cheerfully do all the assignments that producers need completed but no one else wants to do, you get a "penny in the producer jar" each time. Then, when he really wanted to do a story he had to sell to a producer, he'd "cash in the pennies." At that point, he says, you have to start building them up again.

He also talks about "getting over the wall before it's built." By that he means that you have to anticipate roadblocks when pitching a story. If you can get a producer excited about having the story in the newscast, you have an ally when it comes time to convince the news director and others that it's a good story to do.

Michele Harvey is a TV and print reporter in Charlotte, N.C., who has worked with newscast producers for more than 20 years. She says that first and foremost, reporters need to realize that, in the field, they are producers, too.

"You and your photographer need to keep in mind that the producer can't see or hear what you do in the field. You need to let them know about the most exciting video, the most exciting sound. You need to help them by saying, 'This is the sound bite I will use to write my story around and I have a similar one that you can use to promote or showcase the story,'" says Harvey.

Harvey says this collaboration process with the producer starts the minute the story is assigned. "It's not about us and them. You need to leave the morning meeting with everyone in agreement on a vision for the story. If you find the vision doesn't work, you need to let them know how it's changed and offer solutions for any problems that develop," she says.

Harvey says your producer should have confidence in you. "They'll learn to count on you and send you out on the tough stories, the good stories, the stories that will lead the newscast."

WEB WORK

In many newsrooms, newscast producers are also involved in keeping the Web site updated throughout the day. In some shops, like WJHL-TV in Johnson City, Tenn., every producer has been trained to post stories to the Web.

Newscast producers may also be involved in finding good online content to supplement the stories in their newscasts. For example, at KOMU-TV in Columbia, Mo., the producers set aside part of their day to provide the online editors with a list of links and additional content for the Web site. At KPNX-TV in Phoenix, Ariz., producers who find a good link post it directly to the station's site.

Once these links and other additional content are posted, producers can use the good multimedia promotion strategies we've discussed to alert viewers to the content online.

NEWSCASTS OF THE FUTURE

One of the big questions out there right now is how does the traditional newscast fit into an increasingly on-demand, interactive, nonlinear world? Beyond pushing people to a station Web site for multimedia content, can a newscast itself be a multimedia or interactive experience? Some people believe the answer is yes, and research suggests that many Americans would be interested in a new kind of newscast.

The Radio and Television News Directors Foundation (RTNDF) conducted a survey in 2006 to determine where news might be headed. The study found that more than 60 percent of people surveyed would like to "interact with TV news." The researchers defined interacting as "pressing a button to get more information on something you see in a newscast." The study also found that about 40 percent of people would be interested in assembling their own newscasts, although 46 percent had no interest in doing that.[2]

These ideas aren't just theoretical. In September 2006, Nexstar Broadcasting's WYOU-

TV in the Wilkes-Barre–Scranton, Pa., market launched what it believes is the first major network-affiliated interactive local TV newscast in the country. According to the company Web site, the station's 5, 6 and 11 o'clock newscasts focus on one topic that changes daily and sometimes from newscast to newscast. Newsmakers are invited on the show to be interviewed, and viewers call in or e-mail questions. The news director, Ron Krisulevicz, says the station is getting thousands of phone calls every night.

At Northwestern University, Professor Kristian Hammond and a number of graduate students have created News at Seven (newsatseven.com). The university Web site describes it as "a system that automatically generates a virtual news show. Totally autonomous, it collects, parses, edits and organizes news stories and then passes the formatted content to an artificial anchor for presentation. Using the resources present on the Web, the system goes beyond the straight text of the news stories to also retrieve relevant images and blogs with commentary on the topics to be presented."[3]

Pulling from these sources and using text-to-voice software, the system can create original news packages based on the viewer's interests. The fact that the newscast is designed to be viewed online creates all sorts of possibilities for multimedia enhancements—links to the story sources, opportunities to comment on the stories and have other people respond, to name just a few.

But both the News at Seven and WYOU models have their limitations, according to Terry Heaton, senior vice president for Audience Research and Development, a company that consults for news organizations. "These models assume that there will always be passive viewers available for mass distribution—that's a dangerous assumption," says Heaton.

Even though the News at Seven model allows users to customize content, Heaton says the result is designed to be viewed passively. Plus, it takes viewers some time to create the content, and Heaton says people are working more and have less leisure time than they have had for decades.

Heaton believes the traditional "TV News at 6" is going away and that stations need to be focusing their attention on the Web, rather than trying to create a new kind of television newscast. He suggests that a station might hire people with "deep knowledge of important niches in the community" and train them to be reporters. The stories they produce could be used as content for online businesses. Heaton gives the example of a realtor hired to report on the local market; the realtor's stories could be part of an advertising-supported online real estate site.

Heaton says the challenge for television stations right now is that they have to continue to produce newscasts while they try to figure out what a future on the Web might look like. "As I heard someone once say, it's a little like fixing a car while you're driving," Heaton says.

National Science Foundation
Grant No. 0535231

NEWS AT SEVEN

newsatseven.com

Today's News   Archives   Blog   Press   FAQ   About   Contact Us   **InfoLab**

Description

News at Seven gives you the news you want, the way you want it. Each day, **News at Seven** automatically generates a virtual newscast pulled from stories, images, videos and blogs all linked by a common news topic. **News at Seven** presents news, point/counterpoint, opinion, celebrity gossip and the occasional foray into the world of 3D gaming. **News at Seven** isn't just the future, it's the future of the future.

[more]

Press

Wall Street Journal - 1/6/07
"As network news programs continue to struggle, the creators of one news show are trying a new strategy — replacing the producer, the editor and even the news anchor with a computer."

Discovery Channel News - 11/3/06
"A news show that truly speaks to its viewers is the idea behind "News at Seven"..."

Slashdot - 10/25/06
"Automatic Machinima News Broadcasting..."

[more]

News Archives: Editor's Picks

News Update - 2/2/07

Movie Review - 11/20/06

Halloween News Update - 10/31/06

TODAY'S NEWS: August 8th, 2007

News for August 8th, 2007:   view past news
Barry Bonds

From the News at Seven Blog   more

No new show today

Sorry, we are having technical issues with Half-Life 2 so there won't be a new show today. We plan on having a new show up next Wednesday, and continue to work hard on the new version of News at Seven. If any of you are planning on attending...

Comments(0)

News at Seven was developed by Northwestern University's Intelligent Information Laboratory. It is one vision of what the automated newscast of the future might look like.

Source: InfoLab, Northwestern University. Retrieved August 19, 2007, from http://infolab.northwestern.edu/project.asp?id=40.

Al Tompkins, Broadcast/Online Group leader for the Poynter Institute, isn't ready to give up on TV newscasts, yet. "The sky is not falling, but things aren't always going to be as they've been," says Tompkins. "Companies that are generating new products, new ideas are going to be successful."

Tompkins says television news has always been about figuring out what the public wants and needs and then delivering that. He sees some great opportunities for television news stations that can figure out how to capitalize on user-generated content and the delivery of content to mobile devices. We'll talk much more about those two issues in Chapter 12.

TAKING IT HOME

The best journalists are those who spend their whole lives learning—they want to know why things happen, how things work and the impact of it all. But they don't always spend as much time studying their own profession as they should. Reporters and photographers who fully understand newscast production and producers who fully understand the news-gathering process are all too rare. But just as you have an opportunity to make a difference in your newsroom with your multimedia skills, you can also be a leader in creating better newscasts with your understanding of the process.

Beyond the newscast, the multimedia responsibilities of all journalists are growing. For producers, it's becoming essential to have a good understanding of how to write a story for the Web, how to add interactivity and how to promote multimedia content.

Reporters, photographers and all the other journalists in a newsroom should have a solid understanding of what producers do and be able to collaborate with them to create strong newscasts and other multimedia content.

TALKING POINTS

1. Record a local TV newscast. Is there any indication the producer was thinking about the audience? What else could the producer have done to "put the audience first"? Do you think the right choice was made on the lead story? Was it well developed and showcased? Did you notice anything about pacing and flow?

2. Have someone choose a story from a local TV newscast that was included in a newscast tease. Before you watch that tease, watch the story. Try to write a tease for it that

keeps all of the principles of good tease writing in mind. Be sure to include a description of the video you would use. Watch what actually aired. Do you like the original version or your own version better? Why?

3. What do you think about Terry Heaton's assertion that it's wrong to assume that there will always be an audience for television newscasts? If you disagree, describe why. If you agree, how long do you think newscasts can survive? Either way, what should local stations be doing to make sure their newscasts have a longer life?

eLEARNING OPPORTUNITIES

For chapter exercises, practice tools and additional resources, go to the interactive online workbook at http://college.cqpress.com/advancingthestory. You'll find:

- SKILL BUILDING: Test your delivery by recording challenging copy and see how marking your script improves the end result.

- DISCOVER: Check out examples of strong stand-ups and live shots.

- ONGOING STORY: Try your hand at writing a stand-up bridge for this story, screen our version and learn more about why it was done this way.

- EXPLORE: Visit Web sites for resources to help you improve your on-air delivery and write strong stories for print.

10 DELIVERING THE NEWS

At one time, only television and radio journalists had to concern themselves with telling stories out loud. But in a multimedia world, it could be a part of almost any journalist's job. Print reporters may record podcasts or appear as guests on television programs. Newspaper photographers often narrate online slide shows. And broadcast journalists not only have to record narration and appear on camera, more often than not they also have to go live. In this chapter, we'll discuss what it takes to do all of these things well.

All the reporting, writing and editing you've done on your story can be undone if you don't deliver it well. This is the moment of truth, when your journalism must become storytelling. There's a good reason no child ever asks to be read a bedtime article. People respond to stories, and one key difference between a story and an article or a report is the storyteller. As a storyteller, you want to connect with the audience when delivering the news.

It's not easy to make that connection when voicing a story for television or the Web because the audience is faceless and remote. But if you want your stories to have impact, you have to know how to deliver.

VOICING

Vocal delivery is one of the least-discussed elements of multimedia storytelling, but it's critically important to the way a story comes across to the audience. As we've discussed, if you're going to tell a story well on the air or online, you first need to write a script that's designed to be read out loud. But that's just the start. It takes skill and practice to sound both authoritative and conversational when you deliver a script.

SOUNDING NATURAL

Anyone who's ever tried to read a script into a microphone knows that it's not as easy as it may seem. Here are some tips on how to improve the way you sound:

- Breathe correctly. If you learn how to breathe with your abdomen, you'll have better breath support—that is, you'll have control over the breath you need to make sounds. Then you won't find yourself pausing at the wrong time because you need to take a breath. And you won't sound bored because your voice will have energy. Try not to move your shoulders when you breathe. It's easier to do this standing up, which is why many reporters and even some anchors read their scripts while standing.

- Take care of your voice. As any singer will tell you, the voice is an instrument. To get the most out of it, you need to care for it. Don't smoke; it may artificially lower your pitch, but in the long run, it can ruin your voice and your health. Be careful not to strain your voice by shouting yourself hoarse or clearing your throat excessively. Either can damage your vocal cords. Avoid milk products before you record or go on the air, and breathe through your nose to avoid drying your throat. Drink lots of water—not alcoholic, caffeinated or carbonated drinks. It may sound unpleasant, but warm water is the best way to keep your throat moist.

- Relax. Tension in your body will show up in your voice. A tense voice tends to be higher in pitch, which is probably something you're trying to avoid. Take a few deep breaths and relax your shoulders before you begin.

- Get professional help. If you believe you need help with articulation (the process of forming sounds) or the resonance or tone of your voice, consider taking a class in voice and diction or working one-on-one with a voice coach. Some people may also have a heavy regional accent that could prevent them from getting jobs in some parts of the country. In that situation a voice coach can also help.

Not everyone is born with "great pipes," and that's OK. Both Barbara Walters and Tom Brokaw had successful television careers even though they both have minor speech impediments. Your goal should be to make the most out of the voice you were born with and to sound natural when you read a story out loud.

Mental Preparation

As you prepare to record your narration, try not to think about the fact that there's a microphone between you and the audience. In fact, try not to think about the audience at all. Your goal is to communicate as if you're having a conversation with just one person.

Lots of broadcast journalists say they have one specific person in mind when they track—often it's someone older than they are, so their voice has a tone of respect, but it's also someone they know well so they can speak comfortably. Veteran NPR newscaster Carl Kasell likes to imagine he's making a phone call to "Aunt Martha." [1] Some reporters find that actually holding a telephone to their ear while they're reading into a microphone gives them a more relaxed sound.

To put yourself in the right frame of mind to tell your story, think about what you've learned that you're now ready to share. You have to sound like you're interested in telling your story or no one will be particularly interested in listening to it. You're not acting and this isn't a performance, but the way you tell the story should match the content. "The criticism I got early on was that all my stories sounded the same," says reporter Boyd Huppert of KARE-TV in Minneapolis, Minn. "Now when I sit in the booth the first thing I do is think, 'What's this about? Is this happy or sad?' You can go overboard, but over time you find what's comfortable for you."

Intonation

When you read aloud, you want to put more emphasis on some words than others or you'll wind up speaking in a monotone, sounding uninterested and boring your listeners. The trick is to avoid setting up a rhythm with your emphasis that will result in a singsong delivery. Marking your copy will help you find the right intonation.

Scan your script for words that convey important information—usually the subject, verb and object in each sentence—and underline those words. When you read, give those words a little more emphasis than the rest. Ann Utterback, author of the Broadcast Voice Handbook, says to emphasize the words that would help someone understand what the story is about if they're in the kitchen, listening to the TV or radio that's on in the next room.

117 SOT COOKE 3-30048 "Most Christian television that you see is very low quality, it's
118 not very good. And a lot of people have issues with it. And so we want to bring the best
119 of the production world and the best of the media world in with it, and help people do it
120 more effectively and make more entertaining shows."
121
122 NAT: FAITHLIFENOW (DVD) approx 5:00 You want to be successful, God wants you
123 to be successful...
124
125 VO This program, for example, doesn't look like your typical TV ministry, and
126 that's deliberate. The pastors of Faith Life Church in New Albany, Ohio, tape it in
127 their living room: (DVD)
128
129 2-21208 Drenda Keesee "We had someone approach us about doing Christian TV, and
130 we were hesitant /// 21218 We weren't sure we were, quote, TV people, if you know
131 what I'm saying. We met people who said hey, you need to try this, your message is
132 important and people need this message."
133
134 2-21348 Gary Keesee "If you're gonna consider starting TV, it's gonna take you a
135 couple hundred thousand dollars, the first year, to get started. // We were on the line
136 personally for that money. But in the long run, after the first year---we just finished our
137 first year---actually the show is now paying for itself."
138
139 VO It pays for itself, as many TV ministries do, through donations and product
140 sales. The Keesee's daughter Amy does the pitch.
141
142 FAITHLIFE VIDEO: "To order Open for Business..."
143
144 VO Sales of books, DVDs and other products--as opposed to direct appeals for
145 money--provide a significant portion of the income for many TV ministries. They
146 say they have to raise money to stay on the air, just as public television does. But
147 that wasn't always the case.
148
149 SOT 13-210049 Sheen walks into studio
150

Deborah Potter marked this script before recording the track for a 2007 story for the PBS program Religion & Ethics NewsWeekly. Notice the squiggly line marking words she does not want to stress because they repeat what's just been said in a sound bite.

For example, in the following sentence, you would emphasize the words in bold: "A 20-year-old **woman** was seriously **injured** in an **accident** this morning on Route 99." Not: "A **20**-year-old woman was **seriously** injured in an accident this **morning** on Route 99."

There are exceptions to the rule, of course. You might want to emphasize an adverb if it explains what happened. "The man was shaking so **violently** that he dropped the gun." Sometimes, you'll choose to emphasize a word because you want to draw attention to a contrast. "The boy was supposed to wait next to the car, but he was found **under** the car." In this case, you would not emphasize "next to" because there's no reason to draw attention to it.

When you come to the end of a sentence, drop the pitch of your voice. A rising intonation is usually used for a question or an incomplete thought.

Your intonation may also be dictated by the sound bites you use. Pay attention to the words each speaker emphasizes, and adjust your inflection to fit. Huppert reads sound bites out loud before he tracks the narration surrounding the bite. "I read the bite the way I remember the person saying it because that gets me in the right frame of mind," he says. To achieve the same goal, other reporters play back a recording of the bites as they read the script aloud.

Pacing

Pay close attention to the speed of your read. You want to pick a pace that sounds and feels natural to you and that's comfortable for the audience. If you read too slowly, you'll sound ponderous; too quickly and you'll sound rushed and anxious. If you find yourself racing through your story so you won't run long, go back and cut your copy. If you tend to be a fast talker, write shorter sentences and you'll slow down. Don't make the audience struggle to understand what you're saying.

Vary your pacing according to the content of your story. Remember, you want to sound as if you're having a conversation, not declaiming a speech. Nobody talks at the same pace all the time. If you've written the way we've suggested, putting the most important word in a sentence at the end, you'll naturally slow down and emphasize that word.

STAND-UPS

Stand-ups have been around as long as TV news itself. In the early days, they were used to establish that "by golly, a correspondent had been on the scene of the news event [he] just reported," said the late Jim Snyder, who ran TV newsrooms in Washington and Detroit.

WHY DO A STAND-UP?

Because the location is central to the story.

To establish your credibility on an issue.

To demonstrate an action rather than tell about it.

To show a relationship between locations.

To make a transition between locations, characters, time frames or topics.

To draw more attention to what you are saying.

Because you have no pictures (or graphics) to illustrate your point.

That's still the most basic, legitimate reason for going on camera—to establish your credibility on the subject. It's also a way for reporters to build a relationship with viewers, giving them a face to put with the voice. But these days, most reporters and photographers try to produce stand-ups that add more to a story than simple presence. A good stand-up can help the audience make sense out of something complicated. A bad one can bring your story to a screeching halt, make you look foolish or give the audience a good reason to tune out.

For simplicity's sake, we'll use the term stand-up to refer to any on-camera appearance by the reporter, live or on tape. Live shots do pose some different challenges, and we'll address them separately. But all on-camera segments have one thing in common: they're not easy to do well. Talking to a camera is an unnatural act, and you have to make it look like the most natural thing in the world.

Planning a Stand-Up

Too many stand-ups are an afterthought, thrown together at the end of the day just because the news director insists on seeing the reporter on camera in every story, or the newscast producer needs a live shot for pacing. A stand-up should be an essential part of your narrative, adding new information and moving the story forward. Consider these questions before you do a stand-up:

- Why would we want to include a stand-up in this story?

- What information would we convey in a stand-up?

WGAL-TV reporter Susan Shapiro is a master of the active stand-up. To demonstrate how close a murder suspect lived to his victim, Shapiro started her stand-up in front of the man's townhouse, then walked across the parking lot to show where the victim lived.

Source: Courtesy of WGAL-TV.

- Do we have something to show or demonstrate in this stand-up?

- Where and when might we do this stand-up?

- How will the stand-up fit into the finished story?

Stand-ups can serve several different functions, so it's important to know in advance what you're trying to accomplish with an on-camera segment. You might decide to go on camera to demonstrate something rather than just tell about it, or to show a relationship between two locations more clearly than you could by panning with a camera. For example, when Susan Shapiro, a reporter at WGAL-TV in Lancaster, Pa., was covering a story about a woman who'd been killed by her ex-husband, she started her stand-up outside the man's townhouse. "Bottenfield moved into this complex in Denver just a couple of months ago," Shapiro said on camera, looking back and gesturing at the building. "He was living in that end unit." Shapiro then took a few steps across the parking lot as the camera followed her, while saying, "Even though his ex-wife had once filed for a protection-from-abuse order against him, he moved in just across the street from where she lived."

A stand-up can also be used to prepare the audience for a transition between locations, characters, time frames or topics. And a stand-up may be your last resort when there just aren't any pictures or graphics to illustrate a particular point. By going on camera, you can help the audience understand what they can't see.

Before you shoot any stand-up, you need a clear idea of your story structure. You don't need a complete script, but a mental outline is essential. You need to know where your on camera segment will fit in the story, whether you're doing a bridge in the middle or a stand-up close. What information will the audience already know before your stand-up? What will they learn immediately after the stand-up? Sometimes, it's helpful to shoot more than one version in case you decide to change the structure. The important thing is to plan a stand-up that is integral to the story, not one that repeats the obvious or comes out of left field.

Solo Stand-Ups

In Chapter 3, we talked about video journalists (VJs), solo journalists (sojos) or backpack journalists—what some newsrooms still call "one-man bands." No matter what you call it, shooting and reporting your own stories is a challenge, especially when it comes to stand-ups.

Adam Balkin is a technology reporter for NY1 News, a 24-hour New York cable news operation that employs solo journalists. Balkin says stand-ups are often the most difficult shots to get when you're on your own. Framing is a particular challenge. He recommends putting something, such as a pen, on the ground where you want to stand and set focus. "I take a wide shot, hit record, and then go stand by the pen," he says. "I then look to see if there is anything on a building or something on a sign that lines up with the top of my head, so that I can frame properly exactly where I'll be. Then I go back and zoom in on that point." [2]

Thomas Nybo, a contributing reporter for CNN, filed reports from Iraq during Operation Iraqi Freedom. He suggests flipping the display screen on the camera so you can see it from in front of the lens. That way you can see yourself as you're doing your stand-up. Nybo also says that, over the years, he's found that his best stand-ups tend to be the ones that are more tightly framed.

Denise Dowling, an assistant professor of radio/TV at the University of Montana's School of Journalism, suggests that her students use a light stand almost as a dummy to frame their stand-ups when they're alone in the field. "They'll set their light stand up to their height and frame it up as if the top of the light stand was their head." [3]

SOLO STAND-UPS

Chris Mitchell has spent the last seven years as a solo journalist for WMBB-TV in Panama City, Fla., but he still vividly remembers his first day as a reporter-photographer as a "baptism by fire."

"Another reporter showed me how to turn the camera on, how to do a white balance and how to put the tape in," said Mitchell. "Basically, that was it."

Since that first day, Mitchell has trained dozens of reporter-photographers for the station, and he shares this advice for shooting stand-ups on your own:

Set the tripod up at chest height. Once you put the camera on top, it should be just about right.

Check to see that your camera is level and then focus in on a point that approximates where you'll be standing.

Deliver your stand-up, and then check it to see if it's in focus and well framed and that you're happy with the content.

Mitchell says he used to "fret about stand-ups," but now he actually enjoys the challenge of being creative all on his own. For example, in a story about beach renourishment, Mitchell remembers talking with residents who were griping about the color of the new sand. "I framed my stand-up so that you could see me scoop up a handful of sand and then put it directly in front of the lens, so it filled the frame," said Mitchell.

His advice to solo journalists doing stand-ups? "Don't panic, you can do it."

Memorizing

Preparing to go on camera is similar to preparing to record a narration, with one key difference. Unless you're using a teleprompter, you won't be able to read a script because you'll have to look at the camera. The temptation is to memorize what you want to say, word for word, but that's not the most effective approach. If you memorize your script and then start talking, your brain will be fully occupied with remembering it and you won't really be able to focus on what you're saying.

Rather than worry about saying specific words in a particular order, figure out what you're trying to communicate and then just say it. Whenever you can, rehearse a few times before you roll tape or go live, until you feel comfortable with the content. When shooting stand-ups, do as many takes as necessary to get at least two that are usable—one will be a "safety" or backup you can use if there are any technical problems with the first one. Keeping your stand-up short will improve your odds of success.

Use the same techniques as you would when recording narration so that you'll sound interested in what you're saying. When Lesley Stahl covered the White House for CBS News, she often used the phrase "I have to tell you . . ." in her live on-camera reports. It was a simple device to give her stories energy that was natural, not fake.

Action

"The walk to nowhere" has become a cliché, but you still see it all the time—an on-camera segment in which the reporter moves from one place to another for no apparent reason. Active stand-ups are great, but only if they make sense. Let's say you're doing a story about a recall of contaminated spinach and you want to shoot a stand-up at a supermarket. You could push a cart through the produce section and talk about the fact that there's no spinach on the shelves, but your stand-up would be more effective if you simply stood in front of the shelf and pointed out the empty space where the spinach used to be.

Think of a stand-up as your chance to serve as the audience's tour guide. "Use the scene, don't just stand with it behind you," says reporter Kim Griffis of KING-TV in Seattle, Wash. Show the audience something they might miss. Demonstrate how something works. "Just make sure that whatever is coming out of your mouth directly relates to what you are doing with your hands, feet and eyes," says veteran news director Forrest Carr.[4] And don't overdo it. Some active stand-ups are so artificial and contrived that they get in the way of the story and can even damage the reporter's credibility. Consider the case of a reporter who will remain nameless: For a story about red tide contamination in the Gulf of Mexico, he put on his swimsuit and scuba mask and rose out of the water, dripping wet, to do his stand-up. He certainly got the viewers' attention, but not their respect. You're doing journalism, remember, not theater.

While most news directors harp on the need for active stand-ups, there are times when a static stand-up can be appropriate. It's a well-known fact that people respond to a human face—even tiny babies will turn toward a sketch of a face—so going on camera is a good way to draw attention to what you're saying if it's complicated and nonvisual. "Looking the viewer in the eye and telling them something important can be the best way to do it," says Griffis. "You're saying, 'I'm the expert. Trust me.' "

Shooting Stand-Ups

Good stand-ups obviously require close collaboration between reporter and photographer, but sometimes attitudes get in the way. Reporters who stress out about going on camera and photographers who think stand-ups are all about ego may not communicate as well as they should, especially on deadline. So it's important to start talking through the stand-up options well before crunch time. The photojournalist should be involved in deciding what information would be best delivered on camera, choosing a location and determining how to shoot it.

"I love stand-ups," says photojournalist Scott Hedeen of WXIA-TV in Atlanta, Ga. "It's one of the few things I can control." He's more than willing to shoot lots of takes on a stand-up until he gets one that's as good as it can possibly be.

Experienced photographers know how to add visual interest to a longer stand-up by shooting it in multiple takes. This approach allows the reporter to walk the audience through a complex process or demonstrate how something works by illustrating individual steps in a visual sequence. If you wanted to shoot a stand-up showing the correct way to install a child's car seat, for example, you might want a wide shot of the reporter approaching a car and opening the door, a matched tight shot of the reporter's hand opening the door, a medium shot of the door opening, a shot through the opposite door of the reporter putting the car seat in place, tight shots of belts and buckles being threaded and latched and a medium shot of the now-installed seat.

Stand-Ups with Graphics

Another way to help viewers grasp important details in a story is to combine a stand-up with graphics. By shooting the stand-up with the reporter off center in the frame, the photojournalist leaves space for text graphics or a map to be inserted in the control room. For example, in a story about a public hearing on a new school program, WCNC-TV reporter Sterlin Benson Webber included graphics in her stand-up outside the high school where the hearing would be held, reinforcing the ground rules for the evening. The words "Sign up when arrive; Limit to 3 minutes; Only issue," came up on the right side of the screen

Graphics can emphasize important information in a stand-up without breaking the flow of the story. Framing WCNC-TV reporter Sterlin Benson Webber off-center in her stand-up left room on the right for bullet points about that night's public meeting.

Source: Courtesy of WCNC-TV.

as she explained the plan in these words: "Parents and students will be allowed to sign up to speak when they arrive here at East Mecklenburg High School's auditorium. But all speakers must limit their comments to just three minutes. And the student assignment plan is the only issue that parents will be allowed to talk about tonight." Rather than using a full-screen graphic, which interrupts the flow of the story, this approach connects the reporter, the location and the details on the screen in one visual image.

LIVE SHOTS

Going live adds a degree of difficulty to doing stand-ups. There's the pressure of knowing that you have only one chance to get it right, and there's often the stress of having to stay within a strict time limit. Beyond that, the decision to go live may not be made for the best of reasons, leaving reporters fumbling for a way to make their live presence on the air make sense.

The best reason to do a live shot is because something is happening or because you will be demonstrating something while you're on the air. When you're live, the viewer can see what's going on and the anchor can ask pertinent questions. Some reporters will use props when they make sense. For example, if you are going live from the courthouse for a story on the indictment of a local mayor, you might hold up a copy of the indictment as you briefly describe what the grand jury's decision means to the city. It's also common to use live shots for logistical reasons, when there isn't enough time to get a story edited for air. But a so-called black hole live shot from a scene where nothing is happening can seem pointless, and research shows it can actually alienate viewers.[5] Bear that in mind when planning a live shot. Reporters, photographers and producers should all be involved in deciding when and where to go live, and for what purpose.

But be aware that in some newsrooms the producers are required to have live elements in their newscasts, and often the lead story is presented as a live shot whether or

LIVE SHOTS

Mark Becker has been doing live shots for WSOC-TV in Charlotte, N.C., for more than 20 years. He says one way to bring relevance to a "live-for-live's-sake" shot is "simply to take the viewer back, through the reporter's eyes, to the event or the scene, that they covered perhaps hours earlier. Very simply, the reporter is telling what he or she just saw—something that may or may not be on tape—the same way they would excitedly tell a friend or co-worker about something they'd just seen."

For example, if you are live at 6 p.m. on a major street where there was a terrible accident at 6 a.m., Becker says you could start by showing how traffic is moving now, and then explain how it wasn't for most of the morning rush hour, saying something along these lines:

> Anyone who drives home on Main Street knows how brutal traffic can be, even on a good day. Right now both lanes are packed heading out of town. But at least they're moving. Now, imagine this morning, when a lot of these same people were trying to get into work, those two inbound lanes were funneled down into one, all because of a truck that lost control.

Becker says one other way to inject energy into a live shot where something is not going on at the moment is to use the show-and-tell approach. "Often they're called 'active' live shots. This works well where there's been a fire or an accident—where there is something left behind. A reporter can show the damage, or walk and talk to show how a car lost control, moved from the right shoulder to the median, bent a guardrail and flipped over, with the reporter pointing out skid marks or debris along the way," Becker says.

not there is a good reason to be live. So how do you handle what's often called "live for live's sake"? The best advice may be to keep your live presence as short as possible. This will help minimize the chance that the audience will get bored and tune out before you can get to the meat of your story.

KNOW AND TELL

Content

As with every other story form, content is key in a live shot. For most routine shots, you will simply be introducing or delivering a preproduced V/O, V/O-SOT (a V/O with a sound bite or "sound on tape") or package from the field. In these situations, you will most likely have some time to plan what you want to say on camera.

When you know a lot about a subject, it can be a tempting to do a data dump during your live shot, but don't try to tell the audience everything. Instead, figure out the one or two points you want to share about the story, in addition to what's in your preproduced content.

Instead of writing a script for a live shot, many reporters make an outline similar to the "jot outline" we described in Chapter 5. You may also want to include specific numbers and direct quotes from people you're likely to mention in your live shot. Use the notes as a reference if you need them but not as a crutch. Hold the notes out of camera range when possible, and if you have to refer to them, do it deliberately. Looking down and reading a phrase or two from your notes can add credibility to your story; reading more than that can make you look unprepared.

When you're going live, it's important to explain where you are and why you're there at that particular moment. Don't leave the viewer wondering. Begin your live segment with current information—not a reference to something that happened hours ago or that will happen hours from now. When reporter Bridgette Bornstein was covering a bad storm for KSTP-TV in Minneapolis, Minn., here's how she began her live shot: "In just the last few minutes we have seen light flashes across the river, what appear to be transformers blowing. This afternoon we had rain, it changed to freezing rain, changed to hail, and now what we've got is a light snow."

Interact with the environment the same way you would in a stand-up. For ex-

Beginning a live shot with current information lets the viewer know right away why you are where you are. Reporter Bridgette Bornstein started her live report on a snowstorm for KSTP-TV in Minneapolis, Minn., by looking across the river and describing what she had seen there just minutes earlier.

Source: Courtesy of Bridgette Bornstein.

ample, Bornstein turned to look across the river behind her when she referred to the light flashes. But be aware that you can't control the environment when you're live the way you can on tape, and you can't simply do another take if something unexpected happens. That means you need to explain the unexpected when you're live, not ignore it. If cheers break out in the middle of your live shot about a multicar accident, explain that you're standing near a soccer field and someone just scored a goal. Otherwise, the audience will be wondering what the cheering was about and miss the point of your story.

The Live Toss

If your live shot is leading in to a package, don't be redundant by echoing what the anchor says in introducing you or by repeating what you say at the top of your package. Use the live segment to set the scene or put your story in context. ABC News White House reporter Martha Raddatz makes great use of her live "tops," even when there's nothing happening in the shot. When President George W. Bush traveled to Iraq for a summit in 2006, World News Tonight anchor Charles Gibson and Raddatz both went along. Here's how the newscast began that night:

> GIBSON: President Bush and Iraq's Prime Minister Nouri al-Maliki both came here to Amman today, to look for a way to bring the spiraling violence in Iraq under control. They are both here. They were due to meet twice, once tonight, once tomorrow morning. But the Iraqi Prime Minister abruptly cancelled tonight's session. Did he snub the President? Our chief White House correspondent, Martha Raddatz, joins us now from here in Amman. Martha?

> RADDATZ (live): Charlie, the White House is trying to downplay the significance of this. But it is a huge embarrassment when any foreign leader cancels a meeting with the President, especially a foreign leader who has 150,000 of your troops in his country.

> RADDATZ (voice over): It was supposed to be a threesome. But only Jordan's King Abdullah and President Bush appeared for this photo opportunity. . . .[6]

Raddatz uses her live segment to establish the importance of the story, and what she says leads seamlessly into her taped report. It's an essential part of her story, not a throwaway as so many live shots are.

The Live Tag and Anchor Questions

Sometimes a producer will ask you to do both a live toss and a live tag, and sometimes you will be asked to do a live tag only. Too often, reporters look at the tag or "live out" as a throwaway, so they spend little time thinking it through.

However, if you think of the introduction as the appetizer and the package or other pre-produced element as the main course, then the tag should be the dessert. You can use it to provide an additional interesting and relevant fact or detail or to set the stage for future stories. For example, in a story about a tornado touching down in your viewing area, you might mention that tomorrow the Federal Emergency Management Agency will be announcing details on how residents can qualify for aid, and that your station will post the information on its Web site as soon as you get it.

Another element of live reporting is the "anchor question." Sometimes at the end of a live shot, the producer will want the anchor to question the reporter who is on the air live. Unfortunately, not all anchors ask good questions and not all reporters know as much about their stories as they probably should. The most important thing to remember is that it's OK to say you don't know something or to say, "That's a good question; I'll look into it and work on getting an answer." Then be sure to follow up and report the information later.

To avoid this kind of awkward situation, sometimes the anchor or producer will ask the reporter to provide a good question. Again, think of this as an opportunity to get more information into your story. What else would you like viewers to know that you didn't have time to tell them? If you really have nothing more to say, then you need to make that clear to the producer and anchor as well.

Here's an example a live tag that added more information to a story. In a major section of southwestern Florida, the Southwest Florida Water Management District manages water use—locally it's known as SWFWMD (pronounced "swift mud" by local journalists). On this day, reporter Chip Osowski of WFLA-TV in Tampa was previewing a SWFWMD vote that could allocate $85 million more to the Tampa Bay Water desalination plant.

OSOWSKI (on camera): If "Swift Mud" does vote to give the money for funding it will be on a performance-based basis meaning if the plant does not perform, the deal will be dead. Gayle . . .

ANCHOR: And so Chip if the plant does get more funding, how will it be doled out?

OSOWSKI: Well it would be doled out in stages, basically the first 25 percent would be upon an acceptance test, a second payment after the plant had pumped 25 million gallons a day for 4 months, and the final payment would come 12 months later if the plant produces 12 and a half million gallons a day for the first year.

ANCHOR: Okay thanks Chip. That vote is scheduled to be taken at this afternoon's meeting of the water district's managing board in Brooksville. The meeting is open to the public.

Live Only

There are situations, particularly during breaking news, when reporters and sometimes photographers are doing "live only" reporting. There is no videotape relief; it is simply you and the camera working together. In this situation it is critical that you know what you're talking about. In a breaking news situation, this can be particularly challenging, especially if the story is still unfolding and you have very little background information.

If there is action behind you, help viewers understand what they are seeing. For example, you can tell them how many fire trucks are on scene and from which departments, or share how high the flames were when you arrived versus the current situation. As WSOC-TV reporter Mark Becker puts it, "Simply tell what you see and what you hear and what you smell and what you feel."

You might also talk about the information you are trying to gather for the viewer. For example, you might say that when you arrived there were only two fire trucks there, but seven more have arrived in the past 10 minutes and you plan to ask the fire chief to explain what's behind the big boost in resources.

Tell what you know and avoid speculating in these situations. Becker says many reporters try too hard to sound like they know it all when they go on live. "Call it an urge to 'over-report'—to say more than you know for the sake of staying on the air, or to guess at the answer to an anchor's question, rather than look dumb," said Becker. He is adamant that reporters should never assume. "It's frighteningly easy to do when the camera's on, and the pressure's on to beat the competition on a story. It's far better to say 'I don't know,' than to guess that someone was killed in the fire because you see people crying in their front yard. It could have been their cat—or it could just be people overwhelmed by the moment," Becker says.

And no matter whether you are live on a breaking story or doing a typical toss to a package, remember the expression, "Every mic is a live mic." Most practicing journalists can tell you a story about reporters or anchors getting fired for saying something they shouldn't have when they thought the microphone was off. As a rule, you should get into your live position, do a standard mic check and then stand quietly until you hear your cue.

TALKING HEADS

An increasing number of newspapers are requiring their reporters to "do television" these days, often without any preparation. There are plenty of good reasons for print reporters to do these "talking head" interviews beyond the fact that the news organization insists on it. For one thing, you can get the news out to a wider audience than you can reach in the newspaper or online. An appearance on TV may drive readers to the paper or the Web site. And even those who do read the newspaper might care more about the stories if they know what the reporter looks like. You may wind up getting more news tips from people who see you on the air.

For the television station, interviewing a print reporter may enable the newsroom to add expertise on an important story. For example, many small stations don't have a dedicated political reporter, but the local newspaper may have someone who covers nothing but politics and that person may provide valuable insight when a big political story breaks. In addition, TV newsrooms often interview print journalists for stories that the station doesn't have the resources to cover. For instance, the newspaper may have a reporter assigned to cover a trial that's expected to last months, while the television reporter may be in court only on opening day and when the verdict is due. When a surprise witness shows up halfway through the trial, interviewing the print reporter who's been there since the beginning would be an efficient way for the television station to cover the new developments.

But a print reporter being interviewed about a story has to be careful not to look foolish, appear partisan or become a punching bag for an opinionated host. Not only can that undermine your credibility, it could get you sued. In 2005, the Boston Herald was ordered to pay more than $2 million for libeling a judge. Part of the award stemmed from an appearance the newspaper reporter made on television—specifically on the Fox News program The O'Reilly Factor.

Preparation

Before you decide whether to say yes to an invitation to go on television, do your homework and prepare carefully. Know the program and the plan. Is this a news program or a "shout fest"? Listen closely to the questions producers ask before you are "booked" for clues to

DOING TV

Whether you are a print reporter learning TV or a beginning broadcast journalist, the following advice can help you do a better job on the air.

- Know your story. Decide on the two or three main points you want to make about your story. Use details and anecdotes to reinforce points after you have made them. Stick with what you know and respond to questions based on your reporting. Don't be afraid to say you don't know something. Avoid being drawn into a debate or speculation.

- Know the setup. If you're not in the studio, use a monitor or ask the photographer how they're shooting you. Will your hands be in the shot? If you're live, look directly at the camera unless told otherwise but feel free to blink and look down every so often to avoid that frozen deer-in-the-headlights look. Ignore anything going on behind or around the camera and avoid shifting your eyes from side to side—it's distracting and it makes you look unreliable.

- Look good. Dress for TV by avoiding white, large or small patterns and flashy jewelry, especially dangling earrings. You want the viewer to pay attention to your story, not your accessories. The trick from the old movie Broadcast News really does work—pull down your jacket in the back and sit on it to avoid lumpy shoulders. Comb that hair and consider using some makeup. If you're shiny, you may look nervous. At a minimum, use some powder.

- Tell your story. Be brief and direct. Speak in short, complete sentences. Be conversational, and don't overload your answers with acronyms, facts or "official-speak." Define your terms. Correct misinformation politely, but do it. Otherwise you may appear to be confirming or agreeing with erroneous comments. And if you goof, correct yourself. Ask for a monitor so you can see any video used before or during your segment; if you don't see it, it's difficult to respond appropriately.

- Assess the results. Ask for a tape of the program or record it yourself and watch your appearance afterwards. Ask your colleagues for some feedback. It may be painful at first, but there's no better way to improve.

TRADE TOOLS

the approach. Are you the only guest? If not, you will want to know who else will be included and what perspectives the other participants will provide.

Will you be in the studio with the host or anchor, or will you appear remotely from your newsroom or another location? If you are new at this and have the option, you may find it easier to be in the studio where you can interact directly with the host or anchor, versus trying to communicate through a camera lens.

Will the interview be live or on tape? Ask if there will be a setup piece or other information preceding your appearance, and whether any tape will be used during the segment. You'll want to know what information is included so you don't repeat what's already been reported and so you can potentially clear up any contradictions before they occur.

Lessons Learned

Michelle Bearden of the Tampa Tribune says she learned about doing TV news the hard way. "On my first day of working for the television station, I thought I was going in to get training. The news director at the station had told me that the producers would be giving me plenty of help and training before I actually went on the air. But when I got to the station, they had assigned me a TV photographer and they were sending me to cover a visit by the Mormon Tabernacle Choir," Bearden says. "I remember it took me 37 takes to do my first stand-up, and I wrote my first script without any sound bites or a natural sound. It was four and a half minutes long because I thought I had to tell the history of the Mormon Church. So, my first experience with convergence was trial and error—with a lot more error."

Mark Fagan of the Lawrence Journal-World says he also learned a valuable lesson when he first started doing on-camera reports for the newspaper's cable TV outlet. "I'm out for breakfast at a local restaurant. As I'm getting ready to pay the bill, the waiter mentions how he likes my new sports coat. 'Nice jacket,' he says, with a wry smile. 'Thanks,' I tell him. 'Got it for my birthday.' The waiter smiles, then lowers the boom: 'It's a good thing. A bunch of us in the back had been talking about taking up a collection to get you a new one.' Wow. Another lesson learned: Own more than one suit, and make sure it fits. People really do pay attention to such things."

PODCASTING

Broadcast journalists may think they have nothing to learn about recording podcasts and vodcasts. They're just different ways of delivering the news you'd normally do on TV, right? Well, not exactly. Consider how the audience receives what you deliver. Many if not most people listen to podcasts on iPods or other MP3 players, which means they are listening through headphones. That makes podcasting even more intimate and personal than radio. Your voice and the bites and sounds you include in your podcast go right into the listener's ears, so you'll probably want to tone down your delivery. Until you have a good sense of what works, listen to your podcast recordings on headphones and watch your vodcasts on a portable player before posting them.

Print journalists who record podcasts of their stories need to take one additional step and either rewrite their copy so it's easier to read aloud or decide to ad-lib the story. Reading a print story word for word into a microphone usually makes for an awkward sounding podcast. If you decide to ad-lib instead of rewriting, before you start recording make some notes similar to the jot outline we suggest for live shots.

Keep your interest level up as you record; if you sound bored, you'll bore the audience or lose them. If you're ad-libbing a podcast, try to avoid long pauses. "Dead air" is just as deadly on a podcast as it is on the radio, giving the listener every reason to tune out. And don't um and ah if you can help it. It may be natural in conversation, but it's really annoying in your ear. If you do stumble a lot and you can't re-record, just edit out the worst of it. Your audience will thank you.

PRINT POINTERS

Just as print journalists need to understand the fine points of going on camera, television reporters need to understand what's required of them when they're asked to deliver stories for the newspaper or online. When you're first assigned a story for the newspaper or the Web, find out who your editor will be. Talk to that person before starting to write or, if possible, even before reporting. Find out what's expected of the story in terms of content, length, photos and graphics.

Print newsrooms measure story length in column inches, so you need to know what a 15-inch story adds up to in word count. One column inch is about 20 words, so that 15-inch story would run about 300 words. For comparison's sake, the average TV script that runs 1:30 has about 225 words.

Structure

The story structures we discussed in Chapter 5 apply to both print and broadcast, but there are a few terms to remember when you're writing for print. One is the "nut graf," frequently used in newspaper stories. It's a paragraph that usually comes about three or four paragraphs into the story, right after the anecdotal or descriptive lead; it explains the significance of the lead, and it gives the reader a reason to keep going. Some editors call it the "so what" graf. Here's an example from the Washington Post:

> DALIAN, China—Tian Deren is only 58, but poor eyesight means he must be helped across the street. He also has diabetes and is hard of hearing, so earlier this year a son-in-law brought him to a privately run home for the elderly.
>
> Because he is still mobile, Tian isn't relegated to the fourth floor, where the most infirm residents live and where some have been known to throw cups of tea at the staff. His room is clean; the food plentiful. Life is good, he said.
>
> But like many of China's graying citizens, Tian understands that the elderly are now treated differently than they once were, that the country's modernization and one-child-only policy have shifted assumptions about old age.[7]

The third paragraph clearly states what the story is about and explains the point of telling Tian's story—because it epitomizes how China's treatment of the elderly has changed.

Style

Print style used to be substantially different from broadcast style, but newspapers have adapted much of what's best about broadcast writing. Lead paragraphs that used to run on forever are now shorter and snappier. Sentences are shorter, too. So don't stop writing crisp, declarative sentences when you're writing for print.

A few differences persist, however. Attribution comes at the end of a sentence in print as opposed to the beginning in broadcast. For television, you'd write: "Police say the man escaped in a red Toyota," but the print version would be different: "The man escaped in a red Toyota, Lincoln County police spokesman Joe Jones said." Notice that the print version uses a name and title you probably wouldn't mention on the air.

Pay close attention to time references if you're writing for the newspaper. If it happened today and you're writing for the next edition of the morning paper, you obviously can't use a "today" reference. The Associated Press (AP) style guide indicates you also should avoid using the words "yesterday" or "tomorrow" in stories and instead use the day of the week. It's probably a good idea for a multimedia journalist to own copies or buy access to a searchable online version of the AP Stylebook and other AP handbooks for both broadcast and print reporting.

David Cullier, a longtime print journalist, now teaches both broadcast and print students at the University of Arizona. Cullier says he notices that, stylistically, his broadcast students like to use a kind of sign-off on their print stories, such as, "what happens next, only time will tell." That's a weak ending in any medium, but Cullier says it's especially important for print stories to have a summary ending. "It should be something that ties back to the lead, but not an editorialized statement. Often a quote that summarizes the story is used in print," said Cullier.

He suggests that writers start the final paragraph with a one-sentence quote, provide the attribution, and then end the paragraph with a short quote, something like this:

"They told me over and over not to play around with guns," Smith said. "Now that Bobby is dead I wish I would have listened."

Cullier also makes the point that broadcast journalists have the advantage of showing people what's going on with visuals, but print reporters need to show people what's going on with words. "This requires using specifics and facts that illustrate and illuminate. Sometimes people get lazy and just tell what is going on, writing about 'The treacherous river . . .' instead of showing with words: 'The river that has claimed 43 lives in the past decade . . .' This requires more reporting," Cullier says.

TAKING IT HOME

The goal of a storyteller in any medium is to communicate effectively, so strong delivery skills are essential. For some journalists, the techniques we've discussed in this chapter come naturally, but most of us can improve our delivery with practice.

Get in the habit of seeking out critiques of your work from someone whose opinion you value. Make it clear to that person that you want an honest assessment of what you're doing well and what needs improvement.

And be sure to regularly evaluate your own work. Once you've completed one or more stories or live shots, review what you've done. Look for at least one thing you've done well that you'd like to repeat and at least one thing you'd like to improve. Some reporters keep a record of their self-critiques to track their own progress. If you already know what you need to work on, you will also be more prepared to get the most out of sessions with a talent coach or mentor.

TALKING POINTS

1. Find the script of a story you've already produced and that you still have on tape. Mark your copy, looking for words that convey important information (usually the subject, verb and object in each sentence) and underline those words. Now, read your script out loud, giving the underlined words more emphasis. Record yourself doing this if at all possible. Now, go back and listen to your old story—have you improved? Did you notice any other delivery issues? Get in the habit of listening to yourself regularly so you can work on getting better.

2. You are assigned to a story about a new study showing fluorescent lighting is contributing to eyestrain and other concentration problems in many classrooms and offices. Develop several ideas for demonstrative or interactive stand-ups you might do for this story.

3. Choose a story you've already reported and feel you know well. If you were assigned a live shot on this story, which two or three main points would you make? Make notes or create a jot outline for a live shot. Deliver it for an audience and ask for a constructive critique.

eLEARNING OPPORTUNITIES

For chapter exercises, practice tools and additional resources, go to the interactive online workbook at http://college.cqpress.com/advancingthestory. You'll find:

- SKILL BUILDING: Walk through a series of case studies that will test your ethical decision making. Review what one journalism ethics expert would have done in the same situation.

- DISCOVER: Watch a television story produced in response to an ethical dilemma and one story that created an ethical discussion among the community's news media. Decide what you would have done in both cases.

- ONGOING STORY: Handle an ethical problem that may require you to change a major part of the story you've created. Find out what the authors decided to do about the issue.

- EXPLORE: Visit Web sites for links to ethics codes and other ethical decision-making resources.

11 MULTIMEDIA ETHICS

As journalism evolves, so does journalism ethics. With the advent of television, ethical discussions about what video to show and what not to show in a television newscast became part of the routine for broadcast journalists. As the Web took on the role of news and information provider, some old ethical problems became more complicated and some entirely new ethical issues were raised. As we begin our exploration of these issues, it's important to remember that we can never anticipate all the ethical dilemmas a journalist will face. We can only strive to develop a system of ethical decision making.

"Reading about ethics is about as likely to improve one's behavior as reading about sports is to make one into an athlete." The author of that quote, Mason Cooley, was a 20th century aphorist, someone who specializes in summarizing complex truths or ideas in a few words or a simple sentence. Though it's doubtful that Cooley was talking about journalism ethics, there is some truth to the idea that you can never become ethical simply by reading about ethics. You have to think about ethics and practice making good decisions in order to behave ethically.

Many of you have taken entire courses on ethics, and most of you know by now that the discussion of ethics cannot be compartmentalized into a single course or capsulated into a set of rules. Ethics is and should be an ongoing discussion.

THINKING ABOUT ETHICS

Ethics is sometimes defined as "motivation based on ideas of right and wrong." Take a moment to study that phrase. Notice that it doesn't say ethics is defined as "motivation based on what is right and wrong." It says ethics is motivation based on "ideas" of right and wrong. That's an important distinction because making ethical decisions is not necessarily about coming up with the "right" answer, but rather it's about coming up with a defensible answer.

Will you be able to defend your decision to your audience? That's the key to journalism ethics. Though you may not convince your viewer or reader that you made an ethical choice, you will at least be able to explain how you reached your decision. That will satisfy some people and, at the very least, your audience will know that the choice was not made arbitrarily. You can reassure them that a great deal of thought went into the decision-making process.

MULTIMEDIA ISSUES

J. D. Lasica, former senior editor of the Online Journalism Review, says online journalism ethics can be grouped into three broad categories: gathering the news, reporting the news and presenting the news. In this chapter, we'll look at all three. For example, when you as a multimedia journalist are gathering the news, is it OK to ask permission to tape an interview without making it clear that you will also be posting the audio on the Web? You can report the news much more quickly online, but greater speed can also lead to greater risk for error. We'll explore standards of accuracy online and the issue of how corrections are handled. Plus, the line between advertising and news is often blurred even more in the online world; we'll look at how sponsorships and other advertising-supported content are handled across platforms.

Along with new storytelling opportunities, convergence—the practice of communicating complementary information on more than one media platform—brings new ethical challenges to the field of journalism. Print, broadcast and online news media share many of the same ethical principles, however, and most news organizations, regardless of platform, support the Society of Professional Journalists' Code of Ethics:

1. Seek truth and report it. Journalists should be honest, fair and courageous in gathering, reporting and interpreting information.

2. Minimize harm. Ethical journalists treat sources, subjects and colleagues as human beings deserving of respect.

3. Act independently. Journalists should be free of obligation to any interest other than the public's right to know.

4. Be accountable. Journalists are accountable to their readers, listeners, viewers and each other.[1]

The number one principle to seek truth is at the very foundation of all journalism ethics. Journalists should always strive to report the most accurate version of a story possible. At the same time, we must take into account the impact of our work on the people we cover, free ourselves as much as possible from internal or external influences and always be willing to explain our actions to the communities we serve.

On the surface, it may not look so difficult to abide by these principles. Of course journalists should seek the truth and treat their sources with respect. But often the principles themselves are in conflict. Journalists who seek the truth may discover information that will be hurtful to the family of a person involved in wrongdoing. A reporter's membership in a nongovernmental organization may permit that reporter to learn more about a story the group is involved with, but that membership may also compromise the reporter's independence and be difficult to justify to the audience. In many cases, making an ethical decision means choosing not between right and wrong but between right and right.

Despite agreement on general ethical principles, there are also enough differences in the way that print, broadcast and online newsrooms operate to ensure that unique ethical dilemmas do arise. That's why organizations such as the Radio-Television News Directors Association and the National Press Photographers Association have created ethics codes that seek to address some of the specific challenges faced by journalists in the broadcast industry or by photojournalists. CyberJournalist.net, a Web site that focuses on how the Internet, convergence and new technologies are changing the media, has created a Bloggers' Code of Ethics to help guide people using this reporting form. Print organizations like the American Society of Newspaper Editors and the Associated Press Managing Editors have also developed codes to help guide print journalists.

As you've already learned, there are significant operational differences among the broadcast, online and print media. For example, TV and online media both deal with pictures and sound, but the nonlinear capability of the Web lets users choose whether to click through to view a graphic photo or listen to a disturbing audio clip. Broadcast journalists can warn the audience that the pictures they're about to see are graphic, but a newspaper can't alert you to a potentially troubling photograph if it's published on the front page.

The big questions arise when a news organization must decide if its ethical principles are uniform across platforms. If your editorial decision makers believe a graphic is too disturbing to use in the newspaper, is it okay to post it online because the user can choose to view it or not? Or do you need to have ethical policies that are consistent, no matter what medium you use to disseminate the information? This chapter highlights some of the decision-making challenges you'll face as an ethical journalist in a converged media environment.

Corrections on the Web

Most newspapers and television stations around the country have very clear policies on how to handle mistakes that make it into the paper or on the air. You're probably all familiar with the "corrections box" that occasionally appears somewhere in most newspapers. The goal is to alert readers to any errors that were made in the paper's previously published stories. Many TV newsrooms have rules that say a correction must be aired as soon as the mistake

KNOW AND TELL

CORRECTING MISTAKES

A wag once said that being a journalist means never having to say you're sorry. Emerson Stone begs to differ. The former vice president for news practices at CBS News says if it's important enough to report, it's important enough to correct when you get it wrong. This is Stone's 10-point plan for stations wishing to develop or fine-tune a corrections policy.

1. Welcome all who point out your mistakes. Thank them. That sage old Dean, Jonathan Swift (1667–1745), wisely wrote: "A man should never be ashamed to own he has been in the wrong, which is but saying in other words that he is wiser to-day than he was yesterday."

2. No matter is too trivial to correct. See the New York Times' daily corrections of matters as (supposedly) minor as the spelling of names. Those who hear, see or read the news and, out of their own knowledge, perceive a small mistake that goes uncorrected, must ask themselves, "What larger errors do they make that go uncorrected? Can I trust anything they report?"

3. Don't wait. Make the correction on air as soon as its accuracy has been checked.

4. Correct in equivalent news programs. Evening News corrections go in the Evening News, and so on. (You probably don't have the same audience at 11 p.m. and at 5 a.m., so correcting a late-night error in the morning may not do much good.)

5. Avoid burying corrections. Make the correction as prominent in the broadcast as the original error, not thrown away or glossed over.

is confirmed, and some go as far as to say the correction must air again in the same news-cast as the mistake was originally made. For example, if the city budget deficit is reported in error at 6 p.m. on Monday, and the error is discovered at 8 p.m. that same evening, most newsrooms will air a correction in the next scheduled newscast at 10 or 11 p.m.; some will even air the correction a second time at 6 p.m. on Tuesday. The goal is to make sure the correct information reaches the widest possible audience as well as to let people know that accuracy matters to the news organization.

6. Be complete. That means full and clear, including the statement that it is a correction, from which broadcast, who made the error and how it came about. Doesn't hurt to add that you regret it.

7. Tell the whole truth. Procedures like the one directly above sound as if you don't want to tell viewers on the air: "I was wrong; here's how, when, and why." On air, of course, is exactly where corrections are most vital. Responsibility is the key word.

8. Be attuned to catching errors. All staff members need to learn to welcome and get full details of any communication, phoned or written, that alleges an error or states a correction. That information then goes to the proper person for checking and action.

9. Respond directly to complaints. A polite response should go to anyone who alleges an error, once the allegation is checked out and has been properly dealt with, re-gardless of whether the information was right or wrong.

10. Lose the attitude. It is time that we put behind us the days of circling the wagons against claims of error; time to cease those brusque I-haven't-got-time telephone cutoffs or we-stand-by-our-story letters of response. Make some time; get back to the caller promptly, if you really can't talk now. Check out the allegation. Respond by letter if that's the best way. Do the necessary. And again: correct any mistake on the air. (I know: The networks don't do it. Do it.)

Source: "Correcting Mistakes," NewsLab, June 2, 2006, www.newslab.org/resources/corrections.htm.

But things get a little trickier in the Web world. Some online journalism outlets have no formal policy at all for handling corrections. When an error is identified, some organizations simply remove the inaccurate information from the site. Unfortunately, if any online news consumers have read the story earlier in the day, they have been misinformed. Even if they return to the story later, there're not alerted to the fact that what they read earlier was wrong. Most reputable journalism sites do include a correction notice to users somewhere in the story or near it, but policies on how prominent the correction must be vary from organization to organization.

As more and more journalists disseminate information via online sites or through convergence partnerships, the question becomes whether corrections policies should be consistent across media platforms. Take Web archives, for example. Many online newspaper sites archive stories exactly as they appeared in the printed paper's final edition, including any errors. If a correction is necessary, it is indicated at the top of the story or published in a separate box. These news organizations believe that the Web site archive should be the official record of what was published. But a small number of papers have determined that the online archive should include the most accurate version of the story possible. They have developed systems to make the changes necessary to correct a story in the archive. For example, if a suspect's name is misspelled in the printed publication, it will be spelled correctly in the online archive. At the top of the story is a statement noting that the original published version contained an error that has now been corrected. Sometimes the statement will include specifics on exactly what was corrected, sometimes it will not. This approach minimizes the chance that someone will miss the corrections box or notification and republish or simply read inaccurate information. But the story is now altered; it is no longer a record of what was in the paper. So, which approach is the most ethical?

One solution is to simply make your news organization's online corrections policy clear to your users. The San Francisco Chronicle's home page includes a link to "Corrections." This page explains the paper's policy to "promptly correct errors of fact and to promptly clarify potentially confusing statements," includes an e-mail address for reporting errors and lists the most recent corrections from the print edition. That's being transparent—sharing your news organization's policy with the people using your site. This idea of transparency—telling people what you've decided and how you arrived at that decision—is one way that news organizations are accountable for their decisions and can be helpful in dealing with many ethical dilemmas.

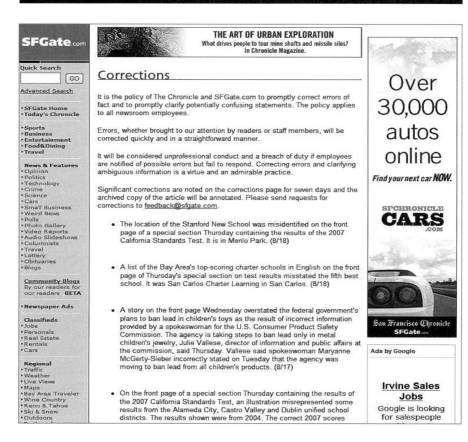

THE ART OF URBAN EXPLORATION
What drives people to tour mine shafts and missile silos?
In Chronicle Magazine.

Corrections

It is the policy of The Chronicle and SFGate.com to promptly correct errors of fact and to promptly clarify potentially confusing statements. The policy applies to all newsroom employees.

Errors, whether brought to our attention by readers or staff members, will be corrected quickly and in a straightforward manner.

It will be considered unprofessional conduct and a breach of duty if employees are notified of possible errors but fail to respond. Correcting errors and clarifying ambiguous information is a virtue and an admirable practice.

Significant corrections are noted on the corrections page for seven days and the archived copy of the article will be annotated. Please send requests for corrections to feedback@sfgate.com.

- The location of the Stanford New School was misidentified on the front page of a special section Thursday containing the results of the 2007 California Standards Test. It is in Menlo Park. (8/18)

- A list of the Bay Area's top-scoring charter schools in English on the front page of Thursday's special section on test results misstated the fifth best school. It was San Carlos Charter Learning in San Carlos. (8/18)

- A story on the front page Wednesday overstated the federal government's plans to ban lead in children's toys as the result of incorrect information provided by a spokeswoman for the U.S. Consumer Product Safety Commission. The agency is taking steps to ban lead only in metal children's jewelry, Julie Vallese, director of information and public affairs at the commission, said Thursday. Vallese said spokeswoman Maryanne McGerty-Sieber incorrectly stated on Tuesday that the agency was moving to ban lead from all children's products. (8/17)

- On the front page of a special section Thursday containing the results of the 2007 California Standards Test, an illustration misrepresented some results from the Alameda City, Castro Valley and Dublin unified school districts. The results shown were from 2004. The correct 2007 scores

On its Web site, SFGate.com, the San Francisco Chronicle promises to leave "significant corrections" posted for seven days, and to include a note about the correction on stories as they're archived.

Source: Courtesy of SFGate.com.

Transparency and Bias

Imagine that you are working in a television newsroom and that your station is a major sponsor of a local golf tournament. Part of the sponsorship agreement is that your sports anchor will have exclusive, pretournament access to interviews with the big-name golfers coming to town. First of all, is there anything wrong with that? Is this an example of paying for a news story? There are no restrictions on what can be asked or used from the interview, but is this an ethical way to gather the news? What if the station's newspaper partner asks your anchor to write a print story from the pretournament interview with star golfer Tiger Woods? Does the station need to make sure the paper knows why the sports anchor is getting an exclusive? Do the viewers and readers need to know? If you don't reveal the nature of the sponsorship agreement, and it eventually comes to light, how might the audience react? This scenario is not at all far-fetched, but the audience is rarely made aware of the situation when it occurs.

This is another example of how transparency can help save you and your news organization from an ethical lapse and the subsequent loss of credibility. If you make the details of a sponsorship agreement clear to everyone involved—both those within the news organizations and the audiences—then you remove the risk of being accused of deception. As an added bonus, the mere act of revealing the arrangement to others may force people in your own news organization to question whether this is an appropriate agreement. That process can help you defend your position if you receive criticism after the arrangement is revealed.

The nature of online journalism also makes it necessary to discuss the ethics of linking the user to information that's been created by others—some of which may be biased. Let's say you're doing a story on the increase in hate crimes in your community. One of the people included in your story is a member of the Creativity Movement, which believes Caucasians are meant to rule the world. Do you link to the organization's Web page to offer people more information about it? If so, do you also need to link to a site that condemns such groups? Most online journalists will tell you that the best solution is to make sure that you clearly identify each link for users to make sure they know where they are going when they click on it. At that point, the user can make an informed choice.

Advertorials and Infomercials

Both television stations and newspapers may sometimes produce special products simply as advertising vehicles. Broadcasters create programs, such as a back-to-school special, to attract advertising dollars to the station, and they use the resources of their news staffs to produce the special. The advertisers typically have no direct control over the content, but the show will certainly feature content that is advertiser friendly. The program most likely will not include any hard-hitting investigations.

In the newspaper business, many papers hire writers from outside the newsroom to produce the content for their special sections, and in that way they avoid any appearance of having their newspeople writing paid content. But not always. The Los Angeles Times found itself in the middle of a major controversy in 1999 when it agreed to sponsor the Staples Center, a new sports and entertainment complex in downtown L.A. What was controversial was that when the Times published a 168-page Sunday magazine supplement about the new facility, the paper split $2 million in advertising revenues with the center. The journalists involved knew nothing about it. Criticism from journalists around the country and inside the Times newsroom led to public apologies from three of the paper's top executives.

But what happens in a converged environment? Is it OK for the newspaper's education reporter to appear in the sponsor-driven television special? Although most print, broadcast and online journalists strive to be ethical, what's acceptable in one medium may or may not be in another.

Most traditional media have very strict policies regarding the presentation of advertising content. Many television stations air "infomercials"—programs devoted to promoting some product or service to the viewers. Some are even designed to look like news programs, but viewers are often notified throughout the show that they are watching paid programming, in other words, not something produced by the station's news staff.

On the print side, there are "advertorials"—advertisements that are designed to look like a news article or editorial regularly published in the paper. These advertorials are identified with a line of type at the top of the story that usually says, "Advertisement," although the size of the type may be so small that it's easily missed.

On the Web, the rules appear to be a little less clear. In 2002, an organization called Consumer Reports WebWatch began tracking a Web advertorial paid for by Sony. According to Sony, the stories were written by freelance journalists, and they featured real consumers who described how technology was affecting their everyday lives. One thing that made the content controversial was the "Related Links" section. Users who clicked to find out more about the technologies described in the articles found themselves exposed to Sony products only. Some of the sites that posted the content published it under the heading of "News," identified it only with the words, "Feature by Sony," and didn't use the word "advertising" at all. So, is it OK for a news Web site to post this kind of content? Should there be specific guidelines about where the content should appear and how it should be identified? The American Society of Magazine Editors suggests this guideline: "On all online pages, there shall be a clear distinction made—through words, design, placement, or any other effective method—between editorial and advertising content."

With the explosion of news organizations that publish their own Web sites and the proliferation of multimedia partnerships around the country, it's probably time for most news operations to develop converged editorial guidelines, so that identification of editorial versus advertising content will be as consistent as possible across platforms. In the case of the TV education special, for example, such guidelines would require the sponsorship of the program be clear to the viewer and to the newspaper's education reporter. If an online product was created in conjunction with the special, the sponsorship would be clearly identified there, too. The goal would be to define the line between advertising and news content as clearly as possible for all involved.

Interview Agreements

Anyone who has ever taken a reader, viewer or user phone call knows that news consumers often have strong loyalty to or dislike for a given news organization. So, just because the management of the television station has decided it wants to partner with the local newspaper, that doesn't mean that the audience is going to be happy about it. And the same holds true for the newsmakers you will be including in your coverage—whether in print, on the air or online.

Most television reporters have had the experience of spending hours, or even days, coaxing someone into giving them an interview, just to hear this: "Oh, you're not planning to put me on TV are you?" In fact, it's not even unusual to conduct an entire interview with lights and camera and microphone and then have the interviewee say, "Now, this isn't going on the air, is it?" Some television reporters have developed a habit of prepping interviewees on the front end by making it clear that the information provided will be used in a newscast. That way the reporters don't waste time and effort getting someone to agree to an interview they might not be able to use on the air.

So, in a multiplatform world, do we owe our interviewees the courtesy of informing them of all the ways that we will be using their words and actions? Print reporters sometimes ask interview subjects for permission to record the audio of an interview. When the interview subject OKs the recording, do you think it is with the understanding that it could be used for more than just taking notes? In fact, those recordings could be posted online or aired on a news broadcast. Should the reporter make that clear to the interviewee?

Should TV reporters who plan to write an online version of their television story make their intent clear to everyone they talk to? It's certainly possible that someone would be willing to talk to a local TV station but not want friends or relatives in other cities to be aware of that fact. However, if the story is posted online, it's accessible to anyone with a computer and Internet access. For example, a lesbian may be quite open about her sexuality with friends and co-workers in Dallas, Texas, but she may not have discussed the issue at all with her family in Little Rock, Ark. If she doesn't know the story is going online, she may feel

NEWS AND SALES: CLARIFYING THE RELATIONSHIP

Good journalism and a station's economic goals can sometimes conflict. But stations risk damaging the foundation of their business if they produce or avoid news stories to please sponsors, or solicit or place advertising in a way that weakens the integrity of their news operation. With that in mind, a group of news and station executives gathered in 2002 under the auspices of NewsLab and the Committee of Concerned Journalists to discuss ways of helping news and sales managers deal with the pressures they face. The group agreed that the following general principles should serve as the basis for all decisions affecting news and sales:

- News content should be determined solely through editorial judgment.
- News sponsors should not dictate or influence news content.
- News content should be clearly distinguishable from advertising content.

To develop written guidelines and to work through most situations involving news and sales, answering these four basic questions will help:

- What are the short-term and long-term consequences of making or not making this sale or arrangement?
- What will viewers and listeners think when they see or hear this on the air? For example: Could this sponsorship influence or appear to influence the content of the story in any way? Could this sponsorship affect the station's brand, image or reputation?
- How will you explain this decision to viewers and listeners, critics and station personnel, and are there any details you would be uncomfortable making public?
- Should this arrangement be in writing?

Adapted from "News and Sales: Clarifying the Relationship," NewsLab, 2006, www.newslab.org/resources/newssales.htm.

it's safe to talk to a local news organization about her feelings as a lesbian regarding a proposed same-sex marriage amendment. But she might be quite disturbed to learn that the story is available online where it can reach a much wider audience, including people back home in Arkansas.

If you consider that two of journalists' primary ethical principles are to minimize harm and to be accountable, it seems clear that multimedia journalists should provide the people they cover with as much information as possible about the ways in which the information they share will be used.

Multimedia News Releases

Journalism isn't the only profession trying to understand and capitalize on the power of multimedia. For many years, public relations practitioners have blanketed newsrooms with paper news releases in the hopes of getting positive coverage for whatever event, product or company they were promoting. But multimedia news releases are becoming increasingly common. These kits often include complete television news stories that stations are free to run, along with supplemental information to be posted on the Web or printed in the newspaper. Television stations have recently come under fire for the way they have used video news releases (VNRs). In some cases, stations have run VNRs as if they were regular news stories without any attribution at all. And the problem is not unique to broadcast newsrooms; there are plenty of examples of newspapers printing press releases without changing a word. Of course, the problem with this is that the news organization usually has not verified the information in the story or alerted the audience to the fact that the story is coming from a nonjournalistic source, leaving the news organization open to charges of deception.

The Radio-Television News Directors Association Code (RTNDA) of Ethics and Professional Conduct states that professional electronic journalists should "clearly disclose the origin of information and label all material provided by outsiders." The group has also created a series of guidelines to help news organizations determine when it's appropriate to use VNRs and when it is not.[2] One of the most important is that news organizations use VNRs only when there is no other way to get the video and the story has clear news value.

Many news organizations have also developed their own policies, which usually include a requirement that the source of the story be clearly identified both verbally and visually. For example, in a story about a new kind of poultry processing, you might not be allowed inside the plant to shoot your own video. In that case, you might include the following line of copy in your story: "As you can see in this video from Tyson Foods, the new machines will change the way each chicken is cleaned." In addition to the verbal reference, you would also want to add a graphic "super" over the video, which would identify the source: Tyson Foods. If you were to use the video online, attribution would be important there as well.

This kind of transparency is essential because it alerts the audience to the fact that you have been unable to verify the accuracy of what you're showing them. What if the machine malfunctions routinely? Certainly, that would not be a part of the news release, so sharing the source of the video allows viewers to apply a healthy amount of skepticism to what they're seeing.

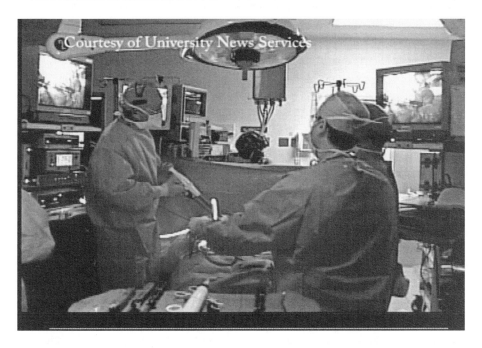

The student-produced newscast at Virginia Commonwealth University has a strict policy of identifying the source of any video not gathered by students involved in the show.

Source: Courtesy of Virginia Commonwealth University School of Mass Communications.

ONLINE ISSUES

In addition to new ethical challenges arising with the advent of multimedia, the online medium itself has created some new ethical dilemmas. Just as television changed the journalism landscape in the 1950s, the Web is changing the way news and information get delivered now. Any time new delivery systems are put in play there is the potential for misuse and abuse. Since one of the primary advantages of online is its accessibility, journalists must be aware at all times that what they put online is there for the world to see.

Blogging

Not too many years ago, journalists around the country were asking themselves whether it was OK for a journalist to write blogs at all. That was at a time when people were confusing the mechanism with the message. Blogs are simply a way to present information; there is nothing inherently unethical or biased about blogs. Still journalists must take care to use them properly.

As we discussed in Chapter 8, a blog is simply an abbreviation for "Web log," a kind of online diary that's regularly updated and often links users to more information about a particular topic. For example, a reporter covering a high-profile trial might produce one or two television stories a day, but might also post multiple blog entries on the case, including links to background stories and PDF files of important documents used in the trial.

Good blogs have a distinct voice; the reader gets a sense of the person writing the blog entry. However, that does not mean the writer should feel free to insert personal bias and unsubstantiated views into a blog. Instead, good blogs are much more like opinion columns in a newspaper. According to the book "The Elements of Journalism," you must keep three criteria in mind when expressing opinion or editorial comment: (1) what you report must be verified and truthful, (2) you must make it clear to your audience what your views and biases are and (3) you must remain independent from the people or issues you cover.[3] So, in the case of the reporter covering the trial, it would be inappropriate for a blog entry to say whether the reporter-blogger thought the defendant was guilty, but the reporter-blogger might be justified in writing about how well the trial was going for the defendant, an observation that would be based on direct observations of the jury's reaction to certain testimony. And that's only if the reporter-blogger had no relationships with any of the people involved in the trial and was not personally vested in the outcome. So, for example, it might be inappropriate for a journalist to serve on the board of local battered women's shelter and then report on a domestic violence trial. It's a fine line and one journalists should walk very cautiously.

And what about the issue of journalists and their personal blogs? Can a journalist who covers the automotive industry maintain a blog for Corvette lovers, for example? Most ethicists will say it depends. "I think the automotive reporter should be circumspect about what opinions he or she offers on the site," says Gary Hill, a news manager at KSTP-TV in Minneapolis and chair of the Ethics Committee for the Society of Professional Journalists. "Clearly the person loves the Corvette or they wouldn't labor on the blog, but does it go further? 'GM is the only American auto manufacturer to ever make a decent muscle car.' If you expressed such an opinion you'd have some explaining to do the next time you had to review a Ford or Chrysler product. Conversely if you decided to write something in your newspaper about a Corvette you would need to disclose that you publish the Corvette blog so readers would know of your love for the car." Again, it comes down to the issue of transparency, making sure that people know of your potential bias.

Many news organizations have developed policies that may prevent employees from blogging on any topic at all, regardless of whether it's on a topic the journalist may cover. Others allow journalists to blog freely about their personal lives but restrict what they write about news stories.

Be sure you ask about your newsroom's policy. If there isn't one, carefully consider whether you are in any way creating an appearance of bias through what you reveal on your personal blog. As Hill says, "A reporter should know that anything they blog can and will be used against them if it suits anybody's purpose to do so."

Plagiarism and Copyright

Although plagiarism is clearly not unique to online journalism, it's so easy to cut and paste information found on the Web that it may be tempting to steal another person's words. However, one word will always protect you from this most egregious of journalism's sins: attribution. Make sure that any time you pull information from another source you identify the source for your reader.

At Emory University in Atlanta, the journalism program has a plagiarism statement on its Web site:

In journalism, source citations are included in the body of the story. The credit should include the name of the person or source, a person's affiliation, and any other information that provides necessary context. The journalist provides attribution for all direct and indirect quotes and paraphrased information and statements. Quotation marks are used even if only a word or phrase of a statement is used. Journalists attribute to specific individuals, organizations or sources and do not create composite sources.

Both direct quotations and paraphrases require attribution. A good paraphrase expresses the ideas found in the source (for which credit is always given) but not in the same words. It preserves the sense, but not the form, of the original. It does not retain the sentence patterns and merely substitute synonyms for the original words, nor does it retain the original words and merely alter the sentence patterns. It is a genuine restatement. It is briefer than its source.[4]

FIGHTING THE PIRATES OF THE PRESS

The Poynter Institute's Roy Peter Clark has been tracking plagiarism cases in journalism for more than 20 years. He offered this background and advice in an online column.

The word plagiarism means "kidnap," and each word-snatch has its own peculiar characteristics. But some patterns repeat themselves time and again.

1. Almost all cases of serious plagiarism are intentional.

2. Serious plagiarism by adults is a moral flaw, not an ethical one.

3. Not all cases of plagiarism are equal.

4. With guidance, supervisors can exercise discretion and match punishments to the severity of the crime.

5. There are special cases in journalism that require special attention, the articulation of standards and practices, and, yes, training.

6. The Internet complicates all of this. Veteran journalists from Spain complained to me of younger reporters who practiced a kind of cut-and-paste journalism from the comfort of their computer chairs.

Suzy Hansen reports in the New York Times that 40 percent of college students admit to Internet plagiarism.

So what's an editor to do?

Students know that plagiarism can lead to grades of F or expulsion from school; professional journalists should know that plagiarism can lead to firing and disgrace.

In addition to understanding how to properly attribute material, you should also familiarize yourself with the laws surrounding the use of copyrighted material. Essentially, anything that appears in a broadcast or is published is considered copyrighted. So, if you pull information from another news source, you are using copyrighted material. That's not always illegal, however. The United States Copyright Office states on its Web site that the doctrine of "fair use" permits news organizations to use copyrighted material from an outside source without permission, but only under certain circumstances.

1. Announce to your staff that plagiarism is a serious problem in all of journalism, and that you assume there will be cases in your newsroom.

2. Insist that serious plagiarism is a firing offense.

3. Publish these, review them every year, make them part of any orientation of new staffers.

4. Develop training sessions on "the tools of originality," with particular attention to note taking, file keeping, methods of attribution and the Internet.

5. Without creating a "rat squad," let staffers know that they can blow the whistle on malpractice in confidence.

6. Train editors how to act on such complaints from both inside and outside the newsroom.

7. Consult with a company about using computer technology to conduct random plagiarism checks on reporters' work.

8. Pray.

9. Pray.

10. Pray.

11. Pray.

Source: Adapted from Roy Peter Clark, "The Global War on Plagiarism: Fighting the Pirates of the Press," PoynterOnline, August 26, 2004, www.poynter.org/content/content_view.asp?id=70511.

In general, these factors are used to determine fair use:

• The purpose and character of the use, including whether such use is of commercial nature or is for nonprofit educational purposes;

• The nature of the copyrighted work;

• Amount and substantiality of the portion used in relation to the copyrighted work as a whole; and

• the effect of the use upon the potential market for or value of the copyrighted work.[5]

In other words, if your state's governor appears on ABC's "Nightline" and makes a controversial statement about working women neglecting their children, you would clearly want to report that information. If you work for an NBC affiliate, you would obviously want to use the video clip of the governor's statement, and the fair use doctrine would allow you to do that. However, fair use would likely not allow you to rebroadcast the entire "Nightline" program on your TV station or Web site. Most legal experts will tell you that the critical issue is to see that no more of the copyrighted work was used than completely necessary to achieve the news reporting purpose, so you must keep that in mind when you are taking information from another source, even with attribution.

Digital Manipulation of Images

Just as ethical journalists do not make up quotes or steal other people's information, they do not manipulate still photos or video in a way that could mislead the audience. Advances in digital imaging hardware and software have made it easier than ever before to manipulate still and moving images in a way that changes the reality of what was there. In August 2006, for example, a freelance photographer who had worked for Reuters for 13 years was fired after it was determined that an image he provided to the news agency had been digitally manipulated to make it look like Israeli war planes had done more bomb damage in Beirut than they actually had.

This kind of digital manipulation is often called "photoshopping," but it can be a problem with video as well. Using slow motion or other effects can make a statement about your subject that you may or may not intend. For example, some research has found that using slow-motion video makes a criminal suspect look guilty. Your reason for using slow motion may be a lack of video, but you should be aware of the unintended impact.

Tom Henry
ON THE ENVIRONMENT

Shortage of water is a global crisis

"Whiskey is for drinking, Water is for fighting over."
— Mark Twain.

I tread carefully as I start today's column with that quote, given there's a debate about whether Twain actually said it. But the point remains: Water tension is getting worse — even in the Great Lakes region.

Lucas County itself is a microcosm of the world's water crisis. While Toledo and other eastern Lucas municipalities have virtually an endless flow from Lake Erie, western townships have wells gone dry.

That brings us to the real crisis: distribution.

There's no equity in how water is dispersed. There are haves and have-nots.

International water expert Peter Gleick said it's no exaggeration to call the situation a crisis because one of every six people on Earth doesn't have access to clean drinking water.

Nearly 5 million people — mostly children — die each year from cholera and other preventable, water-related diseases that all but vanished from the United States 100 years ago. His California-based institute calls the death toll "one of the great tragedies of our time."

Mr. Gleick is co-founder and president of the Pacific Institute for Studies in Development, Environment, and Security. Every other year it publishes an inventory of the Earth's water resources.

"I'm afraid the risks of conflicts over water are growing and not shrinking," he said Tuesday while delivering Bowling Green State University's annual Edward Lamb Peace Lecture to more than 200 people.

What does that mean for us? Probably not much, if we continue to insulate ourselves from human misery and suffering in other parts of the world.

But the United Nations has declared all humans have a right to water. And while a lot of people fear we're moving toward an era of bulk exports and water transfers, few seem to understand that none of the world's poorest regions could deal with water shortages before if they simply had modern sanitation.

Why is the world seemingly more focused on text messaging and palm-sized Internet devices than water treatment?

Mr. Gleick said the human race can do better. He said he would support a tax of up to 5 cents on every $1 bottled water container if the revenue is used to fund improvements.

Congress in 2005 passed the Paul Simon Water for the Poor Act in honor of the late Illinois senator's efforts for water equity. The State Department said the act makes access to safe water and sanitation a foreign-aid policy objective by providing $250 million for global water programs.

Mr. Gleick said that's a "paltry" sum, given the staggering need. But it's a start.

Scientists expect more storms as the Earth's average temperature rises. That's not expected to diffuse water tensions, though. Quite the opposite.

Canada, the most water-rich country, is expected to get wetter. Africa, India, and other parched regions — including the southwestern United States — are expected to get dryer.

The U.S. Census Bureau estimates the world will surpass 6.6 billion people in 2007, twice its 1950 population. By midcentury, the population is expected to surpass 9 billion.

EXAMPLES OF ALTERED PHOTOGRAPHS

The Blade began investigating after determining that a photograph from a March 30 Bluffton University baseball game had been digitally altered by a staff photographer before being submitted to editors. The inquiry found that since January of this year, photographer Allan Detrich submitted 947 photos for publication, of which 79 had been digitally altered. Twenty-seven of the altered photos were published in the newspaper and on toledoblade.com, and an additional 31 were published only on the Web site. Another 21 altered photos submitted were not published.

Above: The original image of the Bluffton University baseball team praying before its first game on March 30 included a pair of legs beneath the No. 19 sign at far right.

Below: The legs have been digitally removed in an altered image that was submitted by the photographer and appeared in the March 31 edition of The Blade.

Left: A photo taken at the Kut-N-Up salon on Sylvania Avenue for The Blade's Toledo 24 series contained a white cord in the upper right of the image. **Right:** When the photographer submitted the image, which was published on toledoblade.com on March 25, the cord had been removed.

Left: A photo taken during the Jan. 27 University of Toledo and Kent State women's basketball game showed players reaching upward. **Right:** A basketball had been added to the image when the photographer submitted it to editors. The image was not selected and did not appear in the paper.

Photos
Continued from Page 1

Mr. Detrich also submitted two sports photographs in which items were inserted. In one he added a hockey puck and in the other he added a basketball, each hanging in mid-air. Neither was published.

The Blade is removing all of Mr. Detrich's photographs from toledoblade.com and blocked access to any of his photographs in the newspaper's archive. The Blade shares its work with the Associated Press, an inter-national news cooperative. On April 6, the AP removed all 59 of Mr. Detrich's photographs from its archives.

Honesty is the fundamental value in journalism.

When a Blade reporter or photographer covers a news event, the newspaper and its readers expect an accurate record of the event.

Reporters and editors are not allowed to change quotes or alter events to make them more dramatic. Photographers and photo editors cannot digitally alter the content in the frame of a photograph to make the image more powerful or artistic.

This principle is widely recognized. In 1991, at the dawn of the digital age, the National Press Photographers Association adopted a "Digital Manipulation Code of Ethics," which all members are required to sign.

That lengthy code makes it very clear that altering the editorial content of a picture is a breach of ethical standards. All Blade photographers are members of the association. All of them have signed the code of ethics, and The Blade follows this code.

This newspaper has a terrific staff of professional journalists. They work hard to bring you the truth in stories and photographs of what is happening in our community, every day of the year. It is especially dismaying to have something like this happen that may cast doubt on our work.

It's impossible to make sense of why this happened, and we are embarrassed by it. But it is important that we are up front and honest with our readers.

Mr. Detrich joined The Blade in 1989 and has won hundreds of newspaper photography awards over the years. He was a Pulitzer finalist in 1998. The work he turned in always appeared to be quality photojournalism, which is why editors had no reason to suspect he was digitally altering photographs.

In this respect, we let our readers down, and we apologize for that and pledge to you that we will do better.

Contact Ron Royhab at: rroyhab@theblade.com

CROSSING AN ETHICAL LINE

Three other news organizations have dealt with the issue of digitally altered photos in the last several years:

■ The Los Angeles Times fired photographer Brian Walski over a satellite phone while he was covering the invasion of Iraq for the newspaper on April 1, 2003. Mr. Walski had taken two separate images and combined them into one image to create a news photograph on March 30, 2003.

Photo editors at the Times' sister paper, the Hartford Courant, discovered the altered image after the Courant had printed it. After a day of research, Colin Crawford, Los Angeles Times director of photography, confronted Mr. Walski. "What Brian did is totally unacceptable and he violated our trust with our readers," Mr. Crawford told Poynter Online, an industry Web site.

■ Adnan Hajj, a Reuters freelance photographer, altered two photos last summer while covering the conflict between Israel and Hezbollah in Beirut.

Mr. Hajj used the cloning tool within Photoshop to alter the amount of smoke in the sky after an aerial bombardment on Aug. 5, 2006. A Reuters investigation confirmed this and found another image of an Israeli F-16 firing defensive flares that was altered to add more flares.

Reuters removed all of Mr. Hajj's images from its database and released the freelance photographer.

Paul Holmes, editor of political and general news at Reuters, told the BBC that senior photographers at the agency "weren't convinced" that cleaning dust off the first image would result in the manipulation the image showed. He said there had been a "lapse in our editing process" but stressed that Reuters had moved swiftly to address the issue and tighten editing procedures.

"There is no graver breach of Reuters standards for our photographers than the deliberate manipulation of an image," Global picture editor Tom Szlukovenyi said in a statement to the BBC.

■ The Charlotte Observer in North Carolina fired photographer Patrick Schneider on July 26, 2006, for manipulating colors in a photo that appeared in the newspaper. Mr. Schneider had been reprimanded for altering photos before.

In this case, the image showed a firefighter on a ladder, silhouetted against the sun and a vividly red sky. It was published in color on the front of the paper's local news section. Observer Editor Rick Thames apologized to the newspaper's readers for the altered photo and announced that Mr. Schneider no longer worked for the paper. "In the original photo, the sky in the photo was brownish-gray. Enhanced with photo-editing software, the sky became a deep red and the sun took on a more distinct halo," the editor's note said.

"Schneider said he did not intend to mislead readers, only to restore the actual color of the sky," the note continued. "He said the color was lost when he underexposed the photo to offset the glare of the sun."

Letters
Continued from Page 1

night-vision goggles, which will help me avoid obstacles while my co-pilot keeps his focus on the gauges inside. Back in the hangar, it took me almost 10 minutes to install and focus my goggles, which is time well spent if they help me see clearly on this dark night. With my goggles down, the first thing I notice is how many stars there are in the sky — literally thousands come into view that I could not see without the help of the goggles.

Although I can see bright objects from very far away, most lighting is not compatible with goggles of this type and I end up seeing many fuzzy bright spots in the air. To make matters worse, my field of view is very limited. Flying with goggles is similar to driving a car while peering through a tube of toilet paper. This requires me to make exaggerated head movements to capture visual information that would be absorbed by my peripheral vision in the day.

I scan the horizon to acclimate to the new view, and I see two aircraft from my squadron rounds with tracers. As the rotor gets up to speed, I can see it form a green blur in my windscreen, so I pay special attention to not let it dip too far down, which would endanger the ground crew and equipment.

Before long we are ready to taxi, and as I start to inch the aircraft forward, I see something out of the corner of my eye. The fireman is making angry arm signals as a figure runs blindly through my rotor arc and across the nose of my aircraft. I immediately recognize the tall frame as one belonging to a junior co-pilot we call "Stomp" on account of his delicate pedal control. Although he is in no real danger of being run over by our slow-rolling helicopter, we speculate on how close he has come to losing his head to the spinning rotor blades that I have lowered to start the taxi process. Since he has no goggles or intercom connection, he is totally unaware of the 42,000-pound giant he narrowly escaped, and he continues with his blissful sprint down the dark flight line.

Generally, flying at night is very deceiving because the objects that help a pilot determine speed and distance just can't be seen on goggles. These "visual cues" that help prevent collisions with other aircraft are often invisible through the goggles.

To make matters worse, the conventional blue lights that illuminate the taxiways dissolve into the green-scope of the goggles, requiring a constant scan under the night-vision device to stay on the tarmac.

When we take off things get harder, and now we move our eyes rapidly from the goggles to the instrument panel to just below the goggles. In this way, a pilot must think in three ways at once and reconcile all the inputs to get from A to B safely. Add bad weather, intermittent radios, and blinding lights into the equation, and night flying carries all the excitement you could hope for. It is our scheduled departure time and the clock is ticking, and we still have to step on it to be out of the danger area by 0500 (5 a.m.) to reduce the risk of being seen and fired upon. We have a demanding schedule to follow, which leaves little room for error, so each pilot must carefully manage his fuel, cargo, and passengers to stay on time line and not get stranded.

After a weapons check and passenger pickup, we are headed to our first stop in Ramadi. Tonight's section leader is a very good pilot we call "Kimo." Kimo is in his early 30s and like several other pilots, he's earned his call sign for a personality trait. Kimo's job to coordinate with controlling agencies, navigate us safely from base to base, and stay on schedule. This may sound easy, but each night we carry more than 200 passengers and countless unmarked parcels, and the darkness coupled with the overwhelming noise in the aircraft breeds miscommunication and error.

As we fly low and fast toward the intended landing site, I drop a little farther back and reflect on how dark it has become since take-off. Just like daylight, there are brighter and darker parts of the night, which is dictated mostly by the position of the moon. If I fall too far behind I run the risk of losing sight of Kimo and getting lost, but if I stay too close, my abrupt movement would cause a collision between us. I was leading a night mission recently when my wingman stayed too close. When we altered our course to avoid an oncoming aircraft, he almost merged with our tail, and I don't want to make the same mistake.

I am still moving into position when I see what appears to be a light beaming out of Kimo's cockpit. In all my time flying at night, it has never been so dark that I could see a flashlight about to T-bone us above the city. I have just enough time to shout "climb" over the radio, an order to which Kimo immediately complies and drags us to over a thousand feet. The Army helicopters have seen us now and maneuver wildly to avoid a midair collision, and a heated exchange occurs over the radio. We discover that the Army pilots heard our radio calls and assumed we were coming from another direction, and since we heard them call clear of the area, we never expected to see them near our path.

We have air traffic controllers to help prevent these things but without traffic radar or adequate facilities, I quickly learn that these types of near-miss incidents are fairly common.

The entire event takes just a few seconds, and we redirect our focus to avoid the numerous obstacles that lie between our position and our intended landing site: a weather balloon, a raging fire that blinds our goggles, and a poorly marked helicopter pad. There is no time to dwell on the near miss; if we become fixated on it, we will start making bad decisions, which will lead to an unpleasant result. In this way, tonight's flight is much like my...

In April 2007, the Toledo Blade published for its readers a full-page explanation of an ethical lapse involving the newspaper. The paper discovered that one of its staff photographers had digitally altered dozens of photos over a period of several months.

(top) This photo of the Bluffton University baseball team appeared on page A-1 of the Blade on March 31, 2007, and on toledoblade.com. It was discovered to have been digitally altered and should not have been published. The photographer digitally removed the legs of a person standing behind the number 19 banner.

(bottom) This is the photograph that should have been published, as it represents a true view of what was happening at the time the photo was taken on March 30, 2007. The staff photographer resigned a few days after the altered photo was discovered. The Blade's policy is to never alter photographs, and these two photos are reprinted with permission of the Blade of Toledo, Ohio, for instructional purposes.

The National Press Photographers Association (NPPA) posted on its Web site this statement about the ethics of digital manipulation:

> As photojournalists, we have the responsibility to document society and to preserve its images as a matter of historical record. It is clear that the emerging electronic technologies provide new challenges to the integrity of photographic images . . . in light of this, we the National Press Photographers Association, reaffirm the

basis of our ethics: Accurate representation is the benchmark of our profession. We believe photojournalistic guidelines for fair and accurate reporting should be the criteria for judging what may be done electronically to a photograph. Altering the editorial content . . . is a breach of the ethical standards recognized by the NPPA.[6]

MULTIMEDIA SOLUTIONS

In earlier chapters, we discussed in detail how converged journalism can help create more powerful storytelling. It may also help in solving ethical dilemmas. In the linear world of television or print, journalists make most of the choices for the news consumer, so the audience is routinely exposed to the content that a journalist or a group of journalists has deemed appropriate. But in the Web world, the consumer has a great deal more choice, and that gives journalists the ability to bring the audience into the ethical decision-making process.

Graphic Images and Sound

No matter whether they work for print, broadcast or online news organizations, most journalists eventually find themselves wrapped up in discussions about the ethical use of graphic images. There is no doubt that a graphic image can be an important aid in reporting the truth of a situation. For example, though many news organizations have policies preventing them from showing video or pictures of dead bodies, dozens of good arguments can be made for violating that policy when you are showing dead bodies in a story about the costs of war. It's tough to adhere to hard-and-fast rules. Most often, conversations about whether to air or publish graphic images occur on a case-by-case basis and revolve around these issues:

- What is the journalistic purpose behind broadcasting or publishing the graphic content?
- What harm may be caused by airing or printing the graphic material?

As we mentioned earlier in the chapter, when the journalistic purpose is strong enough to override the potential for harm, television stations, in particular, have tried to come up with a way to warn the audience when a decision is made to air graphic visuals. You may have even heard an anchor make a statement like this in a local newscast: "We want to warn you, the pictures in this story may be disturbing to some in the audience." The TV station is trying to give viewers the option to change the channel or turn off the TV—especially if they are watching with young children or if they themselves are particularly sensitive to graphic images. Sometimes newspapers will publish less graphic photos on a section front page, and then include a warning about more graphic photos published inside.

However, as we've mentioned, on the Web you can go far beyond a warning; you can actually require your audience to take action in order to view a particular photo or watch a video. You can offer links to photo or video files with an explanation of what the user will see; presumably the user will read this before clicking on the link. With this technique, you are allowing the audience to make an informed decision about viewing the graphic images.

But be aware that the practice of posting graphic images online can also be controversial. According to the Pew Internet & American Life Project, in late spring of 2004, nearly one-quarter of Internet users (24 percent) went online to view some of the most graphic Iraq war images that were deemed too gruesome for newspapers and television to display. But overall, the study showed that Americans are conflicted about the idea of making disturbing images available online. By a 49–40 percent margin, Americans said they disapproved of posting such images.[7]

And it's not just visuals, of course, that can be controversial. If you've ever heard the audio from a 9-1-1 tape, you know that sometimes the sound of a person's voice describing a situation can be as disturbing as seeing the events unfold. At times, however, the content of those tapes does provide important information on such issues as the preparedness of an individual 9-1-1 operator and response times. To minimize the emotional impact, a television station (and, of course, a newspaper) may choose to use a written transcription of the audio. But, to satisfy those who feel "hearing is believing," the entire audio file could be posted on the Web. In this way, you could minimize the harm to your audience as a whole, yet still serve a journalistic purpose.

Using the Web in this way may not always be appropriate. As in every ethical dilemma, there will be those who offer counter opinions. If the journalistic purpose is not strong enough to warrant publishing a photo or airing a video clip, is it strong enough to warrant posting the content online? Should your standards for publication be different for online versus on the air or in the paper? Strong arguments can be made on both sides. However, it helps to remember that you should be accountable to your audience and that ethical decision making is about coming up with defensible answers. News organizations should discuss the issues and be prepared to share with the public what went into their decisions—either through a formal, published statement or informally with members of the public who may contact the news organization about the decisions made.

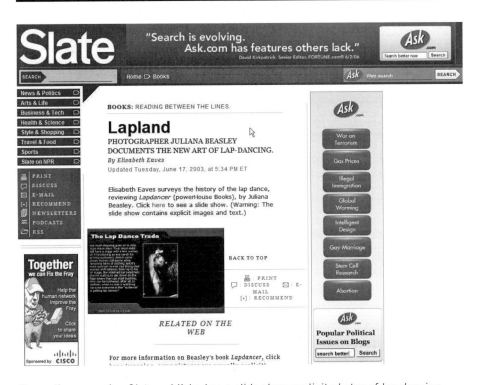

The online magazine *Slate* published as a slide show explicit photos of lap dancing.
Viewers were warned about the nature of the content and could access it only by
clicking on a link.

Source: Courtesy Slate.com.

Access to Information

One of the most exciting attributes of the Web is that it gives the audience access to customized information. For example, if a newspaper conducts an investigation of fire code violations in your community, it would be impossible for the reporter to include in the article
the inspection records for every property. But you can publish the records on the Web, and
you can make the records easily searchable so users can look up specific schools, favorite
restaurants or the local sports stadiums to check on their safety. This capability goes a long
way toward making important stories more relevant for the individual news consumer.

But the capability also raises new ethical questions. There is a great deal of information available online through government and law enforcement agencies. For example, the property appraiser in many communities lists on the Web the owner's name, property value and specific floor plan for every home appraised. A news organization could create a quick link to that information that would make it much easier for casual users to surf the data. What kind of privacy issues does that raise? Has the news organization now made it easier for unscrupulous people to do something illegal like break into a home? Or because the information is already public, has the news organization done nothing more than made public access easier?

These questions have been asked often in regard to the publication of sex offender registries. Because most states require convicted sex offenders to register their names and addresses with local law enforcement, many news organizations have done stories on how the public can access that information, and some have even gone so far as to make accessing the information easier by creating their own searchable databases.

Kelly McBride, an ethics instructor at the Poynter Institute in St. Petersburg, Fla., believes that many newsrooms simply take the attitude that, "if it's legal, we are going to do it." She worries that in the case of the sex offender registry, some readers or viewers might overreact to the coverage, either by retaliating against one of the sex offenders or allowing fears of attack to alter their lives. She says newsrooms "should be obligated to go beyond what is legal and weigh the value of what they are legally allowed to do against the harm or good that can come of it and make a decision on journalistic grounds." [8]

So, what do you think? Just because something is legal doesn't mean it's also ethical. Is it our job to give the public easy access to information that's rightfully theirs? Or do we need to act as gatekeepers on some level in order to protect the public? It's a tough call and one that journalists must routinely make by weighing the importance of telling the truth against the potential for harm.

Access to Sources and Content

One fundamental principle of journalism is that we try to gather as many differing viewpoints as necessary to tell the truth. You'll often be told to get "both sides" of a story, but the reality is that there are many sides to most issues. What your producer or editor is really asking is that you avoid telling a one-sided story, particularly in the case of something controversial.

Newsroom partnerships give us the ability to tell many sides of a story by opening up more access to content and sources. When you combine the resources of print, broadcast and online sites, you naturally bring together more journalists—each with personal sources and reporting experiences—that can be tapped into when a colleague is looking for a different way to tell a story.

Sometimes multiplatform journalism can literally provide reporters with access to information they couldn't get any other way. For example, television reporters often have a much easier time snagging interviews with major business leaders than newspaper reporters do. Galen Meyer, who trains journalists who work for Bloomberg News, says there's something about the allure of being on TV that makes these industry players say yes to an on-air interview when they have already repeatedly turned down a print reporter. By working with a TV partner, a Bloomberg print reporter can sometimes get answers to the questions that are needed to tell a fair and balanced print story. Without the television partnership, the print reporter might have been forced to write nothing more than, "CEO Bill Parks could not be reached for comment."

One thing we discussed earlier in the chapter was the question of whether the interview subject should be informed that the information provided to one medium might be used in another medium. To be absolutely ethical, we believe the television reporter in the scenario described above should alert the interviewee to the possibility that the interview will be used in more than one medium.

DIVERSITY

Some of you may be wondering why the topic of diversity is showing up in a chapter about journalism ethics. Aly Colón is ethics group leader and diversity program chair for the Poynter Institute. He sees diversity as a tool for meeting several of our professional ethical standards:

- Give voice to the voiceless. Diversity can clearly help us achieve this goal. By including people who look different, or think differently, from the population at large, we are giving them voice and diversifying our coverage.

- Act independently. This principle urges us to "seek out and disseminate competing perspectives." In this way, we avoid telling one-sided stories that fail to include minority voices.

- Minimize harm. To achieve this goal, journalists are advised to be compassionate and "treat sources, subjects, and colleagues as human beings deserving of respect, not merely as a means to your journalistic ends." To do that, journalists must understand the people they write about and become aware of the different ways our reporting, writing, editing, producing and photojournalism affects people. It requires us to learn

ETHICS RESOURCES

No matter whether you're working on your college newspaper or for the New York Times, for a tiny radio station in Tupelo, Miss., or for NBC News, there will be times when you feel like you need a little help from some ethics experts in order to make an ethical decision. Sometimes it may be a matter of pulling up a list of questions or reviewing a professional ethics code online. The following information might be just what you need to help in making an ethical decision—either in a converged environment or in a single-platform newsroom.

One of the most thoughtful journalists at work today is ethicist Bob Steele of the Poynter Institute in St. Petersburg, Fla. He has come up with 10 questions to help you reach good ethical decisions:

1. What do I know? What do I need to know?

2. What is my journalistic purpose?

3. What are my ethical concerns?

4. What organizational policies and professional guidelines should I consider?

5. How can I include other people, with different perspectives and diverse ideas, in the decision-making process?

6. Who are the stakeholders—those affected by my decision? What are their motivations? Which are legitimate?

7. What if the roles were reversed? How would I feel if I were in the shoes of one of the stakeholders?

8. What are the possible consequences of my actions? Short term? Long term?

9. What are my alternatives to maximize my truth-telling responsibility and minimize harm?

10. Can I clearly and fully justify my thinking and my decision? To my colleagues? To the stakeholders? To the public?

The simple act of asking these questions can help guide the discussion of an ethical dilemma, and help those involved reach an answer that they will feel they can defend to the audience.

At other times it may help to access the professional codes of ethics from highly regarded journalism organizations. We've already mentioned some of them; these URLs will take you directly to the ethics content posted on the organizations' Web sites.

Radio-Television News Directors Association, "Code of Ethics":

www.rtnda.org/ethics/coe.shtml

Poynter Institute, "Ethics":

http://poynter.org/subject.asp?id=32

American Society of Newspaper Editors, "Credibility":

http://asne.org/index.cfm?id=3

Society of Professional Journalists, "Code of Ethics":

http://spj.org/ethics_code.asp

Cyberjournalist.net, "Bloggers' Code of Ethics":

www.cyberjournalist.net/news/000215.php

All of these organizations developed their ethics codes and guidelines through years of conversations with professional journalists. Their codes are mandatory reading for anyone considering a career in journalism.

Source: For the 10 questions, see Bob Steele, "Ask These 10 Questions to Make Good Ethical Decisions," PoynterOnline, February 29, 2000, www.poynter.org/column.asp?id=36&aid=4346.

about diversity in all areas, including race, ethnicity, culture, class, ideology, religion, abilities, sexual orientation, gender and politics.[9]

The link between ethics and diversity is strong, and multiplatform journalism offers journalists a way to achieve more diversity in their storytelling. Combining resources of multiple media outlets and the opportunity to partner with ethnic media are just two examples of how this can work.

Diverse Resources

When WFLA-TV, the Tampa Tribune and TBO.com decided to get serious about convergence in 1998, WFLA's news director, Dan Bradley, liked to say he had just added more than 130 journalists to his staff. That's because he felt the partnership gave him access to the reporting resources of the Tampa Tribune and Tampa Bay Online. Though many have argued that convergence will diminish the number of voices in the news, it could actually make it possible for the audience to hear from more people with differing perspectives.

Journalists working on deadline often resort to "rounding up the usual suspects" for journalists working on deadline. They wind up going to the same experts and getting reaction from the same newsmakers because they don't have time to seek out new voices. In converged news operations you have the potential for more "feet on the street"—more chances for reporters to encounter people whose ideas or opinions have not yet been heard. And convergence offers more opportunities for reporters to work together to share what they know about covering different communities.

The Web opens up a whole new avenue for disseminating diverse perspectives. The interactivity dimension allows journalists to solicit input, and in that way hear from people who aren't typically included in traditional news stories. News consumers using the site will also have the opportunity to view the comments and join in the conversation.

The traditional audiences for each medium may be exposed to more diverse coverage through the use of multiple platforms. For example, a younger person who doesn't usually read the newspaper may benefit from reading content online that's generated by a print reporter. That story may offer diverse perspectives that the user does not typically encounter.

Partnering with Ethnic Media and Alternative Media

One underused model of convergence involves partnerships with ethnic or alternative media. These news organizations are devoted to providing information to groups of news consumers that are largely underserved by the mainstream media. They feature topics and perspectives that are often missing from mainstream coverage. For example, a study by the National Association of Hispanic Journalists found less than 1 percent of the stories aired in 2002 on network newscasts were about Hispanics. Yet, according to 2000 census data, Hispanics make up 12.5 percent of America's population and have now surpassed blacks as the country's largest minority group.

So, imagine how helpful it would be for a mainstream news organization that was trying to cover an area with a large number of Hispanics to partner with a Spanish-language television or radio station, newspaper or online site. The two organizations could share information about issues that deserved coverage and access to sources on those stories. The partnership would allow both news organizations to reach new audiences with information providing new perspectives.

The same could be said for partnerships with organizations designed to serve blacks or gay and lesbian people or any of the underrepresented communities in a given news market.

TAKING IT HOME

Credibility is the most precious asset a news organization or an individual journalist has. Credibility is the difference between the New York Times and the National Enquirer, NBC News and Entertainment Tonight. Practicing good ethical journalism helps you maintain credibility and preserve the audience's trust. A multimedia journalist faces new challenges in ethical decision making as technology expands both what we're capable of covering and the way we deliver news and information. But journalism's core ethical principles have not changed—our goal is to seek truth and report it, to minimize the harm we do, to act independently of outside influences and to be accountable to the public. Within that framework, ethical journalists arrive at decisions they can comfortably defend and explain to the audiences they serve.

TALKING POINTS

1. Create your own policy for handling corrections in online stories. How will you handle errors on the live site and in your archive? Decide whether you will post this policy on your Web site and be prepared to explain your decision.

2. The U.S. government has released a series of disturbing photographs that show the brutality done to several American prisoners of war. Your news organization has decided not to air the photos in your broadcast, but you will publish them online behind a link. Your job is to write a brief explanation of why the photographs have been posted online.

3. You know that every story you cover is fair game for your news organization's Web site. Come up with a good way to alert everyone you talk to for your stories to the fact that what they say may also be used online.

eLEARNING OPPORTUNITIES

For chapter exercises, practice tools and additional resources, go to the interactive online workbook at http://college.cqpress.com/advancingthestory. You'll find:

• SKILL BUILDING: Walk through a series of case studies that will test your ethical decision making. Review what one journalism ethics expert would have done in the same situation.

• DISCOVER: Watch a television story produced in response to an ethical dilemma and one story that created an ethical discussion among the community's news media. Decide what you would have done in both cases.

• ONGOING STORY: Handle an ethical problem that may require you to change a major part of the story you've created. Find out what the authors decided to do about the issue.

• EXPLORE: Visit Web sites for links to ethics codes and other ethical decision-making resources.

12 GETTING READY FOR THE REAL WORLD

The technological changes affecting journalism today may seem small to those already doing multimedia work, but they have felt like a seismic shift to many traditional journalists who were trained in one primary medium. What makes dealing with these changes even more challenging is that no one is really sure where they're leading or what the field of journalism will look like in the next few years. This chapter will explore what some news organizations are doing to help shape the future and to capitalize on new technologies. It will also help you position yourself to apply for the jobs that currently exist, as well as get you thinking about the types of jobs that might be created for journalists in the future

The media world is changing so rapidly that you might find yourself worrying that your skills will be outdated even before you get that first job. What do news managers really want in a new hire these days? Although it's an age-old question, the basic answer hasn't really changed. They want it all. They want smart, committed people with sound judgment and strong skills, willing to work hard for not much pay. That said, some things are different today.

"Five to ten years ago you were searching for someone who brought one specialty—reporting, photography, weather, sports—to the table," says news director Jim Garrott of WEEK-TV in Peoria, Ill. "Now you are looking for people, especially in smaller markets, who can do multi-tasking . . . providing information for newspaper and radio partners as well as for the Web." That kind of flexibility is vital, says Christine Riser, news director at WJHL-TV in Johnson City, Tenn. "If you think you'll just do a story for TV or the Web or a newspaper you're kidding yourself, and you're not very marketable," she says.

Visual skills are more important than ever in today's newsrooms. "I absolutely think you have to know how to be a photographer because you're going to be asked to shoot," says

Mark Casey, news director at KPNX-TV in Phoenix, Ariz. That's true even in radio news-rooms, says Darren Toms, director of news programming at Clear Channel's WTAM-AM in Cleveland, Ohio. Reporters there carry digital cameras, laptops and minidisc players that allow them to stream audio and video content on the station's Web site. "I never thought a reporter for a radio station would need a camera," Toms says. Five years ago, "I would have said you were nuts." [1]

Advances in communications technology have led to additional changes in today's newsrooms. From YouTube to MySpace to Digg, the rise in user-generated content is affect-ing how journalists connect with the audience. The need to produce content for mobile de-vices from cell phones to Smartphones and even PlayStation Portables has also changed the way journalists do their work. At the same time, the government is adding or reviewing regulations that can affect the way media companies do business. All of these develop-ments could have a bearing on your future career.

THE CHANGING MEDIA LANDSCAPE

When a Virginia Tech student went on a shooting rampage on campus in 2007, some of the first and most memorable reports about the incident came not from journalists but from stu-dents. One graduate student uploaded cell phone video to CNN that captured the sound of gunshots and drew millions of online viewers. At the same time, veteran journalists in Washington were the first to identify the killer, thanks to their sources in law enforcement.[2]

The coverage of the tragedy by both new and old media was a clear illustration of how much the news industry has changed. "Think of just a few years ago, when on a story like this we would look at what the AP [Associated Press] had or what the local papers had," said David Doss, executive producer of Anderson Cooper 360 on CNN. "Now we're looking at PlanetBlacksburg.com, which is the local school Web site down there. We're looking at the school posts online—and MySpace, YouTube, Facebook."[3] NBC News even set up its own Facebook page to solicit input from students who might have known the shooter.[4]

The coverage also highlighted the growth of what's called user-generated content, that is, information—text, audio, video, graphics—created by a medium's users rather than by someone whose job is to produce it for pay.

The term user-generated content applies most often to content created for the Web. When you or your friends create MySpace pages, that's a form of user-generated content. When someone posts video from a birthday party on YouTube, that's user-generated con-tent. When someone writes a comment about a news story on a blog, that's user-generated content.

It's obvious why news organizations care about what's happening on MySpace, YouTube or a personal blog when big news like the Virginia Tech shooting is breaking. But they also care about user-generated content in general, because it affects the relationship between news organizations and their audiences.

The User's Voice

Al Tompkins, leader of the Broadcast/Online Group for the Poynter Institute, believes the rise in user-generated content is due, in part, to the fact that many news organizations had stopped listening to their audiences. "For so many years, audiences have been disenfranchised from the decision-making process on what is news," Tompkins says. Now, he says, the news media have an opportunity to respond and partner with citizens in a way that connects them to content. "We are no longer simply providers," according to Tompkins. "It's going to be really important that we remember that we connect communities, we don't just talk to them."

In choosing "You" as its 2006 Person of the Year, TIME magazine wrote that the Web is a "tool for bringing together the small contributions of millions of people and making them matter."

Source: TIME Magazine.

Chet Rhodes, deputy multimedia editor at Washingtonpost.Newsweek Interactive, agrees that news on the Web is a two-way conversation. "You can't look at your audience and say we don't want to talk to you; that's not what the Web is about," Rhodes says.

Using the Content

The challenge for many news organizations, including washingtonpost.com, is developing systems to manage user-generated content. As we mentioned in the discussion of citizen journalism in Chapter 8, it can be hard to verify the accuracy of information that's gath-

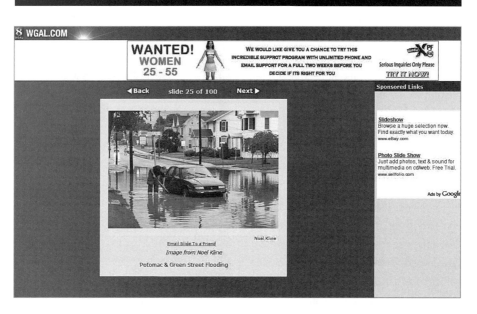

WGAL-TV created slide shows with nearly 300 photos submitted by viewers to help enhance its coverage of major flooding.

Source: Courtesy of WGAL-TV.

ered or created by nonjournalists. But once it's been determined that the information is correct, Rhodes says he has no problem with user-generated content.

"We should be perfectly willing to use any content that moves stories forward," Rhodes says. "We have used cell phone video provided by users—the London bombing video in 2005, for example. We used that without much discussion. It was great content we wanted people to see." Rhodes says one way around the verification issue is to create areas on the Web site where user-generated content can be posted with clear labeling, so the audience understands exactly how much fact-checking the content has received.

Tompkins says when news organizations allow users to also be participants, the users get more invested in the product. He points to the experience of WGAL-TV in Lancaster, Pa., which gave the audience the ability to upload pictures directly to its Web site during a period of intense flooding in 2006. The station recorded 3 million unique visitors to its Web site, and its parent company, Hearst-Argyle, believes WGAL's use of user-generated content was one reason for the huge numbers.

Tompkins says news organizations will succeed by giving their audiences great content, no matter whether that content is generated by the public or by traditional journalists.

NEW DISTRIBUTION METHODS

Technology doesn't just allow people to capture and create news content; it also helps them stay plugged into what's happening in the world when they're on the go. Mobile devices such as iPods, cell phones and other handheld digital technologies are changing the way people access and use information. And more people are using these devices to receive not just text but video. The research firm eMarketer projects that the total number of mobile TV and video subscribers globally will rise from 40 million in 2006 to more than 750 million in 2011.[5]

Rhodes says the change for journalists is "going to be huge. We're going to enter an era where people take the content they want with them and watch or read it whenever they want. That's amazing freedom for an individual."

Newsroom Usage

So, what are newsrooms doing to move into the mobile news arena? They're producing podcasts, sending news reports directly to cell phones, running RSS feeds on their Web sites and more.

When WNYC, a public radio station in New York City, launched the first podcast of a National Public Radio (NPR) program in 2005, the show doubled the number of listeners it reached online in just four weeks.[6] NPR quickly became a leader in podcasting, making its programs across the board available for download. NBC News believes it has expanded its audience by offering free video podcasts of NBC Nightly News and Meet the Press. The video podcasts can be downloaded directly to a computer and then uploaded to a mobile device like an iPod.[7]

At KGO-TV in San Francisco, the station created "abc7news-to-go" to provide news content for cell phone users and those with wireless PDAs. Users sign up to receive text only or video news and weather segments. The station's news director Kevin Keeshan says they're "leveraging the same content over multiple platforms."[8]

In 2006, the station also produced $4\frac{1}{2}$ hours of television news each weekday, three-minute morning and midday webcasts, podcasts, blogs and more. To do all that, KGO journalists have had to learn new skills and change the way they do their jobs.

Today's journalists must be prepared to present the news differently on different platforms. The small screens on most mobile devices are "not great for long form text," says Rhodes of washingtonpost.com. "It's best to produce short summaries or story nuggets for those." But Rhodes believes that newer devices, like the Apple iPhone with its $3\frac{1}{2}$-inch screen, could change that. He says that once more people are using larger screens, longer video clips and stories with more text might work just fine.

Rhodes says the spread of mobile devices also is accelerating the change in the way journalists gather news. "We started a program [in 2006], training print reporters in using video cameras," Rhodes says. "I knew that sooner or later, print reporters were going to figure out that cell phones could shoot video and pictures. We needed to teach them visual grammar." Rhodes says these journalists now have the ability to file video and photos anywhere, anytime, and the public has the ability to receive them—anywhere, anytime.

To deliver news to mobile devices, you'll use many of the techniques you've already learned. For example, the headline writing techniques you learned in Chapter 7 can help you create effective RSS feeds, where the headline is often the only thing the user sees. The procedures we outlined for creating effective webcasts in Chapter 8 also apply to producing content for video-capable cell phones or wireless PDAs.

What we can't tell you for sure is what the future holds for the way journalists do their jobs or the way the audience will consume news. It's unclear, for example, what content people will really want to have access to on their mobile devices. Will they watch entire news programs or just scan the headlines? Many news organizations are now trying to figure this out so they can come up with new ways for people to access news—before the users do it themselves.

MEDIA CONVERGENCE

While many news organizations are distributing their content on multiple platforms, not all of them are doing it alone. Beginning in the mid- to late 1990s, media convergence became a hot topic. At that time, the phrase was often used to describe a partnership between a newspaper and a television station. Sometimes the two share a Web site as well.

The goal for most of the partnerships was to combine the greater newsgathering resources of the newspaper with the video, breaking news and promotional capabilities of the TV station. By January 2007, the American Press Institute's "Convergence Tracker" (www.mediacenter.org/convergencetracker/search) had identified about 80 convergence "news relationships" among U.S. media companies.

Journalists working for Media General, Inc., are learning how to combine still photos and audio clips to create narrated slide shows. Staying on top of the technologies used to gather and present news is critical for today's multimedia journalists.

Source: Courtesy of Alan Rogers.

But several factors appear to have limited the number of these cross-media partnerships. As we've mentioned, many newspapers are now training traditional print journalists to produce video stories, or they're hiring their own video journalists, rather than relying on the use of video from a partner television station. They're using their Web sites as outlets for both audio and video, including webcasts they produce themselves. Similarly, TV stations have realized that the Web is their printing press, and they are using it to publish content they just don't have time for on the air. Because of this, many news organizations are not as interested in developing partnerships as they were in the past.

In addition, federal regulation has put a damper on some kinds of partnerships. The Federal Communications Commission (FCC) has historically tried to prevent a single company from owning both a newspaper and a television station in the same coverage area. (This situation does exist in some markets where the newspaper and TV station were co-owned before the FCC created this rule.) The FCC said it wanted to prevent one corporate owner from controlling too much of the information flow to the public.

But some news organizations argued that the rise of the Internet meant the concern about access to diverse sources of news and information was no longer valid. They pushed the FCC to rewrite the rules to allow more cross-ownership of media outlets, and in 2003 the FCC did. However, after public outcry, congressional action and a court challenge that ended with a Supreme Court ruling, the original rules are still in place. In the meantime, many media companies abandoned their goal of owning both a newspaper and TV station in the same market and having the two work together to produce multimedia content.

Despite all this, some news organizations have continued their convergence efforts, which can be categorized into two approaches: formal partnership and cross-ownership.

Formal Partnerships

Two of the best examples of cross-media partnerships can be found in the Denver market. The Rocky Mountain News and KCNC-TV work together, as do the Denver Post and 9News KUSA-TV. In fact, the Post and 9News share the salary of an employee who oversees stories that the two newsrooms work on together, but they do not share corporate owners. KUSA is owned by Gannett and the Post is owned by MediaNews Group.

"Our partnership is about sharing newsgathering resources and story tips—not we put our stories on their site, or they put their video on our site," says Mark Cardwell, managing editor of new media and strategic development for the Post, who is responsible for the paper's Web site.

The two news outlets also work together on some high-profile projects, Cardwell says. KUSA has started producing a TV version of the Post's major Sunday newspaper package. The paper comes out in the morning and the TV version airs at 6 or 10 p.m. the same day.

The two news organizations do not share a Web site; in fact, they're major competitors online. "They're a monster of an operation," Cardwell says of KUSA. "They often, in terms of page views, beat both the Rocky Mountain News and us in terms of traffic to their site." Cardwell says that as of 2007 the Post's Web site typically ranks second in Web news traffic for the market.

Although these formal, long-term partnerships are relatively rare, many of the points raised in Chapter 8 regarding cross-media team projects are important to remember if you find yourself in one of those situations.

Cross-Owned Convergence

One of the best-known examples of cross-owned convergence is at the News Center in Tampa, Fla. The building houses WFLA-TV, the Tampa Tribune and TBO.com. Media General, Inc. owns all three news organizations.

Just as in the limited partnership described in Denver, the newspaper and TV station work together—sharing resources and tips and working on projects—but the big difference is in the approach online. TBO.com is a shared Web site for both the TV station and the newspaper. You will often find TV station video right alongside a newspaper reporter's stories.

"These days, it's not just about writing for online, but breaking news online is a high priority," says Jim Riley, director of operations for TBO.com. That means reporters for both the TV and newspaper will often write a story for the Web before working on the broadcast or print version. They also produce blogs and podcasts for the online site.

When a WFLA or a Tampa Tribune story is enhanced online, the respective news organizations direct viewers or readers to TBO.com for the content, rather than promoting their own individual Web sites.

In addition, some of the TV station's reporters write fairly regularly for the newspaper, and some of the paper's reporters appear routinely on the station's newscasts. To facilitate all this, the three news organizations visit each other's editorial meetings every day and share planning documents or plan projects together. The company has hired multimedia editors to keep the convergence efforts on track.

Because of the FCC rules mentioned earlier in this chapter, these cross-owned partnerships are still relatively rare, but it's possible you might find yourself working for one at some point in your career.

MULTIMEDIA JOB SEARCHES

Those of you just starting out or in the early stages of your career need to realize that the training you are receiving as a multimedia journalist is going to make you more valuable in the job market. Although gloomy headlines about cutbacks in both print and broadcast newsrooms may be worrisome, the picture is not as bleak as it has been in years past for new journalism grads.

The most recent comprehensive surveys of journalism and mass communications graduates found that the job market improved in 2005, but flattened in 2006. According to the Annual Survey of Journalism and Mass Communication Graduates released in August 2007, "The percentage of 2006 journalism and mass communication bachelor's degree recipients with at least one job offer on graduation was 76.2, comparable to the figure of a year earlier."[9]

The study includes specific data for the fields of print and broadcast. In 2006, 69.9 percent of graduates who had specialized in print journalism had a full-time job. That's compared with 73.0 percent of graduates from a year earlier. For those who had specialized in broadcasting, including broadcast journalism, 67.0 percent of grads were working full time, compared with 64.7 the previous year. Of course, not all of these print or broadcast graduates found jobs in newsrooms, but the overall employment picture in broadcasting appears to be improving.[10]

A couple of other findings in the survey are also worth noting. "Male and female students experienced slightly different job markets in 2006."[11] Of the women surveyed, 76.7 percent found full-time employment, basically unchanged from a year earlier. For men, that percentage was 68.7—a drop from 74.2 percent a year earlier. Also significant are the findings for graduates who are members of a racial or ethnic minority. The employment gap between racial and ethnic minorities and non-minorities was 9.9 percent, up from 7.2 percent a year earlier, meaning it has become harder for minorities to find jobs in mass communications. This disparity has been apparent since the survey was first conducted in 1988.[12] The survey does not offer any explanations for the hiring gaps.

Planning

The planning for a job search begins long before you send out that first cover letter and résumé. If you're still in school, be sure you are taking classes that will expand your skill set, rather than taking the "easy" class or the one that best fits your social schedule.

Perhaps the most important piece of advice to act on while you're still in school is to look for opportunities to get "real world" experience. In many programs, that means an internship. Unfortunately, too often students look at an internship as one more hurdle to clear before graduation, rather than as a launching pad to a career. However, there are countless stories of students who took an internship, made the most of it and turned it into a job offer upon graduation.

Mackenzie Taylor got her job as a direct result of Media General's Multimedia Internship Program. She's now a multimedia reporter for WBTW-TV in the Florence–Myrtle Beach,

S.C., market as well as the Florence Morning News and SCNow.com. The three news organizations are owned by Media General, Inc. As a multimedia reporter, Taylor produces a TV, print and Web version of her story every day.

Each year, Media General hires recent college graduates to work in their convergence markets. The interns are paid a starting reporter's salary, and they're required to work for the company-owned newspaper, TV station and Web site. Taylor was a broadcast major in college but says the internship opened her eyes. "I found I loved doing newspaper stuff as well. I learned I had to collect a lot more information and use a lot more description, but now I really love it," Taylor says.

Her advice to journalists who are still in school? "No matter what you major in, that's not the only thing you'll be doing. Be sure you have enough training to know the fundamentals of TV, newspaper and Web," says Taylor.

In addition to an internship, some schools produce their own news broadcasts or Web sites, and most have a student newspaper. Make no mistake, it's important to get involved in these opportunities to produce stories that will actually be published. The internship and the work samples will become critically important when it comes time to produce your résumé and work portfolio.

No matter how much planning you do or how talented you are, a job search takes a lot of effort. Don't think you can post your résumé on Monster.com and dozens of other online sites or send it by e-mail to hundreds of potential employers and then sit back to wait for job offers to come pouring in. Yes, a few experienced journalists say they've received good offers from employers who just happened to run across their online portfolios. But most people actually have to go looking for work; it doesn't come looking for them.

According to Job-Hunt.org, an online resource for job seekers, relying too much on the Web or e-mail to apply for work is a self-defeating strategy; you can't customize your résumé for specific opportunities and you have no way of knowing if your e-mail was ever received.[13] Think of the Internet as just one of many resources to use in your job search, and begin the hunt by figuring out what you're really looking for.

Ask yourself exactly what kinds of jobs interest you most and what you're most qualified for. Consider where you want to live as well as what you want to do. If you can afford it, you might decide to look for an entry-level job at a small organization in a city you'd like to call home as opposed to a more challenging job in a smaller market where it's cheaper to live.

It's a given that most large news organizations expect more professional experience than small ones. The rule of thumb in journalism is that you'll start in a small market or

GETTING THE MOST FROM AN INTERNSHIP

Mackenzie Taylor is a multimedia reporter for WBTW-TV, the Florence Morning News and SCNow.com in Florence–Myrtle Beach, S.C. She got her job thanks to an internship, and she offers other interns this advice:

- Ask questions. Taylor says she's naturally inquisitive, as most journalists are. Use your reporting skills to find out as much as you can about the way the newsroom works.

- Find a mentor. Taylor says she was assigned to work in the capitol bureau for Media General's South Carolina properties. She credits bureau reporter Robert Kittle with helping her learn as much as she did.

- Offer to help. If you wait to be assigned a task, you might spend a lot of time sitting around or doing work that doesn't interest you. Taylor says she volunteered to write stories for Kittle so often that eventually he let her try it.

- Ask for feedback. Once you get a chance to do some real journalism on your internship, ask your mentor or others to review your work. You won't improve as quickly without constructive criticism.

- Be humble. "Coming out of school, you think you know a lot, but you really don't know what you're doing," Taylor says. Interns need to remember that the newsroom staff can help you or ignore you.

newsroom and work your way up. That's still true for would-be reporters, especially in television.

But other job seekers are finding they can leapfrog the smallest markets if they bring the right skills or apply for the right job. Television news producers, for example, are so highly sought after that some small-market news directors say they can't find any to hire, not even right out of school. Inexperienced photojournalists are also commonly hired in larger markets if their résumé tapes show good potential, and certainly journalists with strong Web skills are in high demand at both TV and newspaper Web sites, so they often bypass the small markets, too.

Whether your challenge in finding a job will be great or small, taking the right approach can help lead you to the best position and the best news organization for you.

Hunting

There are two basic ways to conduct a job hunt—either look for openings or target places you really want to work. You can begin a general search at these online starting points that offer searchable databases of journalism job openings (find more on this book's companion Web site):

- Editor & Publisher
www.editorandpublisherjobs.com/jobs/ep/index.jsp

- Journalism Jobs
www.journalismjobs.com

- Media Bistro
http://mediabistro.com/joblistings

- MediaLine
www.medialine.com/jobs.htm

- Variety Careers
www.variety.com/index.asp?layout=variety_careers

As you look through the listings, pay close attention to all the details—required skills, experience, duties and responsibilities. In late 2006, for example, Village Voice Media was advertising for Web editors:

> The web editor position includes editing and writing compelling daily content, working with editors, staff writers, and freelancers to package multimedia content along with stories, and building an online community through user-generated content. This is an editorial position—content and line editing, and strong news judgment are a must. Ideal candidate will have experience managing a website or blog system and working knowledge of HTML and Photoshop. Responsibilities will also include conceptualizing and executing compelling interactive editorial features (polls, forum questions, interactive maps and timelines), and audio and video editing.[14]

The listing doesn't spell out the number of years of experience required, but if you read between the lines you can tell this isn't a job for beginners. The openings are in Seattle and San Francisco, not exactly starter markets, and the work involves supervising others.

At the same time, the Dothan Eagle newspaper was advertising for an "experienced reporter" for its Ozark bureau, but the job really amounted to an entry-level position for someone with the right credentials:

> We need someone who can dig into this beat, cover city hall and police, but also write human-interest features. We encourage and coach a variety of writing styles, and are a multimedia newsroom. If you're ready to ask questions, look into trends, tell stories about the people of Ozark and you want to grow as a reporter, then we want to see your résumé. At least one year of daily newspaper experience is preferred, and a Bachelor's degree in journalism is required. Recent college graduates with internship experience are encouraged to apply.[15]

The lesson here is that job titles don't tell the whole story, so make sure you read the full listing before you decide whether or not to apply.

Another approach is to search directly on news media company Web sites. Corporations like Gannett, Cox, E. W. Scripps and Media General all have job listings on their sites. One broadcast company, in particular, has created an information campaign to encourage applications from recent college graduates. Nexstar Broadcasting routinely sends e-mails to instructors on college campuses, alerting them to the company's online job postings. The site even includes a tab for "Entry Level" positions, so you can narrow your search to those jobs alone.

Targeting places you really want to work can be even more difficult than sniffing out openings to apply for. You need to figure out exactly what jobs are open and whether you're qualified. Some job seekers will bookmark the Web sites for the organizations they're targeting and then check those sites daily for job postings.

Once you've spotted the right job, make sure you know whom to contact and then craft a personal appeal to that person for consideration. To improve the chances that your request will get through, you may find that you need to do some serious networking before you make an approach.

Networking

Contacts are crucial when it comes to finding a job. Use the connections you've made in previous jobs, internships or in school, and look for additional ways to network with other

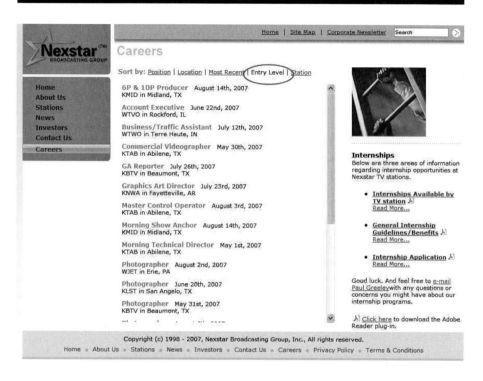

Nexstar Broadcasting Group recognizes that many of its small-market TV stations will be hiring journalists right out of school and has created a Web site that makes searching for those entry-level positions much easier.

Source: Courtesy of Nexstar.tv. Retrieved August 19, 2007, from http://nexstar.tv/careers/?&sort_by=level.

journalists. Some of your instructors may still work for local newsrooms or have significant industry contacts; don't be afraid to ask them for advice.

Don't hesitate to ask for a list of your school's journalism alumni and then use that alma mater connection to contact graduates who are working in a field or in a particular news organization that interests you. Although few of us would feel comfortable doing it, if your Aunt Edna's next-door neighbor's son works for ESPN and that's your dream job, you should seriously consider using that connection to make a contact.

Other options include joining a journalism group—the Council of National Journalism Organizations maintains a list of more than 50 on its Web site at www.cnjo.org. These groups often sponsor workshops or conferences where you can mingle with news professionals and ask for advice or leads about jobs. Some of these organizations, like the Radio-Television News Directors Association, allow job hunters free access to their online listings and let members post résumés. You can also find journalism conferences or workshops to attend by checking www.journalismtraining.org.

Another strategy is to request informational interviews from news managers or other practicing journalists to help you research journalism careers. Never ask for a job during an informational interview, but be sure to take along a copy of your résumé.

WNBC-TV's technology reporter Sree Sreenivasan recommends online networking using LinkedIn (www.linkedin.com), which is sometimes described as MySpace for all kinds of professionals, including journalists. Once you create an account, you can search for people you know who are also members and ask them to connect to you. Their connections then become part of your network, although you can't communicate with them directly. Let's say you're in Sreenivasan's network, and you see that he knows someone at a news organization you'd like to work for. You could send that person a message by way of Sreenivasan, but he would decide whether or not to pass it on. "I have declined to forward messages in some cases when the contact would not be appropriate," he says. "In the old days (i.e., last year), I would have just c.c.-ed my contact and the job seeker. I still do that, on occasion, with very good friends, but this way is better so that the contact can decide whether he/she wants to respond, without the job seeker automatically getting hold of his or her e-mail address." [16] Not everyone finds this process helpful or convenient, but it's one more option to consider to expand your contact list.

JOB APPLICATIONS

When you're looking for a job, you basically have five chances to market yourself: Your cover letter, résumé, portfolio, follow-up calls and a newsroom visit or formal interview. It's important to use each of these chances to your best advantage, but many job applicants don't. News managers say they see the same mistakes over and over—mistakes that land applications in the trash instead of the callback file.

Cover Letters

The quickest way to doom your chances is to send a generic form letter, or get basic facts wrong. Here's an example one TV news director received:

Dear Prospective Employer,

As a journalist working in the field, on the scene of breaking news working long hours, and always on deadline, I find myself pressed but always cognizant of every aspect of the urgency and accuracy behind LIVE, LOCAL and LATE-BREAKING NEWS.

The applicant clearly hadn't done any research—the slogan belonged to a different television station in the market. "Don't be lazy," says Kevin Benz, news director at News8 in Austin, Texas. Address your letter to a specific individual and spell the name correctly. "Google me! Google the station. If you want to be a reporter and you can't find out my name, what does that suggest to me about what kind of a journalist you will be?" If you're applying for an open position, explain how your experience matches the job. Don't talk about what the news organization can do for you; instead describe what skills you can bring to the job. Don't exaggerate your abilities, but do make the strongest case you can in your own favor. And use your cover letter to highlight your skill as a writer—every job in journalism will require you to communicate clearly. Just imagine how quickly this applicant's letter hit the wastebasket:

I want you to no I'm a mature and experienced newsmaker. Above all, my news suaveness put me in a position to receive information in a timely manner, in order to brake news stories.

Use the cover letter to introduce yourself, but don't repeat your entire résumé. You may want to offer some background on your tape or portfolio, however. It's hard for employers to know whether you shot and edited your own stories, just how much of a newscast you wrote or what your specific contributions were to an online story, so tell them in the cover letter.

Résumés

It's becoming almost standard for job seekers to post an online résumé, but many employers still want to see one on paper. If you're applying for your first job, there's no reason to submit a résumé that's any longer than one page. Be specific and candid about your skills and experience.

Many college career centers recommend you put an objective at the top of your résumé, but many news directors say that's a waste of time. Obviously, your objective is to get a job.

Some résumés will follow the objective with a section on education, but that can eas-

HOW *NOT* TO GET A JOB, IN FIVE EASY STEPS

To make sure your job application is rejected, just follow this advice from Kevin Benz, news director, News8, Austin, Texas, and Chip Mahaney, news director, WTVR-TV, Richmond, Va.

1. Don't follow directions. If the ad says to apply by e-mail, send a letter. If it asks for a VHS tape, be sure to send a DVD. The instructions in the ad are a first test for applicants, so do what it says and don't blow it.

2. Fake it. Say you're experienced when you're not; list skills you don't really have and include work samples you didn't produce. Do you really think that will help you land a job in a business that's based on facts?

3. Use gimmicks. They'll definitely get you noticed. Like the applicant who sent a candy bar with a note that read, "I will bring you MOUNDS of great stories." Or the one who sent a shoe, to demonstrate desire to "get a foot in the door." Not a great idea.

4. Stalk the boss. Call every day to make sure your application was received. Twice a day is even better. Show up unannounced to guarantee you won't have a shot at the job.

5. Dress for the tennis court, frat house or nightclub when you come for the interview. If you don't want the job, make sure you don't show up the way the boss should expect you to dress at work. "I can't tell you how many photographers I have not hired because they come in looking like they just got out of jail," Benz said.

ily come a little farther down the page. What most news directors really want to know about you is how much journalism experience you've had. If you are already working in the news business, that should be the first thing a news director sees after your name and contact information. If you report for a student newscast, write for the student newspaper or interned for a news Web site or any other journalism outlet, that kind of information should figure prominently under work experience, too. What you don't want to do is load up the experience section with your lifeguard and waitstaff jobs. If you have enough journalism experience, leave those out altogether; at the most, include one or two.

AMANDA LEE DES ROCHES

JOURNALISM EXPERIENCE
_____

| 2006-Present | VCU InSight | Richmond, VA |

Reporter/Photographer/Anchor
- Research and develop news stories for student produced twice-monthly magazine show aired on WCVW Richmond PBS.
- Produce quality content for the web to enhance news stories.
- On-air delivery of news content.

| 2005 | The Commonwealth Times | Richmond, VA |

Staff writer
- Researched and developed news stories for student produced twice-weekly newspaper.
- Covered general assignment news on VCU's career center and School of Nursing. Assignments ranged from covering business etiquette workshops to male nurse recruitment campaigns and Virginia's future nursing shortage.

TECHNICAL SKILLS
_____

Non-Linear video editing skills, operation of Beta SP camera, operation of Sony XD camera, operation of Canon Mini DV camera, Adobe Premiere, Adobe Audition, Word, Excel, PowerPoint.

EDUCATION
_____

| 2003-Present | Virginia Commonwealth University | Richmond, VA |

Candidate for B.S. in Mass Communications-Broadcast Journalism, August 2006

AWARDS RECEIVED
_____

- Dean's List-Fall 2004, Spring 2005

WORK EXPERIENCE
_____

| 2003-Present | Curves for Women | Ashland, VA |

Fitness Trainer
- Train members on fitness equipment, keep members motivated, maintain more than 500 member records, contract-sales and Curves program applications.

| 1998-2000 | United States Air Force | Colo Sprgs, CO |

Customer Service Technician, Airman First Class
- Maintained records for more than 4,000 personnel, responsible for in-processing of new personnel and issuing and retrieving military identification cards for authorized personnel.
- Supervised and trained newly arrived Airman to the Military Personnel Flight.

Amanda des Roches concentrated her studies on broadcast journalism in college, but right out of school she was hired by the Interactive Media Division at Media General, Inc. The division creates content for dozens of Media General news sites. Her video shooting and editing skills were just what the company was looking for to help create better multimedia content.

Source: Courtesy of Amanda des Roches.

Be specific about your skills, and if you can shoot video, tell what formats you've worked with. If you can edit nonlinear video, name the programs you've used, like Avid, Adobe Premiere or Final Cut Pro. The same goes for your multimedia skills. Describe what you can do and how you've applied your skills on the job or in school, but again, don't exaggerate. Don't say you know HTML if you've only edited tags in Dreamweaver.

List references on your résumé, but don't include any letters of reference with your application unless the job listing specifically requests them. Make sure any person you list as a reference is willing to be contacted and will say something good about you. Most prospective employers won't contact your references until after you've been interviewed, but if you definitely don't want anyone to contact your current employer, say so in the cover letter.

Be aware that any prospective employers who are really interested in hiring you will not check just the references you've listed—they may also call people they know where you've worked or studied. Expect that a future employer will Google you, search for a MySpace or Facebook page, a personal blog or comments you've made in chat rooms. Beware of what you post. Kay Miller, news director at WWSB-TV in Sarasota, Fla., says she's been shocked by what some prospective employees have posted on these sites—everything from pictures of themselves swilling beer to shots of themselves wearing little or no clothing. Miller says she routinely checks these sites before hiring new people, and a risqué page can lose a promising candidate the job. "As a journalist you are only as credible as your last impression you left on your readers or viewers," says Miller. She believes journalists need to do more reputation management for themselves in this age of online access to information. Beyond that, employers will check your online profile for clues to your attitude. "Don't talk bad about any fellow students, co-workers, employers, etc.," says J. J. Murray, news director at KIMT-TV in Mason City, Iowa. "Attitude is everything! Applicants should show a positive attitude even in the toughest of circumstances."

If you're still in school, it's fine to put your grade point average on your résumé but only if it's impressive. Extracurricular activities or hobbies that demonstrate a relevant skill, like foreign languages or travel, are worth including. You can also mention examples that show your leadership abilities or character, but keep the list short. And a word to those applicants with cute or clever e-mail addresses like bootilicious@whatever.com: They make you look frivolous or worse. Get a different one to use on your résumé. The same goes for a voice mail greeting with your dog barking or your favorite song playing. When potential employers call, you want them to be impressed, not turned off.

Résumé Tapes

For television jobs it's still important to provide a résumé tape, although these days most news directors say they'd be happy to receive it on DVD. If you do send tape, your best bet is to use good old-fashioned VHS unless the job listing specifies a different format.

Understand that news directors are busy, so be sure to make a good first impression. "Don't start with yourself on camera introducing you and your tape," says Chip Mahaney, news director at WTVR-TV in Richmond, Va. "This tape is supposed to show me the kind of work you can do." Begin with a simple slate that runs no more than 15 seconds and that shows your name, phone number and e-mail address.

The tape should reflect your professionalism, intelligence and good writing and storytelling skills. For a reporter candidate, most news directors expect to see a montage of four or five creative stand-ups and live shots at the start. "We want to see how you handle yourself on TV," Mahaney says. Dave Busiek of KCCI-TV in Des Moines, Iowa, says he's been known to pop a tape out in as few as three seconds if the applicant shows no on-camera skills. After that, many news directors like to see a range of stories you've done recently, including spot news, general assignment and possibly a feature. Reporter tapes generally don't need to run any longer than 10 minutes.

Often reporter candidates' résumé tapes open with a montage of stand-ups that showcase storytelling ability and presence on camera.

Source: Courtesy of Jessica Chapin.

Photojournalists should put their best work first. Rocky Dailey, former chief photographer at WXMI-TV in Grand Rapids, Mich., says that, ideally, the résumé tape would include general news, a feature, breaking news and possibly an in-depth or series piece. A photo essay is always a good idea—something that showcases the photojournalist's storytelling ability without a reporter. In addition to all that, make certain the stories demonstrate solid shooting and editing skills. So, if you have a story with some great editing but a blue stand-up, don't use it! And remember, chief photographers also want to see what you can do on a nonvisual story; anyone can get great video of a house fire.

Producers should provide an entire newscast. Many also include self-critiques of their shows. These critiques typically outline what the producers were responsible for in the broadcast, what they thought worked well and what might have been improved. Sometimes a news director will also ask the producer to spell out a personal producing philosophy in this critique.

No matter what job you're applying for, include only your best work and don't ever pass someone else's work off as your own. "Repackaging major market internship material doesn't fly," Murray says. "I can tell the difference between a student's own work and something they've repacked from a major market. We want to see stories they've written, shot and

TRADE TOOLS

FINDING A SMALL-MARKET TV JOB

J. J. Murray is the news director at KIMT-TV in Mason City, Iowa, a small market where students can often find jobs right out of college. What is he looking for?

- Students who can speak and write with proper English and grammar skills.
- Students who have a broad-based background in civics, history, politics, crime, law and ethics.
- Students who can report, write, shoot, edit (both linear and nonlinear because not all small-market stations have nonlinear editing) and even do graphics, produce TV stories and write and publish stories for the Web.
- Students who can "one-man-band" a package and a V/O-SOT every day.
- Students who have on-air and off-air skills.
- Reporters who can think like producers and photojournalists.
- Students who have an old-school work ethic where hours and overtime don't matter; they love to work!

edited themselves." Many news directors say they will look past poor video quality if it's the best the applicant can do with the equipment or facilities available. Don't make excuses or cast blame, but feel free to explain the circumstances in your cover letter.

Multimedia Portfolios

Many of the same principles that apply to résumé tapes also apply to multimedia portfolios. Include the best examples of your current work, not everything you've ever done. Don't waste a prospective employer's time. Focus your portfolio on your work, not you. Put just as much effort into creating your portfolio as you did to develop each of the projects you want to highlight, following the principles of clean design and easy navigation.

At a minimum, your portfolio should include your résumé, contact information, examples of your work along with the publication date and source and links to any blogs you maintain. Ideally, you've saved everything you've done electronically—newspaper stories, Flash videos, audio slide shows and so forth. If not, you'll be reduced to hoping that your work is still online with an active URL, always a risky proposition. If at all possible, create a CD or DVD version of your portfolio; just make sure that whatever you burn will work on both PC and Mac platforms.

Pay particular attention to issues of copyright infringement. If you have signed away all rights to your work, you could be open to legal action by including it in an online portfolio.

Interviews

Once you make it to the all-important interview stage, be prepared for what recruiters call the five fundamentals:[17]

- Tell me about yourself.

- Why do you want to work here?

- What are your weaknesses?

- What salary do you expect?

- Don't call us, we'll call you.

Use an open-ended invitation to talk about yourself to provide real-life examples of your accomplishments. Share a story that indicates what you would bring to the job. Show that you've done your homework and are familiar with the company, its news philosophy and the product. You're likely to be asked what you think of it, but that doesn't mean you should

Journalism is about to change completely:
It's time for a whole new type of journalist

Depending on who you ask, the internet has either killed journalism or reinvented it. There's a glut of information out there, half of it's untrue, anyone can publish anything and nothing is private. It's a scary environment for journalism, but it's also reinvigorating readers and revolutionizing the way information is shared.

News outlets need staff who can utilize all that the internet has to offer.

Somewhere between web developers and reporters lie multimedia journalists: a new field for a new era. As a multimedia journalist I have all the traditional journalism skills, but I'm also trained in new types of media like podcasting, blogging, reader interaction and flash animation.

I'm excited to be a journalist in the age of the industry's reinvention, and I'm always seeking jobs where I can combine my creativity, journalistic curiosity and technical knowledge.

Take a look at the multimedia section to see some examples of non-linear and

Home
resume
multimedia
Design
CLiPS
art

Email me

Download my resume

Rachel Youens received a bachelor's degree in journalism from the University of Texas–Austin. To showcase her multimedia and design skills, she created an online portfolio, which includes examples of her video work, slide shows, links to her blogs, as well as magazine and print work. The site also includes her résumé and a personal statement to be used in the hunt for a job. A site like this one might be a useful supplement to the traditional clip portfolio or résumé tape because it showcases multimedia skills.

Source: Courtesy of Rachel Youens.

EMPLOYER PET PEEVES

Many prospective employers have pet peeves when it comes to job applicants. Here are some of them:

- Your voice mail is full. You don't respond to e-mails. "You won't get a second chance if I can't get in touch with you within 24 hours," says J. J. Murray.

- "Don't send me a glamour shot where you look like a porn star," says Kevin Benz. "Your credibility is gone."

- If you apply, be willing to actually move there. "I've had people say they're looking for something closer to home, yet send me a tape anyway," Murray says.

- Don't send stories that are more than six months old. "It shows you're not getting enough practice, doing enough stories, or you're not doing enough good work," says Chip Mahaney.

- "I talk with a lot of college students about positions and they often have trouble articulating why they want the job or why they're interested in television news," says Deana Reece, news director at KVAL-TV in Eugene, Ore.

launch into a full-blown critique. Just be prepared to describe what you saw and say something positive if you can.

When you're asked about your weaknesses, don't try to fudge your answer by focusing on strengths instead. An employer won't see "working too hard" as a weakness. Be brief but candid about what you think you still need to learn and, if possible, tell why the job will help you learn it.

According to Korn/Ferry International, an executive search company, the most common mistake candidates make in interviews is talking too much.[18] Come prepared to ask some questions of your own and listen closely to the answers. The interview is your chance to find out if the job, the boss and the news organization are a good fit for you.

Expect to be asked about your current or previous jobs, but if things haven't gone well don't spend the interview trashing your employer or co-workers. You will be asked why you want to leave, and it's fine to say that you're looking for a new experience or advancement. Just don't say you can't stand your boss, or everyone you work with is a jerk. "We will set traps in an interview to try to draw that out of you," says Benz.

If you're looking for your first job, the initial interview is not the time to raise the issue of salary, benefits or work schedules. The interviewer may bring these topics up, however, so be prepared for questions like, "What kind of salary are you looking for?" One good answer is another question, "What do you generally pay people with my level of experience?" If you've done your homework, you'll have checked the cost of living in the area so you can tell whether their salaries are reasonable.[19] You can also find calculators online to compare the cost of living in hundreds of cities and to estimate moving costs.

Finally, no matter how well or poorly you felt the interview went, always send a brief note or e-mail to thank the person you met with. If you're enthusiastic about the opportunity, say so.

Hiring Tests

When you come in for an interview, you may be asked to take a hiring test. The most common tests cover writing or other skills and current events. J. J. Murray's hiring test at KIMT-TV includes a series of questions about real-world situations to see how applicants would deal with problems at work, including ethical issues.

At WEEK-TV, the current events quiz has 10 questions: five are based on local stories that have been on the station's Web site in the previous week, three questions are national, and the other two involve major local institutions like Caterpillar. "We allow them to sit at a computer and time them," says Garrott. "At no time do I say they cannot use the Internet to find the answers. In the last three years, I have had only one person get 100 percent." Applicants who think the test is designed to test their knowledge miss the point, Garrott says. "It isn't a college test. You need to use everything available to you to find the answers."

CONTRACTS

Journalism jobs these days often come with contracts attached, either "personal services" or union contracts. According to the 2007 survey by the Radio-Television News Directors Association (RTNDA), most TV reporters and anchors and about half of all producers are under contract, and the vast majority of those contracts have noncompete clauses, restricting them from working for a competing station in the same market for a certain period of

TABLE 12.1. STARTING ANNUAL SALARIES

Type of employer	Annual salary
Daily newspapers	$27,000
Weekly newspapers	$24,700
Television	$24,400
Cable television	$30,200
Radio	$27,000
World Wide Web	$31,500

Source: Lee B. Becker et al., "2006 Annual Survey of Journalism and Mass Communication Graduates," University of Georgia, Grady College of Journalism & Mass Communication, August 10, 2007, Appendix Table 33, www.grady.uga.edu/ANNUALSURVEYS/grd06/grdrpt2006_merged_full_v6_Color.pdf, 1.

Note: These are median yearly salaries for 2006 graduates of journalism and mass communication programs.

time.[17] "About the only contracts I see without noncompetes are in states where it's illegal," says Bob Papper, who conducts the RTDNA survey. Many contracts also include standard language giving stations the right to terminate the agreement at any time for any reason on just 60 or 90 days notice.

Signing a contract is intimidating, especially because most contracts are designed to give all the advantages to the employer rather than the employee. Unfortunately, it's tough to make changes to a contract until you've proven your value as a journalist. For that reason, you should not expect to truly "negotiate" a first contract. It is OK to ask for more salary, additional moving expenses or, in the case of a reporter, a better make-up or clothing allowance, but you might not make any headway. Ultimately, employers have most of the power; if you truly want the job, you will probably need to accept their terms. As you become more experienced and more valuable to a news organization, the dynamics of contract negotiations will likely change in your favor.

You've probably heard this before, but it bears repeating: You really don't need to hire an agent to get your first job. It may be counterproductive, in fact. Many news managers in small markets simply won't talk to agents. "If you have agent, use them for advice, not to negotiate [a contract]," says KIMT's Murray. "The best advice is to have a family lawyer look at contracts. It's cheaper to pay by the hour than by a percentage of what little you may make in your first job."

JOURNALISM ENTREPRENEURS

As you already know, journalism is a profession in transition. The economic model that sustained newspapers and broadcast stations for decades has become shaky, and there's lots of gloom and doom talk about the future of the news industry. But there's also plenty of room for optimism about the future of journalism for those who aren't bound to the old ways of doing things. "I think that journalism today, given the upheaval of multimedia and reader-contributed reporting, really does belong to those reporters and editors with an entrepreneurial spirit," says Robert Niles, editor of the Online Journalism Review.[18]

One way to succeed as an entrepreneur is to create your own specialties, whether it's combining sports coverage with database reporting or photojournalism with entertainment reporting. "The people who create combinations of two or more passions and skills will be inventing new jobs for the industry and security for themselves," says Joe Grimm of the Detroit Free Press.

Entrepreneurial journalists may create careers for themselves without holding a full-time job at any one news organization. Freelancing is a challenging way to make a living but it has its rewards, including more flexibility to pursue the stories you want to tell. Freelancers spend a fair amount of time searching for outlets for their work and pitching story ideas, so you have to be a good salesperson to succeed at freelancing. Freelancers usually have had some experience working within a news organization, so they understand what editors or producers want. Without that experience, freelancing might be a tough way to make a living right out of school. You should also research the legal issues involved in freelancing, including copyrights and licensing, before deciding if it's really for you.

Look for freelance opportunities by analyzing the news product you'd like to produce for. Pay attention to bylines, which can tell you what kinds of stories they buy from freelancers. Come up with story ideas that fit the bill and pitch them directly to the supervisor in charge. "Treat any assignment like gold," says Joe Grimm. "Get details on the editor's requirements and fill them to the letter. It is far easier to establish a continuing freelance arrangement with an editor or two than to have to go through all these steps over and over again as you bounce from paper to magazine to Web site." [20]

Networking is just as important to freelancers as it is to jobseekers—maybe even more so. The Freelance Marketplace hosted by MediaBistro (www.mediabistro.com/fm) is a forum where freelancers can showcase their work and, with luck, land assignments. The Society of Professional Journalists also has resources for freelancers online at www.spj.org/freelance.asp.

TAKING IT HOME

Today's journalists have so many options. From the way we gather, present or deliver the news to the job opportunities available, the term "traditional journalist" is becoming obsolete, or perhaps it is simply taking on a new meaning.

Whether you're just getting into the field or already working in a newsroom, you have the potential to envision new forms of storytelling thanks to the rise of multimedia, the growth of user-generated content and the increased capabilities of mobile devices.

As someone in the job market, you will need to highlight versatility and a willingness to experiment and learn. You can't possibly know it all, but if you can show your employer that you have strong journalism skills, an understanding of how those skills are applied across media platforms and a desire to create, you can set yourself apart from other job applicants.

TALKING POINTS

1. Is there something about your local college campus that really matters to nearly everyone? For example, does your football or basketball team have a huge fan base, or is a lack of parking a major issue? How could a student media outlet use this knowledge to engage people and facilitate user-generated content? How could commercial media outlets apply these same strategies to engage the larger community?

2. Review the latest survey of journalism graduates at www.grady.uga.edua/ANNUAL-SURVEYS. Take a look at the hiring gap between men and women as well as between minorities and nonminorities. What do you think might be behind these disparities? What, if anything, should be done to close these gaps?

3. Go online and find a job opening that interests you. List some of the things you would do before sending off your application materials. Show a classmate or two what you've come up with. What would they suggest?

eLEARNING OPPORTUNITIES

For chapter exercises, practice tools and additional resources, go to the interactive online workbook at http://college.cqpress.com/advancingthestory. You'll find:

• SKILL BUILDING: Learn how to create your own multimedia portfolio using a simple template and then saving the content as a Web page to post online.

• DISCOVER: See resume materials created by successful job candidates for both broadcast journalism and multimedia positions.

• ONGOING STORY: Brainstorm strategies for incorporating user-generated content into this story and for delivering the content to mobile devices. Review what the authors came up with for the final multimedia presentation of this story.

• EXPLORE: Visit Web sites for resources to help with your resume and portfolio preparation as well as for the job hunt itself.

Chapter 1

1. David Goetzl, "Go Where the Audience Is: MTV and Rivals Migrate to the Internet and Keep a TV Base," Broadcasting&Cable.com, August 13, 2006, www.broadcastingcable.com/article/CA6361902.html?display=Search+Results&text=sirulnick.
2. "Two-in-Three Critical of Bush's Relief Efforts: Huge Racial Divide over Katrina and Its Consequences," Pew Research Center for the People and the Press, September 8, 2005, http://people-press.org/reports/display.php3?ReportID=255.
3. Excerpted from "Online Papers Modestly Boost Newspaper Readership," Pew Research Center for the People and the Press, July 30, 2006, http://people-press.org/reports/display.php3?PageID=1064.

Chapter 2

1. Marcus D. Rosenbaum and John Dinges, eds., *Sound Reporting: The National Public Radio Guide to Radio Journalism and Production* (Dubuque, Iowa: Kendall/Hunt Pub. Co., 1992).
2. Gary Hanson and Stan Wearden, "The Accuracy of Local TV News: A Study of News Coverage in Cleveland," NewsLab, June 2, 2006, www.newslab.org/research/accurate.htm.

Chapter 3

1. Regina McCombs, "Shooting Web Video: How to Put Your Readers at the Scene," Online Journalism Review, March 2, 2005, www.ojr.org/ojr/stories/050303mccombs.
2. Jakob Nielsen, "Talking Head Video is Boring Online," Jakob Nielsen's Alertbox, December 5, 2005, www.useit.com/alertbox/video.html.
3. Terry L. Heaton, "10 Questions for Lisa Lambden," AR&D, n.d., www.thepomoblog.com/papers/10Q8.htm.

Chapter 4

1. Jim Detjen, "The Beat's Basics," *SEJ Journal,* Summer 2003, www.sej.org/resource/index11.htm.
2. Bradley Wilson, "Establishing a Rapport," Journalism Education Association, 1999, www.jea.org/curriculum/writing/tragedies.html.
3. "Local TV News Project: Beat Reporting on Local Television," Project for Excellence in Journalism, November 2, 2002, http://journalism.org/node/1118.
4. Lori Dorfman and Vincent Schiraldi, "Off Balance: Youth, Race & Crime in the News," Building Blocks for Youth, April 2001, www.buildingblocksforyouth.org/media/media.html.
5. Pat Stith, "A Guide to Computer Assisted Reporting," PoynterOnline, June 3, 2005, http://poynter.org/content/content_view.asp?id=83144.
6. Ibid.
7. ASCII is computer code that represents text.
8. Bob Steele, "Hidden Cameras: High-Powered and High-Risk," PoynterOnline, October 19, 1998, www1.poynter.org/dg.lts/id.5612/content.content_view.htm.
9. Pam Zekman, "Undercover Reporting Tips," IRE Tipsheet no. 1186, Investigative Reporters and Editors, Inc., 2000, www.ire.org/resourcecenter/viewtipsheets.php?number=1186.

Chapter 5

1. "Suggestions for Helping Reporters Focus Stories," www.notrain-nogain.org/list/focus.asp.
2. Robert Krulwich, "Work that Feels So, So Good—and So, So Bad," *Current,* December 16, 2002, current.org/people/peop0223krulwich.shtml.

Chapter 6

1. "Q&A with Travis Fox, Video Journalist for washingtonpost.com," Online Journalism Review, September 18, 2006, www.ojr.org/ojr/stories/600916Junnarkar.
2. "Video Even Less Interactive Than Print (Comment by Regina McCombs)," Teaching Online Journalism, October 29, 2006, http://tojou.blogspot.com/2006/10/video-even-less-interactive-than-print.html.
3. "Transcripts: CNN Newsroom," CNN.com, December 16, 2006, http://edition.cnn.com/TRANSCRIPTS/0612/16/cnr.03.html.
4. Mark Bowden, "Narrative Journalism Goes Multimedia," *Nieman Reports* 54, no. 3 (Fall 2000), www.nieman.harvard.edu/reports/00-3NRfall/Goes-Multimedia.html.
5. "Audio-Video Redundancy," in "Annotated Bibliography of TV News Research," NewsLab, n.d., www.newslab.org/research/bibliography.htm#Audio.
6. "Video Even Less Interactive Than Print (Comment by Angela Grant)," Teaching Online Journalism, October 29, 2006, http://tojou.blogspot.com/2006/10/video-even-less-interactive-than-print.html.
7. Warren Watson, "A Primer on Informational Graphics: Package for Design on Small-Newspaper Info-Graphics," American Press Institute, November 28, 2000, www.americanpressinstitute.org/content/p1465_c1390.cfm?print=yes.
8. Peter Schumacher, "User Feedback Drives Five Principles for Multimedia News on the Web," Online Journalism Review, September 15, 2005, www.ojr.org/ojr/stories/050915schumacher.

Chapter 7

1. "Eyetrack07," Poynter Institute, http://eyetrack.poynter.org.
2. Rosental Calmon Alves and Amy Schmitz Weiss, "Many Newspaper Sites Still Cling to Once-a-Day Publish Cycle," Online Journalism Review, July 21, 2004, http://ojr.org/ojr/workplace/1090395903.php.
3. M. Lynch, "VCU Gets out the Vote," VCU InSight, 2004, www.vcuinsight.org.
4. Based on Cory Bergman, "How to Write for the Web: Lost Remote's Guide for TV Newsrooms," LostRemote.com, 2007, www.lostremote.com/how-to-write-for-the-web.
5. "State of the News Media 2007," Project for Excellence in Journalism, 2007, www.stateofthenewsmedia.org/2007.
6. B. Papper, "Net Worth," *RTNDA Communicator* 61, no. 5 (2007): 12–16.

Chapter 8

1. Webopedia, www.webopedia.com/TERM/C/content_management_system.html.
2. Andrea Miller, "News Alert! When Cable Networks Break In and Why," NewsLab, 2006, www.newslab.org/research/newsalert.htm.
3. "Talking-Head Video Is Boring Online," UseIt.com, December 5, 2005, www.useit.com/alertbox/video.html.
4. David Sifry, "Sifry's Alerts," sifry.com, August 7, 2006, www.sifry.com/alerts/archives/000436.html#summary.
5. "The State of Blogging," Pew Internet & American Life Project, January 2, 2005, www.pewinternet.org/PPF/r/144/report_display.asp.
6. Jane Stevens, "Choosing a Story," University of California–Berkeley Graduate School of Journalism, n.d., http://journalism.berkeley.edu/multimedia/course/choose/.
7. "Ashley Wells' Theory of Interactive Storytelling," NewsLab, June 2006, www.newslab.org/resources/ashley.htm.
8. C. Max Magee, "The Roles of Journalists in Online Newsrooms," Medill School of Journalism, released by Online News Association, November 1, 2006, http://journalist.org/news/archives/MedillOnlineJobSurvey-final.pdf.
9. "Citizen Journalism Expert Jay Rosen Answers Your Questions," SlashDot, 2006, http://interviews.slashdot.org/interviews/06/10/03/1427254.shtml.
10. Steve Outing, "It's Almost Time to Pay for Citizen Journalism," PoynterOnline, November 15, 2005, www.poynter.org/content/content_view.asp?id=91256.
11. Moon Ihlwan, "OhmyNews' Oh My Biz Problem," BusinessWeek.com, November 1, 2006, www.businessweek.com/globalbiz/content/nov2006/gb20061101_539412.htm.

Chapter 9

1. "Newscast Structure," (bibliography), NewsLab, 2006, www.newslab.org/research/bibliography.htm#Newscast.
2. "RTNDF's 2006 Future of News Survey: Section 6, How Do People Want to Get to That Future?" Radio-Television News Directors Association, 2006, www.rtnda.org/resources/future/section6.pdf.
3. InfoLab, Northwestern University, http://infolab.northwestern.edu/project.asp?id=400.

Chapter 10

1. Marcus D. Rosenbaum and John Dinges, eds., *Sound Reporting: The National Public Radio Guide to Radio Journalism and Production* (Dubuque, Iowa: Kendall/Hunt Publishing Co., 1992).
2. Adam Balkin, quoted in John W. Owens, "Strike Up the One-Man Band," Government Video, May 7, 2004, http://governmentvideo.com/articles/publish/article_404.shtml.
3. Denise Dowling, quoted in ibid.
4. Forrest Carr and Andy Friedman, "Caught on Tape," Radio-Television News Directors Association & Foundation, n.d., www.rtnda.org/members/communicator/52_may.asp.
5. Charlie Tuggle, Dana Rosengard, and Suzanne Huffman, "Going Live, As Viewers See It," NewsLab, n.d., www.newslab.org/research/liveshot.htm.
6. "ABC World News," Transcript, November 29, 2006.
7. Maureen Fan, "In China, Aging in the Care of Strangers: One-Child Policy Changes Tradition," *Washington Post,* December 22, 2006, Sec. A.

Chapter 11

1. "Code of Ethics," Society of Professional Journalists, 1996, www.spj.org/ethicscode.asp.
2. "RTNDA Guidelines for Use of Non-Editorial Video and Audio," Radio-Television News Directors Association, April 2005, www.rtnda.org/foi/finalvnr.shtml.
3. Bill Kovach and Tom Rosenstiel, *The Elements of Journalism: What Newspeople Should Know and the Public Should Expect* (New York: Three Rivers Press, 2007), 94–98.
4. "Plagiarism Statement," Emory University, Journalism Program, www.journalism.emory.edu/program/plagiarism.cfm, quoting Floyd C. Watkins and William B. Dillingham, *Practical English Handbook,* 9th ed. (Boston: Houghton Mifflin, 1992), 357–358.
5. "Fair Use," United States Copyright Office, July 2006, www.copyright.gov/fls/fl102.html.
6. www.nppa.org/professional_development/business_practices/digitalethics.html.
7. "Reports: Major News Events," Pew Internet & American Life Project, July 8, 2004, www.pewinternet.org/PPF/r/130/report_display.asp.
8. Joe Strupp, "Ind. Paper Stands behind Sex Offender Coverage," PoynterOnline, February 24, 2004, www.poynter.org/column.asp?id=55&aid=61424.
9. Aly Colón, "Connecting Ethics and Diversity," PoynterOnline, November 17, 2003, www.poynter.org/column.asp?id=36&aid=54476.

Chapter 12

1. Douglas J. Guth, "Media Must Ride Digital Wave, Say Panelists," Cleveland Jewish News, n.d., www.clevelandjewishnews.com/articles/2006/12/08/news/local/digitalwave1208.txt.
2. Peter Johnson, "From DC to Blacksburg, Networks Stayed on Top," *USA Today,* April 18, 2007, Sec. D.
3. David Zurawick, "Alternative Sources Overrun TV News," *Baltimore Sun,* April 18, 2007, www.baltimoresun.com/features/lifestyle/bal-te.to.tv18apr18,0,4361287.story?coll=bal-artslife-today.
4. "The Old College Try," RADAR Magazine, April 17, 2007, www.radaronline.com/exclusives/2007/04/nbcs-vt-massacre-page-on-facebook.php.

5. "eMarketer: Mobile Video to Reach over 750MM Users in 2011," MediaBuyerPlanner, April 12, 2007, www.mediabuyerplanner.com/2007/04/12/emarketer-mobile-video-to-reach-over-750mm-users-in-2011.

6. "Podcast Boosts NPR Show's Audience," CyberJournalist.net, February 9, 2005, www.cyberjournalist.net/news/001903.php.

7. "NBC News Launches Video Podcasts," CyberJournalist.net, November 14, 2006, www.cyberjournalist.net/news/003876.php.

8. Deborah Potter, "Feeding the Beast, the 24/7 News Cycle," *RTNDA Communicator,* December 2006.

9. The most recent survey and other documents about data on graduates in the field can be found at "Annual Surveys of Journalism and Mass Communication," University of Georgia, Grady College of Journalism & Mass Communication, www.grady.uga.edu/ANNUALSURVEYS/grd06/grdrpt2006_merged_full_v6_Color.pdf, 1.

10. Ibid, 3.

11. Ibid, 4.

12. Ibid, 31.

13. "The Dirty Dozen Online Job Search Mistakes," Job-Hunt.org, 2001, www.job-hunt.org/jobsearchmistakes.shtml.

14. "Openings in Newspapers/Wires," JournalismJobs.com, [ad now expired], www.journalismjobs.com/Job_Listing.cfm?JobID=707679.

15. "Openings in Newspapers/Wires," JournalismJobs.com, [ad now expired], www.journalismjobs.com/Job_Listing.cfm?JobID=708014.

16. Sree Sreenivasan, "LinkedIn, Anyone? Social Networking for Professionals," PoynterOnline, October 11, 2006, https://www.poynter.org/column.asp?id=32&aid=102953.

17. Michael Kinsman, "Five Fundamentals for Acing Any Job Interview," California Job Journal, June 11, 2006, www.jobjournal.com/thisweek.asp?artid=1726

18. "Recruiters Reveal Interview Secrets and Employment Gaffes," Korn/Ferry International, May 8, 2006, http://kornferry.com/Library/Process.asp?P=PR_Detail&CID=1580&LID=1

19. To get an idea of the salary picture in general, check the annual survey of journalism graduates at Grady College of Journalism & Mass Communication, www.grady.uga.edu/ANNUALSURVEYS.

20. Bob Papper, "Seize the Pay," *Communicator,* June 2007, www.rtnda.org/communicator/pdfs/062007-16-25.pdf

21. Robert Niles [comment], "Teaching the Future of Journalism," Online Journalism Review, February 15, 2006, www.ojr.org/ojr/stories/060212pryor.

22. Joe Grimm writes the column, "Ask the Recruiter," for the Poynter Institute; the column can be found at www.poynter.org/column.asp?id=77.

23. Joe Grimm, "Ask the Recruiter: How Do I Freelance for a Newspaper?" PoynterOnline, October 27, 2006, https:www.poynter.org/column.asp?id=77&aid=112664.

GLOSSARY OF MULTIMEDIA JOURNALISM

One essential task for a multimedia journalist is to become familiar with some of the key terms each medium uses to describe content, typical job functions, tools and personnel. Here is a glossary of basic terms used in television, online and newspaper journalism. One word of caution—many newsrooms create their own lingo, so what's called a V/O-SOT at one TV station may be called a VO/B in others. However, we're confident you'll find it fairly easy to translate unique terms once you have a fundamental understanding of the overall concepts.

TELEVISION

aircheck. Recording of program for logging, screening or archiving purposes.

anchor lead. What the anchor says on the air to introduce a news package. Also called a *lead-in, anchor intro* or *intro.*

assignment editor. Person who supervises and coordinates the coverage of news events for a newsroom.

B-roll. Often used as shorthand for video.

bird. See *satellite.*

booth. Short for "control booth" or "control room." It houses the producer, director and some other technical staff during the newscast. May be used as a verb to describe a portion of the producer's job, that is, to "booth the show."

cans. Another term for headphones.

capture. See *digitize.*

chyron. See *super.*

CG. Short for "character generation," this is a generic term for text, such as the person's name or location, or numbers superimposed on the television screen. May also be called *chyron* or *super*. See also *side CG.* The term CG also refers to the character generator device that creates these graphics.

cue. Direction to anchor or reporter to begin speaking. May also be used to describe the process of getting audio or video ready for playback, as in "cue the tape."

digitize. To load linear field tape into a nonlinear editing system, thereby converting analog video to digital format; also called *ingest* or *capture.*

director. Person responsible for the technical production of a newscast.

donut. Refers to a story with a live top and tag from the reporter, wrapping around a package or a V/O-SOT.

FS. Short for "full screen graphic," a graphic that fills the entire screen; often used to display complicated information that the audience needs to see to understand.

IFB. Short for "interruptible foldback," an intercom system that allows anchors and reporters to hear what's on the air as well as directions from the producer during a broadcast.

ingest. See *digitize.*

intro. See *anchor lead.*

lead-in. See *anchor lead.*

lineup. See *rundown.*

live shot. Report that has not been recorded but is presented live, often at a news scene.

lock out. See *sig out.*

look live. Recorded "live" shot, when a reporter goes through the motions as if the report were live. Although this technique is sometimes used when technical issues prevent an actual live shot, it's considered poor journalistic practice and raises serious ethical questions.

microwave. Refers to a type of signal from a live truck.

news director. Person responsible for the work of an entire newsroom staff.

OTS. Short for "over the shoulder," a graphic that appears over the anchor's shoulder during a newscast.

package. Story that is preproduced and presented by a reporter, usually introduced by an anchor.

phoner. Story called in by a reporter and broadcast either live or on tape; may also refer to any interview conducted by phone and aired in a newscast. Usually this is accompanied on TV by a graphic that includes a picture and location. Often used when conventional live equipment is not available.

post mortem. Review or critique after the newscast airs.

producer. Essentially a newscast coordinator, this person determines the order and presentation of stories in a newscast and is responsible for much of the writing as well as for timing the show.

reader. A basic, short television story read by the anchor without video or graphic support. Sometimes called a *tell*.

re-ask. For editing purposes, a reporter may re-ask questions on camera after a single-camera interview. Re-asks raise ethical concerns because it's hard to ask a question exactly the same way twice.

remote. Any live program insert from outside the studio.

rundown. Term to describe the blueprint for the newscast; essentially a list of the stories assembled by the producer, shown in the order they will run. Also designates length of each story, its format and which anchor will read it. Also may be called a *lineup*.

satellite. Term for another type of live shot; involves bouncing a live signal from a specially designed truck to a satellite and back to the television station's receiver. This can be done from almost anywhere, but it is expensive. Sometimes referred to as a *bird*.

satellite window. Refers to a block of satellite time; typically purchased in blocks of five to 15 minutes.

side CG. Used to describe a graphic look that incorporates text or numbers, or both, on one side of the screen while keeping the anchor's face or video on the other side of the screen.

sig out. Term used for the last few words a reporter says in a story. Typically includes the reporter's name, the station name or brand and often the story's location. May also be called a *tag out* or a *lock out*.

slot. Position of a story in a newscast; making slot is good, missing slot is bad.

SOT. Stands for "sound on tape," and it is another expression for *sound bite*. It is a portion of a taped interview that has been selected to air.

sound bite. See *SOT*.

split screen. Refers to a production technique that divides the television screen in half with something different in each half. Often used to transition between the studio and a live reporter or to keep the anchor's face on screen while video is rolling in another window on the screen.

stand-up. Reporter's on-camera appearance in a news story, usually not live.

sticks. Term commonly used to describe a camera tripod.

straight live. Reporter simply stands and talks or answers questions from the anchors.

super. See *CG*.

tag. What the anchor says after the news package airs, or what a reporter says live at the end of a package.

tag out. See *sig out*.

technical director. This person pushes the buttons that change cameras and puts tapes and graphics on the air; oversees camera angles, lighting and other technical aspects of a program.

tell. *See reader.*

throw. See *toss.*

toss. Anchor's introduction to a reporter's live shot; sometimes called a *throw.*

VNR. Short for "video news release," and denotes video provided by a public relations firm, company or government agency. Using a VNR without disclosing the source raises ethical concerns.

V/O. Stands for "voice-over." Used in scripting to indicate what portion of narration is covered by video; also used to refer to a story that includes a short video clip, narrated by the anchor or a reporter, usually live.

V/O-SOT. A story, usually read live, with both voiced-over video and a sound bite. Sometimes called a "V/SOT."

vox pop. Short for the Latin "vox populi," meaning "voice of the people"; a gender-neutral term used to refer to what is sometimes still called man-in-the-street, or MOS, interviews.

ONLINE

blog. Short for Weblog; a series of entries to an online journal, posted in chronological order, that can be written by an individual or a group. Video versions are often called *vlogs.*

citizen journalism. News and information gathered and reported by citizens, rather than by professional journalists. Also called *participatory journalism* or *grassroots journalism.*

clip. Segment of audio or videotape that's posted on the Web.

CMS. Stands for "content management system," a software system used to manage the content of a Web site; popular examples include Blogger, WordPress, TypePad, Drupal and Geeklog.

cookie. Computer file that attaches to the hard drives of visitors to a Web site; it tracks what people are doing on a particular site and stores information that allows the site to remember the visitors if they return.

CPM. Cost per thousand impressions (M is the Roman numeral for 1,000); it's the rate advertisers will pay to have an ad displayed on 1,000 page views.

crowdsourcing. Term often used in conjunction with "citizen journalism"; users submit information that is collected into a larger data set for reporting a story. Sometimes called *open source reporting.*

download. To take files from another computer or server for use on your own.

encoding video. Process of changing analog video into digital footage to be read and displayed by a computer.

flaming. Act of posting personal attacks to an online forum or blog.

freeware. Software that's available free for users, generally available for download over the Internet.

FTP. Stands for "file transfer protocol"; a program used to upload files and Web pages to a server.

grassroots journalism. See *citizen journalism.*

hits. Term used to describe a request for a file on a Web server; when you click on a photo or link or answer a poll question online, it's counted as a hit. Sometimes hits are used to measure Web traffic, but measuring unique visitors can be more useful.

HTML. Stands for "hypertext markup language"; a language used to format content so it can be displayed on a Web page.

hyperlinks. Text on a Web site that can be clicked on to take you to another Web page or a different area of the same Web page; often called "links" for short.

JPEG. Stands for "joint photographic experts group"; the most common type of picture file on a Web site, and the file name extension is .jpg. Another common picture file extension is .gif. Pictures must be created or converted to formats like these to display properly on the Web.

lurker. A person who reads discussions on a message board or in a chat room but rarely participates.

mash-up. Term used to describe a Web page that mixes two or more different types of information or services into something new; for example, a mash-up might involve an overlay of traffic data over Google maps.

open source reporting. See *crowdsourcing.*

open source software. Software that is usually free and allows users to see the original source code so they can modify it more easily.

page view. Request for a single page of a Web site; each page view may translate into multiple hits, which is why measuring hits can be misleading.

participatory journalism. See *citizen journalism.*

podcast. Multimedia file distributed over the Internet for playback on mobile devices or personal computers; video versions are often called *vodcasts.*

PPC. Stands for "pay per click"; an advertising system such as Google's AdWords/AdSense where advertisers pay each time a reader clicks on their ads.

RSS. A method for distributing Web site content to another Web site or online application such as a news reader on a cell phone. Some say RSS stands for "rich site summary," and others say it's "really simple syndication."

search engine. Computer software used to search data for specified information; also a site such as Google or Yahoo! that uses such software to look for specific words and display the information for the user.

server. Usually refers to a computer connected to the Internet that is part of a network shared by multiple users.

shovelware. Publishing stories from one medium to another, usually to a Web site, without changing the content significantly, if at all.

style sheet. Set of instructions that tells your computer's Web browser how to display various elements on a Web page; style sheets can dictate font styles and colors, where photos and graphics are located on the page and other elements concerning the way a Web page looks when viewers access it.

tagging. Way to associate a posting with keywords that can be found by search engines.

troll. A person who posts to an online forum or blog to provoke a hostile response from other readers.

unique visitors. The number of people who have visited a particular Web site during a fixed time period (typically 30 days).

upload. To transfer files from your computer to another computer or server.

vlog. See *blog.*

vodcast. See *podcast.*

webcast. Video or audio broadcast that's transmitted over the Web.

XML. Extensible markup language; a language much like HTML but designed to describe online data. It allows you to structure, store and send information.

NEWSPAPERS

banner. A headline extending across the entire page.

body type. Type used for text.

boxcars. See *skyboxes.*

breakouts. Words, phrases or text blocks used to label part of a map or diagram (also called *callouts* or *factoids*).

broadsheet. Standard newspaper page size.

budget. List of news stories scheduled for the next issue of the newspaper.

callouts. See *breakouts.*

caption. See *cutline.*

character. Typeset letter, numeral or punctuation mark.

column inch. Way to measure the length of text or ads; it's an area one column wide and 1 inch long.

copy block. Small chunk of text accompanying a photo spread or introducing a special package of text.

copy editor. Person who edits news copy for content, style and grammar. Copy editors also write headlines and cutlines, and they design pages.

credit. Identifies source for story; for example, Associated Press or Media General News Services.

crop. To indicate where a photo should be trimmed before it runs in the newspaper; usually done by making crop marks in the margins of the photo.

crosshead. See *subhead.*

cutline. Line or block of type providing descriptive information about a photo; also called a *caption*).

dateline. Line in all capital letters at the beginning of a news story that says where the story took place. Originally this also included the date the story took place, hence the name.

deck. Smaller headline that sometimes comes between the headline and the story.

desk. General term to describe the people who edit and design the newspaper.

double truck. Two facing pages on the same sheet of newsprint that are treated as one unit.

dummy. Small, detailed page diagram showing where all elements go; also, the process of drawing up a layout.

extra. Additional edition of a newspaper published at a time other than the usual scheduled publication times; extremely rare since the introduction of Web editions.

factoids. See *breakouts.*

flag. Name of a newspaper as it's displayed on page one; also called a *nameplate.* Sometimes this is mistakenly called the *masthead.*

full frame. Entire image area of a photograph.

graf. Newsroom slang meaning paragraph.

infographic. Short for "informational graphic"; any complex map, chart or diagram used to analyze an event, object or place.

jump. To continue a story on another page; text that's been continued on another page is called the "jump."

layout. Placement of art and text on a page; to lay out a page is to design it.

lede. Another spelling for "lead," the first few lines of an article that introduce the story.

liftout quote. Graphic treatment of a quotation from a story, often using bold or italic type or rules; sometimes called a *pull quote.*

mainbar. The lead or top story in a package of stories on the same topic.

managing editor. Person responsible for all aspects of the news department and has supervisory responsibilities for all the editors.

masthead. A block of information, including staff names and publication data, often printed on the editorial page.

measure. Width of a headline or column of text.

morgue. Newsroom library.

nameplate. See *flag.*

nut graf. Paragraph that explains what a story is about; most often used in news features, the nut graf comes within a few paragraphs of the lead.

pagination. Process of generating a page on a computer.

penetration. Percentage of households in the newspaper market that subscribe.

photo credit. Line that tells who shot a photograph.

press run. Total number of copies printed.

promo. See *teaser*.

proof. Copy of a pasted-up page used to check for errors; to check a page is to proofread it.

publisher. Chief executive responsible for all departments of the newspaper.

pull quote. See *liftout quote*.

rack sales. Papers sold by the single copy either from vending machines or by stores. Also called *street sales*.

rail. Teasers that run in a single column on the left or right side of page one.

refer. Line or paragraph, often given graphic treatment, referring to a related story elsewhere in the paper or in another medium, for example, the newspaper's Web site. Sometimes spelled "reefer."

rules. Lines used to separate columns on a newspaper page.

sidebar. Story accompanying a bigger story on the same topic.

sig. Small standing headline that labels a regularly appearing column or feature.

skyboxes, skylines. Teasers that run above the flag on page one. If they're boxed (with art), they're called skyboxes or boxcars; if they use only a line of type, they're called skylines.

street sales. See *rack sales*.

stylebook. A newspaper's standardized set of rules and guidelines for grammar, punctuation, headline codes, design principles and so forth.

subhead. Heading within the text or story or article, often used to break columns of type into smaller sections and make the page more attractive or easy on the eye. A crosshead is centered in the column; a subhead is usually set left.

tabloid. Newspaper format that's roughly half the size of a regular broadsheet.

teaser. Eye-catching graphic element, on page one or section fronts, that promotes an item inside; also called a *promo*.

INDEX

Boxes, figures and tables are indicated by b, f and t following page numbers.

ABC7 (San Francisco), 10*b*
Access files, 106–107
Accuracy, 51, 132–134
    attribution, 132–133
    checking for, 137
    citizen journalism and, 216
    corrections of mistakes, 274–276, 275*b*
    numbers, 132, 133–134
    producing for the Web and, 198
Action shots, 256–257
Active voice, 129, 172
Adobe Contribute, 194
Adobe Photoshop, 194–195
Advertorials and infomercials, 278–280, 281*b*
Alabama Literacy Test, 18
Alexander, S. L., 91
Alternative media, 299
Alvarez, Mary, 171–172
Ambient sound, 60–61
American Press Institute's "Convergence Tracker,"
        306–307
American Society of Magazine Editors, 279
American Society of Newspaper Editors, 273
Amons, Nancy, 71, 106, 108
Anchors. *See also* Delivering the news
    personal connection of audience with, 13–14
    questions from, 262–263
Anecdotal leads, 127*b*
Animation, 101, 101*b*, 140*b*, 160
Annual Survey of Journalism and Mass
        Communication Graduates (Aug. 2007), 310
Apple iPhone, 306
Applications for jobs, 316–326
Archives of stories, 30–31
Associated Press Managing Editors on ethics, 273
Associated Press (AP) Style Guide, 268
Atkinson, Scott, 174–175
Atlanta Journal-Constitution, 211
Attention getting

in video, 152
    on the Web, 172
Attribution, 132–133
Audience
    connection with, 13–14
    demographics of, 229–230
    diaries or meters to measure, 230, 231
    multitasking and, 2–4
    ratings of TV news, 229–231, 232*b*
    share of, 230–231, 232*b*
Audio. *See* Sound
Audio recorders, 78
Aviles, Tom, 163

Background information, 30
Background interviews, 47–48, 49*b*
Backpack journalists, 75–76, 76*b*
Balkin, Adam, 254
Ball State University's Center for Media Design, 2, 3*f*
Barr, Bryan, 73, 74, 162
Bearden, Michelle, 266
Beat reporting, 83–88
    getting started, 83–86
    resources, 100*b*
    topical beats, 88–102
    tracking the beat, 86–87
    working the beat, 87–88
Becker, Mark, 259*b*, 263
Benz, Kevin, 317, 318*b*
Bergman, Cory, 179, 183, 186
Bias, 277–278
Blackboard, 194
Blind leads, 127*b*
Blocks in newscasts, 228
Bloggers' Code of Ethics, 273
Blogging, 199–204, 200*b*, 201*b*, 202*b*, 203*f*, 205*b*
    ethics and, 273, 284–285
Bloomberg News, 295
Boing Boing, 199, 200*b*

Bornstein, Bridgette, 61, 260–261, 260*b*
Boston Herald, 264
Bowden, Mark, 146
Boyle, Alan, 205*b*
Bradley, Dan, 20, 298
Brainstorming for story ideas, 25*b*
Breaking news
    developing stories vs., 196–197
    handling of, 7
British Broadcasting Corporation (BBC), 75
Broadcasting & Cable magazine on MTV as
        multimedia source, 5
Broadcast to online story, 179–183
Buckley, Bob, 87
Busiek, Dave, 321
Business and economics, 97–100
Business Week, 161–162, 161*b*, 216
"Bus stop test" for focus, 114

Calculators, online, 207, 208*b*
Cameras, 77–78. *See also* Equipment
Campaign coverage, 95
Canadian Broadcasting Company (CBC), 94*b*, 95
Cardwell, Mark, 308
Casey, Mark, 302
CBS Evening News, 14
CBS News, 17
Census Bureau
    population statistics, 55, 56*b*
    Web site, 31
Center for Media Design, Ball State University, 2, 3*f*
Characters in stories, 26
Checklists
    for blogging, 202*b*
    for ethics, 296*b*
    for multimedia journalism, 59*b*
    for storyboarding, 213*b*
    for visual storytelling, 150*b*
Chicagocrime.org, 90, 91*b*
Chicago Tribune, 99*b*
Christmas tree structure, 124–125, 125*f*
Chronicle of Higher Education, 97
Citizen journalism, 215–217, 303
Clark, Roy Peter, 286*b*
Click-to-listen audio files, 56
Clips and scripts, 30–31
Close-ups, 65–66
Closing shots, 66
Clustering, 226
Coates, Jennifer, 221, 222*b*, 223*b*
Cole, Andy, 23
Colòn, Aly, 295
Combs, Candice, 195*b*
Committee of Concerned Journalists, 281*b*
Communication magazine on teases, 239*b*
Community knowledge, 82–83
Computer-assisted reporting (CAR), 105–108
Consumer Reports WebWatch, 279
Contact information for sources, 87

Content management system (CMS), 194
Contracts, employment, 326–327
Conversational style, 131, 174–175, 180*b*
Cooke, Alistair, 131–132
Cooley, Mason, 271
Copyright issues, 258–288
Corrections of mistakes, 274–276, 274*b*
Council of National Journalism Organizations' list of
        journalism groups, 315
Courthouse reporters, 90–91
Cover letters, 316–317
Credibility of reporter, 51
Credibility of sources, 36
Crider, Jeremy, 4*b*
Crime and justice, 88–91
    cop beat, 90*b*
    glossary, 89*b*
Crowley, Candy, 115, 130*b*, 147
Cullier, David, 269
Cutaways, 154
CyberJournalist.net's Bloggers' Code of Ethics, 273

Dailey, Rocky, 321
Daniels, Steve, 133
Data sets, searchable, 204–206, 206*b*
"Deep background," 48
Defense lawyers as sources, 91
Delayed leads, 127*b*
Delivering the news, 247–270, 250*b*
    intonation, 249–251
    live shots, 258–264, 259*b*
    memorizing, 255–256
    mental preparation for, 249
    pacing, 251
    podcasts, 266–267
    print pointers, 267–269
    stand-ups, 251–258, 252*b*
    talking heads, 264–266
    vocal delivery, 247–251, 248*b*
Demographic data, 82
Demographics of TV news audience, 229–230
Denver Post, 308
Depth of coverage in newspapers, 14
Descriptive leads, 127*b*
DeSilva, Bruce, 114
Detail
    in newspaper coverage, 14–15
    in storywriting, 28
Detjen, Jim, 84
Developing stories vs. breaking news, 196–197
Diamond structure, 123–124, 124*f*
Digital manipulation of images, 288–291, 289–290*b*
Distribution methods, changes in, 305–306
Disturbing elements of stories, 13
    display of disturbing images online, 291–292,
        293*b*
Diversity issues, 295, 298–299
Documents
    review of, 116, 210

shooting for TV, 72*b*
Dorfman, Lori, 89
Doss, David, 302
Dotson, Bob, 42, 147, 150*b*
Douglas, Mark, 109
Dowling, Denise, 254
Dube, Jonathan, 55, 180*b*
DuPont-Columbia Award, 104

E-alerts, 31
Economics reporting, 97–100
Editing, 135–137, 153–156, 156*b*, 157*b*
Education reporting, 95–97, 96*b*, 98*b*
Education Week, 97
The Elements of Style (White), 135
E-mail interviews, 45–46
eMarketer, 305
Embargoes, 49–50, 49*b*
Emory University, 285
Emotion in storywriting, 28
Employment contracts, 326–327
Entrepreneurs in journalism, 328
Environmental issues. *See* Health, science and
    the environment
Equipment
    gear list, 79*b*
    lighting, 69, 70*b*
    multimedia journalism, 77–79
    sound equipment, 60, 62*b*, 63*b*
ESPN, 5
Estlow International Center for Journalism and
    New Media, 169
Ethics, 271–300
    access to information, 293–295
    acting ethically, 271–272
    advertorials and infomercials, 278–280
    blogging and, 273, 284–285
    checklist, 296*b*
    copyright issues, 258–288
    corrections on the Web, 274–276
    digital manipulation of images, 288–291,
        289–290*b*
    diversity issues, 295, 298–299
    graphic images and sound, 291–292, 293*b*
    interview agreements, 280–282
    multimedia issues, 272–283, 291–295
    online issues, 284–291
    plagiarism, 285–288, 286–287*b*
    resources, 296–297*b*
    sources of videos, identification of, 282–283,
        283*b*
    transparency and bias, 277–278
Ethnic media, 299
Evaluating sources, 37*b*
Excel files, 106–107, 107*b*
Experts, use of, 30, 56
Eyetools Inc., 169
Eyetrack07 study of Web readers, 169–170, 169*b*

Fact checking. *See* Accuracy
Factiva, 31
Fagan, Mark, 23–24, 266
Fair use doctrine, 287
Fargo Forum, 185*b*
Faw, Bob, 136*b*
Federal Aviation Administration's Web site, 31
Federal Communications Commission (FCC), 308,
    309
Field work, planning for, 74–75
File folders, 86
Finding stories, 24–26
Flash animation, 101, 101*b*, 140*b*
Flow of TV stories, 225–227, 225*t*
Following up on stories, 24
Ford, Celeste, 86, 95
Fox, Travis, 139
Fox News Channel, 78
Framing shots for video, 62–63, 68*b*
Franko, Brad, 167
Freed, Sharon Levy, 146
Freedman, Wayne, 149
Freedom of Information Act (FOIA), 104–105
Freelance Marketplace, 328
Fryer, Joe, 33, 34, 41–42, 112, 121, 154
Future trends, 20–21, 242–245

Gamel, Echo, 223
Games, online, 209, 209*b*
Gannett, 76, 308
Garrott, Jim, 24, 301, 326
Gitner, Seth, 45
Glossary of crimes, 89*b*
Godard, Michele, 13
Goheen, John, 24, 73–74, 163
"Go native," 84
Google
    news.google.com, 31
    www.blogger.com, 31, 32*b*
Government
    as beat topic, 92–95
    videos shot by, 71
    Web sites, 31
Grant, Angela, 155
Graphics, 72–73, 156–162, 159*f*
    ethical issues and, 291–292
    stand-ups with, 257–258, 258*b*
Greenfield, Jeff, 81
Griffis, Kim, 256–257
Griffis, Tim, 71, 149
Grimm, Joe, 328

Hammond, Kristian, 243
"Handshake shots," 66
Hansen, Suzy, 286*b*
Hanson, Jason, 64, 64*b*, 156*b*, 157*b*
Hardy, Larche, 42
Harris, Byron, 28
Harvey, Michele, 241–242

Headline writing for the Web, 183–186, 184b, 185b, 187b
Health, science and the environment, 82, 100–102, 101b, 103b
Hearst-Argyle, 304
Heaton, Terry, 243–244
Hedeen, Scott, 257
Heist, Stan, 58, 62b, 63b, 155b, 156
High-speed Internet connections, 7
Hill, Gary, 285
Hirsch, Rick, 8–9b
Hjelmstad, Pete, 12
Holovaty, Adrian, 90
Hooker, Steve, 69, 70b
Hourglass structure, 122–123, 123f
Houston, Brant, 105
Howard, Cody, 54
HTML, 194, 195b
Huppert, Boyd, 44, 66, 112, 113b, 125, 128, 131, 137, 149, 249

"Ice-breaker" questions, 39–40
Immediacy of broadcasting, 12
Incident reports at police stations, 89
Infomercials, 278–280
Infospace.com, 31, 33b
In-person interviews, 43, 46b
Institutional information, 85b
Interactive graphics, 161–162
Interactives for the Web, 189, 204–209
    searchable data sets, 204–206, 206b
    timelines and maps, 206–207
Internships, 311, 312b
Interviews, 36–50
    agreements, 280–282
    background interviews, 47–48, 49b
    "deep background," 48
    e-mail interviews, 45–46
    getting an interview, 38b
    ground rules, 47–50
    in-person interviews, 43, 46b
    job interviews, 323–326
    "nat sound" stories and, 73–74
    off-the-record interviews, 48
    on-camera interviews, 43–44
    online included as well as TV, 280–282
    openers and closers, 39–40
    phone interviews, 45–46
    policies, 48–49
    questions for, 38–43, 40–41b
    silence during, 42–43
    tough questions, 41–42
    types of interviews, 43–46
    types of questions, 39
    for the Web, 44–45
Intonation when delivering the news, 249–251
Introduction shots, 66
Inverted pyramid structure, 121–122, 122f
Investigative reporting, 102–109

computer-assisted reporting, 105–108
multimedia advantage, 108–109
undercover reporting, 108
using FOI, 104–105

Jensen, Scott, 146
Job searches, 309–316
    cover letters, 316–317
    employer pet peeves, 325b
    hiring tests, 326
    hunting for a job, 313–314, 315b
    internships, 311, 312b
    interviews, 323–326
    job applications, 316–326, 318b
    multimedia portfolios, 323, 324b
    networking, 314–316
    résumés, 317–320, 319b
    résumé tapes, 321–323, 321b
    starting salaries, 327t
Journalism skills, 7–11

Kalodimos, Demetria, 103b
Kasell, Carl, 249
KCNC-TV (Denver), 308
Keeshan, Kevin, 305
Kent State University on accuracy of reporting, 51
Kerr, Euan, 60, 77
KGO-TV (San Francisco), 305
King, Sharon, 238
King, Tim, 73
Koci-Hernandez, Richard, 78
KOMU-TV (Columbia, Mo.), 242
Koppel, Ted, 46b
Korn/Ferry International on mistakes made by job applicants in interviews, 325
KPNX-TV (Phoenix), 6, 242
Krulwich, Robert, 126
Kucharski, Angie, 224b
KUSA-TV 9News (Denver), 308

Lambden, Lisa, 76–77
Larson, John, 26, 120–121b
Lasica, J. D., 272
Lawhorn, Chad, 80, 212
Lawrence Journal-World, 54, 203b, 212
Lawsuits against newspapers, 264
Lawyers as sources, 91
L-cut, 156
Leads, 126–127, 127b, 180b, 222–225
Lehtonen, Amy, 197
LexisNexis, 31
Lighting, 69–71
    placement of subject, 70–71
    technical issues, 69, 70b
Lim, Victoria, 56–57, 112
LinkedIn, 316
Little, Caroline, 20–21
Live shots, 258–264, 259b
    anchor questions, 262–263

content of, 260–261, 260b
  live only, 263–264
  live tag, 262–263
  live toss, 261
Live teases, 236–237
Livingston, Scott, 66
LJWorld.com, 203b
Logging of visual and audio, 141, 143b
Los Angeles Times, 279
Lowe, Caroline, 88

Mahaney, Chip, 321
Maher, Vince, 202b
Main, Alice, 135
Malat, Jonathan, 44, 75, 115, 146
MapQuest, 32
Maps, 82
  clickable, 206–207
  crime maps, 90, 91b
  online, 32, 96b, 99, 99b
Marcus, Dave, 98b
Martin, Meg, 8–9b
Mather, Mike, 84, 151
McBride, Kelly, 294
McCombs, Regina, 67
McMearty, Mike, 20
Media General Broadcast Group, 48, 56
Media General, Inc., 20, 307b, 311
MediaNews Group, 308
Medina, Susan Rossi, 87
Medium shots, 65
Meltzer, Josh, 67, 78
Memorizing the news, 255–256
Mendenhall, Preston, 76, 77
Menell, Jon, 154
Meyer, Galen, 295
Meyerson, Charlie, 184b
Michaelson, Lane, 74, 241
Microphones, 60, 62b, 63b, 79
Microsoft Excel, 106–107, 107b
Miller, Andrea, 196
Miller, Kay, 320
Mitchell, Chris, 255b
Mobile TV and video subscribers, 305–306
Moments to pick for video storytelling, 146, 147b
Morning News (Florence, S.C.), 23
MSNBC, 205b
  flash animation, use of, 101, 101b
  interactive population map, 55, 56b
MTV, 5
Multimedia industry, 5
Multimedia journalism, 2–4, 4b, 5–6, 54–80
  beat reporting and, 99
  checklist for, 59b
  defined, 2
  equipment for, 77–79
  ethics in, 271–300. See also Ethics
  focus of story in, 115
  graphics in, 72–73
  investigative reporting and, 108–109

lighting in, 69–71
  nonvisual stories, 71–74
  planning the story, 74, 140–143, 209–212
  producing for TV and, 240–241
  sound in, 58–61, 62b, 73–74
  teamwork in, 74–75, 212–215
  thinking across platforms, 8–9b, 55–57, 57b, 58b
  video in, 61–69
  working alone in, 75–77
  writing the story and, 115
Multitasking, 2, 3f
Murray, Don, 26
Murray, J. J., 320, 322, 322b, 325b, 326, 327

Nalder, Eric, 85b
National Association of Hispanic Journalists, 299
National Council on Public Polls, 92b
National Press Photographers Association, 290–291
National Public Radio (NPR), 305
Natural sound stories, 73–74, 145–146, 149–150,
    162–163
NBC News, 302, 305
Nelson, Ted, 60
Networking in job search, 314–316
News at Seven (Northwestern University), 243, 244b
Newscast blocks, 228
News.google.com, 31
Newslab, 281b
Newspaper Association of America, 16
Newspapers
  depth of coverage, 14
  detail of coverage, 14–15
  number of daily newspapers available nationwide,
    16
  permanence and portability of, 15
  power of, 14–15
  reporters appearing on television, 264–266, 265b
Nexstar Broadcasting, 243, 315b
Nielsen Norman Group study of Web users, 67
Nielsen People Meter, 230
Niles, Robert, 328
"Nonquestion question," 42
Northwestern University's News At Seven, 243, 244b
Notarangelo, Ann, 84
Note taking, 50–51, 86
  review of, 116
Numbers
  accuracy of, 132, 133–134
  in graphics, 73
Nybo, Thomas, 254

Off-the-record interviews, 48, 49b
OhmyNews, 216
On-camera interviews, 43–44
On-demand news delivery, 5–6, 17
Online. See Web
Online calculators, 207, 208b
Online News Association study on online news skills,
    193–194, 212

Opening shots, 66
Organizational information, 85*b*
Organization of information for writing story, 118
Original Web content, 188–189
Orlando Sun-Sentinel, 189
Orwell, George, 131
Osgood, Charles, 128
Osowski, Chip, 262–263
Outing, Steve, 216
Ownership of newspaper and TV stations by same
     party, 308, 309

Pacing of TV news, 227–228, 251
Papper, Bob, 327
Partnerships, cross-media, 307–309
Peabody Award, 104
People Meters, 230, 231
Permanence of print coverage, 15
Pew Internet & American Life Project
     on blogs, 199
     on display of disturbing images online, 292
Pew Research Center for the People and the Press,
     11, 16–17, 167
Philadelphia Inquirer, 96, 96*b*
Phone calls, 33
Phone directories, 31, 33*b*
Phone interviews, 45–46
Photographers, teamwork with, 74–75
Photojournalists. *See also* Video
     communicating with, 37, 44
     sound and, 60, 61*b*
     teamwork with, 74–75
Photoshopping, 288
Pitching stories for TV, 221*b*
Pitts, Byron, 44, 87
Place in stories, 27
Plagiarism, 285–288, 286–287*b*
Planning the story, 24, 116–119, 119*b*
     additional information, use of, 118–119
     multimedia stories, 74, 140–143, 209–212
     organization, 118
     review of notes and documents, 116, 210
     selection of quotes and sound bites, 116–118
     storyboards, use of, 210–212, 211*b*, 213*b*
Podcasts, 7, 198, 266–267, 305
Police reporters, 88–89, 90*b*
Politics as beat topic, 92–95
Polls
     producing for the Web, 207–209
     reporting on, 92–93*b*
Portability of print medium, 15
Potter, Deborah, 119*b*, 250*b*
Poynter Institute, 169, 286*b*
Pre-interviews, 45
Presentation plan, development of, 215
Price, Dave, 199
Primary sources, 34
Print media, power of, 14–15
Print to online story, 176–179

Producing for the Web, 192–218, 242
     accuracy, 198
     blogging, 199–204, 200*b*, 201*b*, 202*b*, 203*b*,
          205*b*
     breaking news vs. developing stories, 196–197
     citizen journalism, 215–217
     continuous production mode, 196–198
     interactive tools, use of, 204–209
     online calculators, 207, 208*b*
     polls, questionnaires, and quizzes, 207–209, 209*b*
     presentation plan, development of, 215
     sharing resources, 214
     skill set, 193–195, 193*t*
     storytelling, 209
     strategies for constant updates, 197
     unique content, determination of, 213–214
     webcasts and podcasts, 198
Producing for TV, 219–246
     audience and ratings, 229–231
     future trends, 242–245
     journalist producers, 220, 223*b*
     leads, 222–225
     multimedia content, 240–241
     newscast blocks, 228
     news director's expectations for, 224*b*
     pacing, 227–228
     show choreography, 220–229
     story flow, 225–227, 225*t*
     strategic producing and special reports, 231–233
     teases, 233–241, 239*b*
     timing, 228–229
     Web work and, 242
     working with newscast producers, 241–242
     working with promotion producers, 238–240
Project for Excellence in Journalism
     on beat reporting, 88
     on State of the News Media 2007, 190
Public opinion polls, reporting on, 92–93*b*
Pulskamp, Andrew, 197

Questions
     to focus story, 112–115
     for interviews, 38–43, 40–41*b*
Quizzes and questionnaires
     producing for the Web, 207–209, 209*b*
Quotes and sound bites, 116–118, 132–133,
          143–144, 146–149
     leading in and leading out, 148–149

Raddatz, Martha, 261
Radio and Television News Directors Foundation sur-
     vey on future of newscasting, 242
Radio-Television News Directors Association
     Code of Ethics and Professional Conduct, 282
     job searches and postings, 316
     survey on employment contracts, 326–327
The Rainbow Source Book (Society of
     Professional Journalists), 35*b*
Raleigh News & Observer, 106

ADVANCING THE STORY

Ratings of TV news, 229–231, 232*b*
Reading aloud, 135
Reddick, Randy, 81
Relevancy in writing for the Web, 174
Renteria, Juan, 75
Reporters. *See also* Reporting
    credibility of, 51
    personal connection of audience with, 13–14
Reporting, 23–53, 81–110
    accuracy, 51
    beat reporting, 83–88
    caring about the story, 52
    finding stories, 24–26
    interviews, 36–50. *See also* Interviews
    investigative reporting, 102–109
    note taking, 50–51
    research strategies, 28–30
    research tools, 30–33
    sources, 34–36
    story building blocks, 26–28
Research strategies, 28–30, 82
    consulting experts, 30
    following stakeholders, 29–30
    seeking background and data, 30
Research tools, 30–33
    clips and scripts, 30–31
    online sources, 31–32
    phone calls, 33
Résumés, 317–320, 319*b*
Résumé tapes, 321–323, 321*b*
Retrieval systems, 86
Revealing sources, 49
Reverse phone directories, 31, 33*b*
Revising the story, 134–137, 136*b*
    checking for accuracy, 137
    editing, 135–137
    reading aloud, 135
Rhodes, Chet, 303, 304, 305, 306
Richmond Times-Dispatch, 18, 186
Riley, Jim, 309
Riser, Christine, 301
Rocky Mountain News (Denver), 308
Rogers, Carol, 102
Rose, Derek, 34
Rose, Les, 36
Rosen, Jay, 216
Rosenbaum, David, 117*b*
RTNDA/Ball State University survey on TV
    stations with Web sites, 190
"Rule of thirds," 68*b*, 69
Russakoff, Dale, 117*b*

San Francisco Chronicle, 276, 277*b*
San Jose Mercury News, 78, 209, 209*b*
Sarasota Herald-Tribune, 15
Scanlan, Chip, 40–41*b*, 86
Scanners as Web audience, 175–176
Schechter, David, 71
Schiraldi, Vincent, 89

Scholl, Corky, 60, 66
Schuh, Mike, 141, 142*b*
Schwartz, Mike, 21
Science. *See* Health, science and the
    environment
Screening the story, 141
Sculley, John, 158
Searchable data sets, 204–206, 206*b*
Seattle newspapers, 16*b*
Secondary sources, 34, 35
Sequence of video shots, 65–66, 151
Sevareid, Eric, 138
Sex offender registries, 294
SFGate.com, 276, 277*b*
Shapiro, Susan, 253, 253*b*
Share of audience, 230–231, 232*b*
Sharifi, John, 71
Shields, John, 83
Shovelware, 170–171
Show stacking, 221
Siegel, Robert, 39
Sifry, David, 199
Silence during interviews, 42–43
Simmons, Barry, 152
Simplicity
    in graphics, 158–160, 159*f*
    in writing, 128–129, 174–175
Sirulnick, Dave, 5
Sites, Kevin, 76
6News (Lawrence, Kan.), 54
60 Minutes, 154
Skimmers, writing for, 168, 175–176
Slate, 293*b*
Slide shows, 163–165, 164*b*
Snyder, Jim, 251
Society of Environmental Journalists, 103*b*
Society of Professional Journalists
    Code of Ethics, 272
    The Rainbow Source Book, 35*b*
Solopek, Paul, 99, 99*b*
Solo stand-ups, 254, 255*b*
Sony, 279
Sosbe, Kathryn, 90*b*
Sound, 58–61, 62*b*, 143–146
    ambient sound, 60–61
    audio edits, 155–156
    equipment, 60, 62*b*, 63*b*
    ethical issues, 291–292
    natural sound, 73–74, 145–146, 149–150,
        162–163
    online use, 61
    sound bite content, 143–144
    track or "nat sound" stories, 73–74
Sound bites. *See* Quotes and sound bites
Sources, 34–36
    attribution to, 132–133
    beat reporting and, 86
    contact information for, 87
    credibility of, 36

evaluating, 37*b*
multiple sources, need for, 34–35, 35*b*
primary, 34
protecting identity of, 49
secondary, 34
Special TV reports, 231–233
Spokesman-Review (Spokane, Wash.), 204, 206*b*
Sports teases, 235–236
Sreenivasan, Sree, 31, 316
Stacker, Doug, 104
Stahl, Leslie, 151
Stakeholders in stories, 29–30
Stand-ups, 236–237, 251–258, 252*b*
    action shots, 256–257
    with graphics, 257–258, 258*b*
    memorizing the content, 255–256
    planning of, 252–254
    shooting of, 257
    solo, 254, 255*b*
Staples Center (Los Angeles), 279
Starting salaries, 327*t*
Steele, Bob, 108, 296*b*
Stevens, Jane, 210
Stith, Pat, 106
Stone, Emerson, 274*b*
Stoppard, Tom, 128
Storyboards, 210–212, 211*b*, 213*b*
Story building blocks, 26–28
    character, 26
    detail, 28
    emotion, 28
    place, 27
    tension or surprise, 28
Story flow, 225–227, 225*t*
Story mapping, 26, 27*f*
Story structure, 120–121*b*, 120–125, 267–268
    Christmas tree, 124–125, 125*f*
    diamond, 123–124, 124*f*
    hourglass, 122–123, 123*f*
    inverted pyramid, 121–122, 122*f*
Storytelling, interactive, 209
Summary leads, 127*b*
Surprise in storywriting, 28
Surprise, use of, 131–132
Sweeps, 230, 231
Swift, Jonathan, 274*b*
Switchboard.com, 31

Talking heads, 264–266, 265*b*
Tampa Tribune, 20, 56, 58*b*, 109, 298, 309
Taricani, Jim, 49
Taylor, Mackenzie, 311, 312*b*
TBO.com, 20, 56, 58*b*, 109, 298, 309
Teamwork in multimedia journalism, 74–75,
    212–215
Teases for TV news, 233–241, 239*b*
    content knowledge, 233–234
    pitfalls of, 237–238
    sports teases, 235–236

stand-up and live teases, 236–237
viewer benefit and, 234–235
weather teases, 235
Technological change, effect of, 7–11, 10*b*, 301–309
    distribution methods, 305–306
    journalism skills, 306
    media convergence, 306–309, 307*b*
    partnerships, cross-media, 307–309
    systems to manage user-generated content,
        303–305
Television news
    documents, shooting for, 72*b*
    immediacy of broadcasting, 12
    impact of visuals and emotion, 12–13
    producing for, 192–218. *See also* Producing for TV
    reporting for print or Web, 267–269
    as source of major stories, 11
Templin, Julie, 238–240
Tension in storywriting, 28
Testing of job applicants, 326
"Textcasts," 6
Tight shots, 65–66
Timelines, interactive, 206–207
TIME magazine's 2006 Person of the Year, 303*b*
Timing, 141–143, 228–229
Toledo Blade, 289–290*b*
Tompkins, Al, 28, 244–245, 303, 304–305
Toms, Darren, 302
Topical beats, 88–102
    business and economics, 97–100
    crime and justice, 88–91
    education, 95–97
    government and politics, 92–95
    health, science and the environment, 82, 100–102
Topics, developing stories from, 26
Total running time (TRT), 141
Tracking the beat, 86–87
"Track" stories, 73–74
Transparency, 277–278, 283
Tree-shaped structure, 124–125, 125*f*
Tutorials online, 195*b*

Umbrella leads, 127*b*
Undercover reporting, 108
University of Texas School of Journalism study of
    newspaper use of the Web, 171
University of Trier (Germany) Media Studies, 162
User-generated content. *See* Citizen journalism
Utterback, Ann, 249

Video, 61–69. *See also* Visual storytelling
    choosing, 146–147
    framing, 62–63, 68*b*, 69
    identification of sources of, 282–283, 283*b*
    matching sound and, 146–147
    online issues, 66–69
    opens, closes and introductions, 66
    sequences, action and reaction, 65–66, 146, 151
    steady shots, 64–65, 64*b*

Videojournalists, 75–76, 76b
Video news releases (VNRs), 282
Viewer benefit and story teases, 234–235
Virginia Commonwealth University, 283b
Virginia Tech shootings, reporting of, 302
Visual storytelling, 139–166
    attention getting video, 152
    checklist for, 150b
    choosing video, 146–147
    editing, 153–156, 156b, 157b
    graphics, 156–162, 159f
    natural sound stories, 162–163
    "parallel parking," 152–153
    planning the story, 140–143
    sequencing of story, 151
    slide shows, 163–165
    writing to graphics, 160–161
    writing to sound, 147–150
    writing to video, 150–153, 153b
Vocal delivery, 247–251, 248b
Vodcasts, 198

Wall Street Journal, 97
Ward, Bill, 188
Washington Post, 14, 97, 140b, 163, 165b, 268
Watson, Stuart, 104
WBBH-TV (Ft. Myers, Fla.), 12–13
WBFF-TV (Baltimore, Md.), 12b
WBTW-TV (Florence, S.C.), 23
WCNC-TV (Charlotte, N.C.), 197, 206, 207b
Weather teases, 235
Web
    blogs. See Blogging
    broadcast shovelware, 170–171
    corrections on, 274–276
    display of disturbing images online, 291–292,
        293b
    ethics and, 284–291
    how people use, 168–170
    innovation on, 18
    interactivity of, 18
    interviews for, 44–45
    print rehash on, 171
    problems with news on, 170–171
    producing for, 192–218, 242. See also
        Producing for the Web
    reporting on, 15–19, 17t
    sources for research, 31–32
    video shots for, 66–69, 67b
    writing for, 171–176. See also Writing for the Web
Webber, Sterlin Benson, 257–258, 258b
Webcasts, 6, 198
Webster, Brian, 155
WEEK-TV, 326
Weil, Nancy, 90b
Weiss, Joe, 163
Weister, Brian, 65, 163
Wells, Ashley, 212
Wendland, Mike, 8–9
Wertheimer, Dave, 60

West Virginia mine collapse (2006), 34b, 35
WFLA-TV (Tampa, Fla.), 6b, 20, 309
WGAL-TV (Lancaster, Pa.), 19b, 253b, 304, 304b
White, E. B., 135
Whitmeyer, Robin, 198
Wide shots, 65
Williams, Brian, 35
Windows Movie Maker, 163, 164b
WISH-TV (Indianapolis, Ind.), 207
WJHL-TV (Johnson City, Tenn.), 242
WNYC (New York City) radio station, 305
Wooten, Jim, 149
Word choice, 128–132
    active voice, 129
    conversational style, 131
    keeping it simple, 128–129
    powerful words, 129–131
    surprise, use of, 131–132
Working alone in multimedia journalism, 75–77
Writing for the Web, 171–176
    additional content, 188
    attention getting, 172
    blogging, 201
    broadcast to online story, 179–183
    concise and conversational style, 174–175, 180b
    extras, 186–189
    headline writing, 183–186, 184b, 185b, 187b
    interactives, 189
    online writing tips, 180–181b
    original Web content, 188–189
    scanners as audience, 175–176
    style tips, 176b
    time and tense, 172–174, 173b
Writing the story, 111–138. See also Writing for the
    Web
    accuracy, 132–134
    Associated Press (AP) Style Guide, 268
    beginnings and endings, 126–128
    finding the focus, 112–115
    leads, 126–127, 127b
    multimedia focus, 115
    planning the story, 116–119
    questions to focus, 112–115
    revising the story, 134–137, 136b, 137b
    story structure, 120–125
    word choice, 128–132
WSOC-TV (Charlotte, N.C.), 198
WSPA-TV (Spartanburg, S.C.), 173b
W3C, 195b
WVEC-TV (Norfolk, Va.), 199, 201b, 216
WVLT-TV (Knoxville, Tenn.), 239b
WVSN-TV (Miami), 239b
WYOU-TV (Wilkes-Barre–Scranton, Pa.), 243

Yahoo maps, 32
Young Broadcasting Inc., 75

Zamora, Amanda, 186, 196, 201
Zekman, Pam, 108